**SYSTEMS APPLICATION ARCHITECTURE:
COMMON PROGRAMMING INTERFACE**

A  BOOK

THE JAMES MARTIN BOOKS
currently available from Prentice Hall

- Application Development Without Programmers
- Building Expert Systems
- Communications Satellite Systems
- Computer Data-Base Organization, Second Edition
- Computer Networks and Distributed Processing: Software, Techniques, and Architecture
- Data Communication Technology
- DB2: Concepts, Design, and Programming
- Design and Strategy of Distributed Data Processing
- An End User's Guide to Data Base
- Fourth-Generation Languages, Volume I: Principles
- Fourth-Generation Languages, Volume II: Representative 4GLs
- Fourth-Generation Languages, Volume III: 4GLs from IBM
- Future Developments in Telecommunications, Second Edition
- Hyperdocuments and How to Create Them
- IBM Office Systems: Architectures and Implementations
- IDMS/R: Concepts, Design, and Programming
- Information Engineering, Book I: Introduction and Principles
- Information Engineering, Book II: Planning and Analysis
- Information Engineering, Book III: Design and Construction
- An Information Systems Manifesto
- Local Area Networks: Architectures and Implementations
- Managing the Data-Base Environment
- Object-Oriented Analysis and Design
- Principles of Data-Base Management
- Principles of Data Communication
- Principles of Object-Oriented Analysis and Design
- Recommended Diagramming Standards for Analysts and Programmers
- SNA: IBM's Networking Solution
- Strategic Information Planning Methodologies, Second Edition
- System Design from Provably Correct Constructs
- Systems Analysis for Data Transmission
- Systems Application Architecture: Common User Access
- Systems Application Architecture: Common Communications Support: Distributed Applications
- Systems Application Architecture: Common Communications Support: Network Infrastructure
- Systems Application Architecture: Common Programming Interface
- Technology's Crucible
- Telecommunications and the Computer, Third Edition
- Telematic Society: A Challenge for Tomorrow
- VSAM: Access Method Services and Programming Techniques

with Carma McClure

- Action Diagrams: Clearly Structured Specifications, Programs, and Procedures, Second Edition
- Diagramming Techniques for Analysts and Programmers
- Software Maintenance: The Problem and Its Solutions
- Structured Techniques: The Basis for CASE, Revised Edition

SYSTEMS APPLICATION ARCHITECTURE
Common Programming Interface

JAMES MARTIN

with

Kathleen Kavanagh Chapman / Joe Leben

P T R PRENTICE HALL
Englewood Cliffs, New Jersey 07632

Library of Congress Cataloging-in-Publication Data

MARTIN, JAMES (date)
  Systems application architecture : common programming interface /
James Martin with Kathleen Kavanagh Chapman, Joe Leben.
    p. cm.
  "A James Martin book."
  Includes bibliographical references and index.
  ISBN 0-13-785916-3
  1. IBM Systems Application Architecture. 2. Computer interfaces.
3. User interfaces (Computer systems) I. Chapman, Kathleen Kavanagh.
II. Leben, Joe. III. Title.
  QA76.9.A73M3737 1993
  005.2—dc20   93-18129
                                                               CIP

Editorial/production supervision: *Kathryn Gollin Marshak*
Liaison: *Brendan Stewart*
Jacket design: *Bruce Kenselaar*
Manufacturing buyer: *Mary Elizabeth McCartney*

Copyright © 1993 by James Martin

 Published by P T R Prentice-Hall, Inc.
A Simon & Schuster Company
Englewood Cliffs, New Jersey 07632

All rights reserved. No part of this book may be
reproduced, in any form or by any means,
without permission in writing from the publisher.

The publisher offers discounts on this book when ordered
in bulk quantities. For more information, contact:

    Corporate Sales Department
    P T R Prentice Hall
    113 Sylvan Avenue
    Englewood Cliffs, NJ 07632
    Phone 201-592-2863; Fax 201-592-2249

Printed in the United States of America

10 9 8 7 6 5 4 3 2 1

ISBN 0-13-785916-3

Prentice-Hall International (UK) Limited, *London*
Prentice-Hall of Australia Pty. Limited, *Sydney*
Prentice-Hall Canada Inc., *Toronto*
Prentice-Hall Hispanoamericana, S.A., *Mexico*
Prentice-Hall of India Private Limited, *New Delhi*
Prentice-Hall of Japan, Inc., *Tokyo*
Simon & Schuster Asia Pte. Ltd., *Singapore*
Editora Prentice-Hall do Brasil, Ltda., *Rio de Janeiro*

TO CORINTHIA
—JM

TO JOHN AND MY PARENTS
—KKC

TO L.L., THE BEST FRIEND A MAN COULD HAVE
—JL

CONTENTS

Preface *xiii*

PROLOG

1 The SAA Environment *3*

*Why SAA? 4; Structure of SAA 7; SAA Architectures 8;
SAA Applications and Solutions 9;
Vendor Support for SAA 10; Common User Access 14;
Common Communications Support 17;
Architecture Versus Implementation 23;
SAA: Strengths and Weaknesses 24;
SAA: An Open Architecture 25; SAA Implementation 26;
The Future of SAA 26; Conclusion 28; References 28*

2 SAA Application Design *29*

*SAA Design Goals 29; Distributed Computing 30;
Application Components 31; Local Processing 31;
Cooperative Processing 32; Distributed Data Access 33;
Distributed Function Processing 34;
Client/Server Computing 34; Distributed Resources 35;
Distributed Document Access 36;
Distributed Database Access 37; Distributed Files 40;
Data Representation Considerations 42;
Online Processing 44; Application Design 45;
Designing the User Interface 45; Designing Data 46;
Designing Application Logic 46; Designing Communications 47;
Conclusion 47*

PART I PROGRAMMING LANGUAGE INTERFACES

3 High-Level Languages *51*

The C Language 51; COBOL 61; FORTRAN 68; PL/I 75; RPG 83; Conclusion 97

4 The CPI Application Generator Interface *99*

SAA Application Generator Environments 99; Application Generator Interface 100; Application Logic Definition 100; Application Logic Structure 101; Logic Specification 101; Data Definition 107; Data Specification 108; Map Definition 108; Conclusion 115

5 The CPI Procedures Language Interface *117*

Procedures Language Example 118; Expressing Values 119; Procedures Language Statements 121; Program Logic 122; Routines and Functions 122; Conditions and Condition Traps 123; Input and Output 124; Parsing 125; String Pattern Example 125; Numeric Pattern Example 125; Issuing Commands 127; Interacting with the Interpreter 128; Conclusion 129

PART II DATA ACCESS INTERFACES

6 Relational Database Concepts *133*

Tables 133; Table Properties 134; Keys 135; Primary Key 135; Representing Relationships 135; Integrity Constraints 136; Three Views of Data 138; Concurrency 139; Authorization and Privileges 139; Distributed Relational Databases 139; SAA Support for Distributed Database 141; Conclusion 142

Contents

7 The CPI Database Interface 143

Queries 143; The SELECT Clause 144; The FROM Clause 146; The WHERE Clause 146; Other Search Conditions 147; The GROUP BY Clause 150; The HAVING Clause 150; The ORDER BY Clause 150; The UPDATE Clause 151; The UNION Operation 151; The SELECT INTO Statement 151; Updating Data 151; The INSERT Statement 152; The DELETE Statement 152; Cursor-Based Processing 152; Concurrency 153; Data Definition 154; Creating Tables 154; Modifying Tables 157; Defining Views 157; Defining Indexes 158; Authorization 158; Executing SQL Statements 159; Package Processing 160; Embedded SQL Statements 160; SQL Communications Area 162; Dynamic SQL Statements 162; Conclusion 164

8 The CPI Query Interface 165

Queries 165; Report Formatting 167; Commands 168; Processing Query Results 168; Variables 169; Procedures 170; Processing Objects 170; Object Formats 171; The Callable Interface 172; Interface Communications Area 175; Callable Interface Commands 175; Conclusion 178

9 The CPI Resource Recovery Interface 179

Synchronization 179; CPI Database Interface Recovery 180; CPI Resource Recovery 181; Synchronization Point Managers 182; Distributed Resource Processing 183; Resource Recovery Interface Calls 185; Resource Recovery Scenarios 186; Change Commitment with Local Resources 186; Change Commitment with Distributed Resources 187; Conclusion 192

10 The CPI Repository Interface 193

Three Views of Data 194; Entity-Relationship Model 194; The Repository and AD/Cycle 198; Repository Functions 199; Templates 199; Template Format 200; Template Trees 200; Using Templates for Retrieval 202; Repository Function Policies 202; Tool Programs 203; Repository Services 204; Data Services 204; Calling Data Services 204; System Services 207; Calling System Services 208; Built-in Functions 208; Calling a Function 209; Fully Integrated Versus Nonfully Integrated Functions 213; CPI Repository Interface Focus 213; Conclusion 213

PART III NETWORKING INTERFACES

11 Systems Network Architecture *217*

SNA Users 218; Logical Units 218; Logical Unit Functions 219;
Physical Units 220; Control Points 221;
SNA Logical Components 221; SNA Nodes 222; Sessions 223;
LU-LU Sessions 223;
Logical Unit and Network User Relationship 225;
SNA Networking Facilities 225; SNA Functional Layers 228;
Conclusion 233; References 234

12 Logical Unit 6.2 Architecture *235*

LU 6.2 Functions 235; LU 6.2 Versus APPC 236;
Architectural Layers 236; Interfacing with LU 6.2 237;
Architected Protocol Boundary 238;
Protocol Boundary Verb Semantics Versus Programming Syntax 239;
Conversations 239; Application Program View of LU 6.2 239;
Synchronization 240; Parallel Sessions 240; Session Mode Sets 241;
Generalized Data Stream 241; Mapped and Basic Conversations 242;
LU 6.2 Protocol Boundary 243; LU 6.2 Functional Interfaces 243;
Sample Conversations 244;
One-Way Conversation with No Confirmation 244;
One-Way Conversation with Confirmation 248;
Two-Way Conversation 250; Distributed Transaction Example 250;
Mapping Between Syntax and Semantics 253;
Open Versus Closed LU 6.2 Implementations 254;
Application Subsystem LU 6.2 Implementations 254;
APPC LU 6.2 Implementations 254;
CPI Communications Interface 255;
Designing LU 6.2 Conversation Flows 255; Conclusion 256

13 The CPI Communications Interface *257*

CPI-C Concepts 257; CPI-C Calls 258;
CPI-C Conversation Characteristics 263;
CPI-C Call to LU 6.2 Verb Mapping 265;
LU 6.2 Functions Not Supported 265;
Support for Synchronization Point Processing 267;
Sample CPI-C Conversations 268;
One-Way Conversation with No Confirmation 268;
One-Way Conversation with Confirmation 269;
Two-Way Conversation 269;
Protected Conversation with Commit Processing 270;
Distributed Transaction Example 271; Conclusion 272

PART IV   USER INTERFACES

14   Common User Access Interfaces   275

CUA User Interface Models 276;
Advanced Interface Graphical Model 276; Windows 277;
Window Components 278; Secondary Windows 279;
Controls 281; Interaction Techniques 286;
Standard Actions 286; CUA Basic Interface Models 288;
Conclusion 292

15   Common Communications Support User Interfaces   293

CCS Data Stream and Object Architectures 293;
Transmission Objects 293; Data Streams 294;
Document Data Stream Environments 295;
The Interchange Environment 296; The Interactive Environment 296;
The Presentation Environment 296;
Environments and Data Streams 296;
Object Content Architectures 298;
Graphics Object Content Architecture 298; Primitives 298;
Drawing Orders and Segments 299; Picture Generation 303;
Coordinate Spaces and Transformations 304;
GOCA Extended 306; Font Object Content Architecture 306;
Font Resources 307; Font Referencing 307;
The FOCA Approach 308; MO:DCA Data Stream 314;
Document Logical Structure 314; Document Layout Structure 315;
Presentation Space 315;
Relationship of MO:DCA to the Object Content Architectures 315;
MO:DCA Components 317; Intelligent Printer Data Stream 318;
Data Objects 319; Resources 319; IPDS Commands 319;
Conclusion 320

16   The CPI Dialog Interface   321

The CPI Dialog Interface and CUA 321; Dialog Elements 323;
Dialog Services 323; Display Services 324;
Control Services 325; Variable Services 325;
Service Call Formats 325; Using the Dialog Tag Language 327;
Defining an Application Panel 328; Defining Messages 331;
Defining a Command Table 332;
Defining Key Mapping Lists 333; Help Facilities 333;
Defining Help Panels 334; Defining a Help Index 335;
Requesting Help 336; Defining Variables 336;
Conclusion 337

17 The CPI Presentation Interface *339*

CPI Presentation Manager Implementations 339; Windows 340;
Window Hierarchies 340; Window Positioning 341;
Window Interactions 342; Window Characteristics 343; Messages 343;
Synchronous and Asynchronous Message Processing 344;
Application Structure 344;
Application Relationship to the CPI Presentation Interface 346;
User Input 346; User Output 347; Message Paths 348;
User Interface Functions 349; Controls 350;
The Standard Window 351; Dialog Box 352;
Control Window Messages 352; Resources 353;
The Clipboard Facility 354;
CPI Presentation Interface Specifications for Window Processing 354;
Graphics Processing 362; Primitives 362;
Segments 363; Attributes 363; Picture Generation 363;
Retained Data 365; Drawing Mode 367;
Coordinate Spaces and Transformations 367; Clipping 369;
Graphics Specifications in the Presentation Interface 369;
Conformance with CUA 370;
Conformance with CCS Object Content Architectures 371;
Conclusion 371

18 The CPI PrintManager Interface *373*

CPI PrintManager Interface Capabilities 373;
PrintManager Verbs 374; PrintManager Print Options 376;
Print Descriptors 380; Relationship to CCS 381; Conclusion 382

Index *383*

PREFACE

IBM's intent with *Systems Application Architecture* (SAA) is to provide a standard set of interfaces to computing for both application developers and end users. These interfaces are intended to provide a framework for developing computing applications that are consistent and that operate in all of IBM's major computing environments.

One of IBM's motivations for developing SAA is to address the problems caused by the lack of commonality between the different computing environments that it supports. Although many of the same functions are provided in each computing environment, different programs must generally be used to provide these functions. The programs used in the various environments are often dissimilar in how users access their functions and in the results they produce.

SAA provides a strategic direction for the use of IBM computing equipment and software, and has the potential to become a standard that defines a universal computing environment. In this environment, applications can be developed without regard to the underlying hardware or operating system software.

SAA defines three major interfaces. The *Common Programming Interface* (CPI), the subject of this volume, specifies a standard set of programming language facilities and a standard set of high-level services that can be used for applicataion development. The *Common User Access* (CUA) interface specifies how an application developer creates an SAA-compliant user interface. *Common Communications Support* (CCS) defines both a low-level networking infrastructure and high-level services that allow standardized communication among devices, application programs, computing systems, and entire computer networks.

It is becoming increasingly common for enterprises to employ networked computing systems of varying sizes to meet their computing needs. In such an environment, it is often desirable to run the same application, or different pieces of the same application, on more than one type of computing system. This book shows how the languages and application programming interfaces defined by the SAA Common Programming Interface make it possible to implement applications that run in a networked environment using computing systems of various types to satisfy application requirements.

The SAA Common Programming Interface has four major objectives. The first is to provide consistency for the end user from one computing application to another. The second is to enhance the productivity of application developers by providing a common set of languages and high-level services that are available in all the SAA computng environments. The third major objective of CPI is to make it possible for application developers in a particular computing environment to access programs, data, and other resources that are part of a different computing environment. The final major CPI objective is to provide application developers with an enterprisewide application development environment, where designing, modeling, developing, testing, and maintaining applications can be done in an integrated fashion. This book is designed to show information systems managers, application developers, and other technical staff members how the facilities defined by CPI can be used to achieve the objectives that IBM has set for the CPI component of SAA.

This book describes the characteristics of the major CPI programming languages, including C, COBOL, FORTRAN, PL/I, and RPG; the specifications for an application generator, based on IBM'S Cross System Product (CSP); and a procedure language based on IBM's REXX program product. The book also describes the application programming interfaces for the high-level services that are defined by CPI, including the *Common Programming Interface for Communications* (CPI-C) that is used to provide program-to-program communication facilities, the CPI *database interface* that allows computing applications to define, retrieve, and manipulate data stored in relational databases, the CPI *query interface* that allows end users to access and update a relational database and request the formatting of reports using the results of queries, the CPI *dialog interface* that provides services used to define the user interface for an application, and the CPI *presentation interface* that provides formatting services for information presented on displays and printers.

Although the major focus of this book is on the SAA Common Programming Interface, the CPI languages and services provide a means for accessing the facilities that are defined by the other two major SAA components. Therefore, CPI is tightly integrated with the Common User Access and Common Communications Support components of SAA, and this book provides introductory explanations of many of the facilities that make up CUA and CCS. Other companion volumes to this one describe SAA, CUA, and CCS in detail.

The programming languages and high-level services that make up the SAA Common Programming Interface are described in a great many separate IBM publications. And, since the CPI programming interfaces are so closely related to the other two major components of SAA, details concerning various CPI programming interfaces are described in publications relating to the CUA and CCS components of SAA as well. Because of the many interrelationships between the various components of SAA, it is often difficult to find the details required to understand each of the elements making up the SAA Common Programming Interface. With this volume, we have attempted to include, in a single source, all the information that information systems staff members need to obtain a thorough understanding of CPI facilities. It is our hope that this volume will help managers and technical staff members to determine which of the various programming language facilities and high-level services making up CPI will be useful in a particular application situation.

PLAN OF THE BOOK This book begins with a Prolog consisting of two chapters. The first chapter introduces the structure and components of Systems Application Architecture and shows how the SAA Common Programming Interface relates to the other SAA architectural components. The second chapter discusses general issues relating to the design of distributed computing applications in the SAA environment.

Part I then introduces the characteristics of the various third- and fourth-generation languages that are included under the SAA umbrella and that can be used for creating SAA-compliant applications.

Part II begins a detailed discussion of the various application programming interfaces that are defined by CPI and describes those programming interfaces that SAA computing applications can use to access files, databases, and repositories.

Part III describes the programming interfaces that can be used to access SAA networking facilities. The chapters in Part III also introduce some of the facilities that are defined by the Common Communications Support component of SAA.

Part IV discusses the programming interfaces that are used by a computing application to implement the user interface. The chapters in Part IV also introduce the characteristics of the Common User Access component of SAA.

James Martin
Kathleen Kavanagh Chapman
Joe Leben

**SYSTEMS APPLICATION ARCHITECTURE:
COMMON PROGRAMMING INTERFACE**

PROLOG

1 THE SAA ENVIRONMENT

Systems Application Architecture (SAA) is a comprehensive, IBM-developed architecture, consisting of a collection of published software interfaces, protocols, and conventions. SAA includes guidelines for designing an application's end-user interface, standards for common programming language facilities, and common protocols for communicating between the various processors in a distributed system.

The major categories of hardware and software for which IBM has committed to support SAA, at the time of writing, are the MVS and VM systems software for large-system processors, the OS/400 operating system for the AS/400 midrange family, and the OS/2 Extended Edition operating system for its personal systems. These are summarized in Fig. 1.1. It is possible that other environments will be supported over time.

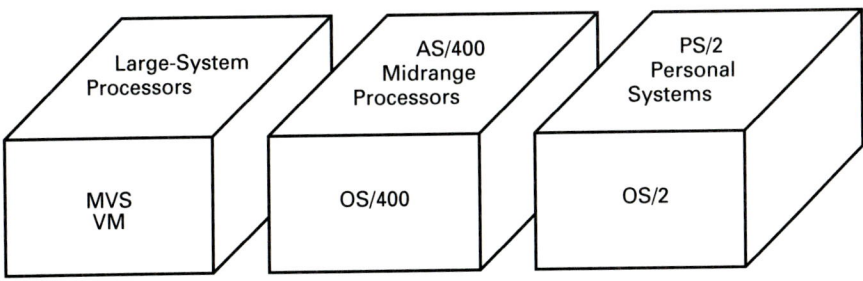

Figure 1.1 SAA interfaces address three categories of hardware and system software.

CCS currently includes support for the following major IBM system software environments:

- **MVS.** *Multiple Virtual Storage* (MVS) refers to a family of operating systems that runs on IBM's large-system processors. Much of the software that runs under the various MVS operating systems is already SAA compliant. All new IBM software for MVS/ESA (Multiple Virtual Storage/Enterprise Systems Architecture), the latest version of MVS, will be SAA compliant. Important MVS subsystems included in SAA are DB2 (Data Base 2) and IMS (Information Management System) for database access and CICS (Customer Information Control System) for transaction processing.
- **VM.** The *Virtual Machine* (VM) systems software is alternative system software for IBM large-system processors. All new IBM software for the VM environment will be SAA compliant. Both the VM/SP and VM/XA versions of VM are included in CCS.
- **OS/400.** *Operating System/400* (OS/400) is the operating system for IBM's AS/400 line of midrange processors. All new IBM OS/400 software will be SAA compliant. The AS/400 processor family and the OS/400 operating system constitute the successor computing environment to IBM's System/36 and System/38 lines of midrange computing systems.
- **OS/2.** *Operating System/2* (OS/2) is the operating system that runs on IBM's Personal System/2 line of small computing systems. OS/2 also runs on many personal computers that are compatible with the PS/2, on many of IBM's older personal computers—such as the PC/AT, and on personal computers compatible with the PC/AT.

An application that is developed in conformance with SAA specifications should operate consistently across all the environments shown in Fig. 1.1. This means the following:

- An SAA application's interface to the end user should appear the same regardless of the environment in which it is run.
- An SAA application should be able to be compiled and run in any of the supported environments without extensive reprogramming.
- An SAA application should be able to communicate with other SAA applications running in any of the environments.

WHY SAA?

Initial development of Systems Application Architecture required a considerable investment of resources on the part of IBM, and additional SAA development work is being done on a continuing basis. Full implementation of the architecture may take a decade or more to accomplish. Why is IBM willing to make such a substantial investment? Not surprisingly, the answer is that IBM felt that such an architecture was needed to ensure its own future growth and continued success in the information systems business. IBM is not alone in making this assessment. Many other major information systems manufacturers are making similar investments for similar reasons. Digital Equipment Corporation's *Network Application Support* (NAS) architecture is a prominent example.

Over the years, IBM's product line has become exceedingly complex. Several different, and basically incompatible, hardware families are now sold and supported. These include the following:

- The System/370 and System/390 lines, with processors ranging from small uniprocessors to various very large processor complexes
- The AS/400 line and its predecessor, the System/3X family
- The 8100
- The Series/1
- The System/88
- Various personal computer and personal workstation lines, including the original PC family, the PS/2 line, and various UNIX workstation models.

In addition to multiple hardware architectures, IBM also has developed, and must continue to support, multiple operating systems. At the time of the initial SAA announcement, IBM offered 14 different operating systems, which provided a wide diversity of interfaces. This diversity also extends to the major system software products used in the different operating environments. Box 1.1 lists key system software products for just a few of IBM's operating systems. Some products operate in more than one environment, but there are still considerable differences even in the same subsystem in moving from one environment to another.

The cost of this complexity is very high, both to IBM and to its customers. For IBM, there is the investment in money and resources that is required to maintain and enhance each of these separate systems and products. Resources have also been consumed in "reinventing the wheel" where multiple products provide essentially the same function, such as IMS/VS and DB2 in database access, ISPF and CMS in time sharing, and JES2 and JES3 in batch job entry facilities. In cases like these, IBM must continue to devote resources to providing the same range of functions in different environments rather than being able to use those resources to add new functions or develop new products. The net result of this for IBM has been a limitation on how rapidly it has been able to enhance or develop critical new system and application software. One obvious concern for IBM is that this situation is having a significant impact on software revenue, which is an increasingly important part of IBM's business.

This product and operating environment complexity has also had a direct impact on IBM's customers. In dealing with enterprisewide needs for computing, companies need to employ all manner of computing systems ranging in size from personal computers through midrange systems, up to large-system host processors. Because of incompatibilities between different systems, companies have

BOX 1.1 System software in the SAA operating environments.

MVS	VM	AS/400	OS/2
System Control			
Info family	SPPF	system management	Presentation Manager
Data Facility	VSAM	storage management	Dialog Manager
VSAM	PSF	Dialog Manager	Batch File Utility
PSF	ISPF	Presentation Manager	
ISPF	GDDM	workstation support	
GDDM	CMS	work management	
TSO	CMS Batch	security	
JES2, JES3	RACF	GDDM	
RACF			
Communication			
VTAM	VTAM	Token-Ring	Token-Ring
NCP	NCP	3270 emulation	3270, 3103, VT100
NetView	NetView	APPC	emulation
DSX	DSNX	SNA upline	APPC
X.25 interface	RSCS	APPN	PC Network
		DSNX	Asynchronous
		X.25 interface	X.25 interface
		NetView alert	NetView alert
		DDM	
Application Enablers			
COBOL	COBOL	COBOL	COBOL
FORTRAN	FORTRAN	FORTRAN	FORTRAN
C	C	C	C
PL/I	PL/I	PL/I	BASIC
CSP	CSP	Application Dev.	Application
ADF	REXX	Tools	Generator
QMF	QMF	RPG	Query Manager
IMS	SQL/DS	BASIC	Database Manager
DB2	CICS	Pascal	
CICS		AS/400 Query	
		SQL/400	
		Database Manager	
		ICF	

often been required to create duplicate system support staffs and application development staffs for each of the different computing system environments. Many of IBM's customers have found it difficult to develop applications that operate in multiple computing system environments or that communicate between environments. The drain on company resources that is caused by dealing with such complexity has slowed the rate at which IBM's customers have been able to develop and install applications. This, in turn, has slowed the rate at which these companies have needed to install new computing capacity. For IBM, growth in its customers computing capacity requirements represents an opportunity for it to sell more hardware and software.

One of IBM's overriding goals in developing and promulgating SAA, then, is to reduce complexity, both for itself and for its customers. Reduced complexity should lead to greater productivity, both for IBM in the development and support of software products, and for IBM's customers in the development and use of computer applications. SAA reduces complexity by defining standard interfaces for both application developers and application users and then supporting those interfaces across IBM's major operating environments.

STRUCTURE OF SAA

The three major IBM computing environments supported by SAA are shown at the bottom of Fig. 1.2. At the bottom are the three hardware environments: the large-system environment, the midrange AS/400 environment, and the personal computer environment. Above that are the system software elements. These include *system control* functions, typically provided by the operating system, that provide a way of accessing and controlling the underlying hardware. *Communication* functions provide the connections between systems and programs that allow them to exchange data. *Application enablers* encompass a range of tools and services that include programming languages, tools for computer-aided software engineering (CASE), application generators, database management systems, teleprocessing monitors, and systems services for data presentation and dialog management. SAA supports IBM's major computing environments through a set of *SAA architectures* and through a set of *SAA applications and solutions* that are built on the SAA architectures.

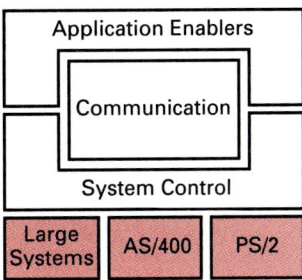

Figure 1.2 Three categories of SAA components support the three IBM computing system environments.

SAA ARCHITECTURES

The SAA architectures provide a standard set of interfaces for developing and using computing applications, regardless of the system on which the application is being developed or run. The three types of interfaces that SAA standardizes are summarized in Fig. 1.3 and are introduced below:

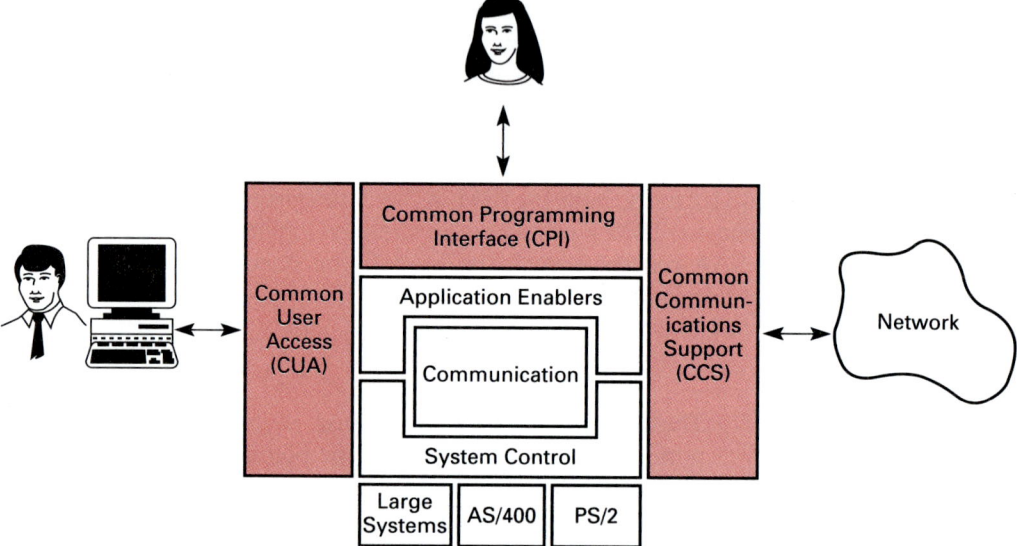

Figure 1.3 SAA defines three architectures that define interfaces to components of SAA.

- **Common Programming Interface.** The *Common Programming Interface* (CPI) architecture, the SAA architecture described in this book, provides specifications for a standard set of languages and a standard set of services that can be accessed using those languages. These languages and services can then be used in a consistent manner by application developers.
- **Common User Access.** The *Common User Access* (CUA) architecture of SAA addresses the interface that SAA applications presents to the end user. CUA includes specifications for the design and use of the screen panels that the end user sees and defines standard techniques for interaction between the end user and the computer system.
- **Common Communications Support.** The *Common Communications Support* (CCS) architecture of SAA specifies standard communication services and protocols that can be used to support the transmission of information between computing systems and between the programs running on them.

This chapter introduces all three of the SAA architectures. Companion volumes to this one describe both the CUA and CCS architectures of SAA in detail [1,2,3].

SAA APPLICATIONS AND SOLUTIONS   In addition to defining the three SAA architectures and providing system software that implements those architectures, IBM and other information technology vendors also provide applications and software solutions that conform to SAA standards and guidelines. These are shown in Fig. 1.4. SAA applications and solutions are designed to be consistent and usable across the entire enterprise, which may include multiple computing environments. SAA solutions are being developed in a great many areas.

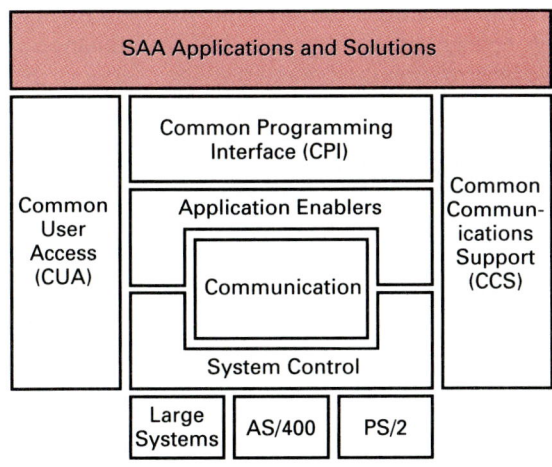

Figure 1.4 IBM and other vendors will supply SAA applications and solutions built on the underlying architectures.

Information and Data

SAA solutions related to information and data provide for both business communications, in the form of notes, memos, reports, and letters, and processing of data in files and databases.

The first set of applications IBM developed that conforms to SAA guidelines is the OfficeVision product family, an integrated set of applications that provide extensive business communication services. OfficeVision functions include electronic mail, address book, calendar management, library services, document processing, and decision support facilities. These functions are provided in a compatible, consistent way by products that run in each of the SAA environments. Connectivity between these products allows information to be exchanged between systems across the enterprise.

In the area of files and databases, IBM provides a family of relational database products, including *DB2* for the MVS environment, *SQL/DS* for the VM environment, and *Database Manager* subsystems for both the OS/400 and OS/2 environments. These products implement a common Structured Query Language

9

(SQL) interface and are being enhanced over time to provide support for providing access to distributed relational data.

Application Development

IBM's key SAA solution in the application development environment is *AD/Cycle*. AD/Cycle comprises a set of integrated CASE tools, with a development platform, that is designed to enhance the productivity and manageability of the application development process. The AD/Cycle tools support all phases of the application development lifecycle, including requirements gathering, analysis, design, coding, testing and debugging, and maintenance. The development platform defines an information model and provides services that enable the tools to be highly integrated.

Information Processing Structure

The communication protocols that are part of the Common Communications Support architecture of SAA allow systems to be interlinked in a variety of ways. Workstations can be linked directly to hosts. Workstations can be linked with each other on a local area network. Hosts can be interconnected in wide area networks. Various local area networks and wide area networks can be interconnected to provide an integrated, enterprisewide network.

Providing system administration facilities for an enterprisewide interconnected system is not a simple task. IBM's solution in this area is *SystemView*, a structure providing a framework for developing system management software products. The SystemView structure defines a consistent interface for users of its products, a common data model for sharing information between products, and guidelines for standardizing and integrating the products.

VENDOR SUPPORT FOR SAA

Many major software vendors other than IBM have announced their support of the SAA standard architectures and will also develop common applications that will run on all of the SAA-supported IBM computing system environments. There is likely to be a rich set of SAA applications available for the IBM environment.

We next provide an introduction to the three major interfaces that SAA defines. Although the major focus of this book is on the Common Programming Interface, we will also introduce the Common User Access and the Common Communications Support interfaces here as well.

Common Programming Interface

It is becoming increasingly common for enterprises to employ computing systems of varying sizes to meet their computing needs. In such an environment, it is often desirable to run the same application on more than one type of computing system. The SAA programming interface standards are designed to support application portability, where an application developed in one environment can be compiled and executed in any of the other environments. In theory, for example, a spreadsheet application for a personal computer that is written in an SAA standard language and that uses only SAA standard services should run on an AS/400 processor simply by making a few minor changes and recompiling it using an AS/400 compiler. This increases application development productivity, since an application need not be rewritten or extensively modified in order to run in another environment. The programming skills that are learned in one environment are also immediately usable in the other environments.

The SAA Common Programming Interface defines a set of languages and programming services that application developers can use in developing SAA applications. The CPI language set includes specifications for procedural languages that are widely used in SAA computing environments, including C, COBOL, FORTRAN, PL/I, and RPG. CPI also includes a specification for an application generator, based on IBM's Cross System Product (CSP), and for a procedure language based on the REXX program product.

The various CPI language specifications define the features that must be included when implementing a language in one of the SAA computing environments. For example, Fig. 1.5 shows the SAA specification for the IF statement in the COBOL language. The specifications for all the SAA language statements are written in a consistent format using a diagramming technique that lists parameters and options in a concise, easy-to-read manner.

CPI also includes specifications for various types of programming services that can be used by an application. These services are defined in terms of the application program interfaces that are used to invoke them:

- **Communications Interface.** The *Common Programming Interface for Communications* (CPI-C) is used to provide program-to-program communication. It is based on SNA's logical unit (LU) 6.2 architecture and includes the services needed to start and end a conversation with a remote program, send and receive data, synchronize processing between programs, and notify a partner of errors in the communication.

- **Database Interface.** The CPI *database interface* allows applications to define, retrieve, and manipulate data from a relational database. It employs the Structured Query Language (SQL), as defined in the *American National Standard Database Language—SQL* standard, and as used in IBM's relational database products, such as DB2, SQL/DS, and the database manager components that run in the OS/400 and OS/2 environments.

- **Query Interface.** The CPI *query interface* allows end users to access and update a relational database and request the formatting of reports using the results of queries. The functions that are part of the query interface are designed to be easy-to-use and accessible via menus. The query interface is based on the Query Management Facility (QMF) that is used with the DB2 database management system.

IF Statement

TSO/E	CMS	OS/400	OS/2	IMS	CICS
X	X	X	X	X	X

The IF statement evaluates a condition and provides for alternative actions in the object program, depending on the evaluation.

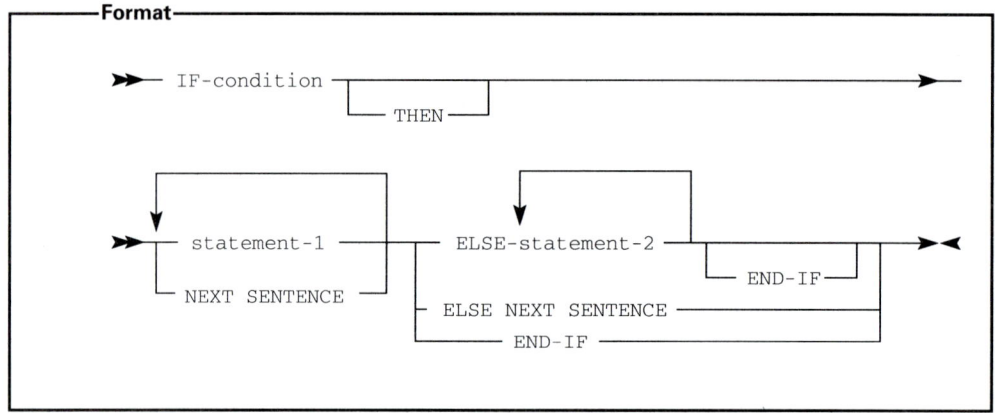

condition
May be any simple or complex condition, as described in "Conditional Expressions" on page 139.

statement-1
statement-2
Can be any one of the following:

- An imperative statement
- A conditional statement
- An imperative statement followed by a conditional statement

NEXT SENTENCE
If the END-IF phrase is specified, the NEXT SENTENCE phrase must not be specified.

ELSE NEXT SENTENCE
May be omitted if it immediately precedes a separator period that ends the IF statement.

END-IF Phrase
This explicit scope terminator services to delimit the scope of the IF statement. END-IF permits a conditional IF statement to be nested in another conditional statement.

For more information, see "Delimited Scope Statements" on page 155.

Figure 1.5 SAA COBOL specification for the IF statement.

- **Dialog Interface.** The CPI *dialog interface* provides services used to control user interaction with the application. These services support the display of information on the screen, the passing of data and function requests from the user to the application, and the flow of panels that make up the dialog. The dialog interface specifications are based on the ISPF and EZ-VU program products.
- **Presentation Interface.** The CPI *presentation interface* provides formatting services for information presented on displays and printers. It includes specifications for both alphanumeric and graphic information. Features supported by the presentation interface include the use of windows, color, fonts, the double-byte* character set for international languages, and both line and picture images. The presentation interface specification is based largely on the GDDM product.

The specifications that make up CPI are intended to provide application developers with a set of languages and services that can be used in any of the supported SAA environments. Although the specifications cover many aspects of an application developer's responsibilities, not every function that is part of application development is included. Certain features that are specific to the hardware or to a particular operating system, such as job control language, installation procedures, tuning considerations, and compiletime and runtime options, are not included in the CPI specifications.

The Common Programming Interface has four objectives:

1. To provide consistency for the end user. This objective is met through the dialog interface and the presentation interface, which provide support for SAA's Common User Access architecture and its goal of providing consistent and easy-to-use end user interfaces.

2. To enhance the productivity of application developers. This objective is met in two ways: through application portability and through skill portability. Applications developed in conformance with the CPI specifications are more easily moved from one computing environment to another with minimal rewriting required to achieve this portability. The standardization of application development languages and services also allows a developer to move more easily between environments and to become productive in a new environment with a minimum of retraining.

3. To make it possible for applications to access programs, data, and other resources that are part of a different computing environment. The communications interface specifies a standard method for program-to-program communication. The database interface and the file statements in the procedural languages allow access to data. Underlying SAA Common Communications Support facilities allow the CPI interfaces to be used to access remote data in a way that is transparent to the application and to the application developer.

*IBM documentation tends to use the term *byte* to refer to a collection of 8 bits while international standards tend to prefer the term *octet.* Since this series of books on SAA describes both IBM architectures and international standards, the authors debated whether to standardize on one term or the other. We decided to compromise. When describing IBM architectures and protocols we typically use the term *byte;* when describing international standards, we typically use the term *octet.*

4. To provide an enterprisewide application development environment, where designing, modeling, developing, testing, and maintaining applications can be done in an integrated fashion. Providing such an environment requires the specifications that make up CPI, and also the full set of application development tools that are consistent with the specifications.

Users and vendors alike are realizing the value of specifying standard application-enabling architectures. Whenever a repetitive aspect of application development can be identified, a standard way of doing it can be specified, a tool to make it happen can be built, and the time it takes to build an application can be reduced.

COMMON USER ACCESS

One key to the effective deployment and efficient use of computer applications is ease-of-use for the end user. The user interface that the end users of an application employ must be well designed and easy to learn. Interfaces should be consistent from application to application in the same environment and from application to application across different computing environments. For example, a database query application running on a 3090 processor complex should employ the same user interface principles as a spreadsheet application running on a personal computer.

The end user interface standards that are part of SAA provide for the development of applications that offer a consistent view to the application user. This promotes user productivity—the learning curve for new applications is reduced, and the user is not required to learn a new interface if an application is moved from one computing environment to another.

SAA Common User Access consists of a set of rules and guidelines that help to guide the development of the interface between a computer application and an end user of that application. The two main aspects of the Common User Access interface concern presentation and user interaction. *Presentation* is concerned primarily with the way in which the computer application presents information to the user of the application. *User interaction* is concerned with the ways in which a user specifies actions and provides information to the application.

Presentation

An application normally displays information to the end user on a screen that is part of a computer workstation or terminal. The way in which that information is formatted and displayed depends on the type of device the user is employing. SAA defines the use of two different types of terminal devices: *nonprogrammable terminals* (NPT)—such as 3270 display terminals—and *programmable workstations* (PWS)—such as a personal computer.

Nonprogrammable Terminal Panel Layout

For a nonprogrammable terminal, a particular arrangement of information appearing on the screen is called a *panel*. The CUA panel layout for a nonprogrammable terminal is shown in Fig. 1.6. All panel types share a common format that divides the panel into five areas:

- **Action Bar.** The action bar area is used to provide the user with a set of action choices that are currently available.
- **Work Area.** The work area is used for the general display or entering of information related to the application.
- **Message Area.** The message area is used by the application to display messages to the user.
- **Command Area.** The command area is used by the user to directly enter commands.
- **Function Key Area.** The function key area is used to display the action choices that can currently be selected using the keyboard's function keys.

```
      Find    Add    Exit    Help
   ─────────────────────────────────────────────────────────
                          Hotel Selector

   Select one from each group by typing the number.
   Then select an action.

        Name of city       1    1. New York
                                2. Paris
                                3. Tokyo

        Price category     1    1. Budget
                                2. Moderate
                                3. Expensive
                                4. Luxury


   Reformatting is complete.  Enter to continue.
   Command ===>    send stat.rpt to toni _____
   Enter    F1=Help    F3=Exit    F10=Actions    F12=Cancel
```

Figure 1.6 Nonprogrammable terminal panel layout.

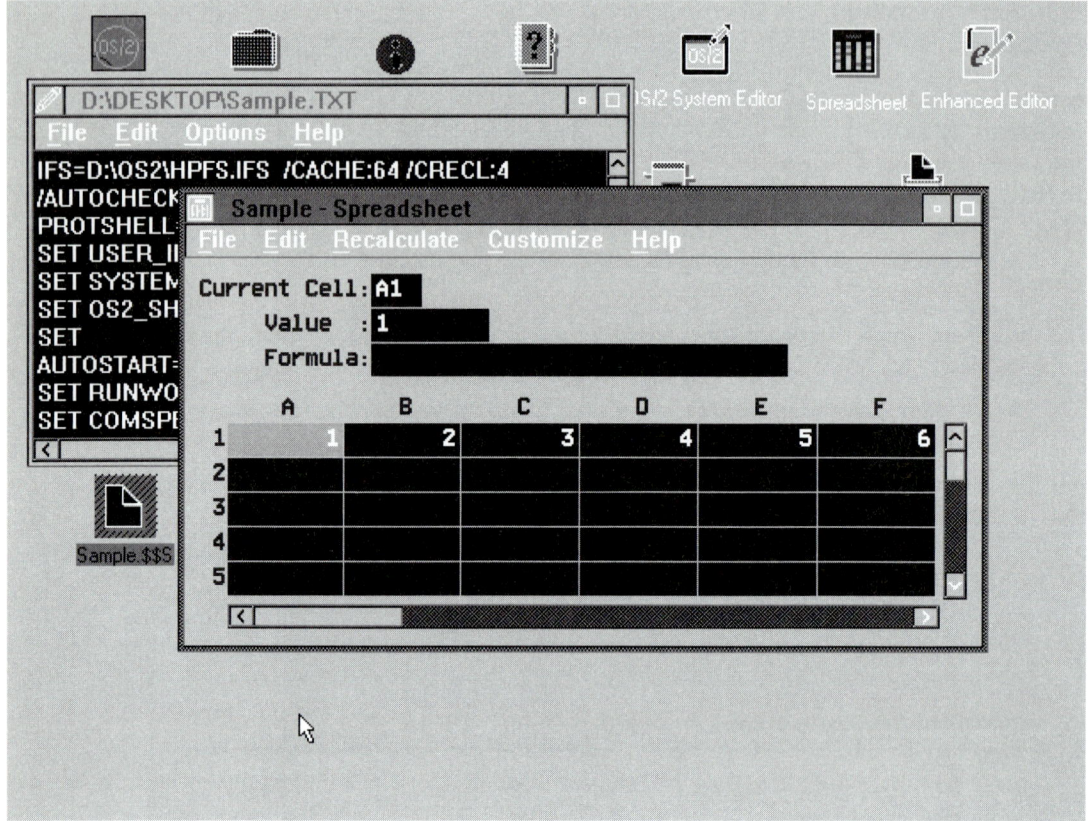

Figure 1.7 Programmable workstation window structure.

Programmable Workstation Window Structure

For a programmable workstation (PWS), such as a personal computer, information is displayed in *windows*. A window is a bounded portion of the display screen that is used to display information. Figure 1.7 shows how the screen of a programmable workstation might look with two windows displayed. CUA defines standard elements that make up a window and provides guidelines on formatting these elements.

Multiple windows can be used to display information from multiple applications simultaneously. Multiple windows can also be used for a single application. CUA defines certain standard ways of using multiple windows. For example, a Help window is used to assist the user in understanding information displayed or choices available in an application panel currently being displayed in some other window.

Panel and Window Information Content Guidelines

In addition to defining standard panel and window layouts, CUA provides guidelines for the use of icons, color, and emphasis in displaying the information content of panels and windows. Guidelines in these areas are designed to allow these facilities to be used in a way that reinforces the user's understanding of how the user interface operates and that is consistent, both within an application and from one application to another.

Interaction Techniques

CUA defines standard methods for user interaction, where the interaction may be used to make a selection, to enter information, or to perform an action such as copying an object or moving a window. CUA defines interaction techniques based on the use of a mouse or other pointing device and on the use of a keyboard.

As part of application interface design, CUA defines standard actions that can be made available to the user as part of the user interface. These actions can be part of a menu bar or may be accessible through the use of function keys or pushbuttons. Many of the standard actions are designed to help the user control the dialog that takes place with the application. Others can be used to directly invoke application functions.

The key benefit to be gained from adhering to the Common User Access rules when designing an application user interface is increased productivity, both for end users and for application developers. End users benefit from reduced learning time as they move from one application to another or from one computing environment to another. Productivity of application developers increases because they need not design the user interface from the ground up for each new application. SAA standard panel and window layouts and standard interaction techniques can be used as a basis for the interface. They can then be modified as necessary to meet each new application's unique requirements. Powerful application development tools are also becoming available that perform much of the processing involved in implementing a CUA-style user interface.

COMMON COMMUNICATIONS SUPPORT

Enterprises not only employ a variety of different computing environments, but they are also beginning to connect different types of computing systems together to create extensive networks of great complexity. In such an environment, it is desirable for applications to be able to communicate with one another and to access resources that are distributed throughout the network.

By defining standard communication techniques, SAA makes it easier to implement networks that interconnect different types of computing systems and that allow applications to communicate with one another using that network. This cross-system communication may be used to access geographically-distributed resources or to develop distributed computing applications, where part of the processing is performed on one system and part on another. The SAA Common Communications Support (CCS) architecture defines consistent methods for exchanging data across a network.

SAA Common Communications Support consists of a set of protocols, services, and standardized data formats that can be used to interconnect applications, systems, networks, and devices in a way that permits useful data interchange. The elements that make up CCS are drawn primarily from SNA, IBM's wide area network architecture, but there are also selected portions of international standards developed by organizations such as ISO, CCITT, and IEEE. CCS elements are divided into six categories: objects, data streams, application services, session services, network services, and data link controls.

Objects

Various types of data, such as text, images, and graphics, can be included in the data streams used to interchange data across the network. Each type of data is contained in the data stream as an *object*. Different object content architectures define the structures of the objects used for different types of data. CCS currently includes definitions for five object content architectures:

1. **Presentation Text Object Content Architecture.** This architecture describes the structure and content of objects containing text information that has been formatted for display.
2. **Graphic Object Content Architecture.** This architecture defines the structure and content of graphic objects that contain such elements as lines, arcs, and character strings.
3. **Image Object Content Architecture.** This architecture describes the structure and content of objects containing bit-mapped data.
4. **Formatted Data Object Content Architecture.** This architecture is used to express the format and meaning of data elements that are stored in files and databases.
5. **Font Object Content Architecture.** This architecture defines the structure and content of objects containing information about type fonts that can be used to control the appearance of printed or displayed text.

Data Streams

A *data stream* is a continuous stream of characters that conforms to a defined format. The format typically specifies the characters that are allowable within the data stream and the syntax and meaning of control codes that are embedded in the data stream. Five data stream definitions are included in CCS:

1. **3270 Data Stream.** This data stream is used for transmitting data between an application program and a 3270-type terminal. A 3270 data stream contains user data, commands, and control codes that govern the processing and formatting of data. For data sent from a program to a terminal, the data stream controls how information is formatted and displayed on the device's display screen or printer. For data sent from a terminal to a program, the data stream controls how the program interprets the data.

2. **Intelligent Printer Data Stream (IPDS).** This data stream is used to send data from an application program to an all-points-addressable printer. IPDS supports presentation of high-quality text, image, vector graphics, and bar code data, and control of device functions such as duplexing and media-bin selection.

3. **Mixed Object Document Content Architecture (MO:DCA) Data Stream.** This data stream is used to store and exchange composite documents, which may consist of a combination of text, graphics, and images. A MO:DCA (often pronounced to rhyme with vodka) data stream consists of data objects and control information, where the data objects can be of different types. The individual object content architectures described previously define the structure of data objects of a particular type.

4. **Character Data Representation Architecture.** This data stream is used to carry character data and information identifying the graphic character set, called a *code page,* used to display or print each character in the data stream.

5. **Revisable-Form-Text Document Content Architecture (RFT-DCA) Data Stream.** This data stream is used to store and exchange text documents in an office information system. An RFT-DCA data stream contains both text representing the content of the document and control information that specifies how the document is to be formatted. RFT-DCA specifies the structure used within the data stream to represent both text and control codes and how systems are to interpret the text and control codes. Revisable-form-text documents are in a form that permits them to be easily modified by anyone who receives the document or has access to it. RFT-DCA is not a strategic data stream and is included in CCS only for migration purposes.

Application Services

Application services are those services that can be requested by SAA application processes. SAA application services enhance the services offered by the network itself by allowing SAA systems to distribute files, exchange documents, and exchange electronic messages. These services are defined by a number of IBM architectures, ISO standards, and CCITT recommendations.

The CCS application services that are included in CCS for the SNA networking environment are the following:

1. **Document Interchange Architecture (DIA).** This architecture defines how documents and requests for document processing services are interchanged between application processes running in SAA systems that are currently communicating with one another.

2. **SNA Distribution Services (SNADS).** This architecture specifies the means by which documents are exchanged between application processes on an *asynchronous* basis. Asynchronous in this context means that the recipient of the document need not be currently active in the network. Documents are stored until the recipient becomes active, at which time the document can be delivered.
3. **Distributed Data Management (DDM).** This architecture defines the way in which remote access to relational databases is handled.
4. **SNA/Management Services (SNA/MS).** This portion of the SNA architecture defines services that allow users to plan, organize, and control the network in a consistent fashion.

The *International Organization for Standardization* (ISO) in Geneva, Switzerland is developing a generalized model of system interconnection, called the *Reference Model of Open Systems Interconnection*, or *OSI Model* for short. The primary purpose of the OSI model is to provide a basis for coordinating the development of standards that relate to the flexible interconnection of systems using data communication facilities. IBM has included OSI protocols in the Common Communications Support interface as a way of supporting communication between IBM and non-IBM systems.

The following OSI protocols are included in CCS as part of application services:

1. **File Transfer, Access, and Management (FTAM).** This is an ISO standard (also adopted by CCITT as a CCITT Recommendation) for the OSI application layer that specifies services and protocols that define a standardized way for accessing and transferring files between open systems.
2. **X.400 Message Handling System.** This is a CCITT Recommendation (also accepted as an ISO international standard) for the OSI application layer that specifies services and protocols that define standard methods for transferring electronic mail messages between open systems.
3. **Association Control Service Element (ACSE).** This is an ISO standard that specifies services and protocols that define how an application running in one open system forms an association with an application running in another open system for the purposes of communication in the OSI environment.

Session Services

Session services are used to establish and terminate communication between two application programs and to transfer data between them. For SNA, CCS employs the formats and protocols that are defined by the *SNA Logical Unit Type 6.2* (LU 6.2) architecture. LU 6.2 provides program-to-program communication across an SNA network. LU 6.2 services are accessed via a protocol boundary that is defined in terms of a set of protocol boundary verbs. Each verb and its associated parameters provides a specific function, such as starting or ending a conversation between programs, sending or receiving data, synchronizing processing, or notifying a program of an error condition.

For OSI, the following session services are included in CCS:

1. **Presentation Layer Protocol.** These protocols provide for connection establishment and release, and data transfer with synchronization and resynchronization capabilities, and the negotiation of presentation contexts that determine how data values are encoded. An associated international standard notation defines how the information content of data can be defined without describing how it is represented in a computer or encoded for transmission and also defines a way of encoding and decoding values for such data types.
2. **Session Layer Protocol.** This protocol provides for both half-duplex and full-duplex transmission, with expedited data transfer and exception reporting.
3. **Transport Layer Protocol.** This protocol provides for multiplexing of transport connections onto a network connection, the use of checksums and sequence numbers for error detection and recovery, and the use of sequence numbers for flow control.

Network Services

The *network services* category in CCS consists of the protocols used to provide routing services across a network. For SNA, it uses the protocols associated with SNA *Type 2.1 nodes*. The architecture of the Type 2.1 node describes how the three variations of the Type 2.1 node can be attached to and exchanges data over an SNA network.

In the OSI environment, the international standards for the Network layer that are included in CCS describe protocols used to attach an SAA processor functioning as an end system to a network implementing the appropriate ISO standards for the OSI architecture. Support is included in CCS for two Network layer protocols:

1. **Connectionless-Mode Network Service.** The protocol to supply the *Connectionless-Mode Network Service (CLNS)* provides a best-efforts or datagram service that includes no error handling or acknowledgment facilities. The CLNS is used in attaching an SAA processor to an OSI network via a Token-Ring LAN subnetwork.
2. **Connection-Mode Network Service.** The protocol to supply the *Connection-Mode Network Service (CONS)* provides a reliable, positive notification of failure service that includes facilities for data transmission with acknowledgments, sequence preservation, and error detection and recovery. The CONS is used in attaching an SAA processor to an OSI network via an X.25 virtual circuit.

Data Link Controls

Data Link Controls in both the SNA and OSI environments are used by the CCS network services and define how two adjacent nodes transmit data in a relatively error-free fashion over a single physical circuit. Data Link Controls are supported in CCS for four types of data links.

- **Synchronous Data Link Control.** Synchronous Data Link Control (SDLC) data links implement point-to-point and multipoint connections in the wide area networking environment. SDLC is used for managing synchronous, code-transparent, serial-by-bit transmissions between nodes that are connected by telecommunications links.
- **Token-Ring LAN.** Token-ring LAN data links are used for transmission across a local area network using a token passing access control method. The token-ring protocols are based on the IEEE 802.2 and 802.5 standards (also described by ISO 8802-2 and ISO 8802-5).
- **CCITT Recommendation X.25.** CCITT Recommendation X.25 defines the interface between a computer and a packet-switched public data network (PSDN). A packet-switched data network implements a virtual circuit that can be used for data transmission.
- **Integrated Services Digital Network (ISDN).** An ISDN data link makes use of a digital circuit provided by a common carrier that conforms to ISDN standards. An ISDN circuit provides end-to-end digital telecommunications services and can be used to support voice and nonvoice services.

The Goal of CCS

The primary goal of Common Communications Support is to provide connectivity between applications across networks in order to support distributed application processing, distributed file processing, and distributed database processing. CCS includes protocols that allow non-SAA systems to participate in the connectivity and to exchange data with SAA systems. An SAA application accesses the various Common Communications Support components through the Common Programming Interface. This is illustrated in Fig. 1.8. For example, if an SAA application needs to communicate with another application, it does so using high-level language statements to invoke the services that are part of the CPI communication interface. These statements generate code that uses the protocols and formats defined by the LU 6.2 component of CCS to accomplish program-to-program communication during program execution. In this way, the application is shielded from the details involved in the CCS protocols. Similarly, an application uses the database interface (SQL) or file I/O statements that are part of one of the CPI languages to access data. The underlying CCS protocols then provide the facilities needed to access distributed data in a manner that is transparent to the application. The CPI presentation interface allows an application to process data that is to be displayed or printed using one of the CCS data streams, again without the application being involved with the details of the CCS protocols and formats.

We now conclude this introductory chapter on SAA by discussing what SAA is and what it is not, describing some of its strengths and weaknesses, and making some predictions about its future.

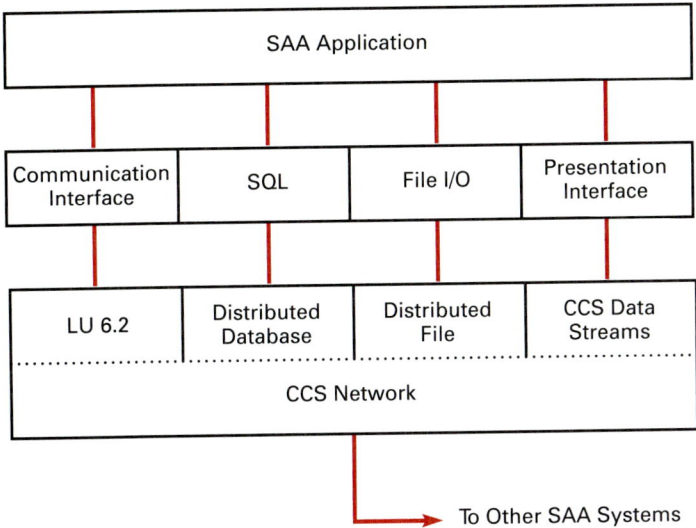

Figure 1.8 The CPI and CCS interfaces work together in handling communication functions for an SAA application.

ARCHITECTURE VERSUS IMPLEMENTATION

SAA is a collection of *architectures* and is not itself a product or set of products. A good architecture relates primarily to the needs of the end users rather than to enthusiasm for particular techniques. And, an architecture should be independent of any particular hardware or software products that implement it. Often products do not implement all functions defined in an architecture because of constraints in the environment in which they are developed and must operate. However, product limitations are not necessarily architectural limitations. Different products may also choose to implement an architecture in different ways. As long as they conform to the rules of the architecture, they can use different techniques to implement the rules. The underlying architecture does not dictate, nor is it affected by, these implementation choices.

Although architectures provide rules for the development of new products, these rules can change. Computing requirements are extensive and are complex to define and implement. The architectures must be able to grow and adapt to new ideas and technologies. This means that the development of architectures like SAA is an evolutionary process.

In describing SAA, IBM has defined the term architecture in the following way:

> An architecture is a set of design principles that define the relationships of and interactions between various parts of a system or network of systems.

As an architecture, SAA defines a set of interfaces that, as we have seen, can be used consistently across multiple computing environments. The specification of these interfaces consists of data formats, protocols, and conventions. They define standard interfaces for end users interacting with applications and systems, for application developers creating programs and applications, and for programs and systems communicating across a network.

Many different hardware and software products have been and are being developed in the different computing environments. For these widely varying products to be used effectively and efficiently by applications in complex configurations involving multiple computing environments, they must be compatible; if compatibility is not achieved, complex interfaces would have to be built for meaningful interaction to take place. One of the primary reasons for developing architectures is to facilitate this compatibility.

By conforming to the SAA architecture, applications can be developed that are compatible with the different hardware and software products and can be used in or interlinked across multiple environments. When new products are developed that conform to the architecture, they will also be compatible and can be used with existing applications without major disruptions.

The goals and standards of architectures are important to both customers and vendors. The architectures must provide customers with a variety of choices for developing applications, and it must allow them to continue using the applications with relative ease as their overall computing environment evolves. Architectures should permit vendors to mass produce hardware or software building blocks that can be used in a variety of different environments. They should also allow the development of new products that are compatible with existing products and can be integrated into existing systems without the need for costly interfaces and program modifications.

SAA: STRENGTHS AND WEAKNESSES

SAA is likely to be the technology that will have the largest affect on IBM customers over the next five to ten years. In many ways, the transition to SAA represents the most significant change in IBM software environments since the introduction of the System/360 in 1964.

As its name implies, SAA is an architecture for building enterprisewide systems of applications. It is a consistent, open set of specifications for how these applications will be built. Today, organizations often mix many types of computers. All the machines serve different, but sometimes overlapping, functions. They are programmed differently, have different user interfaces, and there is little communication between them. It is not easy to build applications that make the best use of differing machine capabilities.

The objective of integrated computing environments is to provide seamless connections between all the machines so information and processes can be distributed freely among them. Additional objectives include the provision of consistent user interfaces for all applications. Such an environment provides programmers with a consistent development model that makes it easy to build applications for distributed computing.

SAA is the architecture that will accomplish these objectives in the IBM environment. It is the architecture that will help IBM customers to build the distributed computing applications of the 1990s. IBM's SAA is an impressive effort to unify IBM's application environments under a single architecture.

However, we must recognize that, at the time of writing, SAA is still in a formative stage. A well-designed architecture should reflect a unified and all-encompassing structure or model within which detailed specifications can be developed. At this point, SAA is more of a collection of interfaces and protocols that have been designated as standard across the SAA-supported computing environments. The underlying model for integrating the various specifications has not yet been fully developed. In a number of instances, the individual interface specifications have been developed based on existing products rather than being designed as part of an overall logical model. Since these products are not fully integrated, the specifications that make up SAA do not yet define a totally seamless environment. As SAA continues to evolve, it will undoubtedly become more complete and comprehensive. IBM's development of an application-development model, AD/Cycle, with its underlying repository, is a step in this direction.

SAA: AN OPEN ARCHITECTURE

There is also the question of whether SAA is truly an open architecture. One of the major limitations of vendor-developed architectures is their proprietary nature. SAA is a proprietary architecture from IBM, not the result of a standards-setting organization. SAA is open in that it specifies a common set of software interfaces across multiple hardware platforms. It supports both proprietary services and protocols, such as SNA and LU 6.2, as well as international standards, including support for ISO protocols for communications.

Even though IBM stresses the openness of SAA, we must understand that SAA plays a critical role in IBM's strategy to increase its dominance in the 1990s in both hardware and software systems. This strategy does not *necessarily* conflict with the needs of IBM's customers, but is important to keep in mind when considering IBM's primary motivation with SAA. IBM customers are currently expressing a growing need for greater connectivity and distributed-processing capability. SAA is designed to meet that need. However, SAA may tend to lock IBM in as a vendor. If SAA becomes the standard for an organization, then IBM or IBM-compatible hardware and software will be preferred in that environment. Competing vendors may be forced either to accept the SAA standard or to develop their own. Customers may then be forced either to accept SAA as the standard or to forgo its benefits.

IBM is responsive to the demands of the marketplace for an open architecture as can be seen in the case of the support for ISO protocols under the SAA umbrella. SAA had originally used IBM's proprietary SNA for communications, but many customers asked for support of the ISO protocols being developed in support of the OSI model. That support has been announced and partially implemented. In addition, much of the marketplace prefers UNIX as the environment for programmable workstations. IBM is responding to this demand with AIX, its version of UNIX, which is evolving to maintain compliance with the communication and programming interfaces of SAA. This will allow IBM customers to use either UNIX or OS/2 as the operating system for programmable workstations.

Still, difficulties remain because the programmer must choose between using the SNA or OSI communications interface. The same problems exist with the programming interfaces, database services, and the user interface. IBM is sensitive to language standards and will most likely continue to support international language standards. The database standards will be driven by its own products, as will the user-interface standards.

SAA IMPLEMENTATION

Another current limitation of SAA is the lack of system software and tools that can be used to develop and execute SAA-compliant applications in all the designated computing environments. IBM has committed to provide products in all environments within two years of the time that an SAA specification is first published. Doing this will be a major challenge for IBM and will continue to be a challenge as SAA expands and evolves. IBM has also indicated that SAA-enabling products may be implemented in different ways. Some products will have versions available in each of the SAA environments—MVS, VM, OS/400, and OS/2. In this case, an application can be developed and run in any of the environments as a stand-alone system and can also be ported from one environment to another. Some SAA functions that are intended to be used where processing is distributed across different systems may be implemented in products that involve *cooperative processing*. With cooperative processing, the user interface processing is performed on a programmable workstation with other application processing being performed on larger systems. In a case like this, the SAA-enabling tool may require both OS/2 and a connected host, with the function not available on a stand-alone basis in any single environment.

THE FUTURE OF SAA

SAA has the potential for having great impact on the future of computing. For IBM, it will eventually reduce the resources required to support overlapping products and allow more resources to be invested in providing new functions and new products. SAA holds the promise of increasing application development productivity for IBM, for other vendors, and for customers. The skills of application developers will be leveraged across multiple environments and the multisystem use of applications will be facilitated.

SAA also facilitates the use of multisystem computing and enterprisewide networks that combine different computing environments. SAA applications will be able to employ various types of distributed processing and distributed database access. Being able to use distributed processing effectively and efficiently is key to IBM's view of the future, where there are workstations on every desk, connected to medium- and large-scale processors acting as departmental and corporate systems. The workstation provides a consistent user interface—based on the Common User Access architecture—to the network and to host systems. The workstation may also perform parts of the application processing, as appropriate to the power of the workstation and the particular application. IBM's hope is that SAA will facilitate application growth, and that application growth will, in turn, drive the demand for IBM's computing systems.

In a broader sense, SAA provides a strategic direction for the use of computing and has the potential to become the standard that defines a universal computing environment. In this environment, applications can be developed without regard to the underlying hardware or operating system. For this to happen, SAA has to be accepted as a de facto standard by vendors and by customers. IBM has been successful in the past with establishing de facto standards. Its System/360 architecture—along with its System/370 and System/390 extensions—underlies the current family of IBM processors that range from very small to very large and also underlies a number of plug-compatible processors. SNA has become a very widely used network architecture, with a large number of non-IBM vendors providing products and interfaces that support SNA. The SQL language is well on its way to becoming a standard for database processing.

For SAA to be successful in achieving widespread acceptance, several things must occur. IBM must, in a reasonable time period, implement the system software and application development tools needed to develop and execute SAA-compliant applications in all the designated computing environments. There is also a need to have a critical mass of SAA applications developed by IBM, by other vendors, and by customers. Finally, SAA must continue to expand and evolve so that it addresses all areas required for true cross-system consistency and connectivity.

SAA has already evolved since its original announcement by adding RPG, PL/I, and the communications interface to the Common Programming Interface, and by adding the Distributed Data Management (DDM) architecture, the Distributed Relational Database Architecture (DRDA), and the OSI protocols to Common Communications Support. The original Common User Access specifications have also been expanded to provide separate models for nonprogrammable terminals and programmable workstations. Areas expected to be addressed within SAA in the future include security, knowledge-based systems, the use of a central repository, and transaction processing.

CONCLUSION   The future of SAA—either in its development as an architecture or its success in terms of implementation—will not be determined in the short term. As with SNA, an architecture of this magnitude may well take eight or ten years before its full impact is felt. In the meantime, even partial observance and implementation can be valuable by providing greater consistency and connectivity across different computing environments.

Now that we have introduced the major components that make up the SAA environment, Chapter 2 begins an examination of the design of distributed computing applications in the SAA environment.

REFERENCES

1. James Martin, Kathleen Kavanagh Chapman, and Joe Leben, *Systems Application Architecture: Common User Access.* Prentice Hall, Englewood Cliffs, NJ, 1991.

2. James Martin, Kathleen Kavanagh Chapman, and Joe Leben, *Systems Application Architecture: Common Communications Support: Distributed Applications.* Prentice Hall, Englewood Cliffs, NJ, 1992.

3. James Martin, Kathleen Kavanagh Chapman, and Joe Leben, *Systems Application Architecture: Common Communications Support: Network Infrastructure.* Prentice Hall, Englewood Cliffs, NJ, 1992.

2 SAA APPLICATION DESIGN

As system software and application development tools have been developed that support SAA, many of the features and benefits of SAA can be automatically incorporated in applications through standard options and defaults provided by each tool. However, even with automatic support, applications need to be properly designed to take full advantage of the cross-system consistency and connectivity possible within SAA. The general design principles that are important in the SAA environment are the subject of this chapter.

SAA DESIGN GOALS

Today, many enterprises are dealing with the issues and problems involved in developing and using complex networks. These networks interconnect different types of processors, ranging from personal computers and intelligent workstations through midrange and large-system processors, using a variety of communications technologies. One of the goals of SAA is to support *connectivity* between computing systems and between applications running on different computing systems. A high degree of connectivity can be the basis for the creation of a distributed computing environment in which networked computers can provide users with access to distributed resources, such as remote files and databases, and in which the processing of an application can be distributed among two or more computing systems.

A second goal of SAA is to increase application *portability*, where an application developed in one environment can be compiled and executed, with little change, in any of the other environments. Portability provides for more efficient and economical operation in several ways. Applications do not have to be extensively rewritten for each environment, thus reducing development costs. As an application evolves and is modified over time, programming resources do not have to be expended maintaining significantly different versions of the application in different environments. Distributed computing applications, where pieces of the application are distributed among two or more computing systems, become easier to implement if the application pieces are not restricted to a particular computing environment.

SAA, and particularly the Common Programming Interface, is concerned with application development *productivity*. When standard programming interfaces are supported across computing environments, programmers and analysts can be more productive. One way that SAA enhances productivity is that developers are not required to learn a new set of skills when moving to a new environment. Having standard services available also increases productivity, since the services can be used as program building blocks, rather than having to be designed, coded, and tested individually for each application.

One of the benefits of SAA is that it is designed to provide the cross-system connectivity and consistency needed in an enterprise networking environment. It is intended to meet the requirements associated with the following types of processing:

- **Distributed computing.** Distributed computing implies that different functions of a computing application execute in different machines, and the different components of an application on each machine work together to solve a common business problem.
- **Distributed resources.** SAA addresses providing access to various types of resources that may be distributed across the network and across different computing environments. These resources can include documents and data stored in files and databases.
- **Online processing.** Online processing involves user interaction that takes place during application processing. Online applications may be interactive or transactional.

We will look at each of these types of processing in more detail in the sections that follow.

DISTRIBUTED COMPUTING

A distributed computing approach supports the distribution of processing power throughout a computer network. In a distributed computing application, each machine attached to the network is assigned functions that it performs best. For example, the functions assigned to host computers and programmable workstations may be completely different. Host computers are best at serving multiple users and coordinating access to large corporate databases. The workstation is best suited for user interface processing and local analysis functions. Some specific application functions might be assigned to one or more computing environments.

Both a host environment and a workstation environment are needed for many business applications. Until now, it has been necessary to assign applications to one environment, forgoing the advantages of the other. With the advent of integrated environments such as that provided by SAA, applications can now more easily be built that take advantage of both environments in a distributed manner.

APPLICATION COMPONENTS

With any one application, there are three components that might be separated using a distributed approach:

- User interface processing
- Application functions
- Data access processing

All three of the above components might be performed on a single machine (host or workstation), or the application can be split between the machines. Depending on how the application is structured, it can generally be placed into one of the following five categories:

- Local processing
- Cooperative processing (distributed dialog processing)
- Distributed data access
- Distributed function processing
- Client/server computing

The following sections discuss each of the above five categories of applications. Keep in mind that complex applications may have some of the characteristics of more than one of these categories.

LOCAL PROCESSING

With *local processing*, as illustrated in Fig. 2.1, all programs and data reside at the same location. The location might be the site of a centralized host, where the user communicates with the application using a terminal attached to the host via a telecommunications link, as illustrated in Fig. 2.1. Local processing can also be implemented using a minicomputer or a programmable workstation on which all application functions are performed.

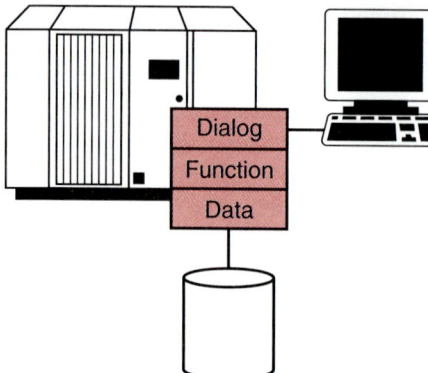

Figure 2.1 With *local processing,* the application's dialog processing, all of its function processing, and its data access processing are performed on the same computing system.

COOPERATIVE PROCESSING

A simple form of distributed computing, illustrated in Fig. 2.2, is one in which all dialog processing functions are implemented on a programmable workstation and other application functions are performed on some other computing system. IBM typically uses the term *cooperative processing* to refer to such a distributed computing environment. However, the term cooperative processing is not precisely defined in the SAA documentation and this term is sometimes used to refer to any type of distributed computing in which more than one computing system is used to execute application functions. A more descriptive term for a distributed computing application in which user-interface processing is performed on a separate computing system might be *distributed dialog processing*.

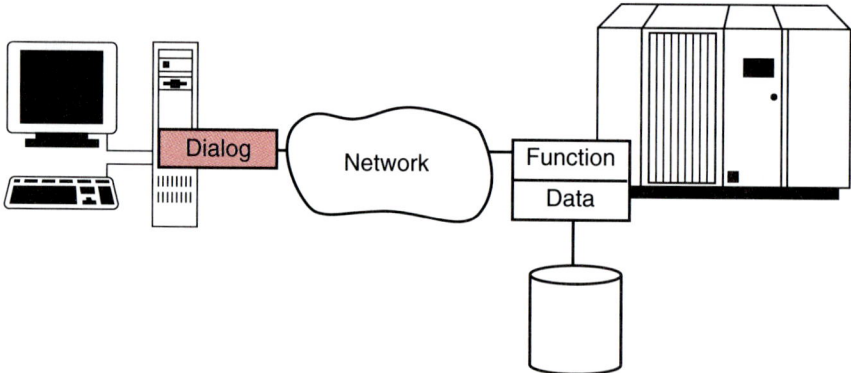

Figure 2.2 With *cooperative processing,* also called *distributed dialog processing,* the dialog processing is performed at the user's location, the function processing and data access processing is performed on a computing system at some other location.

In a distributed computing application that uses cooperative processing, the processing needed to present panels, accept user input, and possibly validate that input is performed on a computing system at the user's location. The application's general processing logic is performed on a computing system at some other location. Data to be displayed is returned to the user's location for formatting and interaction. A communication network connecting the two computing systems allows data entered by the user to flow to the application and data generated by the application to be returned to the user.

Cooperative processing is typically performed using a personal computer for the user interface-related processing and either a midrange or large-system processor to handle other application functions. A personal computer offers several capabilities that can be used to make the user interface easier to use. These features include the following:

- Keystroke tracking
- Field highlighting options
- Color and graphics
- Automatic horizontal scrolling on data entry
- Single keystroke responses
- Multitask windowing
- Use of a mouse pointing device
- Predictable, fast responses to user input

DISTRIBUTED DATA ACCESS Another form of distributed computing, shown in Fig. 2.3, is *distributed data access*. With this type of distributed computing, programs and the data they process reside in computing systems at different locations. Requests for accesses to the data stored in files or databases are sent from the computing systems that perform application processing functions to the computing systems on which the files or databases are maintained. The computing system that maintains the files or databases processes data requests and returns the requested data to the computing systems that perform application and dialog processing functions. This type of distributed computing can be implemented using distributed database systems, distributed file systems, or computing systems on a network that are operating as file servers.

The distributed data access form of distributed computing allows for the widespread access to data often demanded by the demographics of modern business while still maintaining security through centralized access control. This

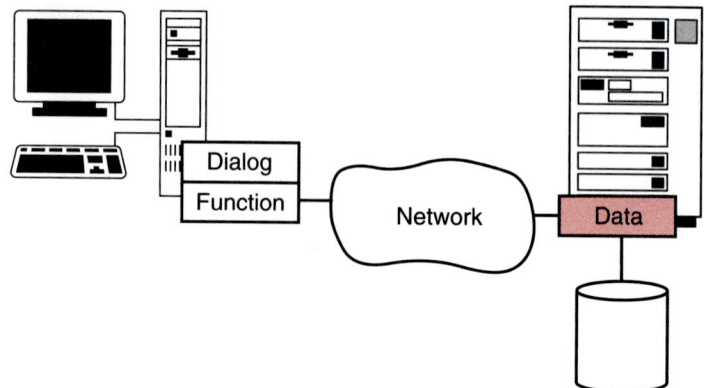

Figure 2.3 With *distributed data access,* the dialog processing and function processing are performed at the user's location; the data access processing is performed by a computing system at some other location.

approach may also be used where local computing systems cannot provide the required data storage capacity.

DISTRIBUTED FUNCTION PROCESSING

Figure 2.4 illustrates a distributed computing application that implements *distributed function processing*. In this environment, application functions are divided into separate components. Each of the components may be executed on a computing system at a different location. Communication facilities are used to invoke functions as they are required and to pass data between components.

Distributed function processing allows the unique processing capabilities of different computing systems to be used to best advantage. For example, graphics processing functions might best be handled by a personal computer, while computationally-intense processing may require the use of a large-system processor. The key to this form of distributed computing is to design the data interfaces between the components in a way that minimizes data transfer.

CLIENT/SERVER COMPUTING

A form of distributed computing that is becoming increasingly widespread is called *client/server computing*. With client/server computing, really a form of distributed function processing, an application issues requests for services that might otherwise be provided locally. For example, the service requests might be for file or database access or for printing services that might otherwise be provided by the local operating system or by calls to a local database management

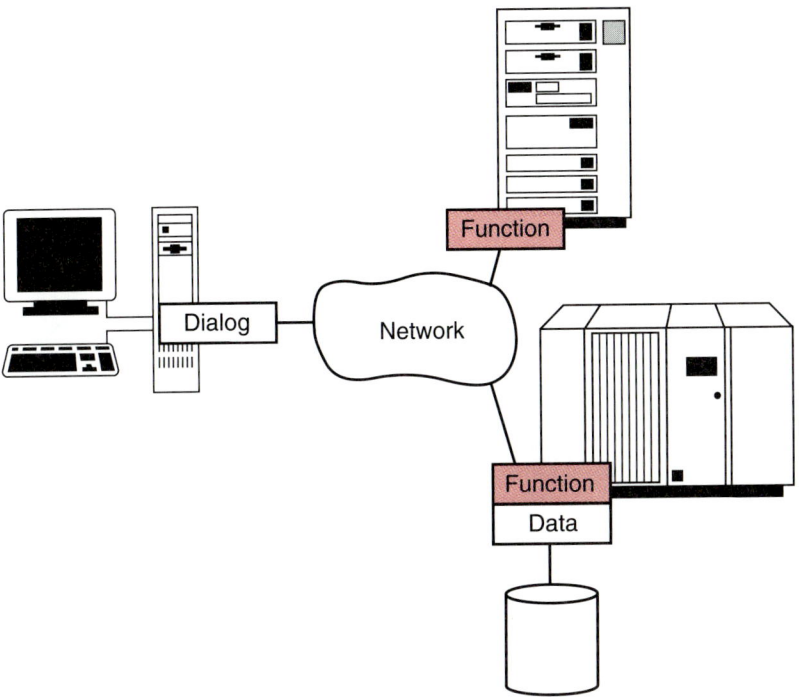

Figure 2.4 With *distributed function processing,* shown here combined with cooperative processing, different application functions are executed on computing systems at different locations.

system. Instead of being processed locally, the service requests are sent across a network to another computing system where they are processed and the results returned to the application that issued the service request. This is illustrated in Fig. 2.5. The application issuing the service requests is called the *client*, and the application running in the remote computing system that processes the requests and provides the results is called the *server*. There can be multiple clients sharing the services of the server, and the client applications need not be aware that processing is not being performed locally.

DISTRIBUTED RESOURCES

In addition to addressing the distribution of computer processing, SAA also addresses providing access to various types of resources that may be distributed across the network and across different computing environments. SAA includes architectures that define methods of accessing different types of data, including the following:

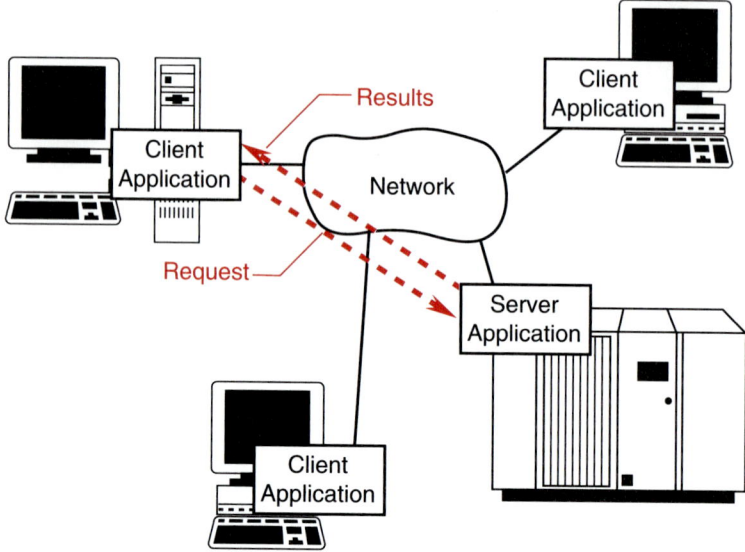

Figure 2.5 With client-server computing, a client application issues a request to a server application, and the server passes results back to the client. A single server can serve many clients.

- Distributed document processing services that provide for the interchange of documents within and between systems.
- Distributed relational database services that allow application programs to access relational databases stored at remote locations.
- Distributed data services that provide for the processing of files stored at remote locations.

DISTRIBUTED DOCUMENT ACCESS

IBM has included in the Common Communications Support component of SAA a series of IBM-developed document-related architectures designed to provide both for the processing of documents and the interchange of documents within and between systems. These architectures define data streams used to generate, store, and interchange documents and different types of objects that can be included within a data stream. By adhering to common object and data stream definitions, a document can easily be created in one environment and processed or displayed in another. CCS also includes support for both IBM architectures and international standards that define how documents and document processing services can be interchanged between systems on both a synchronous and an asynchronous basis.

DISTRIBUTED DATABASE ACCESS

The ultimate goal of SAA's support for a distributed database processing environment is to allow users and applications to be totally independent of the location of the data they process. The user should be able to make requests for data, and the application should be able to issue the appropriate data access statements, without regard to where the data is stored. From a practical standpoint, this complete transparency will take time to achieve, and IBM has defined several forms of distributed database access that provide varying degrees of transparency.

Nontransparent Distributed Database Access

Application programs can employ two forms of distributed database access without requiring the use of any specific CCS application services for distributed database access. These two methods for accessing remote relational databases, described in Box 2.1, require the user or the application to handle access to the database and require no special support from the DBMS software.

Transparent Distributed Database Access

The remaining forms of distributed database processing discussed in this chapter require support from the database management system and provide varying levels of transparency.

Remote Unit of Work Processing

One form of transparent access to remote relational databases is called *remote unit of work* processing. Remote unit of work is the only form of distributed database access currently addressed in CCS.

With remote unit of work processing, the DBMS must be aware that distributed database access is taking place. In this form of distributed database access, data requests are submitted directly from an application component running on one SAA system to a DBMS running on another SAA system. Since a single SQL request can sometimes result in the DBMS making a great many database accesses, the idea of passing the SQL request itself to the remote DBMS can result in a reduction of the network traffic that is required to satisfy the request.

With remote unit of work processing, the remote application itself must handle the releasing of locks through its own COMMIT/ROLLBACK processing. The application must also notify the DBMS if the application fails so the DBMS can take appropriate recovery actions. This form of distributed database processing provides a degree of transparency because the user does not have to know where the DBMS or the data is located. However, the operating system at the

BOX 2.1 Nontransparent distributed database access.

- **Extract Processing.** *Extract processing* is the simplest form of nontransparent distributed database processing. With user-assisted processing, the user (possibly at a personal computer) must know where the data is located and must make a connection with the system on which the desired data is located (possibly on a large-system processor). The user formulates a request to extract the required data from the large-system database and then, in a separate operation, transfers the data back to the personal computer. The user then finally processes the data on the personal computer. With this approach, the user must know where the data is located and must be able to access and interact with both computing systems. Extract processing can also be used to extract nonrelational data from files and to place it in a relational database.

- **Remote Request Processing.** A second form of nontransparent distributed database processing is *remote request processing.* Here, the user interacts with an application running on one computing system to generate a data request. This application then sends the request to a second application located on the computing system that maintains the database containing the requested data. The second application submits the request to the DBMS on that computing system and returns the results of the data access to the first application. This approach is actually a form of client/server computing in which the local application operates as the client (sometimes called the *requester*) and the remote application that has access to the database operates as the server. With remote request processing, CCS facilities are used only for ordinary communication between the client and the server, and the DBMS in the processor that maintains the remote database is unaware that distributed database access is taking place. The data request is submitted to the DBMS by the server application, which looks to the DBMS like any other local application. The DBMS holds and releases locks and performs recovery operations based on the server application. If there is a failure in the network or in the client application that is making the request for data access, the DBMS is unaware of the failure.

application site must be prepared to communicate with the DBMS in the event of an application failure.

IBM has described two other, more powerful, forms of distributed database access, but support for these have not, at the time of writing, been included in CCS. These are described in Box 2.2.

BOX 2.2 More powerful forms of distributed database access.

- **Distributed Unit of Work.** With this form of transparent distributed database access, data in multiple locations can be updated within the scope of a single transaction. The DBMS is responsible for knowing which systems manage the affected data and for coordinating the different accesses and updates. If a problem occurs during a unit of work, the DBMS performs recovery on all systems. With distributed unit of work processing, data can be updated in several locations within a single unit of work. However, separate SQL statements must be used for each location, and a given statement can affect data at only one location. This means that the application must be sufficiently aware of the location of data to avoid issuing an SQL statement that might reference tables residing in more than one location. IBM has announced that CCS will eventually include application services for implementing distributed unit of work processing, but, at the time of writing, DRDA does not yet support it.
- **Distributed Requests.** With this form of distributed database access, a single SQL statement can reference data stored at more than one location. The DBMS is responsible for determining where data is located, accessing it, and coordinating COMMIT/ROLLBACK and recovery processing among the different systems. With this form of distributed database access, the location of the data is totally transparent to the user and to the application. The DBMS provides all the support necessary for distributed database processing. Although IBM has described this form of distributed database access, no plans for its inclusion in CCS have yet been announced.

DISTRIBUTED RELATIONAL DATABASE ARCHITECTURE

The *Distributed Relational Database Architecture* (DRDA), another element of CCS, defines the way in which access to remote relational databases is handled. DRDA builds on the CPI Database Interface (Chapter 7) and on the relational database facilities of the CCS component of SAA. The CPI Database Interface defines a version of Structured Query Language (SQL) that is consistent across the various SAA computing environments. With a consistent language interface, support for distributed database facilities can be performed by an underlying database management system. The DBMS can then process the SQL statements appropriately, regardless of the location of the application and the data. DRDA defines a CCS application service that provides support for the remote unit of work distributed database access described earlier.

DISTRIBUTED FILES   CCS provides comprehensive support for distributed file processing when an application is located on one SAA computing system and the data it processes resides in a file on another SAA computing system.

There are several challenges to providing distributed file processing in the SAA computing environments. Different file systems and different file formats are used in the various SAA computing environments. Also, applications specify file requests using different types of file I/O statements that are part of the SAA languages. The various languages have different file I/O capabilities, and these differences must also be accommodated as part of distributed file processing.

SNA Distributed File Processing

In the SNA environment, distributed file processing services are based on the *Distributed Data Management* (DDM) architecture. DDM defines a standard file model and a set of standard file commands. A file request received from one file system is translated first into DDM standard commands. The request is then routed to the system containing the file to be processed. There, the standard DDM commands are translated into file requests appropriate for the target system. The request is processed, and the results are returned to the requesting system using DDM formats. Figure 2.6 illustrates the different environments that must be supported as part of distributed file processing in SAA.

DDM defines a standard set of commands for passing requests between file systems. These include OPEN, READ BY KEY, READ NEXT, CLOSE, and so on. The portion of DDM that translates the original request into DDM format is

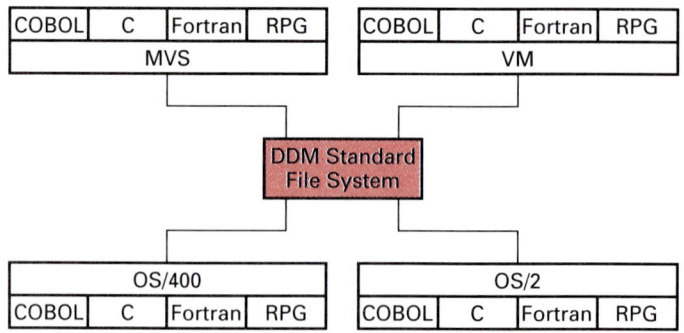

Figure 2.6   The DDM distributed file environment.

called the *source DDM server*. The portion that translates from the DDM format to the format of the receiving system is called the *target DDM server*.

Level 3 of DDM also provides facilities that operate in support of the Distributed Relational Database Architecture (DRDA). DRDA allows application programs to access relational databases stored on remote systems. The DDM facilities required to implement distributed relational databases include definition of a standardized relational database model and an application manager for the Structured Query Language (SQL). The following elements must be packaged by DDM into the proper data stream format for transmission over the network:

- Requests for access to a remote relational database
- Replies from the remote system that maintains the relational database
- Data from the relational database for transmission over the network

OSI Distributed File Processing

File Transfer, Access, and Management (FTAM) provides a set of services in the OSI environment that is similar to that provided by DDM in the SNA environment. A key difference between the two is that IBM's support for DDM allows access to files, individual records, and individual bytes in those records. IBM's implementations of FTAM currently provide only for passing entire files between systems. FTAM specifies protocols for the OSI Application and Presentation layers that define how unstructured, flat, and hierarchical files can be transferred in a standardized way among heterogeneous computing systems, as illustrated in Fig. 2.7.

FTAM makes transparent to users the way in which the data contained in a file is encoded, the particular set of file access method commands used to

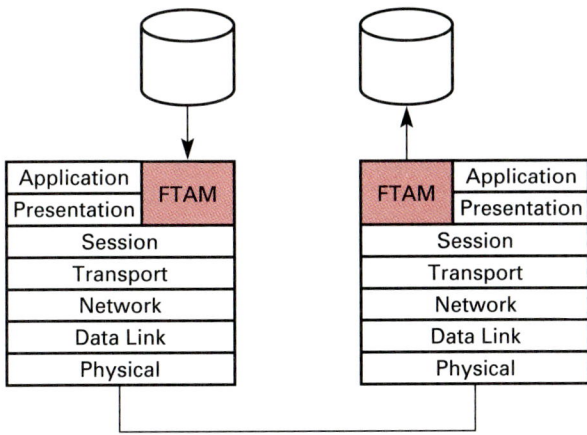

Figure 2.7 File Transfer, Access, and Management (FTAM).

manipulate a file, and the way in which a file is physically organized on the storage medium. With FTAM, one system (called the *initiator*) requests access to another system (called the *responder*). After a dialog has been established between the initiator and the responder, the initiator can send files to and receive files from the responder.

DATA REPRESENTATION CONSIDERATIONS

One area in which the various SAA computing environments differ is in the way they represent data internally. The principle ways in which they differ include the following:

- The order in which the bytes of a binary integer are stored in memory
- Whether ASCII or EBCDIC encoding is used for character data
- How zoned- and packed-decimal fields are treated
- The format used for floating-point numbers
- The way in which double-byte character set (DBCS) data is treated

These differences must be considered when data is being accessed and shared across systems.

Byte-Ordering Differences

Some computing systems are referred to as big-endian systems and others are known as little-endian systems. In a *big-endian* computer system, the highest-order byte of a multiple-byte binary integer is stored in the lowest memory location, and the lowest-order byte is stored in the highest memory location. In a *little-endian* computer system, the highest-order byte is stored in the highest memory location and the lowest-order byte is stored in the lowest memory location. IBM large-system processors are examples of big-endian computers, and computers using Intel microprocessors, such as IBM's personal systems, are examples of little-endian computers. Byte-ordering differences must be resolved when integer data is exchanged over a network between different types of processors.

ASCII and EBCDIC Differences

The ASCII and EBCDIC character sets use different internal representations to define characters. For example, in EBCDIC, the character blank is represented with the hexadecimal value '40'. In ASCII, a blank has the hexadecimal value '20'. ASCII and EBCDIC also have different collating sequences. In EBCDIC, lowercase characters precede uppercase characters, and both precede numbers. In ASCII, numbers precede uppercase characters, which precede lowercase characters. This can cause problems when a character field that contains both numbers and letters is used as part of a sort key or record key. The two character sets also do not support the same set of characters.

Zoned- and Packed-Decimal Data Differences

There are differences between the various SAA computing environments in the sign that is generated for a positive value for a zoned- or packed-decimal field. In the MVS, VM, and OS/2 environments, the sign value hexadecimal 'C' denotes a positive number and the sign value hexadecimal 'D' denotes a negative number. In the OS/400 environment, the sign value hexadecimal 'D' denotes a positive number. Using a signed field in a comparison or as part of a key can cause problems if the data being processed has not all been generated in the same environment.

Floating-Point Format Differences

There are different formats used for floating point data in the different SAA environments. Figure 2.8 summarizes the characteristics of the different formats. These different formats provide different precisions. The System/370 Extended format gives the greatest precision but is not supported in all environments. Using the other formats increases portability but may require checking of intermediate results to protect against exponent underflow or overflow.

Format	Length	Sign	Exponent	Mantissa	Normalization
IEEE Single	32 bits	1 bit	8 bits	23 bits	Binary
IEEE Double	64 bits	1 bit	11 bits	52 bits	Binary
System/370 Short	32 bits	1 bit	7 bits	24 bits	Hexadecimal
System/370 Long	64 bits	1 bit	7 bits	56 bits	Hexadecimal
System/370 Extended	128 bits	1 bit	7 bits	112 bits	Hexadecimal

Figure 2.8 Floating-point formats.

Double-Byte Character Set Considerations

Certain non-Roman languages, such as Japanese, Korean, and Chinese, require more characters than can be represented with one byte, which provides for only 256 different values. For these languages, two bytes are used per character, allowing up to 65,536 different values. The character set based on using two bytes per character is known as the *double-byte character set* (DBCS). Different methods of identifying DBCS data are used, depending on whether the data is in an ASCII or EBCDIC environment. With EBCDIC, control characters mark the beginning and the end of DBCS data. With ASCII, no control characters are used.

The fact that control characters may or may not be used means that a string of data with DBCS characters in it will be a different length depending on the environment in which it is used. Certain printers require the use of control characters with DBCS. Some of the operating systems used in SAA computing environments do not support the use of DBCS data as part of system names. There also may be differences in the set of characters represented when DBCS data is used. All of these considerations must be taken into account when processing DBCS data.

ONLINE PROCESSING

With an online application, the user interacts directly with the application during its processing. The interaction generally consists of information or choices presented by the application to the user and responses or requests returned by the user to the application. The Common User Access portion of SAA provides rules and guidelines for developing a user interface appropriate to this type of user interaction. An online application can be one of two types: interactive or transactional.

Interactive Applications

An *interactive* application, sometimes called a *conversational* application, is one in which the application holds resources for the exclusive use of the user throughout all the exchanges that make up the interaction. Typically, an interactive application is interacting with a single user, with data belonging to that user.

Transactional Applications

A *transactional* application, also sometimes called a *pseudo-conversational* application, typically supports many concurrent users and provides for the sharing of access to data and system resources. With a transactional application, the interchange with a user is broken into a series of short-running tasks, or *transactions*. A transaction consists of one or more logical units of work, where each unit of work has a definite beginning and end. Generally a unit of work will involve a single exchange with the user, receiving a request from the user and then responding to that request. With a transactional application, resources are held only for the duration of a single unit of work. At the end of the unit of work, they are released and reacquired, if necessary, for the next unit of work.

Transactional applications are characterized by their use of the following:

- **Shared Data.** The concurrent users of the application may be accessing records in the same database simultaneously. The application (in cooperation with the underlying database) must provide for maintaining data integrity and recovery across the shared access.
- **Defined Units of Work.** The logical units of work are the basis through which the application controls data manipulation and status. Typically, when a unit of work ends, any changes that have been made to resources are made permanent, or *committed.* This commitment of changes provides a synchronization point for recovery.
- **Coordinated Recovery of Resources.** When a problem occurs in the middle of a unit of work that prevents it from properly completing its processing, any changes that have been made to that point are undone, or *rolled back,* to the state that existed at the beginning of the unit of work. This is done to maintain data integrity by ensuring that all related changes are made to the database and that related records are kept in a consistent state.

Transactional Processing in SAA

The two major IBM transaction processing subsystems are CICS and IMS, both of which run in the large-system environment. CICS and IMS have both been included as part of the SAA environment. Support for shared data, unit of work processing, and resource recovery are provided in the CCS environment through the Distributed Data Management (DDM) architecture and the Distributed Relational Database Architecture (DRDA). As part of CPI, distributed relational databases can be accessed using the CPI Database Interface (Chapter 7) and the CPI Resource Recovery Interface (Chapter 9).

APPLICATION DESIGN

As part of the application design process, there are a number of decisions and choices that can be made that will affect the application's connectivity, portability, and ease-of-use. Use of the different interfaces that are part of CPI should be considered, since they are designed to provide connectivity and portability across SAA environments. The particular interfaces that are chosen will depend on both the application's requirements and the availability of tools that have implemented the interfaces in the environments in which the application will run.

DESIGNING THE USER INTERFACE

For online applications, the design of the user interface is a key activity. As introduced in Chapter 1, the SAA Common User Access architecture defines a set of rules and guidelines for defining the user interface, with separate models provided based on whether the user accesses the application using a personal computer or a character-oriented terminal. The rules and guidelines are based on underlying principles that are aimed at making the interface easy to use. Basing the interface on a CUA model also helps to maintain consistency, both as an application moves from one computing environment to another and as the end user moves from application to application.

With a user interface that has been designed to follow the CUA guidelines, the CPI Dialog Interface (Chapter 16) and the CPI Presentation Interface (Chapter 17) should be considered for use in the application. Both of these interfaces provide support for standard CUA elements and follow CUA rules and guidelines in the formatting and user interaction techniques that they provide.

DESIGNING DATA

When considering an application's requirements for the data it processes, a key question is how data will be stored. If it is in a file, the file processing capabilities of the programming language to be used will be a consideration. If it is in a relational database, the CPI Database Interface (Chapter 7), the CPI Query Interface (Chapter 8), and the CPI Resource Recovery Interface (Chapter 9) can be considered. If access to distributed data is required, the availability of products that implement the desired interface and support the processing of distributed data will be a factor in the decision. If transparent access to distributed data is not fully supported, the application itself may need to perform processing related to cross-system access.

For distributed data, data representation differences may also be a consideration. Problems can be minimized by using programming techniques, such as symbolic parameters and symbolic variables, and by avoiding the use of characters that are not part of the character sets used in all the environments in which the application will run.

DESIGNING APPLICATION LOGIC

An application's basic processing requirements will in large part determine the programming language that is most appropriate to use. Beyond this choice, there are some general principles that can be followed when designing an application's logic that will improve its portability and suitability for use in a distributed computing environment.

Application portability can be enhanced by following a principle of separation, or isolation, in designing the logic of the application. According to this principle, you first identify any common functions that are frequently used within one or more applications. These functions may be installation-specific, or they may be more general functions that are defined within SAA but have not yet been implemented in the tools you are using. You then develop a generalized version of each function that can be invoked as a service or utility by the applications you are generating. In developing these services or utilities, define and use a standard interface for invoking them, and document both the functions and their interfaces. Separating out common functions in this way will increase development productivity by making them reusable. It will also make it easier to change them if an application is moved to a new computing environment, since the changes will have to be made in only one place. Functions that are dependent on the particular computing environment used for execution should also be identified and handled in a way that isolates them from the rest of the application. This will make them easier to modify if an application is moved to a different computing environment.

A second principle to follow is that of modularity. This principle states that an application's processing should be broken into separate modules, where each module is highly independent and self-contained. Making modules independent of each other makes it less likely that a change to one module causes changes to be required to other modules, making the application more portable. Using separate modules for functions related to user interface processing, data access, and general processing logic makes an application easier to split apart for use in a distributed computing environment. Guidelines for developing independent and self-contained modules are as follows:

- A module performs a single function.
- A module has one entry point and one exit point.
- Control is always returned to the calling module.
- Each variable has a single use.
- The number of parameters passed is minimized.
- Use of shared storage is minimized.

DESIGNING COMMUNICATIONS

In a distributed computing or distributed data environment, it may be necessary for programs to directly communicate with one another. This may be needed to coordinate the commitment or recovery of resources controlled by different programs or simply to communicate processing results from one program to another. For program-to-program communication across a network, the CPI Communications Interface (Chapter 13) can be considered.

CONCLUSION

This chapter has examined general design techniques that can be employed in creating computing applications that execute in the SAA environment. Chapter 3 begins our detailed exploration of the SAA Common Programming Interface by examining the characteristics of the conventional programming languages that have been included as part of CPI.

PART I PROGRAMMING LANGUAGE INTERFACES

3 HIGH-LEVEL LANGUAGES

This chapter describes the conventional programming languages that are included in the Common Programming Interface component of SAA. These include the industry's most widely used programming languages: C, COBOL, FORTRAN, PL/I, and RPG. Each of these languages has its own particular strengths and has characteristics that make it well suited to handle particular types of processing. Selection of a language to use for the development of a computing application will continue to be based on the processing requirements of a given situation. IBM's goal is to provide compatible versions of the CPI languages in all the various SAA environments, thus making it easier to distribute applications across environments. In many instances, the CPI interface has been based on national or international standards, which helps to provide compatibility not only across SAA environments but with non-SAA environments as well. In the sections that follow, we will examine the CPI interface for each of the SAA high-level languages.

THE C LANGUAGE   The C language is suited to a wide variety of programming tasks. It has been used to develop system software, application software, including text processing and graphics packages, and engineering, scientific, and commercial applications. C supports the use of a number of different data types. It can function with machine-level entities at a very low level or with aggregate data types, such as arrays and structures, that allow high-level control.

The C language itself is quite compact, with a limited number of statements and facilities. However, most implementations of the language also include an extensive library of functions that have themselves been written in C. These functions provide for input/output processing, mathematical manipulations, exception handling, string and character manipulation, dynamic memory management, and date and time value manipulation. The use of a function library helps to increase program portability, since a consistent application program interface to the library functions can be provided for each language implementation.

The CPI C language specification is designed to be in conformance with the American National Standard for Information Systems—Programming Language C (X3.159-1989) and with the International C Standard (ISO - IEC 9899-1990 (E)). Implementations are available in the MVS, VM, OS/400, and OS/2 environments.

C Example

Figure 3.1 shows an example of a program written in C. This program shows how the C language can be used with the CPI query interface. The *include* statements at the beginning of the program bring in sets of library functions that can then be referenced later in the program.

C Data Definition and Use

The C language allows for the definition and use of data objects that are either constants or variables. A constant is a data object whose value does not change during program execution. The data types that can be used for constants are listed in Box 3.1. Variables may have their values changed during execution. When a variable is declared, it may have a data type, storage class, and other attributes specified for it. Box 3.2 lists the data types that can be associated with variables. Scalar data types define the basic types of data. More complex data structures can be derived from combinations of the scalar data types. Box 3.3 summarizes the storage classes that can be assigned to a variable.

Data values can also be represented using *expressions*, formed using constants, variables, and operators. Box 3.4 contains a list of the operators that can be used in expressions. Unary expressions combine one operator with one operand, as in the following examples:

```
++count1;
pointer1 = &wordlength;
*pointer1 = charcount;
```

Binary expressions consist of two operands joined by an operator, as in these examples:

```
a + b;
wordlength = charcount;
```

```c
/********************************************************************/
/* Sample Program:  DSQABFC                                         */
/* C Version of the SAA Query Callable Interface                    */
/********************************************************************/

/********************************************************************/
/* Include standard and string "C" functions                        */
/********************************************************************/
#include <string.h>
#include <stdlib.h>

/********************************************************************/
/* Include and declare query interface communications area          */
/********************************************************************/
#include <DSQCOMMC.H>

int main()
     {

struct dsqcomm communication_area;       /* DSQCOMM from include */

/********************************************************************/
/* Query interface command length and commands                      */
/********************************************************************/
signed long command_length;
static char start_query_interface[] = "START";
static char set_global_variables[]  = "SET GLOBAL";
static char run_query[] = "RUN QUERY Q1";
static char print_report[] = "PRINT REPORT (FORM=F1";
static char end_query_interface[] = "EXIT";

/********************************************************************/
/* Query command extension, number of parameters and lengths        */
/********************************************************************/
signed long number_of_parameters;   /* number of variables       */
signed long keyword_lengths[10];    /* lengths of keyword names  */
signed long data_lengths[10];       /* lengths of variable data  */

/********************************************************************/
/* Variable data type constants                                     */
/********************************************************************/
static char char_data_type[] = DSQ_VARIABLE_CHAR;
static char int_data_type[]  = DSQ_VARIABLE_FINT;

/********************************************************************/
/* Keyword parameter and value for START command                    */
/********************************************************************/
static char start_keywords[] = "DSQSCMD";
static char start_keyword_values[] = "USERCMD1";

/********************************************************************/
/* Keyword parameter and values for SET command                     */
/********************************************************************/
#define SIZE_VAL 8
char set_keywords [3][SIZE_VAL];     /* Parameter name array       */
signed long set_values[3];           /* Parameter value array      */
```

Figure 3.1   C language example.

(Continued)

```
/*********************************************************************/
/* MAIN PROGRAM                                                      */
/*********************************************************************/

/*********************************************************************/
/* Start a Query Interface Session                                   */
/*********************************************************************/
     number_of_parameters = 1;
     command_length = sizeof(start_query_interface);
     keyword_lengths[0] = sizeof(start_keywords);
     data_lengths[0] = sizeof(start_keyword_values);
     dsqcice(&communication_area,
             &command_length,
             &start_query_interface[0],
             &number_of_parameters,
             &keyword_lengths[0],
             &start_keywords[0],
             &data_lengths[0],
             &start_keyword_values[0],
             &char_data_type;

/*********************************************************************/
/* Set numeric values into query using SET command                   */
/*********************************************************************/

     number_of_parameters = 3;
     command_length = sizeof(set_global_variables);
     strcpy(set_keywords[0],"MYVAR01");
     strcpy(set_keywords[1],"SHORT");
     strcpy(set_keywords[2],"MYVAR03");
     keyword_lengths[0] = SIZE_VAL;
     keyword_lengths[1] = SIZE_VAL;
     keyword_lengths[2] = SIZE_VAL;
     data_lengths[0] = sizeof(long);
     data_lengths[1] = sizeof(long);
     data_lengths[2] = sizeof(long);
     set_values[0] = 20;
     set_values[1] = 40;
     set_values[2] = 84;
     dsqcice(&communication_area,
             &command_length,
             &set_global_variables[0],
             &number_of_parameters,
             &keyword_lengths[0],
             &set_keywords[0][0],
             &data_lengths[0],
             &set_values[0],
             &int_data_type[0];

/*********************************************************************/
/* Run a Query                                                       */
/*********************************************************************/
    command_length = sizeof(run_query);
    dsqcic(&communication_area,&command_length,&run_query [0]);

/*********************************************************************/
/* Print the results of the query                                    */
/*********************************************************************/
    command_length = sizeof(print_report);
    dsqcic(&communication_area,&command_length,&print_report[0]);
```

Figure 3.1   (Continued)

```
/****************************************************************/
/* End the query interface session                              */
/****************************************************************/
    command_length = sizeof(end_query_interface);
    dsqcic(&communication_area,&command_length,&end_query_interface[0]);
    exit(0);
}
```

Figure 3.1   (Continued)

C Language Statements

The C language defines a relatively small number of different types of statements, most of which relate to the flow of control within a program. These statements are described in Box 3.5. The C language also has a set of preprocessor directives that specify actions that should take place during the compilation process. These directives are listed in Box 3.6.

C Library Functions

The C language supports the definition and use of *functions*. A function is called by name, may have a set of input parameters that can be passed to it, and may return a value. The body of a function consists of a block statement containing the data definitions, declarations, and statements needed to perform the processing required to return the proper value. A source program may define and use its own functions. It may also invoke functions that have been defined separately.

The C library includes general-purpose functions and macros that can be used by any C program. The functions provided in the library include the following:

- Error handling, including the processing of messages and signals.
- Time manipulation, including returning the time and converting it to various formats.
- Searching and sorting arrays.
- Mathematical functions, such as sine, cosine, square root, absolute value, and Bessel functions to solve differential equations.
- Conversion of string values to other data types.
- Input/output operations for processing stream files in either formatted or character mode and for processing direct files.
- Handling of function arguments.
- Generation of pseudo-random numbers.
- Dynamic memory management, including reserving and freeing storage.
- Environment interaction.
- String operations, including searching, comparing, copying, moving, and concatenating string values.
- Character manipulation, including testing for types of character values, converting between upper and lower case, and manipulating multibyte character values.

BOX 3.1 C language constant data types.

- **Integer.** A numeric value expressed in decimal, octal, or hexadecimal notation. A decimal constant contains any of the digits 0 through 9. An octal constant contains any of the digits 0 through 7. A hexadecimal constant contains any of the digits 0 through 9 and a through f. Examples:

    20597 (decimal)   0aff07 (hexadecimal)   03175 (octal)

- **Float.** A numeric value expressed in scientific notation. Example:

    7.315e2 (7.315 × 10^2)

- **Character.** A single character, from the C character set, enclosed in single quotation marks. The value used to represent the constant is a binary code value that identifies the character in the character set used on the particular system executing the program. Examples:

    'a' '?'

- **String.** A series of characters enclosed in double quotation marks. Example:

    "Now is the time!"

- **Enumeration.** A numerical value corresponding to a particular entry in a list of identifiers. In the following example, the enumeration constants, contained in braces, are **red, white, green, blue,** and **yellow;** the values in parentheses below the **enum** statement are the numerical values associated with the constants:

    ```
    enum colors {red, white, green, blue, yellow}
                 (1)    (2)    (3)    (4)   (5)
    ```

BOX 3.2   C language variable data types.

Scalar Data Types

- **Character.** Holds any member of the computing system's character set. It can also be treated like an integer value and can be defined as signed or unsigned. Example:

    ```
    char first_name = "Ralph";
    ```

- **Floating-Point.** Contains numeric values in floating-point format. Example:

    ```
    float big_num = 100.43e5;
    ```

- **Integer.** Contains a numeric value. It can be defined as signed or unsigned. It also can be defined as short or long, which affects the maximum size of the variable. Example:

    ```
    int errswitch = 0;
    ```

- **Pointer.** Holds the address of a data object or function. Pointers are commonly used to pass the address of a variable to a function, to access dynamic data structures, or to access elements of an array or members of a structure. The following example defines **pointerx** as a pointer to an integer object:

    ```
    int *pointerx;
    ```

- **Enumeration.** Holds an enumeration constant value. The following example defines **current_color** as an enumeration variable and indicates that the value of **current_color** is taken from the enumeration data type **colors**:

    ```
    enum colors {red, white, green, blue, yellow};
    enum colors current_color = blue;
    ```

Derived Data Types

- **Array.** Contains an ordered group of data objects, where all the data objects have the same data type. An array can be defined with multiple

(Continued)

BOX 3.2 *(Continued)*

dimensions. The following example defines a two-dimensional array with 15 elements of type **int**:

```
int results[5][3];
```

- **Structure.** Contains an ordered group of data objects where different objects can be of different data types. The following example defines **night_class** as a structure variable, containing the objects defined in the structure data type **class**:

```
struct class {int class_code;
       char instructor;
       char location;
       int time_period;};
struct class night_class;
```

An individual object can be referenced using the variable name and object name: **night_class.location.**

- **Union.** An object that can hold any one of a set of named members, which can be of any data type. The following example defines **length** as a union variable, containing one member from the union data type **measure,** which can be **length.meters** or **length.yards**:

```
union measure {float meters;
        int yards;};
union measure length;
```

BOX 3.3 C language variable storage classes.

- **Auto.** A variable with the **auto** storage class must be defined and used within a single block.
- **Register.** A variable with the **register** storage class indicates that the variable will be heavily used and should be placed into a machine register for faster access.
- **Extern.** A variable with the **extern** storage class can be referenced outside the source file in which it is defined.
- **Static.** A variable with the **static** storage class retains storage throughout program execution and can be used only within one source file.

BOX 3.4   C language operators.

Unary Expression Operators

Increment	++	Adds 1 to the value of the operand
Decrement	--	Subtracts 1 from the value of the operand
Plus	+	Maintains value of the operand (multiply by +1)
Minus	-	Negates the value of the operand (multiply by -1)
Logical negation	!	Yields value true if the operand evaluates to false
Bitwise negation	~	Yields the ones complement of the operand
Address	&	Yields a pointer to the location of the operand
Indirection	*	Yields a reference to the location to which a pointer points
Cast	(*type*)	Converts the value of the operand to the data type specified by *type*
Size	*sizeof*	Yields the size of the operand in bytes

Binary Expression Operators

Bitwise AND	&	Compares the two operands bit-by-bit and sets a resulting bit pattern. If both bits are 1, the resulting bit is set to 1; otherwise, the resulting bit is set to 0.
Bitwise exclusive OR	^	Compares the two operands bit-by-bit and sets a resulting bit pattern. If both bits are 1 or both bits are 0, the resulting bit is set to 0; otherwise, the resulting bit is set to 1.
Bitwise inclusive OR	|	Compares the two operands bit-by-bit and sets a resulting bit pattern. If both bits are 0, the resulting bit is set to 0; otherwise, the resulting bit is set to 1.
Logical AND	&&	If both operands have a nonzero value, the expression has a value of 1; otherwise, it has a value of 0.
Logical OR	||	If either operand has a nonzero value, the expression has a value of 1; otherwise, it has a value of 0.
Conditional	?:	Evaluates a condition. If the condition is true, the first of two subsequent expressions is used as the expression value; otherwise, the second expression is used.
Assignment	=	Gives the value of the right operand to the left operand.
Comma	,	Evaluates the left operand and uses the value of the right operand as the value of the expression.

BOX 3.5   C language statements.

- **Block.** Groups together data definitions, declarations, and statements so they are treated as a unit. The beginning and the end of the block are marked by braces ({ }).
- **Break.** Terminates and exits from a **loop** or **switch** statement.
- **Continue.** Terminates the current iteration of a loop and returns control to the condition part of the loop.
- **Do.** Performs a loop where the body of the loop is executed once before the loop condition is evaluated.
- **For.** Executes a statement iteratively based on the evaluation of expressions.
- **Goto.** Unconditionally transfers program control to a specified statement.
- **If.** Conditionally executes a statement based on evaluation of an expression.
- **Null.** Performs no operation.
- **Return.** Terminates the execution of the current function and returns control to the caller of the function.
- **Switch.** Transfers control to one of a series of statements within the switch statement body based on evaluation of an expression.
- **While.** Executes a loop repeatedly until a specified condition is no longer met.

BOX 3.6   C language preprocessor directives.

- **#Define.** Causes the preprocessor to replace all subsequent occurrences of an identifier or macro with specified source text.
- **#Undef.** Ends the scope of a **#define** directive.
- **#Error.** Causes the preprocessor to generate an error message and terminate the compilation.
- **#Include.** Causes the preprocessor to replace the directive with a specified file.
- **#If, #ifdef, #ifndef, #elif, #else, #endif.** These directives control whether the immediately following source statements are passed to the compiler based on the evaluation of an expression or the testing of a condition.
- **#Line.** Specifies a value to be used as the line number of the next source statement.
- **#.** A null directive that performs no action.
- **#Pragma.** An implementation-defined instruction to the compiler.

COBOL

The COBOL (COmmon Business Oriented Language) language was designed to support the needs of business data processing. It has a number of features that makes it easy to handle a variety of file and record types and to produce different types of output, including formatted reports. The Englishlike appearance of COBOL language statements promotes readability of COBOL programs, which helps to make programs easier to maintain.

The CPI specification for COBOL is largely based on the American National Standard Programming Language—COBOL, ANSI X3.23-1985, Intermediate Level. This standard is identical with ISO standard 1989-1985. The specification also includes some elements from ANSI X3.23-1985, High Level, and IBM enhancements to the standard. Implementations are available in the MVS, VM, OS/400, and OS/2 environments.

COBOL Example

Figure 3.2 shows an example of a COBOL program. This program performs the same processing as the C language example shown previously, illustrating the use of the query interface. It shows the basic structure of a COBOL program, which consists of four major divisions:

- **IDENTIFICATION DIVISION.** Provides documentary information about the program, such as its name, author, the date it was written, and the date it was last compiled.
- **ENVIRONMENT DIVISION.** Provides information about the system environment in which the program is compiled and run. This can include use of specific collating sequences, character sets, and currency signs, and information about the external names that are used to reference files used by the program.
- **DATA DIVISION.** Describes and defines various types of data, including files, constants, and variables used by a program.
- **PROCEDURE DIVISION.** Defines the actual processing to be performed by the program.

COBOL Data Definition And Use

COBOL supports the use of two types of data: file data and program data. *File data* consists of a group of records existing on some external storage medium. *Program data* is used only internally by the program.

File Data.

In the Environment Division, a file is given a name by which it is referenced within the program and is associated with an external name used to identify the file in the particular operating system environment in which the program is run. The file's organization and access mode are specified. The organizations and

```cobol
      ******************************************************************
      *   The following is a VS COBOL II version of the query          *
      *   callable interface *** DSQABFC0 **.                          *
      ******************************************************************
       IDENTIFICATION DIVISION.
       PROGRAM-ID. DSQABFC0.
         DATE-COMPILED.
       ENVIRONMENT DIVISION.
       DATA DIVISION.
       WORKING-STORAGE SECTION.
      **************************
      * Copy DSQCOMMB definition - contains query interface variables.
      **************************
       COPY DSQCOMMB.

      * Query interface commands

       01   STARTQI     PIC X(5)   VALUE "START".
       01   SETG        PIC X(10)  VALUE "SET GLOBAL".
       01   QUERY       PIC X(12)  VALUE "RUN QUERY Q1".
       01   REPT        PIC X(21)  VALUE "PRINT REPORT (FORM=F1".
       01   ENDQI       PIC X(4)   VALUE "EXIT".

      * Query command length
       01   QICLTH      PIC 9(8) USAGE IS COMP-4.
      * Number of variables
       01   QIPNUM      PIC 9(8) USAGE IS COMP-4.
      * Keyword variable lengths
       01   QIKLTHS.
            03  KLTHS   PIC 9(8) OCCURS 10 USAGE IS COMP-4.
      * Value lengths
       01   QIVLTHS.
            03  VLTHS   PIC 9(8) OCCURS 10 USAGE IS COMP-4.
      * Start Command Keyword
       01   SNAMES.
            03  SNAME1  PIC X(7) VALUE "DSQSCMD".
      * Start Command Keyword Value
       01   SVALUES.
            03  SVALUE1 PIC X(8) VALUE "USERCMD1".
      * Set GLOBAL Command Variable names to set
       01   VNAMES.
            03  VNAME1  PIC X(7) VALUE "MYVAR01".
            03  VNAME2  PIC X(5) VALUE "SHORT".
            03  VNAME3  PIC X(7) VALUE "MYVAR03".
      * Variable value parameters
       01   VVALUES.
            03  VVALS   PIC 9(8) OCCURS 10 USAGE IS COMP-4.
       01   TEMP        PIC 9(8)            USAGE IS COMP-4.

       PROCEDURE DIVISION.
      *
      * Start a query interface session
            MOVE 0 TO QICLTH.
            INSPECT STARTQI TALLYING QICLTH FOR CHARACTERS.
            MOVE 0 TO TEMP.
            INSPECT SNAME1 TALLYING TEMP FOR CHARACTERS.
            MOVE TEMP TO KLTHS(1).
```

Figure 3.2   COBOL language example.

```
      MOVE 0 TO TEMP.
      INSPECT SVALUE1 TALLYING TEMP FOR CHARACTERS.
      MOVE TEMP TO VLTHS(1).
      MOVE 1 TO QIPNUM.
      CALL DSQCIB  USING DSQCOMM, QICLTH, STARTQI,
                         QIPNUM, QIKLTHS, SNAMES,
                         QIVLTHS, SVALUES, DSQ-VARIABLE-CHAR.
*
* Set numeric values into query variables using SET GLOBAL command.
      MOVE 0 TO QICLTH.
      INSPECT SETG TALLYING QICLTH FOR CHARACTERS.
      MOVE 0 TO TEMP.
      INSPECT VNAME1 TALLYING TEMP FOR CHARACTERS.
      MOVE TEMP TO KLTHS(1).
      MOVE 0 TO TEMP.
      INSPECT VNAME2 TALLYING TEMP FOR CHARACTERS.
      MOVE TEMP TO KLTHS(2).
      MOVE 0 TO TEMP.
      INSPECT VNAME3 TALLYING TEMP FOR CHARACTERS.
      MOVE TEMP TO KLTHS(3).
      MOVE 4 TO VLTHS(1).
      MOVE 4 TO VLTHS(2).
      MOVE 4 TO VLTHS(3).
      MOVE 20 TO VVALS(1).
      MOVE 40 TO VVALS(2).
      MOVE 84 TO VVALS(3).
      MOVE 3 TO QIPNUM.
      CALL DSQCIB  USING DSQCOMM, QICLTH, SETG,
                         QIPNUM, QIKLTHS, VNAMES,
                         QIVLTHS, VVALUES, DSQ-VARIABLE-FINT.
*
* Run a query.
      MOVE 0 TO QICLTH.
      INSPECT QUERY TALLYING QICLTH FOR CHARACTERS.
      CALL DSQCIB USING DSQCOMM, QICLTH, QUERY.
*
* Print the results of the query.
      MOVE 0 TO QICLTH.
      INSPECT REPT TALLYING QICLTH FOR CHARACTERS.
      CALL DSQCIB USING DSQCOMM, QICLTH, REPT.
*
* End the query interface session.
      MOVE 0 TO QICLTH.
      INSPECT ENDQI TALLYING QICLTH FOR CHARACTERS.
      CALL DSQCIB USING DSQCOMM, QICLTH, ENDQI.
      STOP RUN.
```

Figure 3.2 *(Continued)*

access modes that are supported are listed in Box 3.7. The Environment Division can also provide information about sorting and merging or checkpointing a file. The Data Division contains one or more record descriptions for each data file and each sort or merge file used by the program. The following is an example of a record description. Level numbers are used to group together related fields in the record and allow them to be treated as a unit.

```
01  EMPLOYEE-RECORD.
    05  EMPLOYEE-NAME
        10   FIRST-NAME      PIC X(15).
        10   LAST-NAME       PIC X(15).
    05  EMPLOYEE-NO          PIC 9(6).
    05  WAGE-RATE            PIC 9999V99.
    05  ADDRESS.
        10   STREET          PIC X(20).
        10   CITY            PIC X(15).
        10   STATE           PIC X(15).
        10   POSTAL-CODE     PIC X(6).
```

Program Data.

Program data is also defined in the Data Division. Level numbers can be used to define data items as individual items or as groups of related items. A data item definition specifies the data type of the item, its size, and how it is represented in storage. It may also provide editing characteristics used to format the data, an initial value for the item, and dimension specifications for data in the form of a table or array. Box 3.8 lists the data types supported in COBOL.

COBOL Statements

COBOL statements can be divided into the following general categories:

- **Imperative statements.** Imperative statements specify actions to be taken by the program. Actions include arithmetic operations, data manipulation, input/output processing, and program flow and control. Box 3.9 lists the imperative statements that are part of the CPI COBOL specification.
- **Conditional Statements.** Conditional statements are statements that are executed only when a specified condition occurs. Box 3.10 lists the conditions that may occur and the statements associated with the conditions.
- **Compiler-Directing Statements.** Compiler-directing statements specify actions for the compiler to perform. They are listed in Box 3.11.

BOX 3.7 COBOL file organizations and access modes.

File Organizations

- **Sequential.** In a sequential file, the sequence of the records is based on the physical order in which they are placed in the file. Only sequential access can be used with a sequential file.
- **Indexed.** In an indexed file, each record has an embedded key. An index associated with the file provides a logical path to each record based on its key. All access modes can be used with an indexed file.
- **Relative.** In a relative file, each record has an associated relative record number that determines its location within the file. All access modes can be used with relative files.

Access Modes

- **Sequential Access.** With sequential access, records are accessed sequentially within the file. For a sequential file, the sequence is the physical sequence in which they were written. For an indexed file, the sequence is by ascending key values. For a relative file, the sequence is by ascending relative record number.
- **Random Access.** With random access, records are retrieved or written based on a specified key value or random record number.
- **Dynamic access.** With dynamic access, individual input/output requests specify whether access is to be sequential or random.

BOX 3.8 COBOL data types.

- **DISPLAY.** Data that is stored in character form and can contain any alphanumeric value.
- **INDEX.** Data items used to reference an element of a table or array.
- **BINARY.** Data items containing numeric values stored in binary format.
- **PACKED-DECIMAL.** Data items containing numeric values stored in internal decimal format, using four bits for each digit, plus four bits for the sign.
- **COMPUTATIONAL-3.** An IBM extension that is equivalent to PACKED-DECIMAL.
- **COMPUTATIONAL-4.** An IBM extension that is equivalent to BINARY.
- **COMPUTATIONAL.** Data items containing numeric values. The format used to store the value is system-dependent.

BOX 3.9 COBOL imperative statements.

Arithmetic Operations
- ADD
- SUBTRACT
- MULTIPLY
- DIVIDE
- COMPUTE

Data Manipulation Operations
- ACCEPT (DATE,DAY,TIME)
- INITIALIZE
- INSPECT
- MOVE
- SET
- STRING
- UNSTRING

Input/Output Operations
- OPEN
- CLOSE
- READ
- WRITE
- DELETE
- REWRITE
- ACCEPT
- DISPLAY
- START
- STOP
- SORT
- MERGE
- RELEASE
- RETURN

BOX 3.9   *(Continued)*

Program Flow and Control Operations
- PERFORM
- CALL
- CANCEL
- EXIT
- GOBACK
- STOP RUN
- GO TO
- ALTER

BOX 3.10   COBOL conditional statements.

Condition	Statements Used With
ON SIZE ERROR	ADD, COMPUTE, DIVIDE, MULTIPLY, SUBTRACT
ON OVERFLOW	CALL, STRING, UNSTRING
INVALID KEY	DELETE, READ, REWRITE, START, WRITE
AT END	RETURN, READ
AT END OF PAGE	WRITE
general expression	IF, EVALUATE, SEARCH

BOX 3.11   COBOL compiler-directing statements.

- COPY
- EJECT
- SKIP1/2/3
- TITLE

FORTRAN

The FORTRAN (FORmula TRANslator) language was developed to perform tasks involving mathematical computations and complex manipulations of numeric data. It is used most commonly for scientific and engineering applications and continues to be popular with those whose work places an emphasis on mathematical computation. Although it supports complex calculations, the language itself is relatively simple and easy to learn.

The CPI specification for FORTRAN includes all elements defined in the American National Standard Programming Language— FORTRAN, ANSI X3.9-1978 (FORTRAN 77), which is identical with ISO standard 1539-1980. The specification also includes a number of extensions to the standard developed by IBM. Implementations are available in the MVS, VM, OS/400, and OS/2 environments. Figure 3.3 contains an example of a FORTRAN program. Again, this shows the use of the query interface.

FORTRAN Data Definition

FORTRAN supports several different types of data, as described in Box 3.12. These data types can be specified for constants, variables, and arrays. Values can also be represented using expressions. Box 3.13 lists the operators that can be used as part of expressions. Certain FORTRAN statements can be used to specify the characteristics and arrangement of data. These are described in Box 3.14.

FORTRAN Program Structure

FORTRAN supports the definition and use of functions and subroutines. A *subroutine* is a program unit that can be called from within another program by a CALL statement. A *function* is a procedure that is invoked directly by its name and that returns a value. A function can be one of three types:

- Intrinsic Function. An intrinsic function is supplied by the FORTRAN processor. There are a large number of intrinsic functions included as part of FORTRAN as defined by SAA. They provide commonly used arithmetic functions, such as sine and square root, logical functions, bit operations, and various types of data conversion.
- Statement Function. A statement function is defined in a single statement and is used internally within the program in which it is defined.
- External Function. An external function is defined as a program unit, and can be invoked by other program units.

FORTRAN statements used to define and use functions and subroutines are shown in Box 3.15.

```fortran
C************************************************************************
C Sample Program: DSQABFF
C FORTRAN Version of SAA Query Callable Interface
C************************************************************************
C
C Processing:
C
C       a. Start a Query Manager session using the Callable Interface.
C       b. Set Global Query Manager numeric variables.
C       c. Get Global Query Manager numeric variables.
C       d. Run a Query Manager query using the Callable Interface.
C       e. Print a report using the Callable Interface.
C       f. Exit the Query Manager session.
C
C Prerequisites:
C
C       a. Create the SAMPLE database.
C       b. Create a table, T1, with data in it.
C       c. Create a query, Q1, which selects data from table T1.
C       d. Create a form, F1, that displays data for query Q1.
C
C************************************************************************

        PROGRAM DSQABFF

C************************************************************************
C Include and declare query interface commmunications area.
C
C Note that the Include file naming rules are system specific.
C************************************************************************

        INCLUDE 'DSQCOMMF.FOR'

C************************************************************************
C Query interface command lengths and commands
C************************************************************************

        INTEGER COMMAND_LENGTH
        CHARACTER START_QUERY_INTERFACE*5,
     +            SET_GLOBAL_VARIABLES*10,
     +            GET_GLOBAL_VARIABLES*10,
     +            RUN_QUERY*12,
     +            PRINT_REPORT*21,
     +            END_QUERY_INTERFACE*4

C************************************************************************
C Query command extension, number of parameters and lengths
C************************************************************************

        INTEGER NUMBER_OF_PARAMETERS,
     +          KEYWORD_LENGTHS(10),
     +          DATA_LENGTHS(10)

C************************************************************************
C Variable data type constants
C************************************************************************

        CHARACTER CHAR_DATA_TYPE*4,
```

Figure 3.3 FORTRAN language example. *(Continued)*

```
     +              INT_DATA_TYPE*4
C*******************************************************************************
C Keyword parameters and values for START command
C*******************************************************************************

       CHARACTER*8 START_KEYWORDS(1),
     +             START_KEYWORD_VALUES(1)

       INTEGER*4 DUMMY_START_KEYWORD_VALUES(1)
       EQUIVALENCE (START_KEYWORD_VALUES, DUMMY_START_KEYWORD_VALUES)

C*******************************************************************************
C Keyword parameter and values for SET and GET commands
C*******************************************************************************

       CHARACTER*8 SET_KEYWORDS(3)
       INTEGER     SET_VALUES(3)

       CHARACTER*8 GET_KEYWORDS(3)
       INTEGER     GET_VALUES(3)

C*******************************************************************************
C Declare command length and return code variables
C*******************************************************************************

       INTEGER   CLEN, RC

C*******************************************************************************
C Start a query interface session
C*******************************************************************************

       DATA START_QUERY_INTERFACE /'START'                   /
       DATA SET_GLOBAL_VARIABLES  /'SET GLOBAL'              /
       DATA GET_GLOBAL_VARIABLES  /'GET GLOBAL'              /
       DATA RUN_QUERY             /'RUN QUERY Q1'            /
       DATA PRINT_REPORT          /'PRINT REPORT (FORM=F1'   /
       DATA END_QUERY_INTERFACE   /'EXIT'                    /
       DATA CHAR_DATA_TYPE /DSQ_VARIABLE_CHAR/
       DATA INT_DATA_TYPE  /DSQ_VARIABLE_FINT/
       NUMBER_OF_PARAMETERS = 1
       COMMAND_LENGTH       = CLEN(START_QUERY_INTERFACE)
       KEYWORD_LENGTHS(1)   = CLEN(START_KEYWORDS(1))
       DATA_LENGTHS(1)      = CLEN(START_KEYWORD_VALUES(1))
       START_KEYWORDS(1)    = 'DSQMODE'
       START_KEYWORD_VALUES(1) = 'INTERACTIVE'
       RD = DSQCIFE(DSQCOMM,
     +              COMMAND_LENGTH,
     +              START_QUERY_INTERFACE,
     +              NUMBER_OF_PARAMETERS,
     +              KEYWORD_LENGTHS,
     +              START_KEYWORDS,
     +              DATA_LENGTHS,
     +              DUMMY_START_KEYWORD_VALUES,
     +              CHAR_DATA_TYPE)

       PRINT *, 'RETURN CODE =', DSQ_RETURN_CODE
```

Figure 3.3 *(Continued)*

```
C*******************************************************************
C Set numeric values into query using SET command
C*******************************************************************

      NUMBER_OF_PARAMETERS = 3
      COMMAND_LENGTH       = CLEN(SET_GLOBAL_VARIABLES)
      SET_KEYWORDS(1)      = 'MYVAR01'
      SET_KEYWORDS(2)      = 'SHORT'
      SET_KEYWORDS(3)      = 'MYVAR03'
      KEYWORD_LENGTHS(1)   = CLEN(SET_KEYWORDS(1))
      KEYWORD_LENGTHS(2)   = CLEN(SET_KEYWORDS(2))
      KEYWORD_LENGTHS(3)   = CLEN(SET_KEYWORDS(3))
      DATA_LENGTHS(1)      = 4
      DATA_LENGTHS(2)      = 4
      DATA_LENGTHS(3)      = 4
      SET_VALUES(1)        = 20
      SET_VALUES(2)        = 40
      SET_VALUES(3)        = 84
      RC = DSQCIFE(DSQCOMM,
     +             COMMAND_LENGTH,
     +             SET_GLOBAL_VARIABLES,
     +             NUMBER_OF_PARAMETERS,
     +             KEYWORD_LENGTHS,
     +             SET_KEYWORDS,
     +             DATA_LENGTHS,
     +             SET_VALUES,
     +             INT_DATA_TYPE)

      PRINT *, 'RETURN CODE =', DSQ_RETURN_CODE

C*******************************************************************
C Get numeric values using GET command
C*******************************************************************

      NUMBER_OF_PARAMETERS = 3
      COMMAND_LENGTH       = CLEN(GET_GLOBAL_VARIABLES)
      SET_KEYWORDS(1)      = 'MYVAR01'
      SET_KEYWORDS(2)      = 'SHORT'
      SET_KEYWORDS(3)      = 'MYVAR03'
      KEYWORD_LENGTHS(1)   = CLEN(GET_KEYWORDS(1))
      KEYWORD_LENGTHS(2)   = CLEN(GET_KEYWORDS(2))
      KEYWORD_LENGTHS(3)   = CLEN(GET_KEYWORDS(3))
      DATA_LENGTHS(1)      = 4
      DATA_LENGTHS(2)      = 4
      DATA_LENGTHS(3)      = 4
      GET_VALUES(1)        = 20
      GET_VALUES(2)        = 40
      GET_VALUES(3)        = 84
      RC = DSQCIFE(DSQCOMM,
     +             COMMAND_LENGTH,
     +             GET_GLOBAL_VARIABLES,
     +             NUMBER_OF_PARAMETERS,
     +             KEYWORD_LENGTHS,
     +             GET_KEYWORDS,
     +             DATA_LENGTHS,
     +             GET_VALUES,
     +             INT_DATA_TYPE)
```

Figure 3.3 *(Continued)*

```
      PRINT *, 'RETURN CODE =', DSQ_RETURN_CODE

C***************************************************************************
C Run a query
C***************************************************************************

      COMMAND_LENGTH = CLEN(RUN_QUERY)
      RC = DSQCIF(DSQCOMM,
     +            COMMAND_LENGTH,
     +            RUN_QUERY)

      PRINT *, 'RETURN CODE =', DSQ_RETURN_CODE

C***************************************************************************
C Print the results of a query
C***************************************************************************

      COMMAND_LENGTH = CLEN(PRINT_REPORT)
      RC = DSQCIF(DSQCOMM,
     +            COMMAND_LENGTH,
     +            PRINT_REPORT)

      PRINT *, 'RETURN CODE =', DSQ_RETURN_CODE

C***************************************************************************
C End the query interface session
C***************************************************************************

      COMMAND_LENGTH = CLEN(END_QUERY_INTERFACE)
      RC = DSQCIF(DSQCOMM,
     +            COMMAND_LENGTH,
     +            END_QUERY_INTERFACE)

      PRINT *, 'RETURN CODE =', DSQ_RETURN_CODE

      END
```

Figure 3.3 *(Continued)*

FORTRAN Processing Statements

FORTRAN processing statements can be used to assign values to variables and array elements, to control the sequence of execution of the program, and to perform I/O operations. These statements are listed in Box 3.16. FORTRAN has one compiler directive, the INCLUDE statement, which can be used to include source statements from another file as part of a program.

BOX 3.12   FORTRAN data types.

- **INTEGER.** Data used for numeric values in integer format. INTEGER*2 items are two bytes long, and INTEGER*4 items are four bytes long.
- **REAL.** Data used for numeric values in floating-point format. REAL*4 items are four bytes long (single precision) and REAL*8 items are eight bytes long (double precision).
- **COMPLEX.** Data used for complex numbers, consisting of a real part and an imaginary part. COMPLEX*8 items are eight bytes long and COMPLEX*16 items are 16 bytes long.
- **LOGICAL.** Data used to represent the values **"true"** and **"false."** LOGICAL*1 items are one byte long, and LOGICAL*4 items are four bytes long.
- **CHARACTER.** Data stored as a string of characters that may contain any character from the FORTRAN character set. A character substring, representing a contiguous portion of a character string, can also be defined.

BOX 3.13   FORTRAN expressions.

Arithmetic Expression Operators

```
** Exponentiation
*  Multiplication
/  Division
+  Addition or identity
-  Subtraction or negation
```

Character Expression Operators

```
// Concatenation
```

Relational Expression Operators

```
.LT.   Less than
.LE.   Less than or equal to
.EQ.   Equal to
.NE.   Not equal to
.GT.   Greater than
.GE.   Greater than or equal to
```

Logical Expression Operators

```
.NOT.   Logical negation
.AND.   Logical conjunction
.OR.    Logical inclusive disjunction
.EQV.   Logical equivalence
.NEQV.  Logical nonequivalence
```

BOX 3.14 FORTRAN data characteristics statements.

- **COMMON.** Specifies a storage area that can be shared by two or more program units.
- **DATA.** Provides initial values for variables, array elements, and character substrings.
- **DIMENSION.** Specifies the dimensions of an array.
- **EQUIVALENCE.** Specifies that two data items (variable, array element, or character substring) are to share the same storage.
- **IMPLICIT.** Specifies data types to be assigned implicitly when one is not specified explicitly.
- **PARAMETER.** Specifies names for constants.
- **SAVE.** Specifies variables, arrays, or common blocks defined in a subprogram that are to be available to the calling program after the subprogram completes execution.

BOX 3.15 FORTRAN program structure statements.

- **PROGRAM.** Identifies a program unit as a main program.
- **FUNCTION.** Identifies a program unit as an external function.
- **SUBROUTINE.** Identifies a program unit as a subroutine.
- **ENTRY.** Establishes an alternate entry point for a function or subroutine.
- **RETURN.** Ends the execution of a function or subroutine and passes control back to the program unit that invoked it.
- **CALL.** Invokes a subroutine.
- **EXTERNAL.** Identifies a name as the name of an external function.
- **INTRINSIC.** Identifies a name as the name of an intrinsic function.

BOX 3.16 FORTRAN processing statements.

Assignment Statements

- **=.** Used in an assignment statement to assign the value of an expression to a variable, array element, or character substring.
- **ASSIGN.** Assigns the value of a statement label to a variable.

Flow Control Statements

- **IF / ELSE IF / ELSE / END IF.** Used in constructs to control execution of statements based on the evaluation of logical expressions.
- **DO.** Executes a set of statements iteratively until a specified condition is met.
- **GO TO.** Transfers control to a specified statement label.
- **CONTINUE.** A statement having no effect.
- **END.** Terminates execution of a program unit.
- **STOP.** Terminates execution of a program unit and displays a specified value to the user.
- **PAUSE.** Suspends execution of a program unit and displays a specified value to the user. Execution resumes when the user intervenes.

PL/I

The PL/I (Programming Language/I) language was developed by IBM to meet the needs of scientific, engineering, commercial, and system programming applications. It combines many of the features found in COBOL, FORTRAN, and ALGOL, with the addition of features that support structured programming constructs. The CPI specification for PL/I is based on IBM PL/I products rather than on national or international standards. Implementations are available that can be used in the MVS and the VM environments. Figure 3.4 contains an example of a simple PL/I program.

PL/I Data Definition

Variables can be defined in a DECLARE statement. The different data types and other attributes that can be used in defining data are listed in Box 3.17. If attributes are not declared explicitly, they are assigned by default. The DEFAULT statement can be used to specify the defaults to use for different data types.

```
A:  PROCEDURE;
    DECLARE RATE FLOAT (10),
            TIME FLOAT (5),
            DISTANCE FLOAT (15),
            MASTER FILE;
    CALL READCM (RATE, TIME,
        DISTANCE,MASTER);

READCM:
    PROCEDURE (W,X,Y,Z);
    DECLARE W FLOAT (10),
            X FLOAT (5),
            Y FLOAT (15),
            Z FILE;
    GET FILE (Z) LIST (W,X,Y);
    Y = W * X;
    IF Y > 0
        THEN RETURN;
        ELSE PUT LIST('ERROR READCM');
    END READCM;
END A;
```

Figure 3.4 PL/I language example.

Values can be represented using expressions, which combine constants, variables, and function references with various operators. The operators that can be used in expressions are shown in Box 3.18. Arrays can be used as operands within an expression. The specified operation is performed on each element of the array, with an array as the result.

PL/I Program Structure

PL/I programs are structured as a set of one or more *external procedures*. (An external procedure is one that is compiled separately.) One of the procedures is specified as OPTIONS(MAIN), and this procedure initially receives control when the program is invoked. Other procedures can be invoked from within the program with a CALL statement. A procedure can also contain internal procedures nested within it. An internal procedure is also invoked with a CALL statement. A procedure can also be defined as a function by using the RETURNS attribute. A function is invoked directly by name and returns a value. Figure 3.5 shows an example of an external procedure (TPROD) defined and invoked as a function. A recursive procedure, defined with the RECURSIVE option, can invoke itself.

A PL/I program can also contain *begin-blocks*. A begin-block is a set of statements delimited by a BEGIN statement and an END statement. The begin-block structure affects the scope of the declaration of names and the allocation of some variables. A begin-block is executed when normal program flow reaches it. Figure 3.6 contains an example of a PL/I program with an internal procedure and begin-blocks.

The CPI PL/I specification includes a number of built-in functions and procedures. They provide the following types of processing:

- **String-Handling Functions.** Simplify the processing of bit, character, and DBCS strings.
- **Arithmetic and Mathematical Functions.** Provide mathematical operations, determine properties of arithmetic values, and control conversion during arithmetical operations.
- **Array-Handling Functions.** Operate on array arguments and return an element value.
- **Condition-Handling Functions.** Allow the program to investigate the cause of enabled conditions.
- **Storage Control Functions.** Control the storage requirements and locations of variables and the value assignment, conversion, and number of generations of variables.
- **Input/Output Functions.** Determine the current state of a file.
- **Date and Time Functions.** Access the system date and time.

PL/I Processing Statements

PL/I processing statements allow the application developer to define and manipulate data, perform I/O operations on stream and record files, structure a PL/I program, manage the flow of control within a program, and handle conditions that arise during program execution. The statements that are supported are listed in Box 3.19.

PL/I also includes statements that provide compile-time directives to the compiler. These statements are listed in Box 3.20.

```
MAINP:   PROCEDURE;
         DCL TPROD ENTRY (BIN FLOAT (53),
                          BIN FLOAT (53),
                          BIN FLOAT (53),
                          LABEL) EXTERNAL
             RETURNS (BIN FLOAT(21));
         GET LIST (A,B,C,Y);
         X = Y**3+TPROD(A,B,C,LAB1);
LAB1:    CALL ERRT;
         END MAINP;

*PROCESS;
TPROD:   PROCEDURE (U,V,W,Z)
             RETURNS (BIN FLOAT(21));
         DCL (U,V,W) BIN FLOAT(53);
         DECLARE Z LABEL;

         IF U > V + W
             THEN GO TO Z;
             ELSE RETURN (U*V*W);
         END TPROD;
```

Figure 3.5 PL/I program structure—use of a function.

```
A: PROCEDURE OPTIONS(MAIN);
   statement-1
   statement-2
   B: BEGIN;
      statement-b1
      statement-b2
      CALL C;
      statement-b3
      END B;
   statement-3
   statement-4
   C: PROCEDURE;
      statement-c1
      statement-c2
      statement-c3
      D: BEGIN;
         statement-d1
         statement-d2
         GO TO LAB;
         statement-d3
         END D;
      statement-c4
      END C;
   statement-5
LAB: statement-6
   statement-7
   END A;
```

Figure 3.6   PL/I program structure—internal procedure and begin-blocks.

BOX 3.17 PL/I data types and attributes.

Coded Arithmetic Data

- **BINARY or DECIMAL.** Defines the *base* of the data item.
- **FIXED or FLOAT.** Defines the *scale* of the data item.
- **PRECISION.** Specifies the *precision* of the data item, using number of digits and optionally, a scaling factor.
- **REAL or COMPLEX.** Specifies the *mode* of the data item.

String Data

- **BIT, CHARACTER, or GRAPHIC.** Specifies the variable as a bit variable, character variable, or graphic variable. (Graphic variables are used for DBCS data.)
- **VARYING.** Specifies the variable as being of variable length.
- **PICTURE.** Specifies the properties of a character data item by specifying a picture character for each position in the item.

Data Aggregates

- **Array.** An *n*-dimensional collection of elements that have identical attributes.
- **Structure.** A hierarchical aggregate whose elements need not have identical structures. A structure may be given dimensions, defining an array of structures.

General Attributes

- **INITIAL.** Specifies an initial value for a variable.
- **ALIGNED or UNALIGNED.** Specifies whether a data element must be aligned on a storage boundary.
- **AUTOMATIC, STATIC, CONTROLLED, or BASED.** Specifies the manner in which storage is allocated for a variable, as follows:
  — **AUTOMATIC.** Storage is allocated upon entry to the block that contains the storage declaration.
  — **STATIC.** Storage is allocated when the program is loaded.
  — **CONTROLLED.** The program controls the allocation and freeing of storage for the variable. Multiple allocations of a variable stacks generations of the variable.
  — **BASED.** The program controls the allocation and freeing of storage for the variable. Multiple allocations of a variable are available and can be identified by a locator variable.

BOX 3.18   PL/I expressions.

Arithmetic Expression Operators

+	(prefix or infix)	Identity or addition
−	(prefix or infix)	Negation or subtraction
*		Multiplication
/		Division
**		Exponentiation

Bit Expression Operators

¬	Logical not
&	Logical and
|	Logical or

Comparison Expression Operators

<	Less than
¬<	Not less than
<=	Less than or equal to
=	Equal to
¬=	Not equal to
>=	Greater than or equal to
>	Greater than
¬>	Not greater than

Concatenation Expression Operator

|	Concatenation

BOX 3.19 PL/I Processing statements.

Data Definition and Manipulation Statements

- **DECLARE.** Defines the attributes and scope of name for a variable or other type of name.
- **DEFAULT.** Specifies data-attribute defaults for different data types.
- **= (Assignment).** Evaluates an expression and assigns its value to one or more target variables.
- **ALLOCATE.** Allocates storage for controlled variables.
- **FREE.** Frees storage used by controlled variables.

Input/Output—Record-oriented Data Transmission Statements

- **CLOSE.** Dissociates a file definition from the file with which it was associated.
- **DELETE.** Deletes a record from a file.
- **LOCATE.** Sets a pointer to the location of the next record in a sequential output file.
- **OPEN.** Associates a file definition with a file and makes it available for processing.
- **READ.** Makes a record from a file available for processing.
- **REWRITE.** Replaces a record in a file.
- **WRITE.** Adds a record to a file.

Input/Output—Stream-oriented Data Transmission Statements

- **DISPLAY.** Displays a message on the user's terminal or the system console.
- **FORMAT.** Controls the formatting of data being transmitted using stream-oriented transmission.
- **GET.** Assigns values from an input stream to one or more variables.
- **PUT.** Transmits values to an output stream.

(Continued)

BOX 3.19 *(Continued)*

Program Structure Statements

- **BEGIN/END.** Delimits a begin-block.
- **PROCEDURE/END.** Delimits a procedure.

Flow Control Statements

- **DO/END.** Delimits and repetitively executes a set of statements called a *do-group*.
- **LEAVE.** Transfers control out of a do-group to the statement following the END statement and terminates the do-group.
- **IF/THEN/ELSE.** Evaluates an expression and controls the flow of execution based on the results of the evaluation.
- **SELECT/WHEN/OTHERWISE/END.** Evaluates an expression and performs one of a series of actions based on the results of the evaluation.
- **NULL.** The null statement (;) performs no action. It may be used as part of an IF or SELECT statement.
- **CALL.** Invokes a procedure.
- **RETURN.** Terminates execution of a procedure and returns control to the procedure that invoked it.
- **GO TO.** Transfers control to the statement with the specified label.
- **STOP.** Immediately terminates the program.
- **DELAY.** Suspends execution of the program for a specified period of time.

Condition Handling Statements

- **ON.** Causes an action to be executed when a particular error or condition, such as end-of-file or end-of-page, occurs.
- **REVERT.** Cancels the action specification on any ON statement for a specified condition.
- **SIGNAL.** Raises a specified condition.

BOX 3.20   PL/I compiler-directing statements.

- ***PROCESS.** Specifies compile-time options.
- **%INCLUDE.** Incorporates external text into the source program.
- **%NOPRINT.** Suspends printing of the source listing until a %PRINT statement is encountered.
- **%PAGE.** Skips the program listing to a new page.
- **%PRINT.** Resumes printing of the source listing.
- **%SKIP.** Causes a specified number of blank lines to be included in the program listing.

RPG

RPG (Report Program Generator) is a language that was originally designed to be an easy-to-use report generator. With RPG, the application developer specifies the layout of inputs and outputs and the calculations to be performed. The general logic required to read inputs, write outputs, check sequences, and perform processing of totals is provided by the RPG compiler. As RPG has evolved over the years, a number of logic and file control facilities have been added. These facilities allow RPG to be used not only for basic report writing and inquiry but also to perform a variety of complex functions in both batch and interactive applications.

The CPI specification for RPG is largely based on the RPG/400 language implemented under OS/400. Implementations are available in the MVS, VM, and OS/400 environments. Figure 3.7 contains portions of an RPG program. This partial program shows an example of the use of the CPI PrintManager interface. The portions shown illustrate input specifications, calculation specifications, and output specifications.

RPG Program Cycle

The basic logic for an RPG program, called the *program cycle,* is supplied by the RPG compiler. This logic represents the series of steps the program performs for each input record. Figure 3.8 contains a flow chart representation of the program cycle. Depending on the specifications coded, a particular program may or may not use each step in the cycle. The basic processing performed at each step includes the following:

1. RPG processes all heading and detail lines.
2. RPG reads the next input record and sets indicators that identify the record and any control breaks that have occurred.

```
     ***********************************************************
     *                                                         *
     *              FILE SPECIFICATIONS                        *
     *                                                         *
     ***********************************************************
     *..1....+....2....+....3....+....4....+....5....+....6....+....7...
     *
     * Define output file
     *
     FQPRINT  O  F    132     OF        PRINTER       KPRTCTLLINE
     ***********************************************************
     *                                                         *
     *              INPUT SPECIFICATIONS                       *
     *                                                         *
     ***********************************************************
     *..1....+....2....+....3....+....4....+....5....+....6....+....7...
     *-----------------------------------------------------------*
     * IBM-supplied constants                                    *
     *-----------------------------------------------------------*
     I/COPY EKICONR
     *-----------------------------------------------------------*
     * Print descriptor name.                                    *
     *                                                           *
     * In this example note that the "universal" print descriptor*
     * name format is used.  This is to make the code as system- *
     * independent (and portable) as possible.                   *
     *                                                           *
     * This example also assumes that this print descriptor already *
     * exists and that it contains the following print options.  *
     *                                                           *
     *      Option Name: DUPLEX                                  *
     *          Default:        YES                              *
     *          Rule:           List                             *
     *          Valid Values: YES, NO, TUMBLE                    *
     *                                                           *
     *      Option Name: COPIES                                  *
     *          Default:        1                                *
     *          Rule:           Range                            *
     *          Valid Values: 1-255, zero decimal places         *
     *-----------------------------------------------------------*
     I              'PRDNAME=IBM Print Ma-C         CPRDNM
     I              'nager Options'
     *-----------------------------------------------------------*
     * General Declarations                                      *
     *-----------------------------------------------------------*
     IGENVAR    DSW
     *    Success/failure return code
     I                                       B   1   40SUCCES
     *    General counter
     I                                       B   5   80COUNT
     *    Level of structure
     I                                       B   9  120LEVEL
     *    Loop index
     I                                       B  13  160I
     *    Initialization options
     I                                       B  17  200OPTS
     *    Application Anchor Block Handle
     I                                       B  21  240HAB
```

Figure 3.7   RPG program example.

```
*     Handle for Print Session
I                                           B  29   320HPRM
*     Number of Items Returned
I                                           B  33   360ITMRTN
*     Number of Items Remaining
I                                           B  37   400ITMRMN
*     Number of elements in OPTARY
I                                           B  49   520OPACT
*     Name of Print Descriptor
IPRDEVR         DS
I                                           B   1    40PRDEL
I                                               5    84 PRDENM
*     Buffer (reserved for future use)
IBFRVAR         DS
I                                           B   1    40BUFRL
I                                               5     6 BUFR
*     Write Buffer
IWBUFF          DS
I                                               1   132 BUFF
*     Document length and name
IDOCVAR         DS
I                                           B   1    40DOCNML
I                                               5    14 DOCNME
*----------------------------------------------------------------*
* Miscellaneous Constants                                        *
*----------------------------------------------------------------*
I                 'YES, NO, TUMBLE'   C          DUPVVA
I                 '0, 1, 255'         C          CPSVVA
I                 'Setting an invalid p-C        INVM1
I                 'rint option...'
I                 'An error message sho-C        INVM2
I                 'uld be output...'
I                 'List of current prin-C        CURPOP
I                 't options:'
******************************************************************
*                                                                *
*             CALCULATION SPECIFICATIONS                         *
*                                                                *
******************************************************************
*..1....+....2....+....3....+....4....+....5....+....6....+....7...
*================================================================*
* Start a PrintManager process                        (SPRINIT)  *
*================================================================*
C                     Z-ADD0         OPTS
C                     MOVE HNULL     HAB
C                     CALL 'SPRINIT'
C                     PARM           OPTS
C                     PARM           HAB
C                     MOVE HAB       SUCCES
C                     MOVE 'SPRINIT' 'FNM
C                     EXSR CHKNUM
*----------------------------------------------------------------*
* Invoke SPRGEEM with an indexc value of 0 to get the total
* number of additional error messages.
*----------------------------------------------------------------*
C                     Z-ADD0         INDX
C                     CALL 'SPRGEEM'
C                     PARM           ERRINF
```

Figure 3.7 *(Continued)*

(Continued)

```
C                     PARM           INDX
C                     PARM           ERRID
C                     PARM           ERRDL
C                     PARM           ERRMSG
C                     PARM           TOTCNT
C                     PARM           SUCCES
 *----------------------------------------------------------------*
 * Output the error identifier and error value for each
 * additional error message.
 *----------------------------------------------------------------*
 * DO 1 to TOTCNT times...
C           1         DO    TOTCNT   INDX
 *
 * Get the additional error message
 *
C                     CALL  'SPRGEEM'
C                     PARM           ERRINF
C                     PARM           INDX
C                     PARM           ERRID
C                     PARM           ERRDL
C                     PARM           ERRMSG
C                     PARM           TOTCNT
C                     PARM           SUCCES
 * If didn't get the eror message, don't try to output it
C           SUCCES    IFEQ  000000000
C                     GOTO  SKPOUT
C                     END
 * Fill in the output fields and output the information
 *
 * Output the constant line saying "Error Message:"
C                     MOVE  *BLANK   MSGSTR
C                     MOVE  *BLANK   OFLD
C                     MOVE  ERRID    MFLD1
C                     MOVE  MSGSTR   OFLD
C                     EXCPTPRINT                        Print
 * Move the error message into a structure such that we can
 * output it on multiple lines
C                     MOVE  ERRMSG   ERMM2
 * Output the first 132 characters of the message
C                     MOVE  *BLANK   OFLD
C                     MOVE  ERMM2A   OFLD
C                     EXCPTPRINT                        Print
 * Output the next 124 characters of the message
C                     MOVE  *BLANK   OFLD
C                     MOVE  ERMM2B   OFLD
C                     EXCPTPRINT                        Print
C           SKPOUT    TAG
 * End DO 1 to TOTCNT times
C                     END
 *----------------------------------------------------------------*
 * The storage for the ERRINFO structure returned by SPRGERI
 * must be freed using SPRFERI.
 *----------------------------------------------------------------*
C                     CAll  'SPRFERI'
C                     PARM           ERRINF
C                     PARM           SUCCES
 * End "IF not successful"
C                     END
```

Figure 3.7   *(Continued)*

```
 * Return to the caller
C                   ENDIT     TAG
C                             ENDSR
 ********************************************************************
 *                                                                  *
 *                    OUTPUT SPECIFICATIONS                         *
 *                                                                  *
 ********************************************************************
 *..1....+....2....+....3....+....4....+....5....+....6....+....7...
OQPRINT   E                   PRINT
O                             OFLD      B0132
```

Figure 3.7 *(Continued)*

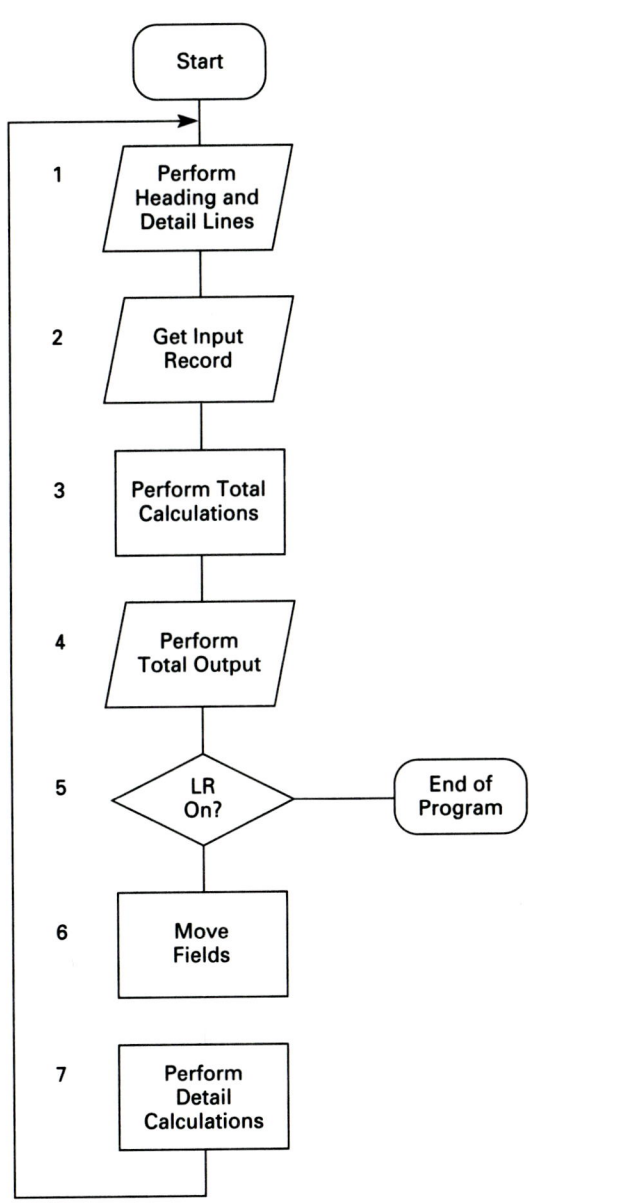

Figure 3.8 RPG program logic cycle.

3. Based on control breaks, RPG performs total calculations.
4. Based on control breaks, RPG processes output total lines.
5. If the last record (LR) indicator is on, the program ends; otherwise, processing continues.
6. Fields from selected input records are moved to a processing area.
7. RPG processes detail calculations, as defined in the calculation specification.

RPG Program Structure

An RPG program consists of a series of *specifications*. Each type of specification relates to a particular set of functions. These specifications are formatted, and each entry must start in a specific position. The types of specifications defined for RPG include the following:

- **Control Specifications.** Provide information about program generation and execution.
- **File Description Specifications.** Define all files in the program.
- **Extension Specifications.** Describe arrays and tables used in the program and specify how they are initialized.
- **Line Counter Specifications.** Indicate the forms length and length of overflow lines for each printer file.
- **Input Specifications.** Describe data structures, records, and fields in input files and specify how they are used by the program.
- **Calculation Specifications.** Describe calculations to be done by the program and specify the order in which they are performed.
- **Output Specifications.** Describe records and fields in output files and indicate when they are written.

The following sections describe in more detail each of the types of specifications.

Control Specifications

The control specification statement provides information about program generation and execution. Entries included in the control specification statement are described in Box 3.21.

File Description Specifications

File description specifications identify each file used by the program. A file can be used for input, output, or both. Multiple files can be used as input, and RPG provides the logic to match the files on specified fields. The processing of a file may be controlled by the RPG program cycle or by the application program through the use of calculation operations. The entries that can be used as part of a file description are shown in Box 3.22.

Extension Specifications

Extension specifications describe arrays, tables, and record address files. A record address file consists of a set of relative record numbers that are used to access records in another file. The entries in an extension specification are described in Box 3.23.

Line Counter Specifications

Line counter specifications specify page length and form length for printer files. Possible entries are listed in Box 3.24.

Input Specifications

Input specifications are used to describe input files and data structures. For input files, record identification entries describe an input record and its relationship to other records in the file. Field description entries describe individual fields. Input specification entries for files are listed in Box 3.25. For data structures, there are data structure statement entries describing the data structure as a whole and data structure subfield entries that describe subfields within the structure. Entries for data structures are shown in Box 3.26.

Calculation Specifications

Calculation specifications define operations to be performed on data processed by the program. Many different types of operations can be performed as part of a calculation. These include the following:

- **Arithmetic Operations.** Perform standard arithmetic operations on numeric data.
- **Comparison Operations.** Compare two values and set an indicator based on the results of the comparison.
- **Move Operations.** Transfer values from one field to another.
- **Declarative Operations.** Define fields, parameters used in a CALL statement, and names that are the destination of a branching operation.
- **Subroutine Operations.** Define a group of calculations as a subroutine or invoke a subroutine.
- **Indicator Operations.** Set indicators on or off.
- **Structured Programming Operations.** Perform a group of calculations iteratively or conditionally.
- **Call and Branching Operations.** Invoke another program or branch around operations when specified conditions occur.
- **File Operations.** Allow the program to directly control files. They can be used to open, close, read, write, and update a file.

- **Information Operations.** Provide access to debugging and time facilities.
- **Data Area Operations.** Retrieve, write, or unlock a data area.

The specifications indicate when the calculation is to be performed, the data and operations to be used for the calculation, and tests to be performed on the results of the calculation. The entries that are part of the calculation specifications are shown in Box 3.27.

Output Specifications

Output specifications are used to describe output files. Record line entries describe records that make up the file and under what conditions they are written. Field description and control entries describe fields in a record and when they are written. Entries in an output specification are listed in Box 3.28.

Indicators

Much of the program-specified processing that can take place is based on the use of *indicators*, which can be set on and off. Some indicators are defined internally by RPG and can be used in various types of operations. These include

- **First Page Indicator.** Can be used to write heading and detail records before processing the first input record.
- **Last Record Indicator.** Indicates that the last record from an input file has been processed.
- **Matching Record Indicator.** Indicates whether the matching fields from two files contain the same values.
- **Return Indicator.** Indicates to the internal RPG program logic that control should be returned to the calling program.

Other indicators are defined as part of the program's specifications. These include

- **Overflow Indicator.** Indicates when the last line on a page has been printed.
- **Record Identifying Indicator.** Indicates that a designated record type has been selected for processing.
- **Control Level Indicators.** Indicates that a control break (change in sequence number) has occurred in a designated field.
- **Field Indicators.** Indicates whether a designated field meets a specified condition, such as whether the field's value is blank, equal to zero, greater than zero, or less than zero.
- **Resulting Indicators.** Indicates a record-not-found condition, an end-of-file condition, or an exception or error condition for a file operation; or contains the results of a test on an arithmetic operation result field.

Compiler Directive Statements

Compiler directive statements can be used to control processing that takes place during compilation. These statements are listed in Box 3.29.

BOX 3.21   RPG control specifications.

- **Debug.** Whether DEBUG and DUMP operations will be used.
- **Currency Symbol.** The character used as the currency symbol.
- **Date Format.** The day/month/year format used for dates.
- **Date Edit.** The separator character used with dates.
- **Inverted Print.** The characters used as decimal notation and as a separator in numeric fields.
- **Alternate Collating Sequence.** Whether the normal or alternate collating sequence is used.
- **Sign Handling.** Whether a sign is forced on input and output of zoned numeric fields.
- **1P Forms Position.** Whether the first print line is printed only once or repeatedly.
- **File Translation.** Whether a file translation table will be used to translate for data in specified files to translate to an alternate collating sequence.
- **Transparency Check.** Whether RPG should check for DBCS values.
- **Program Identification.** A unique name assigned to the program.

BOX 3.22 RPG file description specifications.

- **File Name.** A unique name assigned to the file.
- **File Type.** Whether the file is used for input, output, update, or combined input/output.
- **File Designation.** Whether the file is a primary file, secondary file, record address file, array or table file, or full procedural file.
- **End of File.** Whether all records from this file must be processed before the program can end.
- **Sequence.** Whether match fields are in ascending or descending order.
- **File Format.** File is program described.
- **Record Length.** The length of logical records.
- **Mode of Processing.** Whether random or sequential processing will be used.
- **Length of Key Field or Record Address Field.** Length of key or record address value used to access the file.
- **Record Address Type.** Describes keys or relative record numbers used to access the file.
- **Type of File Organization or Additional Areas.** Whether the file is indexed, relative record, or processed without keys.
- **Overflow Indicators.** Indicator to use for PRINTER file overflow condition.
- **Key Field Starting Location.** Record position in which the key field begins.
- **Extension Code.** Whether extension specifications or line counter specifications are included for this file.
- **Device.** Whether the file is a PRINTER file, on disk, sequentially organized, or accessed by a user-supplied routine.
- **Continuation Lines.** Whether continuation lines are used for this specification to specify additional options for this file.
- **Name of Label Exit.** The name of the routine used to process a file accessed by a user-supplied routine.
- **File Addition/Unordered.** Whether records can be added to this file.
- **File Condition.** Whether RPG or the program will open this file.

BOX 3.23   RPG extension specifications.

For Arrays and Tables

- **From File Name.** An array or table file to be loaded at prerun time.
- **To File Name.** File to which an array or table is to be written.
- **Table or Array Name.** The name of the array or table described in this specification.
- **Number of Entries Per Record.** Number of array or table entries in each array or table input record.
- **Length of Entry.** Length of each array or table element.
- **Packed/Binary, Signed Left/Right.** Data format used for array or table elements.
- **Decimal Positions.** Number of positions to the right of the decimal in array or table elements.
- **Sequence.** Whether data used to load the array or table is in ascending, descending, or unspecified sequence.

For Record Address Files

- **From File Name.** Name of the record address file.
- **To File Name.** Name of the file processed using record numbers from the record address file.

BOX 3.24   RPG line counter specifications.

- **File name.** File name of the PRINTER file from the file description specification.
- **Line Number—Number of Lines Per Page.** Number of printing lines available.
- **Form Length.** Indicates that the previous value is the form length.
- **Overflow Line Number.** The line number of the overflow line.

BOX 3.25 RPG input specifications—files.

Record Identification Entries

- **File Name.** The file name for this file as it appeared in the file description specification.
- **Sequence, Number, Option.** Whether sequence checking is to be performed and if there can be multiple records with the same sequence number.
- **Record Identifying Indicator, Position, Not, C/Z/D, Character, AND/OR.** Definition of the record identification codes that identify a particular record type. They specify the locations of the codes, the part of the character that acts as the code, the actual value of the code, and the indicator associated with this record type. The record type can be associated with a general indicator, control level indicator, halt indicator, return indicator, or look-ahead field.

Field Description Entries

- **Packed/Binary, Sign Left/Right.** The format of the field and the use of preceding or following signs.
- **Field Location.** The location of the beginning and the end of the field.
- **Decimal Positions.** Number of decimal positions in a numeric field.
- **RPG Field Name.** The name of the field.
- **Control Level.** For a control field, the control level indicator associated with this field.
- **Matching Fields.** For a field used to match against another file, the match field code associated with this field.
- **Field Record Relation.** Association of this field with a particular record type.
- **Field Indicators.** The values (blank, zero, plus, minus) in this field that will cause the specified indicator to be turned on.

BOX 3.26   RPG input specifications—data structures.

Data Structure Statement Entries

- **Data Structure Name.** The name of the data structure being defined.
- **Option.** Whether the data structure is used for program status or in a data area.
- **Occurs *N* Times.** The number of occurrences for a multiple-occurrence data structure.
- **Length.** The length of the data structure.

Data Structure Subfield Entries

- **Packed/Binary, Sign Left/Right.** The format of the field and the use of preceding or following signs.
- **Field Location.** The location of the beginning and the end of the field.
- **Decimal Positions.** Number of decimal positions in a numeric field.
- **RPG Field Name.** The name of the field.

BOX 3.27   RPG calculation specifications.

- **Control Level, Conditioning Indicators.** Under what conditions the calculation is performed in relation to various indicators.
- **Factor 1.** The field or data value used as the first operand.
- **Operation.** The specific operation to perform.
- **Factor 2.** The field or data values used as the second operand.
- **Result Field, Field Length, Decimal Positions, Half Adjust.** The field that will contain the result of the calculation and its characteristics.
- **Resulting Indicators.** Conditions tested for and indicators set based on the value in the result field.

BOX 3.28   RPG output specifications.

Record Line Entries

- **File Name.** The name of the file.
- **Type.** The record type, which can be a header, detail, total, or exception record.
- **Fetch Overflow.** Whether overflow lines should be used for a PRINTER file.
- **Space and Skip, Space Before, Space After, Skip Before, Skip After.** For a PRINTER file, spacing to be done when this record is printed.
- **Output Indicators, AND/OR.** Conditions under which this line is written, in terms of indicators that are on.
- **EXCPT Name.** Name associated with exception records.

Field Description and Control Entries

- **Output Indicators.** Conditions under which this field is included in the record, in terms of indicators that are on.
- **Field Name.** Name of the field.
- **Edit Codes.** Type of editing performed on the field, including zero suppression and punctuation.
- **Blank After.** Whether the field is set to blanks after the output operation is completed.
- **End Position in Output Record.** Location of the end of the field.
- **Packed/Binary, Sign Left/Right.** The format of the field and the use of preceding or following signs.
- **Constant or Edit Word.** A literal value that always appears in this field or an edit word used to format the field, including the use of currency symbols, commas, periods, and signs.

BOX 3.29 RPG compiler directives.

- **/TITLE.** Heading information for the program listing.
- **/EJECT.** Skip to a new page in the program listing.
- **/SPACE.** Space the specified number of lines in the program listing.
- **/COPY.** Include records from the specified file as part of this source program.

CONCLUSION

This chapter described the characteristics of the various conventional programming languages that are included in the Common Programming Interface component of SAA. Chapter 4 continues Part I by describing the CPI Application Generator Interface.

4 THE CPI APPLICATION GENERATOR INTERFACE

An application generator is a development facility designed to simplify and speed up the process of building and maintaining computing applications. Rather than specifying application logic in detail through a series of procedural statements in a programming language, the application developer selects and combines higher-level application functions, and the application generator then translates the functions into a form suitable for execution.

SAA APPLICATION GENERATOR ENVIRONMENTS

As part of SAA, the CPI Application Generator interface is designed to provide application compatibility and portability across all the SAA computing environments. As currently implemented, the use of a CPI Application Generator product involves three phases:

- **Application definition.** The *application definition* phase includes specifying processing logic, defining data to be used by the application, and defining screen and printer formats to be used for data display.
- **Application generation.** The *application generation* phase uses the various definitions that make up the application and prepares the application for execution in a specific computing environment.
- **Application execution.** The *application execution* phase takes place after the application definition and generation phases have been completed successfully. Once the application has been generated, it can be executed repeatedly in a particular environment.

The SAA Application Generator interface is currently implemented in IBM's Cross System Product (CSP) family of products. CSP products have a two-part structure:

- **Application Development.** An *Application Development* (AD) part of a CSP product supports the definition and generation of an application. The AD portion generates the application in a form that is basically independent of hardware and operating system considerations.
- **Application Execution.** An *Application Execution* (AE) part of a CSP product supports running the application in a particular hardware and system software environment. The AE portion is responsible for adapting the application to the specific environment in which it is being run.

Generally, an Application Development product running in one environment can generate a version of the application capable of being executed in any of the supported environments. This promotes application portability across systems, since an application can easily be built on one system and then run on another. At the time of writing, not all environments have both AD and AE products implemented. Check the current documentation for specific implementations of CSP to see what functions are supported in each environment.

APPLICATION GENERATOR INTERFACE

The intent of the CPI Application Generator interface is to allow an application to be developed using development software that operates in any of the supported computing environments and then executed using execution software in that same environment or in any of the other supported environments. However, compliance with the Application Generator interface that is part of CPI addresses only the Application Execution phase. The interface specifies the elements that can be used to define processing logic, to describe data contained in files, databases, or tables, and to format screen and printer displays. Support for the interface in a particular environment is measured in terms of the interface elements that can be executed using an AE product implemented in that environment.

APPLICATION LOGIC DEFINITION

The types of processing that can be performed by an Application Generator interface application includes functions such as accessing data in files and databases, executing logic tests, performing computations, editing and reformatting data, moving data between records and screen and printer displays, sending output to displays and printers, and accepting input from the user.

Processing logic is defined as a set of *logic blocks*. A logic block can be either a process or a statement group. A *process* includes an I/O operation, which is specified as the *process option* for the process. A process can also include processing statements for performing functions in addition to the I/O operation. A *statement group* consists of a series of processing statements that perform some logical function but does not include any I/O processing. A statement group can be invoked as a subroutine from a process or from another statement group. One process can also invoke another process.

APPLICATION LOGIC STRUCTURE   The processes and statement groups that make up an application have a hierarchical structure. Figure 4.1 illustrates a possible application structure. There are one or more *main processes* at the top of the hierarchy. When an application is invoked, these main processes are executed sequentially. A main process can invoke *nested processes* and statement groups. Nested processes and statement groups can in turn invoke other nested processes and statement groups. This type of structure conforms to the top-down flow that characterizes structured programming.

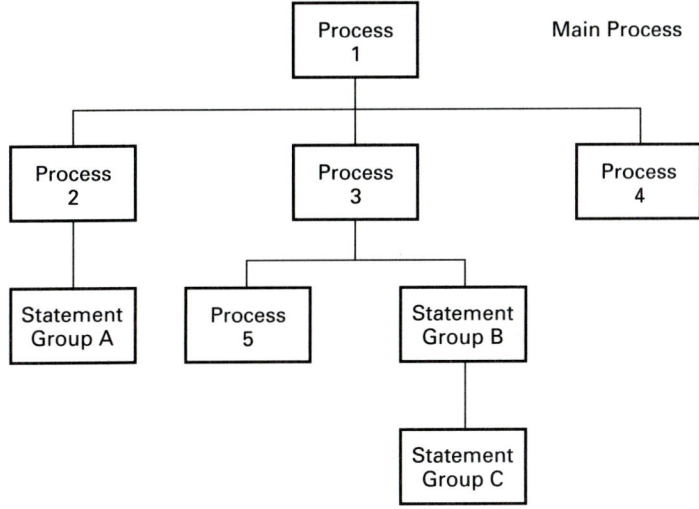

Figure 4.1   Hierarchical logic structure of an application.

When there are multiple main processes, the default is for control to pass from one main process to the next sequentially. However, flow statements can be used to alter this sequence by passing control directly to a named main process or to another application.

LOGIC SPECIFICATION   Application logic is defined by providing application specification information, application structure information, and application processing statements. Application specification information defines general information about the

BOX 4.1 Application specification elements.

- **Allow Implicits.** Specifies whether implicit data item definitions should be created.
- **Application Name.** Specifies the name of this application.
- **Bypass Edit PF Keys.** Specifies up to five keyboard function keys the application user can employ to bypass map edits when inputting data.
- **Called Parameter List.** Specifies parameters received by a called application.
- **Help Map Group Name.** Specifies the name of the map group containing user-defined help maps for this application.
- **Help PF Key.** Specifies the function key to be used to request help.
- **Map Group Name.** Specifies the map group containing maps used as process objects in this application or passed as parameters to a called application.
- **Message File.** Specifies the name of a user-created message file.
- **PF1-12=PF13-24.** Specifies that function keys 13-24 perform the same functions as function keys 1-12.
- **Prologue.** Consists of unformatted lines of text describing the application.
- **Table and Additional Records List.** Specifies a list of the tables referenced by this application and of records used as an additional working-storage area, a call argument, or a record redefinition.
- **Type.** Specifies the method of processing for this application. The following types can be specified:
  — **Main Transaction.** Defines an application that interacts with a user at a display device, where the application does not return control to a calling application or program when it terminates.
  — **Batch Transaction.** Defines an application that does not interact with a user at a display device, where the application does not return control to a calling application or program when it terminates.
  — **Called Transaction.** Defines an application that interacts with a user at a display device, where the application returns control to a calling application or program when it terminates.
  — **Called Batch.** Defines an application that does not interact with a user at a display device, where the application returns control to a calling application or program when it terminates.
- **Working Storage.** Specifies the name of the record to be used as the primary working-storage area. Any other records to be used as working-storage are specified in the Table and Additional Records List.

application as a whole, including its name, type, the map group it uses, and so on. Box 4.1 lists the elements that are part of application specification.

Application Structure

Application structure information is used to define individual processes and statement groups. It provides a name for the process or statement group and defines the process option for a process. It also defines the overall structure and logic flow for the application. The elements that can be specified as part of application structure are shown in Box 4.2.

BOX 4.2 Application structure elements.

- **Application Flow Logic.** Defines flow statements associated with main processes in this application. Flow statements transfer control directly from one main process to another.
- **Application Process List.** Lists the main processes for this application and defines specifications for each process.
- **Application Structure List.** Lists all processes and statement groups in their top-down, hierarchical structure.
- **Process Description.** Consists of a text string that describes a process.
- **Process Error Routine.** Specifies the name of an error-handling subroutine that is invoked if an error occurs during the execution of the I/O operation specified as the process option.
- **Process Name.** Specifies the name of the process.
- **Process Object.** Specifies the name of a record or map accessed by the process option.
- **Process Option.** Specifies the I/O function performed by this process. The following options can be specified:
    — **ADD.** Places a new record in a file or database.
    — **CLOSE.** Closes a file, disconnects a printer, or releases unprocessed rows in a set of SQL rows selected by UPDATE, SETUPD, or SETINQ.
    — **CONVERSE.** Displays a map on a terminal screen and waits for the user to enter input. When the user presses the Enter key or a function key, the data entered by the user is validated as specified in the map definition. If the data is not valid, the map is redisplayed with a message prompting the user to correct the data in error.

(Continued)

BOX 4.2 *(Continued)*

- **DELETE.** Removes a record from a file or database.
- **DISPLAY.** Sends a map to a printer or terminal screen.
- **EXECUTE.** Used for a process that has no I/O function to perform.
- **INQUIRY.** Reads a record from a file or database.
- **REPLACE.** Puts a changed record back into a file or database.
- **SCAN.** Reads the next record in a file or database.
- **SETINQ.** Selects a set of SQL rows for later retrieval with the SCAN process option.
- **SETUPD.** Selects a set of SQL rows for later retrieval with the SCAN process option. The rows can then be updated with the UPDATE option or deleted with the DELETE option.
- **SQLEXEC.** Executes an SQL statement constructed by the application. This allows the use of SQL facilities not directly supported as process options, such as multirow inserts, deletes and updates, and GRANT, REVOKE, CREATE, and DROP processing.
- **UPDATE.** Reads a record from a file or database with the intent of replacing or deleting the record.

• **SQL Statement.** Specifies the SQL statement used for a process that accesses a relational database. An entire statement can be generated for a process that uses the SQLEXEC process option, or an SQL statement generated from one of the other process options can be modified. The following options can be used with the SQL statement:

- **Execution Time Statement Build.** Allows an SQL statement to be built or modified dynamically at execution time.
- **Model SQL Statement Generation.** Generates a model DELETE or UPDATE SQL statement for an SQLEXEC process.
- **UPDATE or SETUPD Process Name.** Specifies the name of a process that selects rows to be replaced by a process with the REPLACE process option.

• **Statement Group Description.** Consists of a text string describing a statement group.

• **Statement Group Name.** Specifies the name of statement group.

Application Processing

Processing statements are used within processes and statement groups to specify detailed processing, including data movement and calculations, condition testing, and invoking of statement groups, processes, and other applications. The application processing statements that can be used are summarized in Box 4.3.

BOX 4.3   Application processing statements.

- **Arithmetic.** Performs arithmetic calculations, including addition, subtraction, multiplication, division, and remainder.
- **CALL.** Invokes another application or program, with control returning to this application when the called application or program terminates.
- **DXFR.** Invokes another application or program and terminates the current application.
- **FIND.** Invokes a process or statement group if the value in a data item is found as a value in a specified table column.
- **IF.** Executes a set of processing statements based on the results of one or more comparisons specified as part of the IF statement.
- **MOVE.** Moves the contents of one item to another or one data structure to another.
- **MOVEA.** Moves the contents of one array to another or initializes an array.
- **PERFORM.** Invokes a process. When the invoked process completes, control returns to the statement following the PERFORM.
- **RETR.** Obtains data from a table based on a search argument.
- **SET.** Positions the cursor in a map field, changes the attribute byte for a map field, sets an SQL row data item to null, clears a display, clears a record, causes a printer to skip to a new page, or establishes a position in a file.
- **TEST.** Determines the state of an operand and invokes a statement group or branches to a main process as a result of the state.
- **Unconditional Branch.** If used in a process or statement group, invokes a statement group, with control returning to the calling process or statement group when the invoked statement group completes. If used as a flow statement, transfers control to a main process with no return when that process completes.
- **WHILE.** Repetitively executes a set of statements until one or more specified conditions are met.
- **XFER.** Invokes the execution of another application or program and terminates the current application.

Special Function Words

The CPI Application Generator interface also defines a set of reserved words, called *special function words*, that provide specific functions or pieces of information, such as an application termination function or the current system date. These words, shown in Box 4.4, are typically used as part of processing statements. Certain special function words can also be used as part of map specification. Special function words are typically used in displaying error messages, checking I/O operations, invoking service routines, and setting switches.

BOX 4.4 Special function words.

- **EZEAID.** Indicates which function key was pressed to signal input during a CONVERSE process option I/O operation.
- **EZEAPP.** Used to store an application name for use with DXFR and XFER.
- **EZECLOS.** Terminates the application.
- **EXECNVCM.** Used as a switch to determine whether data commitment is performed automatically for each CONVERSE operation.
- **EZECOMIT.** Commits all changes to data since the last commit point.
- **EZEC10.** Checks a character data item with a check digit for modulus 10.
- **EZEC11.** Checks a character data item with a check digit for modulus 11.
- **EZEDAY.** Contains the current system date in Julian format.
- **EZEDTE.** Contains the current system date in YYMMDD format.
- **EZEFEC.** Used as a switch to determine whether application processing continues after a hard I/O error in a file or database.
- **EZEFLO.** Causes the flow statements for the current main process to be executed.
- **EZEG10.** Generates a modulus 10 check digit for a character data item.
- **EZEG11.** Generates a modulus 11 check digit for a character data item.
- **EZEMNO.** Contains the number of a message to be written to the user on the next screen display operation.
- **EZEMSG.** Specifies a variable field on a map to be used for displaying messages.
- **EZEOVER.** Used as a switch to control arithmetic overflow processing.
- **EZEOVERS.** Used to check for the occurrence of arithmetic overflows.

BOX 4.4 *(Continued)*

- **EZEROLLB.** Rolls back changes to data made since the last commit point.
- **EZERTN.** Causes an immediate return from an invoked process or statement group to the invoking process or statement group.
- **EZERT8.** Contains a return code generated by an I/O operation for a serial, relative, or indexed file.
- **EZESQCOD.** Contains a return code generated by the most recent SQL I/O operation.
- **EZESQLCA.** Contains the SQL communications area returned by an SQL I/O operation.
- **EZESQRD3.** Contains the third integer return value in the SQL communications area, which is the number of rows processed by the SQL operation.
- **EZESQRRM.** Contains the substitution variables associated with the return code in EZESQCOD.
- **EZESQWN1.** Contains the second warning byte from the SQL communications area, which indicates whether data truncation has occurred.
- **EZESQWN6.** Contains the sixth warning byte from the SQL communications area. The meaning of the byte varies with the database manager being used.
- **EZETIM.** Contains the current system time in the format HH.MM.SS.
- **EZETST.** Contains the number of the first row in a table or the first element in an array that met the search conditions in a FIND, RETR, IF, or WHILE statement. Following a MOVEA statement, it contains the subscript of the last element modified in the target array.
- **EZEUSR.** Contains the system-dependent user identifier.

DATA DEFINITION

An application typically processes data stored in a file or database. The data definition portion of an application specification describes that data. The data is defined by specifying the characteristics of individual data items and the way in which a set of data items is structured as a record in a file or a row in an SQL database.

Data definition also includes defining data that is used during application processing but that is not saved after execution. This data is defined as working storage data items and records. Tables of data values can also be defined for use in editing and validation processing.

DATA SPECIFICATION

Data is defined using data structure, record specification and table specification information. The following sections describe these three aspects of data specification.

Data Structure

The data structure information describes individual data items, specifying things such as the item's name, length, and type. It also describes the way in which data items are grouped into records or rows in an SQL database table. Box 4.5 lists the data structure elements that can be used. A data item can be defined as local or global. If it is *local*, the data item can be used only in the record or SQL row currently being defined. If it is *global*, it can be included, by name, in other record or row structures in the application.

Record Specification

Record specification information defines the organization associated with a record, along with other information, such as the record name and the file or database with which the record is associated. Possible elements are shown in Box 4.6. The elements that can be specified for a particular record depend on the organization specified.

Table Specification

Table specification information defines sets of data values that can be used as part of application processing or for editing of data entered in a map. The elements that can be specified are listed in Box 4.7.

MAP DEFINITION

An application's user interface is specified by defining screen and printer display formats in elements called *maps*. Maps define the layout of data that is displayed or entered during application execution and can also specify editing to be performed on the data. Each map is part of a map group, which consists of the maps used for a particular application.

Maps can contain constant fields and variable fields. Constant fields are used to display protected information, and variable fields allow the user to enter data. The CPI Application Generator interface provides extensive editing capabilities for the data entered in a variable field. Editing options can also be used to format data before it is displayed.

BOX 4.5 Data structure elements.

- **Data Item Bytes.** Specifies the number of bytes needed to store a data item.
- **Data Item Decimal Positions.** Specifies the number of positions to the right of the decimal point for a numeric data item.
- **Data Item Description.** Text description of the data item.
- **Data Item Key.** Specifies whether a column in an SQL row is part of the table's key.
- **Data Item Length.** Specifies the maximum number of characters or digits in a data item.
- **Data Item Level.** Specifies the placement of a data item relative to other data items in a data structure.
- **Data Item Name.** Specifies the name of a data item.
- **Data Item Occurs.** Specifies the number of times a data item repeats.
- **Data Item Read-Only.** Specifies whether a data item in an SQL row can be written to the database or only read.
- **Data Item Scope.** Specifies whether the data item is local or global.
- **Data Item SQL Column Name.** For an SQL row data item, specifies the column name by which the item is known to the database manager.
- **Data Item SQL Data Code.** For an SQL row data item, identifies the data type of the data item to the database manager.
- **Data Item Type.** Specifies the format of a data item. Possible types are as follows:
    - **BIN.** Binary number.
    - **CHA.** Character data.
    - **DBCS.** Double-byte character data.
    - **HEX.** Hexadecimal data.
    - **MIX.** DBCS data mixed with single-byte data.
    - **NUM.** Numeric characters with positive sign in F format.
    - **NUMC.** Numeric characters with positive sign in C format.
    - **PACF.** Packed decimal characters with positive sign in F format.
    - **PACK.** Packed decimal characters with positive sign in C format.
- **Record Structure.** Specifies the format of data items within a record.
- **SQL Row Record Structure.** Specifies the data items that make up a row in an SQL table.
- **Table Structure.** Specifies the data items that make up a row in a data table.

BOX 4.6 Record specification elements.

- **Alternate Specification For.** Specifies the name of an existing record or SQL row whose data item structure is to be used for this record or SQL row.
- **Default Key Item.** For an SQL row, specifies the name of the data item to be used as the search field in default SQL statements built for an alternate specification of an SQL row.
- **Default Selection Conditions.** Specifies default search criteria for an SQL row.
- **File Name.** Associates a record with a physical file for serial, relative, and indexed files.
- **Organization.** Specifies how the file or database associated with a record or SQL row is organized. Possible organizations are
  - **Indexed.** Records are in a file and are accessed by a key that is specified in the record ID item element.
  - **Redefined Record.** An alternate data structure for an existing record.
  - **Relative.** Records are in a file that is an ordered set of fixed length records. Records are accessed by means of a relative record number, which is carried in the record ID item element.
  - **Serial.** Records are in a file and stored in sequential order.
  - **SQL Row.** The record represents a row in an SQL database table.
  - **Working Storage.** Defines a storage area for data items used during program execution.
- **Prologue.** Consists of a text description of the record.
- **Record ID Item.** Names the data item that contains the record key for an indexed file or the relative record number for a relative file.
- **Record Name.** Specifies the name of the record.
- **Redefinition For.** Identifies the name of the record being redefined when the record organization is redefined record.
- **SQL Table Names.** Specifies the names of the SQL database tables associated with the SQL row being defined.

A map is created by "painting" it directly on the terminal screen. The application developer determines the map layout by entering each field in the position where it should appear when the map is displayed on a screen or printer. Constant fields are defined by typing the appropriate information at the desired position. Variable fields are defined by using special character codes. As fields are being defined, or "painted," formatting characteristics and editing checks can be assigned to them.

BOX 4.7   Table specification elements.

- **Column Definition.** Defines a data structure describing each row in the table.
- **Contents Definition.** Defines the data values stored in the table.
- **Prologue.** Consists of a text description of the table.
- **Table Name.** Specifies a name for the table.
- **Type.** Specifies how the table is to be used. Possible types are
  - **Unspecified.** The table is used only for reference by processing statements.
  - **Match Valid.** The table can be specified as a map variable field edit routine. Data entered by the user must match a value in the table.
  - **Match Invalid.** The table can be specified as a map variable field edit routine. Data entered by the user must not match any value in the table.
  - **Range Match Valid.** The table can be specified as a map variable field edit routine. Data entered by the user must be within one of the ranges of values contained in the table.

Map definition consists of map specification and map structure information, each of which is described next.

Map Specification

Map specification defines options related to the map as a whole, such as its size and position on the screen. Map specification elements are shown in Box 4.8. They can be used to

- Assign a name to a map
- Specify a map's size and position on the screen
- Specify the initial position of the cursor within a map
- Associate a help map with a map
- Specify function key usage
- Specify how certain types of data are displayed
- Specify the device types with which a map can be used

Maps can be defined with a size that is smaller than the screen size. Such maps are known as partial maps. Multiple partial maps can be displayed on the screen at the same time provided that they

- Do not overlap.
- Can be completely contained within the screen area.
- Are arranged vertically and not side-by-side.

Map Structure

Map structure defines the individual fields that make up the map, along with options related to individual fields. Map structure elements are shown in Box 4.9. Map structure elements can be used to

BOX 4.8 Map specification elements.

- **Bypass Edit PF Keys.** Assigns function keys that allow the user to bypass field edits that have been defined for fields. This statement identifies the function keys that can be used for this purpose for a map.
- **Cursor Field.** Identifies the map field in which the cursor appears when the map is first displayed.
- **Device Selection.** Specifies the device types on which this map can be displayed or printed.
- **Fold Input.** Specifies whether character data entered into variable fields in this map should be converted to uppercase.
- **Help Map Name.** Identifies the help map to be displayed when help is requested for this map.
- **Help PF Key.** Specifies the function key that the user can use to request help for this map.
- **Map Name.** Assigns a name to the map. The name consists of a map group name and a map name. The map group name identifies a group of maps used with one application.
- **Position.** Specifies where this map is located when displayed on a terminal screen. The values entered are for the line and column coordinates of the upper-left corner of the map.
- **Size.** Specifies the number of lines and columns contained in this map. The map size must be no larger than the screen or page size of the smallest device associated with this map.
- **SO/SI Take Position.** When DBCS data is used in the large-system and midrange environments, special characters (SO and SI) are used to delimit the DBCS data. This statement specifies whether SO/SI characters are to be represented by blanks in printed output.

BOX 4.9   Map structure elements.

- **Constant Field.** Defines a constant field, which is used to display protected information.
- **Field Attribute.** Specifies formatting and processing characteristics associated with a field. The different attributes that can be specified are as follows:
  - **Color.** Specifies the color used to display a field on a color device.
  - **Cursor.** Identifies this as the field in which the cursor should be positioned when the map is first displayed.
  - **Data Type.** Specifies whether a field will accept any character or only numeric data.
  - **Extended Highlighting.** Specifies the use of a highlighting technique when the field is displayed. Highlighting techniques include blinking, reverse video, and underlining.
  - **Light Intensity.** Specifies the brightness used when displaying the field. Possible intensities are normal, bright, and dark (not visible).
  - **Light Pen Detectable Field.** Specifies that a field can be selected with a light pen.
  - **Modified Data Tag.** Determines how the modified data tag for the field is set when a map is first displayed. The modified data tag indicates whether the contents of a field have been changed.
  - **Outlining.** Creates lines at the edges of fields on DBCS devices or to define a constant field that is to be displayed with a box around it.
  - **Protection.** Specifies whether data can be entered in a field.
- **Help Map.** Identifies a map as a help map.
- **Message Field.** Identifies a variable field as the map message field. It is used to display application- and system-defined messages to the user.
- **Variable Field.** Defines a variable field (one into which a user can enter data). The following types of special variable fields can also be defined:
  - **Array.** Defines a variable field that is part of an array of fields. A map array is specified by giving the same name to each field in the array and following the name with a subscript value.
  - **DBCS.** Defines a variable field that will contain DBCS data.
  - **MIX.** Defines a variable field that can contain a mixture of single-byte and DBCS data.
- **Variable Field Edit.** Defines different types of edits performed on the data that is entered or displayed. Possible edits include the following:

(Continued)

BOX 4.9 *(Continued)*

- **Currency Symbol.** Specifies that a currency symbol should be inserted when data is displayed in the field and that the user can include a currency symbol when entering data in the field.
- **Data Type.** Specifies the type of data that is allowable in the field. Possible types are character, numeric, DBCS, and mixed single-byte and DBCS.
- **Date Edit.** Specifies the format to be used for a field containing a date. The date is displayed in the format specified and data entered is checked to be sure it is in the correct format.
- **Decimal Positions.** Specifies the number of positions to the right of the decimal point for numeric fields. For data being displayed, a decimal point symbol is inserted at the appropriate position. For data being entered, a decimal point symbol can be included.
- **Description.** Provides a text string that describes the variable field. It is used for documentation only.
- **Edit Error Message Numbers.** Specifies the number of an error message to be displayed when a particular type of error occurs. Different error types for which a message can be displayed are data type error, edit routine error, input required error, minimum input error, and value error.
- **Edit Routine.** Specifies the name of a processing routine or edit table used to edit the data in this field. Edit tables can be used to match against valid or invalid values or to check against ranges of valid values. The processing routine can be a system-supplied check digit routine or an application-defined routine.
- **Fill Character.** Specifies the character used to fill unused positions when a field is displayed.
- **Fold.** Specifies whether lowercase alphabetic characters entered by the user should be converted to uppercase.
- **Hexadecimal.** Specifies that only hexadecimal digit values (0-9, A-F) can be entered in the field.
- **Input Required.** Indicates whether data must be entered in this field.
- **Justify.** Specifies whether data is to be left-justified, right-justified, or left as is. Data entered and data displayed are aligned within the field as specified here.
- **Maximum Value.** Specifies the largest value that can be entered into a numeric field.
- **Minimum Input.** Specifies the minimum number of characters that must be entered in a field.
- **Minimum Value.** Specifies the smallest value that can be entered in a numeric field.

BOX 4.9 *(Continued)*

> — **Numeric Separator.** Specifies whether a numeric field contains separator characters, such as commas. If separator characters are used, they are inserted in data being displayed and allowed in data entered by the user.
> — **Sign.** Specifies whether a sign is used with a numeric field, and if so, where it appears. It is inserted for displayed data and allowed for entered data.
> — **Zero Edit.** Specifies the display format for numeric fields with a zero value. The format depends on values specified for decimal positions, currency symbol, numeric separators, and the fill character.
> - **Variable Field Edit Order.** Specifies the order in which fields on a map are edited.
> - **Variable Field Name.** Assigns a name to a variable field. The application can refer to the field by this name for processing.

- Define a field as a constant field, variable field, or message field.
- Assign attributes, such as color, emphasis, protection, and data type, to a field.
- Define edits to be applied to data that is entered or displayed in a variable field.
- Identify a map as a help map.

CONCLUSION

This chapter described the CPI Application Generator interface that is implemented by IBM's Cross System Product (CSP) family of application generators. The CPI Application Generator interface defines a flexible method for generating applications without requiring conventional programming. Chapter 5 concludes Part I by describing the CPI Procedures Language interface. Implementations of the CPI Procedures Language interface can be used to write procedures for a variety of purposes, including controlling the system software environment.

5 THE CPI PROCEDURES LANGUAGE INTERFACE

The CPI Procedures Language interface is based on the IBM program product REXX. REXX is a procedural language, in many ways similar to conventional programming languages like COBOL and FORTRAN. However, it possesses certain unique characteristics:

- The language processors that implement the interface are interpreters, rather than compilers, and the language contains features specifically designed to allow programs to be developed and debugged interpretively.

- The language has powerful character string manipulation capabilities and automatic data typing.

- The language allows commands to be issued to the surrounding system environment. A program is able to determine the environment in which it is running and then issue commands appropriate to that environment.

- The basic language statements are relatively simple and easy to use. However, the large number of built-in functions, and the ability to define additional functions, makes the language very powerful.

The products that implement the Procedures Language interface are

- VM Procedures Language VM/REXX Interpreter
- TSO/E REXX Interpreter
- OS/2 Procedures Language 2/REXX Interpreter
- OS/400 Procedures Language 400/REXX Interpreter

PROCEDURES LANGUAGE EXAMPLE

The following is an example of a simple Procedures Language program that accepts a line of input and calculates the average number of letters per word in the entered line:

```
/* Sample Procedures Language Program */
say "Enter a line of text"
pull linein
total = 0
do num = 1 by 1 until linein = ""
   parse var linein word linein
   total = total + length(word)
end
say "The average number of letters per word is"
   format(total/num,,0)
```

The following describes the purpose of each line in the program.

- The first line is a comment.
- The **say** instruction displays the quoted message on the user's display.
- The **pull** instruction accepts a line of input from the user.
- The **do** instruction contains an assignment statement that initializes the value of the variable **total** to **0.**
- The **do** loop is repeated until the **linein** variable contains no more words.
  — As part of the **do** loop, the variable **num** is initialized to **1** and incremented by 1 each time the loop executes.
  — The **parse** instruction takes the value currently in the variable **linein,** extracts the first word in the value and places it in the variable **word,** and then places the remainder of the value back in the variable **linein.**
  — The assignment statement uses the **length** function to determine the length of the word currently in **word,** and adds that length to the variable **total.**
- When all the words in the line of text have been processed, the **do** loop ends, and a message is displayed that includes a calculated value that is the average number of letters per word.
- The **exit** instruction then ends the program.

The following is what a user might see when executing the previous program in the OS/2 operating system environment.

```
[C:\]rexx1
Enter a line of text
this is a sample line of text
The average number of letters per word is 3
```

EXPRESSING VALUES

The Procedures Language supports the use of variables and different types of constants. For example, in the following assignment statement, **total** is a variable and the value 0 is a number:

```
total = 0
```

Box 5.1 lists the different types of data values that can be defined in the Procedures Language. Values are assigned to variables using assignments. The **drop** instruction can be used to reset variables to an uninitialized state.

Variables and constant values can be combined into expressions using various types of operators. The following expression calculates a value by dividing the value in **total** by the value in **num**:

```
total/num
```

The different types of operators that can be used to construct expressions are summarized in Box 5.2.

Values can also be generated by invoking functions. In the following instruction **format** is a function that returns a rounded and formatted number:

```
say "T.he average number of letters per word is "
   format(total/num,,0)
```

BOX 5.1   Data value types.

- **Numbers.** Numbers can be expressed in either decimal form or in exponential notation. A number value can include a plus or minus sign and a decimal point.
- **Literal strings.** A literal string is a sequence of characters enclosed in single or double quotation marks. Any characters can be included in a literal string.
- **Hexadecimal strings.** A hexadecimal string is a sequence of hexadecimal digits (0-9, A-F) enclosed in single or double quotation marks followed by the character X. For example, '02FF'X is a hexadecimal string. Hexadecimal strings are interpreted as hexadecimal values.
- **Binary strings.** A binary string is a sequence of binary digits (0 or 1) enclosed in single or double quotation marks followed by the character B. For example, "11000101"B is a binary string. Binary strings are interpreted as binary values.

BOX 5.2 Operators.

Arithmetic Operators

+	Addition
−	Subtraction
*	Multiplication
/	Division
%	Division with return of integer part of result
//	Division with return of remainder
**	Raise to a power

Comparison Operators

=	Equal (numerically or when padded, etc.)
\	Not equal
> <	Greater than or less than (same as not equal)
< >	Less than or greater than (same as not equal)
= =	Identically equal
\ = =	Not identically equal
>	Greater than
<	Less than
\ >	Not greater than
\ <	Not less than
> >	Strictly greater than
< <	Strictly less than
\ > >	Strictly not greater than
\ < <	Strictly not less than
> =	Greater than or equal to
< =	Less than or equal to
> > =	Strictly greater than or equal to
< < =	Strictly less than or equal to

Note: the NOT character (¬) can be used in place of the backslash (\).

BOX 5.2 *(Continued)*

Logical Operators

&	AND
|	Inclusive OR
&&	Exclusive OR
\	Logical NOT

String Concatenation

(blank)	Concatenation with one blank in between
||	Concatenation with no blank in between
(abuttal)	Concatenation with no blank in between

When the **say** instruction is interpreted and executed, the **format** function is invoked and the value it returns is displayed as part of the **say** message. The Procedures Language includes a large number of built-in functions and also provides the capability for defining additional functions.

In addition to defining data types and operators, the Procedures Language also includes detailed rules for how arithmetic is performed. These rules allow different implementations of the language to all return the same results for computations even though the underlying machine architectures might have differences that could affect the results of computations. The **numeric** instruction allows a program to specify the precision and notation to be used in arithmetic operations.

PROCEDURES LANGUAGE STATEMENTS

The statements that make up a Procedures Language program can consist of keyword instructions, assignments, or commands. Keyword instructions, such as **say, pull, do/end,** and **exit,** provide the basic processing capabilities of the Procedures Language. Assignments are used to give variables new values. Commands are passed to the environment in which the Procedures Language program is being processed. The environment processes the command and returns control to the program. The format and function of a command is determined by the particular environment to which it is passed (VM/CMS, MVS/TSOE, OS/2, AS/400). The Procedures Language includes facilities for determining the current active environment and for sending commands to a specified environment.

The following sections examine the key processing capabilities provided by the keyword instructions and built-in functions that are defined as part of the Procedures Language.

PROGRAM LOGIC

Generally, control flows from one program statement to the next until an **exit** instruction ends the program. Certain keyword instructions can be used to execute statements repetitively or conditionally. In the sample program shown earlier, the **do** instruction caused a set of statements to be executed repeatedly until a particular condition occurred. Instructions for specifying the flow of control are listed in Box 5.3.

ROUTINES AND FUNCTIONS

A *routine* is a sequence of instructions that can be invoked by name. The following code shows an example of a routine that calculates the total area of a box based on its length, width, and height:

Box 5.3 Program logic flow instructions.

- **Do..end.** Used to group instructions together and execute them repetitively. The repetition can be a specified number of times or conditional.
- **Iterate.** Used to alter the flow within a repetitive **do** loop. It stops execution of instructions within the group and passes control back to the **do** instruction.
- **Leave.** Causes an immediate exit from one or more repetitive **do** loops. It passes control to the instruction following the **end** clause.
- **If..then..else.** Specifies conditional processing of an instruction, or group of instructions, based on the evaluation of an expression.
- **Nop.** Has no effect and can be used as the target of **then** or **else** when no action is to be taken for certain conditions.
- **Select.** Used to specify actions to be taken for several different alternative conditions.
- **Exit.** Used to unconditionally end program execution.
- **Signal.** Causes a change in the flow of control when a specified condition occurs. It is typically used to trap error and failure conditions.

```
/* Box area routine */
    .
    .
boxarea: procedure
 arg length,width,height
 area = 2*(length*width) + 2*(width*height) +
   2*(length*height)
 return area
```

An *internal routine* is a routine that is defined within the program in which it is invoked. An *external routine* is a routine that is defined outside of the invoking program. External routines can be written in the Procedures Language or in other languages that support the required interfaces. Certain routines, called *built-in functions*, are part of the Procedures Language language processor.

A routine can be invoked as a subroutine by calling it with a **call** instruction:

```
call boxarea var1, var2, var3
say "Box size is " result
```

The **call** instruction transfers control to the named routine, which can be either internal or external. When the **return** instruction is reached in the called routine, control returns to the statement following the **call.** Any value specified as part of the **return** instruction is then available in the variable **result.**

A routine can also be invoked as a function:

```
say "Box size is " boxarea(var1,var2,var3)
```

The value returned by the **return** instruction directly replaces the function invocation. A function call can be made to either an internal or an external routine.

The Procedures Language keyword instructions used to define and invoke routines are summarized in Box 5.4.

CONDITIONS AND CONDITION TRAPS

Condition traps are used to interrupt the normal flow of execution when a particular condition occurs and to pass control to a specified routine. A condition trap can be set with the **call** or **signal** instruction:

```
call on error errorroutine
signal on failure
```

The conditions for which traps can be set are listed in Box 5.5. If a name is specified following the condition, such as **errorroutine** in the **call** instruction, control is passed to that routine if the condition occurs. If no name is specified, control is

BOX 5.4   Defining and invoking instructions.

- **Call.** Used to invoke a routine.
- **Return.** Used to pass control from a routine or function back to the point of invocation in the invoking program.
- **Procedure.** Used in an internal routine to specify variables from the main program that are available to the internal routine and to protect other variables from being affected by the routine. Only variables specifically named in the **procedure** instruction are available to or affected by the internal routine.
- **Arg.** Used to access arguments passed to a routine and to assign them to variables.

BOX 5.5   Trap conditions.

- **Error.** Raised if a command indicates an error condition upon return.
- **Failure.** Raised if a command indicates a failure condition upon return.
- **Halt.** Raised if an external attempt is made to interrupt and terminate execution of the program.
- **Notready.** Raised if an error occurs during an input or output operation.
- **Novalue.** Raised if an uninitialized variable is used in certain situations.
- **Syntax.** Raised if a language processing error is detected.

passed to a routine with the same name as the condition. So the **signal** instruction would pass control to the routine **failure** if the failure condition occurred.

INPUT AND OUTPUT

The Procedures Language uses a character-oriented form of input and output. A Procedures Language program has

- One or more character input streams
- One or more character output streams
- One external data queue for interprogram communication

The input and output streams are processed serially, on either a character-by-character or line-by-line basis. There is a default input stream and a default output stream. Other streams can be specified by name. The external data queue is processed on a line-by-line basis.

Box 5.6 lists the instructions and functions used to process input streams, output streams, and the external data queue.

PARSING

Parsing involves splitting up a string, under control of a template, and placing the resulting substrings into variables. It is done with the **parse** instruction. The sample program shown earlier contains the following instruction:

```
parse var linein word linein
```

The above instruction parses the value in the variable **linein,** placing the first word in the variable **word** and the rest of the value back in the variable **linein.**

There are a number of possible sources for the string that is parsed by a **parse** instruction. Box 5.7 shows the different forms the **parse** instruction takes with different sources of input.

The template that controls the parsing consists of a list of variables separated by blanks, patterns, or both. The simplest form of template is a list of variable names, as shown in the previous sample **parse** instruction. A template can also contain a pattern that indicates where the string is to be split in determining the values to be assigned to the variables. A string pattern specifies a particular character or group of characters that must be matched within the string. A numeric pattern specifies the character position at which the split takes place.

String Pattern Example

Assume the variable **fullname** contains the value **Chapman, John,** and the following statement is executed:

```
parse var fullname with lastname ',' firstname
```

All the data preceding the comma is placed in the variable **lastname,** and the data following the comma is placed in **firstname.** Therefore, the variable **lastname** now contains the value **Chapman,** and the variable **firstname** now contains the value **John.** Note that the data that makes up the pattern (the comma) is not included in the parsed data.

Numeric Pattern Example

The next example illustrates the use of a numeric pattern. Assume that the variable **param1** contains the value **count=12,** and the following statement is executed:

BOX 5.6   Stream instructions and functions.

Input Stream Instructions and Functions

- **Charin.** Reads a named input stream as characters.
- **Linein.** Reads a named input stream as lines.
- **Pull.** Reads the default input stream as lines if the external data queue is empty.
- **Parse pull.** Reads the default input stream as lines if the external data queue is empty.
- **Parse linein.** Reads the default input stream as lines.
- **Chars.** Returns the number of characters currently available in an input character stream.
- **Lines.** Returns the number of completed lines that remain in an input stream.
- **Stream.** Used to determine the state of an input stream or to carry out an operation on it.

Output Stream Instructions and Functions

- **Charout.** Writes to an output stream as characters.
- **Lineout.** Writes to an output stream as lines.
- **Say.** Writes to the default output stream as lines.
- **Stream.** Used to determine the state of an output stream or to carry out an operation on it.

External Data Queue Instructions and Functions

- **Pull.** Reads a line from the queue.
- **Parse pull.** Reads a line from the queue.
- **Push.** Adds a line to the head of the queue.
- **Queue.** Adds a line to the end of the queue.
- **Queued.** Returns the number of lines currently in the queue.

BOX 5.7 PARSE instruction sources of input.

- **Parse arg.** The input consists of strings that are passed as part of an argument list.
- **Parse linein.** The input consists of the next line from the default input stream.
- **Parse pull.** The input consists of the next string from the external data queue.
- **Parse source.** The input consists of a system-dependent string that describes the source of the program being executed.
- **Parse value.** The input consists of the expression following the keyword **value**.
- **Parse var.** The input consists of the value in the variable specified following the keyword **var**.
- **Parse version.** The input consists of information describing the language processor being used.

```
parse var param1 with first6 7 rest
```

Here the value 7 in the pattern indicates that the data should be split at position 7, with the first 6 characters going in the variable **first6** and the rest of the data in the variable **rest**. Therefore, the variable **first6** now contains the value **count=** and the variable **rest** now contains the value **12**. Numeric patterns can specify either absolute or relative positions.

String and numeric patterns can be combined in the same template, allowing very powerful parsing operations to be performed. Parsing can also be performed on a series of strings. This is particularly useful for processing a set of argument values that has been passed as part of the invocation of a function.

ISSUING COMMANDS

A particularly powerful capability of the Procedures Language allows a Procedure Language program to interact with the external environment in which it is executing. It does this by issuing commands or subcommands that take the form of character strings. The character string is passed to the external environment, where it is processed, and a return code is returned to the Procedures Language program. For example, in the OS/2 environment, a Procedures Language program could include the statement

```
dir
```

The Procedures Language interpreter first determines that the statement is not a keyword instruction, an assignment statement, or a label. Since it is none of these, the character string "**dir**" is passed to OS/2, which interprets it as the command to display a list of the files contained in the current directory.

A variable can also be used to provide the command value:

```
say "Enter a file name"
pull filename
commandval = "TYPE" filename
commandval
```

Here the variable **commandval** is used to construct the command. If the user were to enter **list3.txt** after the **Enter a file name** prompt, the character string **type list3.txt** would be passed to OS/2.

The **address** built-in function can be used to determine the name of the currently active environment. The **address** instruction can also be used to specify a specific environment to which a command is to be sent.

INTERACTING WITH THE INTERPRETER

The Procedures Language includes certain keyword instructions that allow a program to interact with the interpreter, or language processor, under which it is running. The **interpret** instruction can be used to execute an instruction that has been built dynamically within the program. The **options** instruction can be used to specify how the language processor should handle DBCS data. The **trace** instruction can be used to control the displaying of information about program statements for debugging purposes.

The Procedures Language also defines application programming interfaces that can be used by programs written in other languages to access certain services provided by the language processor. When control is passed from the Procedures Language program to another program, such as when an external routine is invoked or a command is executed in the external environment, these application programming interfaces can be used. The variable pool interface supports functions that allow Procedures Language variables to be fetched, set, and dropped. Exits can be used to

- Process host commands
- Process external functions
- Halt processing
- Do initialization processing
- Manipulate the external data queue
- Do session I/O
- Do termination processing
- Test the external trace indicator

CONCLUSION This chapter has examined the Procedures Language interface that can be used to write conventional application programs and also to issue commands to the external environment in which the program is executing. Chapter 6 begins Part II on data access interfaces by introducing relational database concepts.

PART II DATA ACCESS INTERFACES

6 RELATIONAL DATABASE CONCEPTS

Several of the interfaces in the CPI architecture are concerned with data access. These include

- **Database Interface.** The CPI Database Interface provides for access to data stored in relational databases. It includes facilities for defining, retrieving, and manipulating relational data. The interface is defined in terms of SQL language elements.
- **Query Interface.** The CPI Query Interface, like the CPI Database Interface, provides a way of processing data in a relational database. In addition to basic database processing capabilities, it has facilities designed to make it easier to access the data and to format the display of accessed data.
- **Resource Recovery Interface.** The CPI Resource Recovery Interface provides a method of change management that allows changes to multiple resources to be coordinated. It provides services that allow changes made to a set of resources to all be made permanent (committed) or all undone. The resources can all be located on the same system, or they can be distributed across several different systems.
- **Repository Interface.** The CPI Repository Interface defines sets of services that can be used to define, collect, manipulate, and control information stored in a repository. These services are provided by a repository manager, and the CPI Repository Interface defines the way in which an application program can request these services from the repository manager.

In this chapter we examine some of the relational database concepts that underlie these CPI interfaces.

TABLES

With the relational data model a database is represented by, and perceived by its users as, a set of *tables* that contain *rows* and *columns*. A table represents an *entity type*—the type of person, object, or concept about which information is stored. A column represents an *attribute* of the entity type—one type of information stored about the entity. A row represents a particular *entity occurrence*, or *entity instance*. A particular row contains a set of *data items*, or *values*, one for each column in the table. An example of a possible table is shown in Fig. 6.1.

Employee

Employee-Name	Sex	Birth-Date	Employee-Number	Department-Number	Skill-Code	Job-Title	Salary
Jones	M	100335	373	04	73	Accountant	2000
Blanagan	M	101019	871	17	43	Plumber	1800
Lawrence	F	090932	355	04	02	Clerk	1100
Rockefeller	M	011132	963	09	11	Consultant	5000
Ropley	M	021242	597	17	43	Plumber	1700
Smith	M	091130	188	04	73	Accountant	2000
Ralner	M	110941	645	04	02	Clerk	1200
Horace	F	071235	161	17	07	Engineer	2500
Hall	M	011030	190	17	21	Architect	3700
Fair	F	020442	292	09	93	Programmer	2100

Figure 6.1 The Employee table.

This table represents the Employee entity type. The columns in the table represent the kinds of information stored about employees. Each row in the table stores a set of data items that describe a particular employee.

TABLE PROPERTIES

The tables that make up a relational database have certain properties associated with them:

- Each row-column entry in a table consists of a single, or *atomic,* data item; repeating groups are not allowed. A data structure from which repeating groups have been removed in order to place the data into tabular form is called a *normalized data structure.*

- All the data items in a given column are of the same type.

- Each column in a table has a unique name within that table.

- In the relational data model, the sequence of the rows and columns in a table is not meaningful; the rows and the columns can be viewed in any sequence without affecting either the information content or the semantics of any function that uses the table. It is possible to impose a sequence on the rows or columns of a table if this is necessary for processing. However, the basic definition of a relational table does not assume any particular sequence.

KEYS

It is possible to define a column, or a set of columns, that uniquely identifies each row. This column, or set of columns, is called the table's *key*. In many cases, an individual column can be found that uniquely identifies each row. For example, in the Employee table shown in Fig. 6.2, the Employee-Number column has a unique data item value in each row and can serve as the table's key.

Employee

Employee-Number	Employee-Name	Sex	Birth-Date	Department-Number	Skill-Code	Job-Title	Salary
373	Jones	M	100335	04	73	Accountant	2000
871	Blanagan	M	101019	17	43	Plumber	1800
355	Lawrence	F	090932	04	02	Clerk	1100
963	Rockefeller	M	011132	09	11	Consultant	5000
597	Ropley	M	021242	17	43	Plumber	1700
188	Smith	M	091130	04	73	Accountant	2000
645	Ralner	M	110941	04	02	Clerk	1200
161	Horace	F	071235	17	07	Engineer	2500
190	Hall	M	011030	17	21	Architect	3700
292	Fair	F	020442	09	93	Programmer	2100

Figure 6.2 The Employee table with key field.

With many tables, two or more columns must be combined to provide unique identification. Two or more columns that are combined to serve as a key are called a *composite key*.

PRIMARY KEY

A key can be defined as a *unique key*, which specifies that no two rows have the same key value. In many cases, a table has more than one possible unique key. For example, in this particular Employee table, the Employee-Name column also happens to have unique data item values. The different possible keys for a table are called *candidate keys*. One of the candidate keys can be chosen as the key for the table by designating it as the *primary key* when the table is defined.

REPRESENTING RELATIONSHIPS

Another characteristic of the relational data model is that all relationships between entity types are expressed in the form of data stored in the tables. In the example shown in Fig. 6.3, we can express the relationship between an employee and a department by using data item values in the Department-Number column of the Employee table and data item values in the Dept column of the Department table.

Employee

Employee-Number	Employee-Name	Sex	Birth-Date	Department-Number	Skill-Code	Job-Title	Salary
373	Jones	M	100335	04	73	Accountant	2000
871	Blanagan	M	101019	17	43	Plumber	1800
355	Lawrence	F	090932	04	02	Clerk	1100
963	Rockefeller	M	011132	09	11	Consultant	5000
597	Ropley	M	021242	17	43	Plumber	1700
188	Smith	M	091130	04	73	Accountant	2000
645	Ralner	M	110941	04	02	Clerk	1200
161	Horace	F	071235	17	07	Engineer	2500
190	Hall	M	011030	17	21	Architect	3700
292	Fair	F	020442	09	93	Programmer	2100

Department

Dept	Location
02	Detroit
01	New York
04	Chicago
03	Miami
17	Houston
09	Denver

Figure 6.3 Employee and Department tables.

Representing all relationships through stored data has two advantages. First, it makes a relational database easy to use, since the user or application program does not have to be aware of structural relationships. Second, it contributes to data independence. Where application programs are dependent on structural relationships, and explicitly refer to them in navigating the database, changes made to structural relationships may require that changes be made to application programs. With a relational database, changes in relationships are made simply by changing data, and such changes are less likely to require changes in application programs.

INTEGRITY CONSTRAINTS

The relational data model also includes two *integrity constraints* that concern the data item values that can be placed in tables. These two integrity constraints are called *entity integrity* and *referential integrity*.

Entity Integrity

The *entity integrity* rule states that no column that is part of a primary key can have a null value. This rule is necessary if the primary key is to fulfill its role of uniquely identifying the rows in a table. If a particular primary key value could be completely or partially null, there would be some particular row that could not be distinguished from other rows. The database management systems that are used in the various SAA environments ensure that a primary key does not contain a null value.

Referential Integrity

It is possible for one table to contain a column, or set of columns, that contain data item values drawn from the same set of values as the column or columns that form the primary key in some other table. This column or set of columns is called a *foreign key*. In the example shown in Fig. 6.4, the Manager-Number column in the Department table is a foreign key because each Manager-Number is drawn from the Employee-Number values in the Employee table, the set of valid employee numbers.

Department

Department-Number	Location	Manager-Number
04	Chicago	127
05	Chicago	null
01	New York	301

Employee

Employee-Number	Employee-Name	Salary
301	Hansen	2000
482	Michaels	1800
127	Robinson	1100
185	Donatelli	5000
079	Smith	1700
246	Chapman	2000

Figure 6.4 Foreign key.

The referential integrity rule states that every foreign key value in the first table must either match a primary key value in the second table, or it must be wholly null. In other words, any value of Manager-Number in the Department table must either be null, or it must match an Employee-Number value in the Employee table. The referential integrity rule guarantees that the Department table will not reference a manager who does not have an entry in the Employee table. Thus, the referential integrity rule lets us ensure that a department is not managed by someone who is not an employee. Allowing a null value in the foreign key, however, does allow the Department table to contain a row for a department that currently has no manager.

THREE VIEWS OF DATA

In talking about the data stored in a database, it is common to look at the data in at least three different ways. The following are descriptions of these three different views of the database:

- **User View.** This is the collection of data items and their relationships, as perceived by an individual application program or group of related application programs. A user view generally encompasses only a small subset of the data items that are stored in a database.
- **Logical Data Model.** This is the entire collection of data items, and their relationships, that will be stored in one database. The logical data model documents the enterprise's overall view of the database. It is a logical map that identifies *all* the data stored in a database and combines all the individual user views into one integrated structure. It is not likely that any application program would ever require access to all the data items documented by the logical data model.
- **Physical Data Structures.** These are the files, indexes, and other storage structures that are used to physically implement the logical data model on the storage medium.

A key benefit to this approach to data definition is an increase in data independence at the application program level. Generally, an application program is not concerned with any physical storage issues. These are handled by the database management system. If changes are made in the area of physical definition, to improve performance or to reflect changes in the database, application programs are not affected and can continue to be used without change. Changes can also be made at the logical level without affecting application programs. Data items and rows can be added to and deleted from the database and data item formats changed, and only those programs that directly process the data items in question are affected.

The CPI Database Interface supports the use of user views. Virtual tables, or *views*, can be created based on one or more existing tables. The interface also supports the definition of *base tables*, which are tables not derived from other tables. Base tables are part of the logical data model. Generally, the CPI Database Interface does not address the definition and use of physical data structures. This is left to the individual database managers in each of the SAA environments. However, it does include the definition of indexes.

An *index* is a set of pointers into a table based on values in one or more table columns. If an index is unique, it ensures that no two rows have the same values for the column or columns on which the index is based. When a table has a primary key, an associated unique index ensures that primary key values are unique. An index can also be used to provide faster access to a table or to provide a way of processing the table rows in a specified sequence.

CONCURRENCY

One of the goals of a database management system is to allow multiple end users and application programs to have access to the same shared data at the same time, which is known as *concurrent access*. However, providing concurrency brings with it some potential problems. If two programs are permitted to make changes to the same row of a table at the same time, the two programs may interfere with one another in a variety of ways.

The various SAA database management systems support concurrent access and all allow more than one user or program to access a given piece of data at the same time. In order to handle the problems associated with concurrent access, the database management systems provide systems of *locks*. Locks control whether and in what way other programs or users can access the data that a particular user or program is currently using. The locking system ensures that no program accesses data that has been changed by another program before the changes are completed. A commitment process determines when changes made to a database are considered permanent. An application program or user can determine that particular changes are to be either committed or rolled back. The database management systems will also automatically roll back uncommitted changes when certain types of failures occur.

AUTHORIZATION AND PRIVILEGES

The centralized storage of data in databases, and the accessing of this data by multiple end users and application programs, brings with it a need for security. To provide for security facilities, the SAA database management systems include an authorization mechanism that permits different users to be allowed or denied access to different parts of a database and controls the operations a user can perform on data that can be accessed. This authorization mechanism is based on granting privileges to different users.

DISTRIBUTED RELATIONAL DATABASES

One of the ultimate goals of SAA is to define a distributed relational database environment, in which the location of the data being processed is totally transparent to the user and to the application program. The user should be able to make requests for data, and the application should be able to issue the appropriate SQL statements, without regard to where the data is stored. As we described in Chapter 2, from a practical standpoint, this complete transparency will take time to be achieved.

Box 6.1 reviews the five forms of distributed database access that IBM has defined and that were described in Chapter 2.

BOX 6.1 Forms of distributed database access.

Nontransparent Distributed Database Access

- **Extract Processing.** The simplest form of distributed database processing is *extract processing*. Here, the user, possibly at a personal computer, makes a connection with the system where the desired data is located, possibly on a large-system processor. The user then formulates a request to extract the required data from the large-system database and then transfers the data back to the personal computer. The user then initiates processing of the data on the personal computer. With this approach, the user must know where the data is located and must know how to access and interact with both the personal computer and the host computer that maintains the database. Extract processing can also be used to extract nonrelational data from files and to place it in a relational database.

- **Remote Request Processing.** With *remote request processing,* the user interacts with an application program running on computing system A to generate a data request. A function, called a *requester,* running on computing system A then sends the request to a function, called a *server,* running on computing system B that maintains the database containing the required data. The server running on computing system B submits the request to the DBMS and returns the results of the data access to the requester running on computing system A. The requester then passes the data to the application program. With remote request processing, the DBMS in the database processor is unaware that distributed processing is taking place. The data request is submitted to the DBMS by the server function, which appears to the DBMS as any other local application. The DBMS holds and releases locks and performs recovery on behalf of the server function. If there is a failure in the network or if the application program that accesses the requester fails, the DBMS is unaffected by the failure.

Transparent Distributed Database Access

- **Remote Unit of Work Processing.** With *remote unit of work processing,* an application program can access a single relational database maintained on a single remote computing system. The application program can issue multiple SQL statements as part of a single unit of work (or transaction). With remote unit of work processing, the requester and server functions maintain state information relative to the progress of the transaction across the multiple SQL statements, and commitment/rollback is performed for the transaction as a whole. This

Chap. 6 Relational Database Concepts 141

BOX 6.1 *(Continued)*

is the only form of transparent distributed database processing that is supported in SAA at the time of writing.

- **Distributed Unit of Work Processing.** With *distributed unit of work processing* an application program can access the data maintained in multiple remote databases maintained by multiple separate computing systems. All the data can be updated within the scope of a single transaction. However, a single SQL statement can process data that is maintained by only one computing system. Because multiple sites may be involved, management functions operating in each computing system must support protocols that allow commit/rollback and recovery processing to be synchronized across the various systems. Typically, the management function operating in the computing system that executes the requester acts as the coordinator for commit/rollback and recovery processing. IBM has committed to providing support for distributed unit of work processing within SAA.

- **Distributed Request Processing.** An even more powerful form of distributed database processing is *distributed request processing*. With distributed request processing, a single SQL statement can reference data that is maintained by multiple separate computing systems. Again, the requester and server management functions must coordinate commitment/rollback and recovery processing among the different computing systems. With this form of processing, the location of the data and the location of the application processing is totally transparent to the user and to the application program. The DBMS provides all the support necessary for providing transparent access to data maintained by any number of computing systems. Support for distributed request processing will probably eventually be included in SAA, but, at the time of writing, IBM has not yet announced definite plans for it.

SAA SUPPORT FOR DISTRIBUTED DATABASE

The SAA approach to distributed database is to provide support for it as part of CCS. CCS currently includes the *Distributed Relational Database Architecture* (DRDA), which is designed to provide programs with access to relational data stored on remote computing systems. At the time of writing, DRDA addresses only the remote unit of work form of distributed database access. Application programs using the CPI Database Interface or the CPI Query Interface can access data stored in remote relational databases provided the database management system they are using has implemented

DRDA. With this approach, the application is unaware of whether the database is remote or local, and the processing required because of the distributed nature of the data is transparent to the application program.

CONCLUSION This chapter has examined the basic relational database concepts on which the various data access interfaces that CPI defines are based. Chapter 7 examines the first of the data access interfaces described in Part II—the CPI Database Interface.

7 THE CPI DATABASE INTERFACE

As we introduced in Chapter 6, the CPI Database Interface provides for access to data stored in relational databases. It includes facilities for defining, retrieving, and manipulating the data stored in relational tables. The interface is defined in terms of SQL language elements. SQL is a standardized language, and the SAA specification reflects the International Standards Organization/IEC 9075-1989(E) Database Language SQL standard and the American National Standards Institute X3.135-1989 Database Language SQL standard.

The CPI Database Interface addresses the logical definition of data and the processing of data by a user, which can be either a person or an application program. It does not define how data is stored or managed on a physical level. With this approach, an application program can be moved from one SAA environment to another with minimal changes to the program. Storage and management of data can be optimized in each SAA environment to provide greater processing efficiency.

QUERIES A key operation in processing relational databases is the accessing of selected data from one or more tables. With SQL, this is done using *queries* that select and combine data from one or more base tables or views to produce a *result table*. In SQL, a query is formulated using a SELECT statement or a SELECT clause within another SQL statement.

The simplest form of query consists of a SELECT clause followed by a FROM clause, as in the following example:

```
SELECT    QUOSUPP, QUOPART, PRICE
FROM      QUOTATIONS
```

The SELECT clause specifies the names of the columns that are included in the result table. The FROM clause specifies the table or tables from which the data is selected. (All the SQL examples in this chapter reference the tables shown in Fig. 7.1.)

INVENTORY

INVPART	PNAME	ONHAND
124	BOLT	900
125	BOLT	1000
105	GEAR	0
106	GEAR	700
171	GENERATOR	500
172	GENERATOR	400
134	NUT	900
135	NUT	1000
181	WHEEL	1000
205	BAND	450
206	MOTOR	225
221	AXLE	1500
222	AXLE	25
231	AXLE	75
232	AXLE	150
241	WHEEL	300

QUOTATIONS

QUOSUPP	QUOPART	PRICE	TIME	ONORD
51	124	1.25	5	400
51	125	0.55	5	0
51	134	0.40	5	500
51	135	0.39	5	1000
51	221	0.30	10	10000
51	231	0.10	10	5000
52	105	7.50	10	200
52	205	0.15	20	0
52	206	0.15	20	0
53	124	1.35	3	500
53	125	0.58	3	200
53	134	0.38	3	200
53	135	0.42	3	1000
53	222	0.25	15	10000
53	232	–	15	0
53	241	0.08	15	6000

SUPPLIERS

SUPSUPP	NAME	ADDRESS	CODE
51	DEFECTO PARTS	16 JUSTAMERE LANE, TACOMA WA	20
52	VESUVIUS INC.	512 ANCIENT BLVD., POMPEII NY	20
53	ATLANTIS CO.	8 OCEAN AVE., WASHINGTON DC	10
54	TITANIC PARTS	32 SINKING STREET, ATLANTIC CITY NJ	30
57	EAGLE HARDWARE	64 TRANQUILITY PLACE, APOLLO MN	30
61	SKYLAB PARTS	128 ORBIT BLVD., SYDNEY AUSTRALIA	10
64	KNIGHT LTD.	256 ARTHUR COURT, CAMELOT ENGLAND	20

Figure 7.1 Inventory, Quotations, and Suppliers tables.

THE SELECT CLAUSE

The SELECT clause can include the keywords ALL or DISTINCT. The clause ALL, which is the default, causes duplicate rows to be included in the result table; the clause DISTINCT eliminates duplicate rows. Column names can be specified directly, as shown above. The * character can be used to specify that all the columns in a table should be included in the result table:

```
SELECT    INVENTORY.*, QUOSUPP, QUOPART
FROM      INVENTORY, QUOTATIONS
```

Various types of expressions can also be used to specify a column. The rules for forming and using expressions are defined as part of the CPI Database Interface specification. One type of expression that can be used to specify a result column is a function:

```
SELECT    QUOPART, SUM(ONORD)
FROM      QUOTATIONS
```

The different functions that are included in the CPI Database Interface are listed in Box 7.1.

BOX 7.1 SQL functions.

Column Functions

- **AVG.** Returns the average of a set of numbers.
- **COUNT.** Returns the number of rows or values in a set of rows or values.
- **MAX.** Returns the maximum value in a set of values.
- **MIN.** Returns the minimum value in a set of values.
- **SUM.** Returns the sum of a set of numbers.

Scalar Functions

- **CHAR.** Returns a string representation of a date/time value.
- **DATE.** Returns a date from a value.
- **DAY.** Returns the day part of a value.
- **DAYS.** Returns an integer representation of a date.
- **DECIMAL.** Returns a decimal representation of a numeric value.
- **FLOAT.** Returns a floating point representation of a number.
- **HOUR.** Returns the hour part of a value.
- **INTEGER.** Returns an integer representation of a number.
- **LENGTH.** Returns the length of a value.
- **MICROSECOND.** Returns the microsecond part of a value.
- **MINUTE.** Returns the minute part of a value.
- **MONTH.** Returns the month part of a value.
- **SECOND.** Returns the seconds part of a value.
- **SUBSTR.** Returns a substring of a string.
- **TIME.** Returns a time from a value.
- **TIMESTAMP.** Returns a timestamp from a value or a pair of values.
- **VALUE.** Returns the first argument that is not null.
- **VARGRAPHIC.** Returns a graphic string representation of a character string.
- **YEAR.** Returns the year part of a value.

THE FROM CLAUSE

The FROM clause specifies one or more table or view names that are the source of the data included in the result table. A correlation name can be assigned to a table or view in the FROM clause:

```
SELECT    I.*, QUOSUPP, QUOPART
FROM      INVENTORY I, QUOTATIONS Q
```

In the forgoing example, the correlation name I has been assigned to the INVENTORY table, and the correlation name Q has been assigned to the QUOTATIONS table. The correlation name is then used for column references that include the table name, as shown in the SELECT clause. Correlated queries will be discussed further later in this chapter.

THE WHERE CLAUSE

A WHERE clause can be included in a SELECT statement in order to cause data from only selected rows to be included in the result table:

```
SELECT    *
FROM      QUOTATIONS
WHERE     QUOPART = 124
```

The WHERE clause specifies one or more search conditions that identify the rows to be included. A search condition is based on a comparison of values. The comparison operators that can be used are

- =   equal
- < >   not equal
- <   less than
- >   greater than
- < =   less than or equal to
- > =   greater than or equal to

The values being compared can come from a column name, a constant, a program variable, a function, or a special register. The search condition comparison can also use expressions formed using arithmetic operators (+, –, *, /) or the CONCAT operator:

```
            SELECT     QUOSUPP, QUOPART
            FROM       QUOTATIONS
            WHERE      PRICE * ONORD > 500.00
```

Subqueries

A WHERE clause can contain a SELECT clause as part of a search condition. This type of nested query is known as a *subquery*:

```
        SELECT    QUOPART, PRICE
        FROM      QUOTATIONS
        WHERE     QUOSUPP = (SELECT SUPSUPP
                             FROM    SUPPLIERS
                             WHERE   NAME = 'VESUVIUSINC.')
```

If a subquery refers to a column of a table that is part of a higher level query, this is known as a *correlated reference*:

```
        SELECT    QUOSUPP, QUOPART, PRICE
        FROM      QUOTATIONS Q
        WHERE     PRICE = (SELECT MIN(PRICE)
                           FROM    QUOTATIONS
                           WHERE   QUOPART = Q.QUOPART)
```

This query lists the supplier number (QUOSUPP), part number (QUOPART), and price for the row in the QUOTATIONS table that has the minimum price for that part. Using the correlation name, Q, allows the column reference to QUOPART to be unambiguous.

OTHER SEARCH CONDITIONS

There are certain specific conditions that can be tested for as part of a search condition, using keywords with defined meanings. For example, you can test for a value in a list of values by using IN:

```
            SELECT    QUOSUPP, QUOPART
            FROM      QUOTATIONS
            WHERE     QUOPART IN (105, 135, 205)
```

Box 7.2 shows the different conditions that can be tested for as part of a search condition.

BOX 7.2 SQL search conditions.

- **ALL.** Used with subquery that returns multiple values. The condition is true if the comparison is true for all values returned:

        SELECT   QUOPART, ONORD
        FROM   QUOTATIONS
        WHERE   ONORD >= ALL (SELECT ONORD
                                  FROM   QUOTATIONS
                                  WHERE   PRICE > 500.00)

- **AND, OR.** Used to combine multiple conditions:

        SELECT   QUOSUPP, QUOPART, PRICE
        FROM   QUOTATIONS
        WHERE   QUOPART = 124 AND PRICE > 1.30

- **ANY.** Used with a subquery that returns multiple values. The condition is true if the comparison is true for any value returned:

        SELECT   QUOSUPP, QUOPART, PRICE
        FROM   QUOTATIONS
        WHERE   PRICE > ANY (SELECT PRICE
                                 FROM QUOTATIONS
                                 WHERE ONORD > 0)

- **BETWEEN.** Compares a value with a range of values:

        SELECT   QUOSUPP, QUOPART, PRICE
        FROM   QUOTATIONS
        WHERE   QUOPART BETWEEN 105 AND 135

- **EXISTS.** Used with a subquery. The condition is true if any rows are returned by the subquery:

        SELECT   QUOPART, PRICE
        FROM   QUOTATIONS
        WHERE   EXISTS (SELECT *
                            FROM QUOTATIONS
                            WHERE PRICE > 1000.00)

BOX 7.2 *(Continued)*

- **IN.** Compares a value with a list of values:

        SELECT   QUOSUPP, QUOPART, PRICE
        FROM   QUOTATIONS
        WHERE   QUOPART IN (105, 135, 205)

- **LIKE.** Searches for strings that have a certain pattern:

        SELECT   SUPSUPP, NAME, ADDRESS
        FROM   SUPPLIERS
        WHERE   ADDRESS LIKE "% MN%'

- **NOT.** Used to test for the inverse of a condition. Can be used directly with BETWEEN, IN, LIKE or NULL:

        SELECT   QUOSUPP, QUOPART, PRICE
        FROM   QUOTATIONS
        WHERE   QUOPART NOT IN (105, 135, 205)

    Can be used with one or more complete conditions:

        SELECT   *
        FROM   QUOTATIONS
        WHERE   NOT (QUOPART < 200 AND (PRICE > 1.00
                   OR TIME <10))

- **NULL.** Tests for null values:

        SELECT   *
        FROM   QUOTATIONS
        WHERE   PRICE IS NULL

- **SOME.** Used with a subquery that returns multiple values. The condition is true if the comparison is true for any value returned:

        SELECT   QUOSUPP, QUOPART, PRICE
        FROM   QUOTATIONS
        WHERE   PRICE > SOME (SELECT PRICE
                                 FROM   QUOTATIONS
                                 WHERE ONORD > 0)

THE GROUP BY CLAUSE

A GROUP BY clause can be used to process a particular set of rows as a group. The group consists of those rows that have the same values in the specified grouping column or columns:

```
SELECT      QUOPART, MIN(PRICE)
FROM        QUOTATIONS
GROUP BY    QUOPART
```

The forgoing example groups the rows in the QUOTATIONS table by part number (QUOPART) and then selects the minimum price in each group.

THE HAVING CLAUSE

A HAVING clause specifies search conditions that can have the same form as the search conditions in a WHERE clause. With HAVING, the search conditions are applied separately to each group of rows as specified by a GROUP BY clause:

```
SELECT      QUOPART, SUM(ONORD)
FROM        QUOTATIONS
GROUP BY    QUOPART
HAVING      SUM(ONORD) > 0
```

Here, a group is included in the result table only if the sum of the ONORD field for that group is greater than zero. A HAVING clause can be used without a GROUP BY clause, in which case it is applied to all rows as one group.

THE ORDER BY CLAUSE

The ORDER BY clause specifies a sequence for the rows of the result table:

```
SELECT      QUOPART, QUOSUPP, PRICE
FROM        QUOTATIONS
ORDER BY    QUOPART, PRICE DESC
```

One or more column names are specified. The values in these columns are used to sort the rows in the result table. Sorting can be in either ascending (ASC) or descending (DESC) sequence. Instead of specifying a column name, it is also possible to refer to the column by number, specifying its relative position in the SELECT clause:

```
ORDER BY 1, 3 DESC
```

THE UPDATE CLAUSE

The UPDATE clause identifies columns that can be updated in a subsequent UPDATE statement. It is primarily used with cursor-based processing and is discussed further later in this chapter.

THE UNION OPERATION

The UNION operation can be used to create a result table by combining two other result tables:

```
SELECT     QUOPART PRICE
FROM       GSAQUOT
WHERE      QUOSUPP = QUERYSUPP
    UNION
SELECT     QUOPART PRICE
FROM       COMMQUOT
WHERE      QUOSUPP = QUERYSUPP
```

Either UNION or UNION ALL can be specified. UNION eliminates duplicate rows in the result table; UNION ALL leaves duplicate rows in the result table.

THE SELECT INTO STATEMENT

As part of an application program that contains SQL statements, a SELECT INTO statement can be used to assign the result table values to program variables:

```
SELECT     SUPSUPP, CODE
INTO       :SUPPNO, :SUPPCODE
FROM       SUPPLIERS
WHERE      NAME = :SUPPNAME
```

A program variable that is used as part of an SQL statement is known as a *host variable*. When used in an SQL statement, the variable name is preceded by a colon (:). A SELECT INTO statement must return at most one row of data, and the values from that row are assigned to the variables specified by the INTO clause. Host variables can also be used to provide data used in the SQL statement. In the forgoing example, a host variable is used to provide a value for the WHERE clause.

UPDATING DATA

In addition to retrieving data from a database with the SELECT statement, SQL provides facilities for updating data. The INSERT statement can be used to add rows to a table or view. The DELETE statement can be used to delete rows, and the UPDATE statement can be used to replace values in one or more rows.

THE INSERT STATEMENT

The INSERT statement can directly specify the values to be inserted, either in the form of constants or by referring to host variables:

```
INSERT     INTO INVENTORY
VALUES     (126, 'BOLT', 0)
```

or

```
INSERT     INTO INVENTORY (INVPART, PNAME)
VALUES     (:TRPART, :TRNAME)
```

Specifying column names allows data to be inserted in selected columns. Other columns are initialized with null values.

An INSERT statement can also select one or more rows from some other table to be inserted. This is done with a SELECT clause:

```
INSERT     INTO TESTINV
    SELECT     *
    FROM       INVENTORY
    WHERE      PRICE IS NOT NULL
```

THE DELETE STATEMENT

A DELETE statement removes one or more rows from a table:

```
DELETE   FROM QUOTATIONS
WHERE    QUOSUPP = :TRANSSUPP
         AND QUOPART = :TRANSPART
```

The search condition specified in the WHERE clause identifies the rows to be deleted.

CURSOR-BASED PROCESSING

When an SQL query, issued from within an application program, is expected to return multiple rows, the values returned cannot be simply assigned to host variables. Instead, a *cursor* is used to process the rows one at a time. The cursor must be defined and associated with a particular SELECT statement. This is done with the DECLARE CURSOR statement:

```
DECLARE    PARTCURSOR CURSOR FOR
    SELECT     INVPART, PNAME, QUOSUPP, PRICE
    FROM       INVENTORY, QUOTATIONS
    WHERE      INVPART = QUOPART AND
               PRICE > :MINPRICE
    ORDER BY INVPART QUOSUPP
```

An OPEN statement for the cursor causes the SELECT statement to be executed and the results table created:

```
OPEN      PARTCURSOR
```

A FETCH statement is used to retrieve each row and store it in host variables for whatever further processing is required:

```
FETCH     PARTCURSOR
INTO      :PARTNO, :PARTNAME, :SUPPNO, :PRICE
```

When all the rows have been processed, the cursor is closed with a CLOSE statement:

```
CLOSE     PARTCURSOR
```

When processing rows with a cursor, it is possible to update or delete a particular row:

```
DECLARE              QUOTCURSOR CURSOR FOR
    SELECT               *
    FROM                 QUOTATIONS
    WHERE                QUOSUPP = :TRANSSUPP
    FOR UPDATE OF PRICE
        .
        .
        .
    UPDATE               QUOTATIONS
    SET                  PRICE = :CALCPRICE
    WHERE CURRENT OF QUOTCURSOR
        .
        .
        .
    DELETE               FROM QUOTATIONS
    WHERE CURRENT OF QUOTCURSOR
```

To update a column, it must be specified in the FOR UPDATE OF clause in the DECLARE CURSOR statement. The WHERE CURRENT OF clause in the UPDATE or DELETE statement causes the row currently associated with the cursor to be updated or deleted.

CONCURRENCY   When data is being updated in an environment in which shared access to databases is allowed, steps must be taken to ensure that data integrity is maintained and that changes made by one user do not affect another user. SQL assumes that the database management system will automatically place locks on any resources needed to make a change to a database and will release the locks when the change processing is completed. Generally, an application program is unaware of this lock processing.

An application program can affect how long locks are held through a process called *change commitment*. The program is able to specify during its execution that changes made up to a particular point are to be considered committed, or permanent, or that the changes should be rolled back, or undone. The point in a program where changes are committed or rolled back is known as a *commit point*. When a commit point is reached, any locks being held on resource are released.

The termination of a program's execution is always considered to be a commit point. If the program terminates normally, the changes are committed; if the program terminates abnormally, changes are rolled back. The program can explicitly define a commit point during its execution by issuing a COMMIT or ROLLBACK statement:

```
COMMIT WORK
```

or

```
ROLLBACK WORK
```

The SQL interface also includes a LOCK TABLE statement that allows a user to control shared access to a particular table:

```
LOCK TABLE INVENTORY IN SHARE MODE
```

A table can be locked in either SHARE mode or EXCLUSIVE mode. With SHARE mode, other users are allowed to access the table only for read-only operations. With EXCLUSIVE mode, no one else is allowed to access the table. The lock on the table is released when a commit point is reached.

DATA DEFINITION

Certain SQL statements can be used to define or modify objects, such as tables, views, and indexes. The statements for each type of object are described below.

CREATING TABLES

The CREATE TABLE statement is used to define a new table:

```
CREATE TABLE QUOTATIONS
     (QUOSUPP    SMALLINT NOT NULL,
      QUOPART    SMALLINT NOT NULL,
      PRICE      DECIMAL(5,2),
```

```
            TIME         SMALLINT,
            ONORD        INTEGER,
            PRIMARY KEY(QUOSUPP,QUOPART))
```

Each of the columns in the table is named, and its data type specified. Box 7.3 lists the data types that are supported in the SQL interface. The PRIMARY KEY clause can be used to define a primary key for the table. A unique index must be created for the primary key. In some database management systems, the index is

BOX 7.3   SQL data types.

String Data

- **BIT Data.** Data that is not associated with a coded character set.
- **SBCS Data.** Data in which every character is represented by a single byte.
- **MIXED Data.** Data that may contain a mixture of characters from a single-byte character set and a double-byte character set.
- **GRAPHIC Data.** Data in which every character is a double-byte character.

Numeric Data

- **Small Integer.** A binary integer with a precision of 15 bits, whose value ranges from –32,768 to +32,767.
- **Large Integer.** A binary integer with a precision of 31 bits, whose value ranges from –2,147,483,648 to +2,147,483,647.
- **Floating Point.** A floating-point representation of a real number. Single precision floating-point uses 32 bits, and double precision floating-point uses 64 bits.
- **Decimal.** A packed-decimal or zoned-decimal number with an implicit decimal point.

Date/Time Data

- **Date.** A three-part value representing year, month, and day using the Gregorian calendar.
- **Time.** A three-part value representing hour, minute, and second using a 24-hour clock.
- **Timestamp.** A seven-part value representing year, month, day, hour, minute, second, and microsecond using the Gregorian calendar and a 24-hour day.

created automatically. For other systems, the user must create the index, and the table is not made available for processing until the index has been created.

Referential Integrity

The CREATE TABLE statement can also be used to define referential constraints that exist between tables:

```
CREATE TABLE QUOTATIONS
       (QUOSUPP     SMALLINT NOT NULL,
        QUOPART     SMALLINT NOT NULL,
        PRICE       DECIMAL(5,2),
        TIME        SMALLINT,
        ONORD       INTEGER,
        PRIMARY KEY(QUOSUPP,QUOPART),
        FOREIGN KEY SUPPCONST (QUOSUPP)
                    REFERENCES SUPPLIERS
                    ON DELETE CASCADE,
        FOREIGN KEY PARTCONST (QUOPART)
                    REFERENCES INVENTORY
                    ON DELETE SET NULL)
```

The FOREIGN KEY clause specifies that the named column or columns must have a value that matches one of the primary key values in the referenced table. In this example, each column value in QUOSUPP must match a primary key in the SUPPLIERS table. The table being defined (QUOTATIONS) is known as the *dependent table*. The referenced table (SUPPLIERS) is known as the *parent table*.

The ON DELETE clause specifies the action to be taken if an attempt is made to delete a row from the parent table, where the primary key value matches a foreign key in the dependent table. The delete rules that can be specified in an ON DELETE clause are summarized in Box 7.4.

BOX 7.4   Referential integrity delete rules.

- **RESTRICT.** The row in the parent table is not deleted and an error condition occurs.
- **CASCADE.** The row in the parent table is deleted and any rows in the dependent table with a matching foreign key value are also deleted.
- **SET NULL.** The row in the parent table is deleted. Any row in the dependent table with a matching foreign key value has the foreign key fields set to null.

MODIFYING TABLES An ALTER TABLE statement can be used to add a column to a table or to add or delete primary and foreign keys:

```
ALTER TABLE INVENTORY
    ADD BIN SMALLINT

ALTER TABLE QUOTATIONS
    FOREIGN KEY PARTRC1 (QUOPART)
    REFERENCES INVENTORY
    ON DELETE SET NULL
```

Definitions and descriptions of tables, views, indexes, and other objects are maintained in a catalog by the database management system. The COMMENT ON statement can be used to add or replace a comment associated with a table or a table column:

```
COMMENT ON COLUMN QUOTATIONS.ONORD
    IS 'Quantity on order'
```

An entire table can be deleted with a DROP statement:

```
DROP TABLE QUOTATIONS
```

When a table is dropped, any objects dependent on that table, such as views or indexes, are also deleted.

DEFINING VIEWS A view is a logical, or virtual, table that is derived from one or more base tables or other views. A view is created with a CREATE VIEW statement:

```
CREATE VIEW ORDERS (SUPPNAME, PARTNUM, PARTNAME, ONORD,
PRICE, TOTALPRICE)
    AS SELECT NAME, QUOPART, PNAME, ONORD, PRICE,
PRICE * ONORD
        FROM INVENTORY, QUOTATIONS, SUPPLIERS
        WHERE INVPART = QUOPART
            AND SUPSUPP = QUOSUPP
            AND ONORD > 0
```

The statement names the view and, optionally, the columns that make up the view. A SELECT clause then specifies the source of the data that can be accessed using the view.

A comment can be added to or replaced in the view's catalog description by using a COMMENT ON statement:

```
COMMENT ON TABLE ORDERS
       IS 'Outstanding orders'
```

A view can be deleted with a DROP statement:

```
DROP VIEW ORDERS
```

DEFINING INDEXES

Indexes are created with the CREATE INDEX statement:

```
CREATE INDEX XQUOT
       ON QUOTATIONS (PRICE DESC)
CREATE UNIQUE INDEX XQUOT2
       ON QUOTATIONS (QUOSUPP, QUOPART)
```

The statement specifies the column or columns on which the index is to be created. A column can be used in either ascending (ASC) or descending (DESC) sequence. Specifying UNIQUE ensures that no two rows will have the same value for the index key.

An index is deleted with the DROP statement:

```
DROP INDEX XQUOT
```

An index associated with a primary key cannot be dropped.

AUTHORIZATION

Every SQL statement that is executed is associated with an *authorization ID*, which in turn is associated with a set of *privileges*. The database management system checks the authorization ID to ensure that the program or person executing the SQL statement has the authority to do so.

A user that has the authority to create a table also has the authority to retrieve or modify data in that table, alter the table, and define and drop views and indexes based on the table. The user also has the authority to grant other users the right to access the table. This is done with the GRANT statement:

```
GRANT SELECT, DELETE, INSERT, UPDATE
      ON QUOTATIONS
      TO KKC01, CLW03
```

Privileges can be granted to individual users by specifying their authorization IDs. Privileges can also be granted to all users by specifying TO PUBLIC. The different privileges that can be granted are summarized in Box 7.5. Privileges can be granted for either a table or a view.

Privileges that have been granted to other users can be revoked with a REVOKE statement:

```
REVOKE ALL
       ON QUOTATIONS
       FROM CLW03
```

BOX 7.5   GRANT privileges.

- **ALL.** Grants all table privileges.
- **ALTER.** Grants the privilege to use the ALTER TABLE statement.
- **DELETE.** Grants the privilege to use the DELETE statement.
- **INDEX.** Grants the privilege to use the CREATE INDEX statement.
- **INSERT.** Grants the privilege to use the INSERT statement.
- **REFERENCES.** Grants the privilege to create and drop referential constraints in which this table is the parent.
- **SELECT.** Grants the privilege to use the SELECT statement.
- **UPDATE.** Grants the privilege to use the UPDATE statement. Specific column names can be specified, and then only those columns can be updated.

EXECUTING SQL STATEMENTS

There are several ways in which SQL statements can be executed. SQL database management systems typically include a facility that allows a user at a display terminal to enter SQL statements and then see results immediately displayed on the terminal. This is known as *interactive SQL*.

SQL statements can also be embedded within an application program. *Static SQL* statements are coded in a source program and then processed by a precompiler. The precompiler checks the syntax of the SQL statements and converts them into appropriate host language statements that invoke the database management system. As part of the program preparation process, a *package*, or *access plan*, is prepared. The package contains control structures and SQL statements in executable form. The package establishes a linkage between the application program and the data it accesses and is used when the program is executed. When a program is executed, the database management system checks that the package is still consistent with the databases being used. If changes have been made that affect the package, a new package is prepared.

An application program can also contain SQL statements that are prepared dynamically. A *dynamic SQL* statement is constructed during program execution and then executed directly. Not all SQL statements can be prepared and executed dynamically.

PACKAGE PROCESSING

The creator of an application program has the right to use the associated package to execute the program. This privilege can be granted to other users with a GRANT statement and revoked with a REVOKE statement:

```
GRANT    EXECUTE
         ON PACKAGE QUOTUPDT
         TO JALAK

REVOKE   EXECUTE
         ON PACKAGE QUOTUPDT
         FROM JALAK
```

A package can be deleted with a DROP statement:

```
DROP    PACKAGE QUOTUPDT
```

EMBEDDED SQL STATEMENTS

The CPI Database Interface supports the use of embedded SQL statements with all the SAA programming languages, including C, COBOL, FORTRAN, PL/I, RPG, and the Procedures language. The SQL statement is enclosed by delimiters that are language specific. Box 7.6 shows examples of an embedded SQL statement in each of the languages.

There are certain SQL statements that are used only as an embedded statement in an application program. The BEGIN DECLARE and END DECLARE statements are used to identify variables that are used as host variables:

```
      EXEC SQL   BEGIN DECLARE SECTION   END-EXEC.
   01 PARTINFO.
      05 PARTNO      PIC S9(4)    COMP.
      05 PARTNAME    PIC X(15).
      05 SUPPNO      PIC X9(4)    COMP.
      05 PRICE       PIC S999V99  COMP-3.
      05 ONHAND      PIC S9(5)    COMP.
      05 ONORD       PIC S9(5)    COMP.
      EXEC SQL   END DECLARE SECTION     END-EXEC.
```

The variables are defined according to the rules and syntax of the language in question.

BOX 7.6 SQL statement delimiters.

C Language

```
EXEC SQL SELECT SUPSUPP, CODE
         INTO :SUPPNO, :SUPPCODE
         FROM SUPPLIERS
         WHERE NAME = :SUPPNAME;
```

COBOL

```
EXEC SQL SELECT SUPSUPP, CODE
         INTO :SUPPNO, :SUPPCODE
         FROM SUPPLIERS
         WHERE NAME = :SUPPNAME
END-EXEC
```

FORTRAN

```
EXEC SQL SELECT SUPSUPP, CODE
C        INTO :SUPPNO, :SUPPCODE
C        FROM SUPPLIERS
C        WHERE NAME = :SUPPNAME
```

PL/I

```
EXEC SQL SELECT SUPSUPP, CODE
         INTO :SUPPNO, :SUPPCODE
         FROM SUPPLIERS
         WHERE NAME = :SUPPNAME;
```

Procedures Language

```
EXEC SQL 'SELECT SUPSUPP, CODE',
         'INTO :SUPPNO, :SUPPCODE',
         'FROM SUPPLIERS',
         'WHERE NAME = :SUPPNAME'
```

RPG

```
C/EXEC SQL SELECT SUPSUPP, CODE
C+         INTO :SUPPNO, :SUPPCODE
C+         FROM SUPPLIERS
C+         WHERE NAME = :SUPPNAME;
C/END-EXEC
```

The CONNECT statement is used to connect the application program to an application server that provides database management services:

```
EXEC SQL    CONNECT TO :APPSERVER;
```

The INCLUDE statement can be used to bring source text into the program from an external file or library:

```
EXEC SQL    INCLUDE SOURCE.EDIT;
```

The text included can contain host language statements and SQL statements other than the INCLUDE statement.

SQL COMMUNICATIONS AREA

When an SQL statement is executed as part of an application program, the database management system returns information to the program about the results of the execution. This information is returned in a data area known as the *SQL Communications Area*, or SQLCA. The fields that are contained in the SQLCA are described in Box 7.7.

A description of the SQLCA area can be included in the program by issuing an INCLUDE statement for it:

```
EXEC SQL    INCLUDE SQLCA;
```

The application program can test the fields in the SQLCA to see if the statement executed successfully, and if not, what caused the problem. The SQL statement WHENEVER can be used to check the SQLCA for a certain condition and to take a specified action if the condition occurs:

```
EXEC SQL    WHENEVER NOT FOUND
            GOTO UNMATCHED;
```

The conditions that can be tested are listed in Box 7.8.

DYNAMIC SQL STATEMENTS

Dynamic SQL statements are constructed during program execution, rather than being coded as source statements and compiled as part of the program. A dynamic SQL statement is constructed in the form of a character string. During program execution, the character string is translated into an executable form, and the SQL statement is executed. For certain SQL statements, the statement can be put into executable form and executed with the EXEC IMMEDIATE statement:

BOX 7.7   SQL communications area fields.

Field Name	Data Type	Description
SQLCAID	CHAR(8)	Contains an eye catcher ('SQLCA') for storage dumps.
SQLCABC	INTEGER	Contains the integer length (136) of the SQLCA.
SQLCODE	INTEGER	Contains an SQL return code.
SQLERRML	SMALLINT	Contains the integer length of the SQLERRMC field.
SQLERRMC	VARCHAR(70)	Contains information that is substituted for variables in the descriptions of error conditions.
SQLERRP	CHAR(8)	Contains a three-letter code identifying the database management system product.
SQLERRD	ARRAY	Contains six integer variables that contain diagnostic information.
SQLWARN	ARRAY	An array holding a set of eleven 1-byte warning indicators, some of which contain product-specific information.
SQLSTATE	CHAR(5)	Contains a return code indicating the outcome of the most recently executed SQL statement.

BOX 7.8   WHENEVER conditions.

- **NOT FOUND.** A condition that results in an SQLCODE of +100.
- **SQLERROR.** A condition that results in a negative SQLCODE.
- **SQLWARNING.** A condition that results in an SQLWARN0 of 'W' or a positive SQLCODE other than +100.

```
        EXEC SQL    EXECUTE IMMEDIATE :STATEVAR;
```

The host variable :STATEVAR contains the statement string.

Certain types of SQL statements must be prepared, or translated into executable form, with a PREPARE statement and then later executed with an EXECUTE statement:

```
        EXEC SQL    PREPARE DYNAMSTATE
                    FROM :STATEVAR;
        EXEC SQL    EXECUTE DYNAMSTATE
                    USING :VAR1, :VAR2;
```

When the statement being constructed is a SELECT statement, the program needs information about the columns in the results table in order to provide a data area suitable for processing the results. The DESCRIBE statement can be used to obtain this information:

```
        EXEC SQL    PREPARE DYNAMSTATE
                    FROM :STATEVAR;
        EXEC SQL    DESCRIBE DYNAMSTATE
                    INTO :SQLDA;
            .
            .
            .
        EXEC SQL    FETCH DYNCURSOR
                    USING DESCRIPTOR :SQLDA;
```

Once the information has been obtained, it can be used in a FETCH, OPEN, or EXECUTE statement to provide the necessary host variables description.

CONCLUSION

This chapter has described the CPI Database Interface that defines how the data stored in relational databases is processed using SQL statements. Chapter 8 describes the CPI Query interface that defines a more user-oriented method for accessing the data in relational databases.

8 THE CPI QUERY INTERFACE

The CPI Query Interface, like the CPI Database Interface, provides a means for processing the data stored in a relational database. In addition to providing basic database processing capabilities, the CPI Query Interface has facilities for both accessing and updating relational data and for formatting the display of accessed data. IBM provides products in each of the SAA computing environments that implement the CPI Query Interface:

- **MVS and VM.** Query Management Facility
- **OS/400.** OS/400 Query Management
- **OS/2.** OS/2 Query Manager

The facilities of a product that implements the CPI Query Interface can be accessed by both end users at terminals or workstations and by application programmers using one of the SAA-supported programming languages. Application programs access the facilities of a product implementing the CPI Query Interface by issuing calls to a *callable interface* that is defined by the CPI Query Interface specification.

QUERIES   The CPI Query Interface supports the use of SQL statements for processing data in a relational database. The SQL facilities that can be used include SELECT expressions, data definition statements, authorization functions, and basic updating facilities. The specific statements available are listed in Box 8.1.

When an SQL statement is issued through the CPI Query Interface, it is referred to as a *query*. Queries can be issued by an end user or an application program that is accessing the facilities defined by the CPI Query Interface. Queries

BOX 8.1 SQL statements allowed as queries.

SELECT Expressions

```
SELECT
    FROM clause
    WHERE clause
      GROUP BY clause
    HAVING clause
    ORDER BY clause
UNION, UNION ALL
```

Basic Data Access Statements

```
DELETE
INSERT
SELECT INTO
UPDATE
```

Data Definition Statements

```
ALTER TABLE
COMMENT ON
CREATE INDEX
CREATE TABLE
CREATE VIEW
DROP
```

Authorization Statements

```
GRANT
REVOKE
```

can also be stored and assigned a name and then later retrieved by name and executed.

Following is an example of a query that could be processed by a product implementing the CPI Query Interface:

```
SELECT    QUOSUPP, QUOPART, PRICE, ONORD
FROM      QUOTATIONS
ORDER BY  QUOSUPP, QUOPART
```

As in Chapter 7, the queries in this chapter all refer to the relational database tables illustrated in Fig. 7.1.

REPORT FORMATTING

When a query contains a SELECT expression that returns data, the data can be displayed online or printed. The CPI Query Interface includes a report formatting facility that can be used to format the data when it is displayed or printed. The set of specifications that define a report format is contained in an object called a *form*. The CPI Query Interface specifies the options that are available in defining a form object.

COLUMN Fields

A form object consists of different types of fields. COLUMN fields define the formatting to be used for the different columns that make up the report. For each column the user can define the following COLUMN fields:

- **Data Type.** Defines the data type of the data in the column as NUMERIC, CHAR, GRAPHIC, or DATE/TIME.
- **Column Heading.** Defines the text to be used as a heading for the column.
- **Usage.** Determines how a column is used in the report. Possible values are
  - **Blank.** Column is included.
  - **OMIT.** Column is omitted.
  - **BREAKn.** Column is used for a control break at level *n*, where *n* can range from 1 to 6.
  - **AVERAGE, COUNT, FIRST, LAST, MAXIMUM, MINIMUM, SUM.** Determines the value shown for the column at subtotal and total levels.
- **Indent.** Specifies the location of a column within a row.
- **Width.** Specifies the width of the column.
- **Edit.** Specifies formatting characteristics for the column, based on data type.
- **Seq.** Can be used to order the columns in a report.

BREAK Fields

BREAK fields specify information associated with control breaks. Heading text and footing text can be specified, along with its alignment. Blank lines can be specified as appearing before or after the heading or footing text. A page break, column headings, and the positioning of break summary information can also be specified.

PAGE and FINAL TEXT Fields

PAGE fields are used to define page heading and footing information. Page heading and footing text can be specified, along with its alignment and blank lines that are to precede or follow it.

FINAL TEXT fields define text that appears at the end of the report. The text itself, its alignment, and blank lines preceding it can be specified.

OPTIONS Fields

OPTIONS fields specify various formatting options. With these fields the user can specify

- Line spacing between detail lines.
- Whether values print in a break column on every line or only when the value changes.
- Whether asterisks are used to mark different levels of breaks.
- Whether a wrapped column is split between pages.
- Whether column heading, break summary, and final summary separator lines are included.

COMMANDS

The CPI Query Interface includes a set of commands that can be used to process queries and the results returned by queries. As mentioned earlier, a query can be issued directly, or it can be stored as a named object and then executed later with a RUN QUERY command. For example, suppose the following query has been saved under the name SUPQUERY:

```
SELECT   SUPSUPP, NAME, INVPART, PNAME, TIME, ONHAND, ONORD
FROM     SUPPLIERS, INVENTORY, QUOTATIONS
WHERE    INVPART = QUOPART
         AND SUPSUPP = QUOSUPP
         AND SUPSUPP = 53
```

The above query could then be executed by specifying:

```
RUN QUERY SUPQUERY
```

PROCESSING QUERY RESULTS

When a query is submitted online directly by an end user, the query results are displayed on the user's display. A form can be used to control the formatting of the data that is displayed. If a form has been defined and stored, it can be specified as part of the RUN QUERY command:

```
RUN QUERY SUPQUERY (FORM=SUPPFORM
```

The forgoing command will cause the form SUPPFORM to be used to format the results of SUPQUERY.

The CPI Query Interface does not specify the way in which a query or form is stored. The details of this are left to each query product that implements the CPI Query Interface. The CPI Query Interface does specify rules for constructing names, and each product implementation must support the use of query and form names in commands like RUN QUERY by retrieving and using the specified objects.

A PRINT command can be used to produce a hard copy listing of the results of a query:

```
PRINT REPORT (FORM=SUPPFORM
```

As with RUN QUERY, the form to use to format the report can be specified as part of the command. Other options that can be specified as part of PRINT REPORT are listed in Box 8.2.

BOX 8.2 PRINT REPORT options.

- **WIDTH.** Maximum number of characters per print line.
- **LENGTH.** Maximum number of lines per page.
- **FORM.** Name of form to use to format data.
- **PRINTER.** Name of printer to use to produce the report.
- **DATETIME.** Specifies whether system date and time are included on the bottom of each page.
- **PAGENO.** Specifies whether a page number is included on each page.

Query results can also be saved in a database table by issuing the SAVE command:

```
SAVE DATA AS SUPDATA
```

If the table named in the SAVE command already exists, the results data replaces data already in the table. If the table does not exist, a new table will be generated using column names and data types based on the columns in the query.

VARIABLES

A query can contain comments and can reference variables:

```
          -- This query lists selected fields from the
          -- SUPPLIERS, INVENTORY, and QUOTATIONS tables
          -- for a specified supplier number.
          --
          SELECT    SUPSUPP, NAME, INVPART, PNAME, TIME,
                    ONHAND, ONORD
          FROM      SUPPLIERS, INVENTORY, QUOTATIONS
          WHERE     INVPART = QUOPART
                    AND SUPSUPP = QUOSUPP
                    AND SUPSUPP = &SUPPLIER
```

Comments begin with two hyphens (--). An ampersand that precedes a name identifies the name as a variable.

Prior to running the query, a value can be assigned to a variable by issuing a SET command:

```
              SET GLOBAL (SUPPLIER = 53
              RUN QUERY SUPQUERY
```

The SET command specifies a variable name, without an ampersand, and the value to which the variable is set.

PROCEDURES

A procedure is a set of query commands that is processed as a unit. Each command in a procedure must be enclosed in single quotes. As with an individual query, a procedure can be named and stored and then later retrieved and run as a unit. For example, the following commands could be defined as a procedure named SUPPROC:

```
              'RUN QUERY SUPQUERY'
              'PRINT REPORT (FORM=SUPPFORM'
              'SAVE DATA AS SUPDATA'
```

The procedure can then be executed with the following command:

```
              RUN PROC SUPPROC
```

As with queries and forms, the CPI Query Interface does not define the processes used to name and store a procedure or the way in which those processes are invoked. Each query product is free to specify the details concerning these processes.

PROCESSING OBJECTS

In the CPI Query Interface, stored queries, forms, and procedures are all considered to be *objects*. Certain commands can be used to perform processing on objects. A hard copy listing of an object can be produced with the PRINT command:

```
             PRINT QUERY SUPQUERY
             PRINT FORM SUPPFORM
             PRINT PROC SUPPROC (PRINTER=PRINTLOC1
```

A printer name can be specified to cause the output to be printed on a particular printer.

ERASE can be used to remove an object from the database where it is stored:

```
                  ERASE QUERY SUPQUERY
                  ERASE FORM SUPPFORM
                  ERASE PROC SUPPROC
                  ERASE TABLE SUPDATA
```

ERASE can also be used to remove a table.

Objects can be moved between operating environments by using the EXPORT and IMPORT commands. EXPORT places a copy of the object in a specified file. IMPORT brings in a copy of an object from the specified file:

```
               EXPORT QUERY TO QUERYFILE
               IMPORT QUERY FROM QUERYFILE
```

EXPORT and IMPORT can be issued for a query, procedure, form, or table. When EXPORT is used for a table, a file format can be specified:

```
           EXPORT TABLE TO HOLDTABLE (DATAFORMAT=IXF
```

Currently, IXF is the only format supported for table data. IXF is not an SAA-defined data interchange format. It can be used to exchange data between two like implementations, for example, between one QMF system and another QMF system. IBM's intent is to eventually define an interchange format that will allow tables to be interchanged between any two query products that implement the CPI Query Interface.

OBJECT FORMATS

The CPI Query Interface does define interchange formats that can be used to export queries, procedures, and forms. Queries and procedures use a *panel* format. In this format, objects are written out as fixed-length records with a logical record length of 79. The content of the object—either queries or commands—consists of a series of text strings.

Forms are written in an encoded format using variable-length records of up to 7290 characters. The encoded format defines a set of record types, with specific formats for each record type. The different record types are described in Box 8.3.

BOX 8.3 FORM record types.

- **Header (H).** The *Header* record identifies the stored object as a form. It also identifies the product used to produce the object and other descriptive information for the form as an object.
- **Value (V).** A *Value* record provides the value associated with a given FORM field, where the field's value can be represented by a single data item. The field is identified in the record by a field number.
- **Table Description (T).** A *Table Description* record describes the content and format of a table of values that follows as a set of *Table Row* records. The Table Description record identifies the table, the number of rows and columns it contains, and the field number and data length for each column.
- **Table Row (R).** A *Table Row* record contains the data values for one row in a table.
- **End-of-Object (E).** The *End-of-Object* record marks the end of the object, or FORM.
- **Application Data (*).** An *Application Data* record contains data associated with the object, such as comments describing the object.

THE CALLABLE INTERFACE

As we introduced earlier in this chapter, the CPI Query Interface defines a callable interface that application programs can use to access query functions by issuing program calls. All query commands available to end users can also be issued through the callable interface. At the time of writing, the callable interface is supported for C, COBOL, FORTRAN, and Procedures Language programs.

The callable interface consists of the following elements, which are described in the following sections:

- Function calls
- Interface Communications Area
- Return variables

Function Calls

A query command is executed by issuing a function call to a query callable interface module. The syntax of the function call reflects the syntax for function calls in the particular programming language being used. There are two types of calls that can be used. The first passes a command to be executed to the callable interface. The second passes a command and one or more variables.

For C, COBOL, and FORTRAN, the first format of call uses three parameters, which reference the Interface Communications Area, a field containing the length of the query command, and a field containing the query command to be executed. In Procedures Language the only parameter required is the query command itself. Box 8.4 contains examples of a function call without variables in each of the languages.

> **BOX 8.4 Function calls without variables.**
>
> **C**
> ```
> dsqcic(&communication_area,&command_length,
>         &run_query[0]);
> ```
>
> **COBOL**
> ```
>     CALL DSQCIB USING DSQCOMM, QLEN, QUERY
> ```
>
> **FORTRAN**
> ```
>     RC = DSQCIF(DSQCOMM,
>                 COMMAND_LENGTH,
>                 RUN_QUERY)
> ```
>
> **Procedures Language**
> ```
>     call DSQCIX 'RUN QUERY Q1'
> ```

Certain query commands, such as the SET and GET commands, require reference to variables. For C, COBOL, and FORTRAN, the call used for this type of command contains the following parameters:

- **Interface Communications Area.** Defined structure used to pass information between the application program and the query processor.
- **Command Length.** Length of the command to be executed.
- **Command.** Command to be executed, represented as a character string.
- **Number of Parameters.** Number of variables included with the command.
- **Variable Length.** Length of the variable name that follows.
- **Variable.** Name of a variable.
- **Value Length.** Length of the value associated with a variable.
- **Value.** Value associated with a variable.
- **Value Type.** An indicator of a variable's type as unsigned character or long integer.

Based on the value specified for the number of parameters, each of the following parameter fields occurs that number of times. So if the number of parameters is 3, there are three variable length fields, three variable fields, and so on.

In the Procedures Language, the command is followed by a variable list containing pairs of variable names and variable values. Box 8.5 shows examples of this type of call in each of the programming languages.

BOX 8.5   Function calls with variables.

C

```
dsqcice(&communication_area,
        &command_length,
        &command,
        &number_of_parameters,
        &keyword_lengths[0],
        &keyword_names[0],
        &data_lengths[0],
        &data_values[0],
        &data_types[0]);
```

COBOL

```
CALL DSQCIB USING DSQCOMM, COMMAND-LENGTH, COMMAND,
                  NUMBER-OF-PARAMETERS,
                  NAME-LENGTHS, NAMES,
                  VALUE-LENGTHS, VAR-VALUES,
                  VAR-TYPES
```

FORTRAN

```
  RC = DSQCOFE(DSQCOMM,
+              COMMAND_LENGTH,
+              NUMBER_OF_PARAMETERS,
+              KEYWORD_LENGTHS,
+              KEYWORD_NAMES,
+              DATA_LENGTHS,
+              DATA_VALUES,
+              DATA_TYPES)
```

Procedures Language

```
call DSQCIX 'SET GLOBAL (SUPPLIER=53, PART=027)'
```

Interface Communications Area

The *Interface Communications Area*, or DSQCOMM, is a storage area allocated within the application program. It contains a set of variables that are set by the query processor and can be referenced by the application program after a call to determine the results of command processing. Box 8.6 lists the fields that are contained in the Interface Communications Area.

BOX 8.6 Interface communications area.

- **Return Code.** Indicates the status following the processing of a command. Possible values are
    - **DSQ_SUCCESS.** Command processed successfully.
    - **DSQ_WARNING.** Command processed with warning conditions.
    - **DSQ_FAILURE.** Command not processed successfully.
    - **DSQ_SEVERE.** Severe error, session terminated.
- **Instance Identifier.** Identifier established during processing of the START command.
- **Completion Message.** Message ID of the message that would have been displayed to the user after command processing completes, if the command had been issued by an end user.
- **Query Message ID.** Message ID of a query message, if the command resulted in query processing.
- **START Command Parameter in Error.** Parameter in error when a START command fails due to a parameter error.
- **Cancel Indicator.** Indicates whether the user cancelled command processing while the query processor was running a command.

Return Variables

In addition to the variables that are part of the Interface Communications Area, there are other variables that contain information about the completion of a query command. These values can be accessed by the application program by issuing a GET command that references the appropriate variable names. Box 8.7 describes the variables that have been defined for the callable interface.

CALLABLE INTERFACE COMMANDS

There are two additional query commands that are associated only with the callable interface and cannot be issued directly by an end user: START and EXIT.

BOX 8.7 Return variables.

Command Message Variables
- **DSQCIMNO.** Contains the message number of the message that would be displayed on the user's terminal indicating successful completion or an error during processing.
- **DSQCIMSG.** Contains the message text of the message that would be displayed on the user's terminal.

Query Message Variables
- **DSQCIQNO.** Contains the message number of the query message that would be displayed when an error occurs during the processing of a query.
- **DSQCIQMG.** Contains the message text of the message that would be displayed if an error occurs.
- **DSQISQL.** Contains the SQL return code from the database manager.

Product Variables
- **DSQAAUTH.** Current connect authorization ID.
- **DSQAPRNM.** Current default printer nickname.
- **DSQCATTN.** Last command cancel indicator.
- **DSQAROWS.** Current number of rows fetched for data.
- **DSQAROWC.** Current data is completed.
- **DSQAMODE.** Current processing mode.

In addition, the SET and GET commands have a different format from those issued by an end user.

The START Command

The START command is issued at the beginning of the program to specify how the query session is to operate. There are three parameters that can be specified as part of the START command:

- **DSQSMODE.** Specifies whether subsequent commands are executed in interactive or batch mode. In interactive mode, a terminal is associated with the application program. Query results, messages, and other interactions are displayed on the terminal, and inputs are accepted from the user at the terminal. In batch mode, there is no interaction with a user at the terminal.

- **DSQSCMD.** Specifies the name of a file that is used to start the query session.
- **DSQSRUN.** Specifies the name of the query procedure to process after initialization is started.

The EXIT Command

The EXIT command terminates a query session and is issued when query processing is completed.

The SET and GET Commands

The SET and GET commands take on a different format when used with the callable interface. Rather than including the variable references as part of the command string, variable references are included as additional function call parameters. Box 8.8 shows how a GET command would be used in a COBOL program and a Procedures Language program to access a value in a return variable.

BOX 8.8 Sample GET calls.

COBOL

```
CALL DSQCIB USING DSQCOMM, COMMAND-LENGTH, COMMAND,
                  NUMBER-OF-PARAMETERS,
                  NAME-LENGTHS, NAMES,
                  VALUE-LENGTHS, VAR-VALUES,
                  VAR-TYPES
```

where the call parameters have the following values:

```
COMMAND-LENGTH              10
COMMAND                     GET GLOBAL
NUMBER-OF-PARAMETERS        1
NAME-LENGTHS                7
NAMES                       DSQISQL
VALUE-LENGTHS               9
VAR-VALUES                  SQLCODE
VAR-TYPES                   DSQ-VARIABLE-CHAR
```

Procedures Language

```
call DSQCIX 'GET GLOBAL (SQLCODE=DSQISQL)'
```

CONCLUSION This chapter has examined the CPI Query Interface that defines an alternative to the CPI Database Interface for accessing the data stored in relational databases. The CPI Query Interface is implemented in query products that allow end users and application programs to formulate database queries. Chapter 9 describes the CPI Resource Recovery Interface that can be used in constructing transaction processing applications.

9 THE CPI RESOURCE RECOVERY INTERFACE

The CPI Resource Recovery Interface provides a method of change management that allows changes that have been made to multiple resources to be coordinated. It provides services that allow changes made to a set of resources to all be made permanent (committed) or all undone (backed out). The resources can all be located on the same computing system, or they can be distributed across several different systems.

SYNCHRONIZATION Resource recovery is based on the concept of *synchronization*. An application program is able to specify, during its execution, either that changes made up to that point are to be considered *committed*, or made permanent, or that the changes should be *backed out*, or undone. The point in a program's execution at which changes are either committed or backed out is called a *synchronization point*. At the time that a program declares a synchronization point, it must know that the different resources affected by the changes that the program has made up to that point are in synchronization with one another. If a failure occurs, and the program needs to be restarted, resources can be restored to the condition in which they existed at the most recent synchronization point, and the program's execution can be restarted from that point.

The processing that takes place between one synchronization point and the next is called a *logical unit of work*. A logical unit of work includes all the changes that are either committed or backed out. For the CPI Resource Recovery Interface, these changes can be made to different types of resources, and the resources can be either local or remote.

A program's first synchronization point is established when the program begins execution. Another synchronization point is also established when the program terminates. If a program does not explicitly specify other synchronization points, the entire processing of the program represents a single logical unit of work. This is illustrated in Fig. 9.1. If a program whose processing represents a single unit of work terminates normally, all changes that the program has made to resources under its control are committed. If the program terminates abnormally, all changes that the program has made to resources under its control are backed out. This approach might be appropriate for a program that executes quickly, possibly processing a single short transaction each time it executes.

```
              ⎧  Program Start.
              ⎪     :
   Unit of    ⎨     [Program processing code.]
   Work       ⎪     :
              ⎩  Program End.
```

Figure 9.1 Single unit of work.

If a program executes for a longer period of time, perhaps processing a series of transactions, where each transaction is independent of the others, it is often desirable to establish a separate synchronization point after completing the processing of each transaction. With this approach, the program treats the processing associated with each transaction as a separate logical unit of work, as illustrated in Fig. 9.2 Resource recovery services can be used to define synchronization points as the program executes.

```
                   Program Start.
   Unit of    ⎧       :
   Work 1    ⎩    [Commit/rollback for transaction 1.]
   Unit of    ⎧       :
   Work 2    ⎩    [Commit/rollback for transaction 2.]
                       :
                       :
   Unit of    ⎧       :
   Work n    ⎩    [Commit/rollback for transaction n.]
   Unit of    ⎧       :
   Work
   n + 1          Program End.
```

Figure 9.2 Multiple units of work.

CPI DATABASE INTERFACE RECOVERY

The CPI Database Interface defines COMMIT and BACKOUT statements that can be used for resource recovery activities associated with relational database processing. The COMMIT statement establishes a synchronization point for database resources and causes all database changes that the program has made, up until the point at which the COMMIT statement is executed, to be committed. The BACKOUT statement causes all changes that the program has made to database resources under its control since the most previous synchronization point to be backed out, thus restoring those database resources to the condition in which they existed at the time the most previous synchronization point was established.

The COMMIT and BACKOUT statements that a program executes apply only to relational database resources that are directly accessible to that program. If the program is running in a local processing environment, it can access databases controlled by the database management system running in the same computing system as the application program. IBM's intent with SAA database recovery is also to provide support for distributed database processing. As we introduced in Chapters 2 and 6, IBM has defined three levels of distributed database processing, of which only the first is supported by SAA at the time of writing:

- **Remote Unit of Work.** An application program is able to access relational databases maintained by a single database management system on a single remote computing system. The application program can issue multiple SQL statements as part of a single remote unit of work, but all must be for databases on the same remote system. The CPI Database Interface COMMIT and BACKOUT statements can be used with a remote unit of work.

- **Distributed Unit of Work.** An application program can access data in relational databases maintained on multiple separate computing systems. Changes can be made to databases on different systems as part of a single unit of work, but a single SQL statement can reference data that is maintained by only one computing system. IBM has committed to providing support for distributed unit of work processing within SAA but has not as yet done so as of the time of writing.

- **Distributed Request.** With *distributed request processing,* a single SQL statement can reference data that is maintained by multiple separate computing systems. At the time of writing, IBM has not committed to providing distributed request processing as part of SAA.

The CPI Database Interface currently supports a connection between an application program and a single database server at a time. To change the connection and connect to a different database server, the program must first issue a COMMIT or ROLLBACK statement to either commit or roll back any changes it made to resources associated with the first database server. Thus, with the version of the CPI Database Interface current at the time of writing, only changes for databases under the control of a single computing system can be included in a logical unit of work.

CPI RESOURCE RECOVERY

The services defined by the CPI Resource Recovery Interface are more generalized than those defined by the CPI Database Interface. CPI Resource Recovery services can be applied to resources of different types, and protected resources can be located on the same computing system, or they can be distributed across different computing systems.

The CPI Resource Recovery Interface defines three types of protected resources:

- **Protected Databases.** Resource recovery is used to control changes made to data in databases.
- **Protected Conversations.** With a protected conversation, a program can include conversation partners in synchronization operations. The system maintains the state of the conversation, for each partner, at the time of the last synchronization point. If a backout occurs, the conversation can also be restored to its state at the previous synchronization point.
- **Product-Specific Protected Resources.** Other types of resources, specific to a particular environment and product, can also be protected. An example of this is the CMS shared file system for VM/ESA.

A resource can be identified as protected in one of two ways. It can be defined as protected as part of the definition of the resource itself, or an application program can explicitly request that a resource that it accesses be protected.

SYNCHRONIZATION POINT MANAGERS

System resources that can be changed in a coordinated or synchronized manner are called *protected resources*. Each type of protected resource, such as a protected file or relational database, is controlled by a *resource manager* that actually makes changes to the protected resource on behalf of application programs. For example, a program makes calls to a database management system to make changes to a relational database. A database management system is an example of a resource manager.

A program accesses a *synchronization point manager* (syncpoint manager) to control changes that the program is either committing or backing out. A synchronization point manager is an operating system component that coordinates change processing among the various resource managers that are controlling protected resources. The CPI Resource Recovery Interface allows an application program to communicate with a syncpoint manager.

Two-Phase Commit Protocol

When a program wishes to establish a synchronization point by committing changes that it has made to all the protected resources it is accessing, the program issues a request to the syncpoint manager for the Commit service. The syncpoint manager then uses a *two-phase commit* protocol to commit the changes to all the protected resources that have been changed by the program requesting the Commit service. The following describes the processing that the syncpoint manager performs in each of the two phases of the Commit operation:

Phase 1.

The syncpoint manager sends Prepare-to-Commit messages to each of the resource managers that are controlling protected resources to which the program requesting the Commit operation has access. Each resource manager that receives a Prepare-to-Commit message determines if the changes that have been made by the program to the particular protected resource under its control can be committed at that time. If the changes can be committed, the resource manager responds positively to the syncpoint manager; if the resource manager cannot commit the changes at that time, it responds negatively.

Phase 2.

If *all* the resource managers respond positively to the syncpoint manager's Prepare-to-Commit messages, the syncpoint manager sends a Commit message to each of the resource managers. Each resource manager then commits the changes made by the program to the protected resource under its control, and all changes to the protected resources under the original program's control are then made permanent. The syncpoint manager then informs the application program that the Commit operation completed successfully.

If any resource manager is unable to commit the changes and responds negatively to the syncpoint manager's Prepare-to-Commit message, the syncpoint manager sends a Backout message to each of the resource managers. All the resource managers then back out all changes that the application program made since the last synchronization point. The syncpoint manager then informs the application program that the Commit operation failed and that all changes have been backed out. The program can then restart itself from the most recent synchronization point if desired.

DISTRIBUTED RESOURCE PROCESSING

The change coordination services defined by the CPI Resource Recovery Interface can be applied to resources that are distributed across different computing systems. When a program issues a request for a Commit service, the syncpoint manager on the local computing system communicates with the syncpoint managers on all other affected computing systems. Based on the responses that the local syncpoint manager receives from the remote syncpoint managers, changes are either committed on all affected systems or all changes are backed out.

Changes to distributed resources may involve multiple application programs that are communicating across systems, as shown in Fig. 9.3. When the conversation between two programs is defined as a *protected conversation*, one program can include the other in synchronization operations. The system maintains information about the state of the conversation at each synchronization point. In the

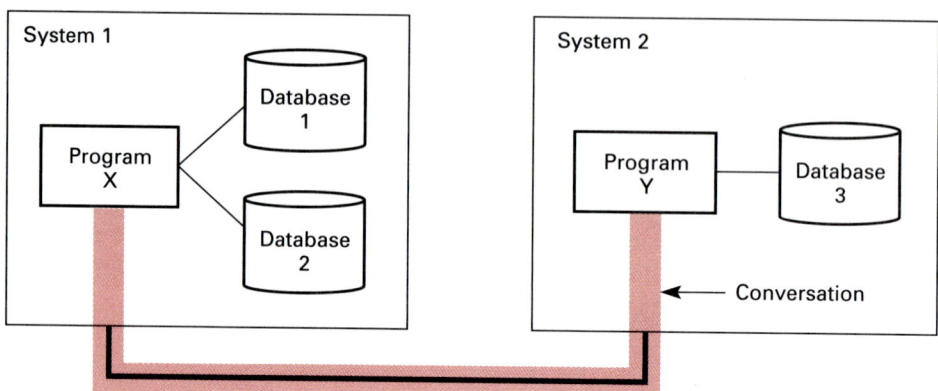

Figure 9.3   Cross-system communication.

event of a backout or a restart, the conversation can also be restored to its state at the time of the synchronization point.

Resources can be coordinated across a series of conversations. In this case, commit processing takes place across a *commit tree*, as shown in Fig. 9.4. The program that issues the original request for the Commit service is at the root of the tree. Each program in the tree that is a conversation partner with the root receives a Take-Commit notification. That program then issues a request for a Commit service of its syncpoint manager. This causes each program in the next set of branches in the tree to receive a Take-Commit notification. All programs in the tree must issue a request for the Commit service, and all must complete successfully, before any of the changes are committed. If any program in the tree causes a Backout operation to take place rather than a successful Commit, all the changes are backed out and a Backed-Out indication is returned to all the other programs.

Any program can also issue a request for the Backout service. A Take-Backout notification is then propagated down the commit tree. A program that

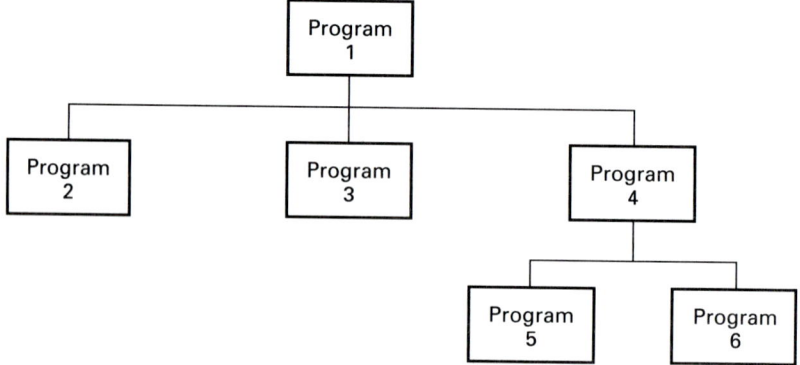

Figure 9.4   Commit tree.

receives a Take-Backout notification issues a request for the Backout service to continue the backout processing. A Take-Backout notification can also be generated by a system failure or other problem that causes a resource manager to initiate a Backout operation.

RESOURCE RECOVERY INTERFACE CALLS

The CPI Resource Recovery Interface defines an application programming interface that takes the form of two callable services: a Commit service and a Backout service.

The Commit Service

A program makes a request for the Commit service by issuing the following call:

```
CALL SRRCMIT(return_code)
```

The **return_code** parameter is used by the system to return a value that indicates the result of the Commit operation. Possible **return_code** values for the Commit service are listed in Box 9.1.

BOX 9.1   SSRCMIT return codes.

- **RR_OK.** The Commit operation completed successfully.
- **RR_COMMITTED_OUTCOME_PENDING.** The Commit operation completed, but the state of one or more protected resources is not known. This may indicate a system or application failure.
- **RR_COMMITTED_OUTCOME_MIXED.** The Commit operation completed, but one or more resources have returned to a previous synchronization point. This may indicate that commit processing has been abnormally interrupted by operator intervention.
- **RR_PROGRAM_STATE_CHECK.** The Commit operation failed and changes have been neither committed nor backed out.
- **RR_BACKED_OUT.** The Commit operation failed, and all protected resources have been returned to the previous synchronization point.
- **RR_BACKED_OUT_OUTCOME_PENDING.** The Commit operation failed, and the state of one or more protected resources is not known. This may indicate a system or application failure.
- **RR_BACKED_OUT_OUTCOME_MIXED.** The Commit operation failed and one or more protected resource has had its changes committed rather than backed out. This may indicate that commit processing has been abnormally interrupted by operator intervention.

The Backout Service

The Backout service is requested by issuing the following call:

    CALL SRRBACK(return_code)

The return codes for SRRBACK are shown in Box 9.2.

BOX 9.2 SRRBACK return codes.

- **RR_OK.** The Backout operation completed successfully.
- **RR_BACKED_OUT_OUTCOME_PENDING.** The Backout operation completed, but the state of one or more protected resources is not known. This may indicate a system or application failure.
- **RR_BACKED_OUT_OUTCOME_MIXED.** The Backout operation completed, but one or more protected resources has had its changes committed rather than backed out. This may indicate that commit processing has been abnormally interrupted by operator intervention.

RESOURCE RECOVERY SCENARIOS

The following scenarios illustrate the use of resource recovery calls in typical application situations. The first set of scenarios are for situations where a single application program is performing the processing. The second set includes distributed resources and a conversation between application programs.

CHANGE COMMITMENT WITH LOCAL RESOURCES

Figure 9.5 illustrates program flows for committing and backing out changes when protected resources are all under control of a single application program.

Successful Commit

The first example in Fig. 9.5 shows a successful Commit operation. An SRRCMIT call is issued, the syncpoint manager coordinates with the resource managers to have all changes committed, and the application program receives a return code that indicates that the Commit operation was successful.

Unsuccessful Commit

In the second example in Fig. 9.5, a failure occurs somewhere during the commit processing. All changes are backed out, and the application program receives a return code indicating that changes were backed out.

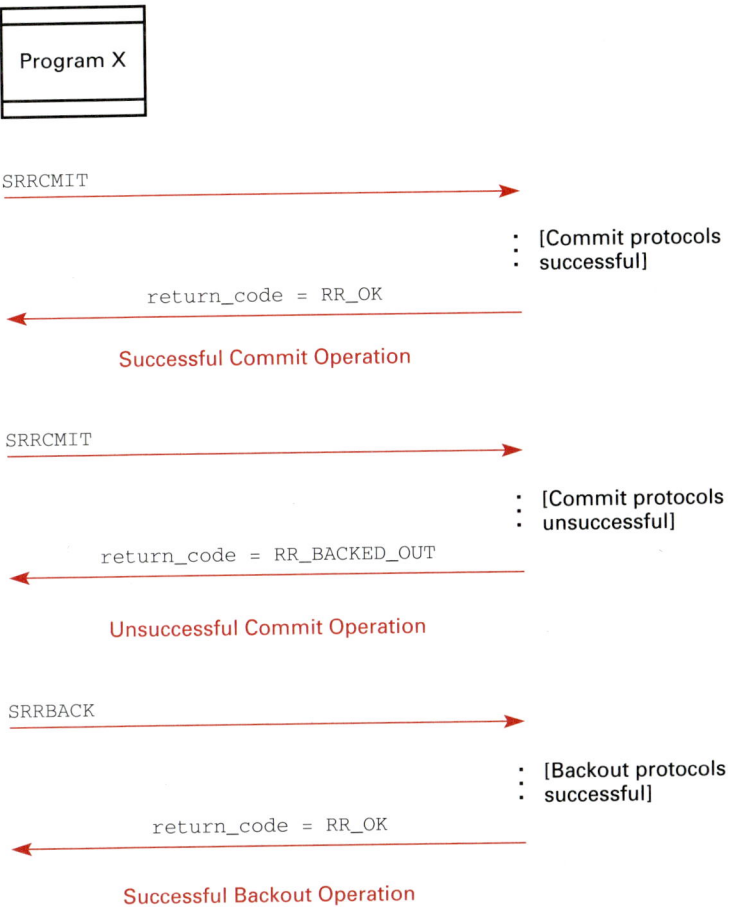

Figure 9.5 Change commitment with local resources.

Successful Backout

The third example in Fig. 9.5 shows a successful Backout operation. An SRRBACK call is issued, all changes are backed out, and the application program receives a return code indicating that the backout was successful.

CHANGE COMMITMENT WITH DISTRIBUTED RESOURCES

The next set of scenarios show change commitment processing that involves a conversation between two application programs. In these examples, calls and indicators from the CPI Communications Interface (CPI-C) are used to illustrate conversation processing. The resource recovery interface does not require the use of CPI-C.

However, CPI-C does include the facilities necessary to support synchronization processing.

Successful Commit

Figure 9.6 illustrates the program flows for a successful Commit operation with distributed resources and a conversation between application programs. The following steps are involved:

1. Program Y is in receive state.
2. Program X issues a Commit request with an SRRCMIT call.
3. Program Y receives a Take-Commit notification through the **status_received** indicator.
4. Program Y issues an SRRCMIT call.
5. The syncpoint manager on each system works with local resource managers to commit all changes. The syncpoint managers coordinate with each other to see that all Commit operations were successful.
6. Both programs receive a return code indicating that the Commit operation was successful.

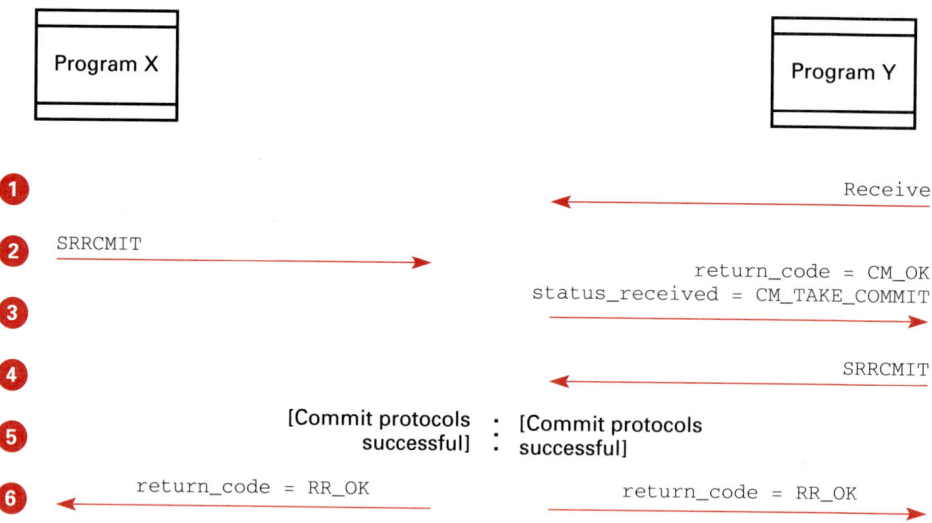

Figure 9.6 Successful Commit with distributed resources.

Unsuccessful Commit

Figure 9.7 shows a Commit operation that is unsuccessful. The processing steps are as follows:

1. Program Y is in receive state.
2. Program X issues a Commit request with an SRRCMIT call.
3. Program Y receives a Take-Commit notification through the **status_received** indicator.
4. Program Y issues an SRRCMIT call.
5. For some reason, changes to a protected resource are unable to be made permanent, making one of the Commit operations unsuccessful. The syncpoint managers then initiate Backout operations so that all changes are backed out. Protected resources and the conversation are all returned to their state at the time of the previous synchronization point.
6. Both programs receive a return code indicating that the changes were backed out rather than committed.

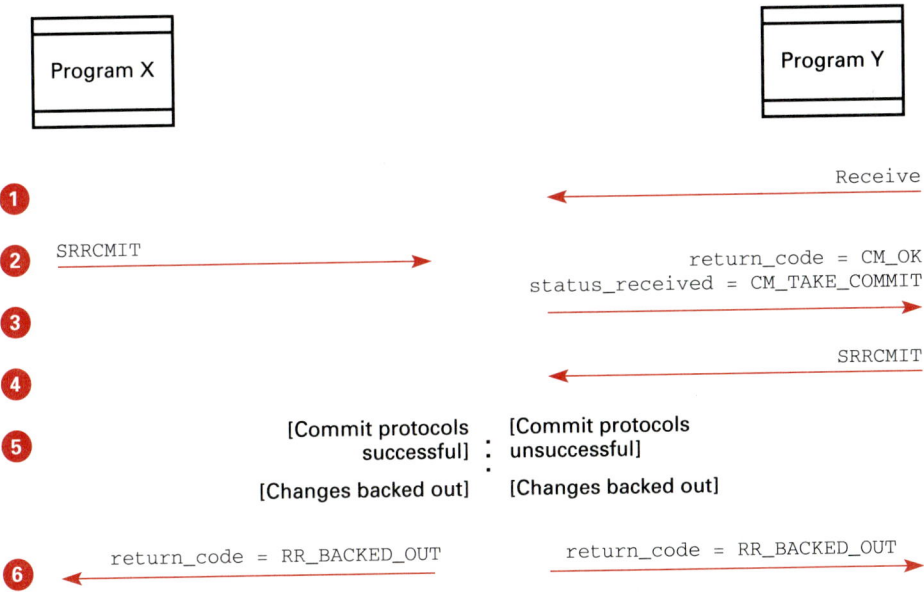

Figure 9.7 Unsuccessful Commit with distributed resources.

Commit with Partner Program Backout

Figure 9.8 shows the processing that occurs if a partner program responds to a Take-Commit notification with a Backout request rather than a Commit request:

1. Program Y is in receive state.
2. Program X issues a Commit request with an SRRCMIT call.
3. Program Y receives a Take-Commit notification through the **status_received** indicator.

4. Program Y has detected a problem that prevents it from committing its changes and issues an SRRBACK call.

5. The syncpoint manager on each system works with local resource managers to back out all changes. The syncpoint managers coordinate with each other to see that all Backout operations are completed.

6. Program X receives a return code indicating that changes were backed out rather than committed. Program Y receives a return code indicating that its Backout request was successfully completed.

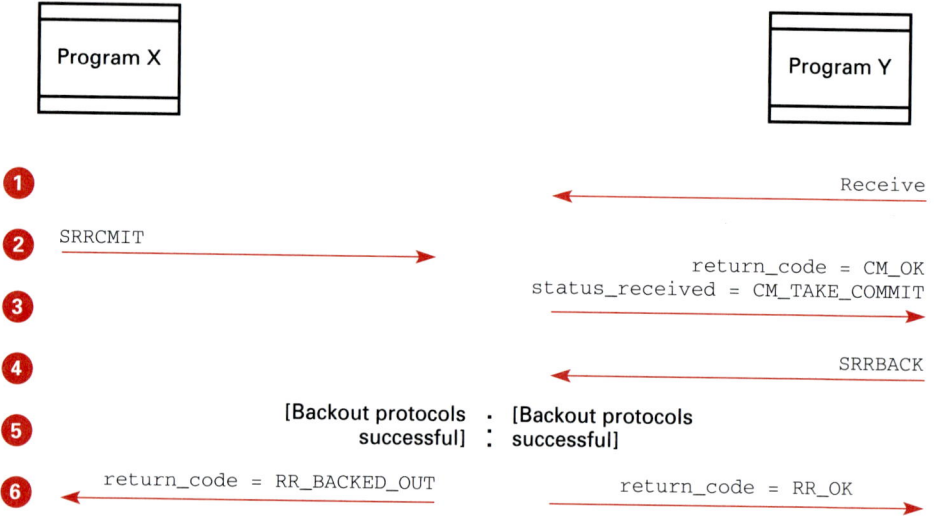

Figure 9.8 Commit with partner program Backout.

Successful Backout

Figure 9.9 shows the program flows for a successful backout with distributed resources. The steps involved are as follows:

1. Program Y is in receive state.
2. Program X issues a Backout request with an SRRBACK call.
3. Program Y receives a Take-Backout notification through the return code.
4. Program Y issues an SRRBACK call.
5. The syncpoint manager on each system works with local resource managers to back out all changes. The syncpoint managers coordinate with each other to see that all Backout operations were successful.
6. Both programs receive a return code indicating that the Backout was successful.

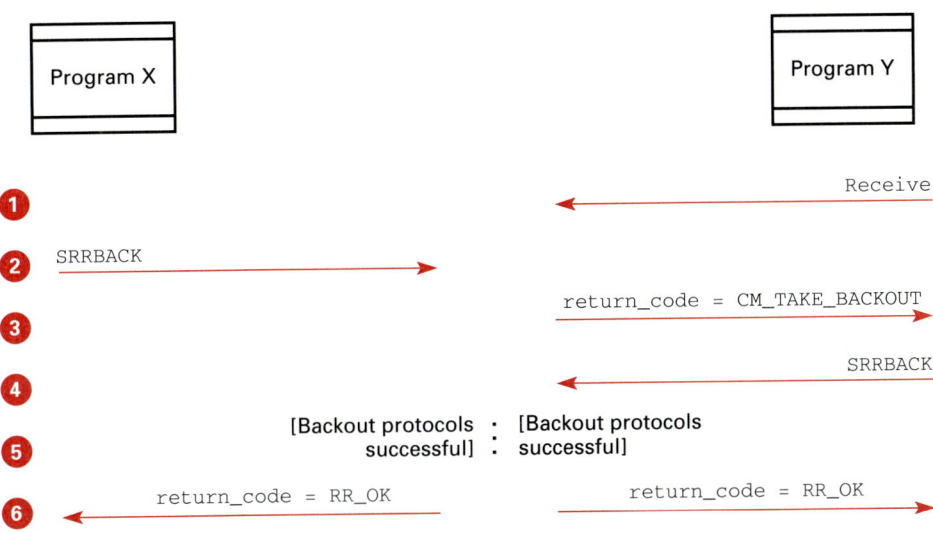

Figure 9.9 Successful Backout with distributed resources.

Wide Area Networking

Figure 9.10 illustrates the program flows used when a resource failure to a protected resource occurs outside of Commit or Backout processing. The following steps apply:

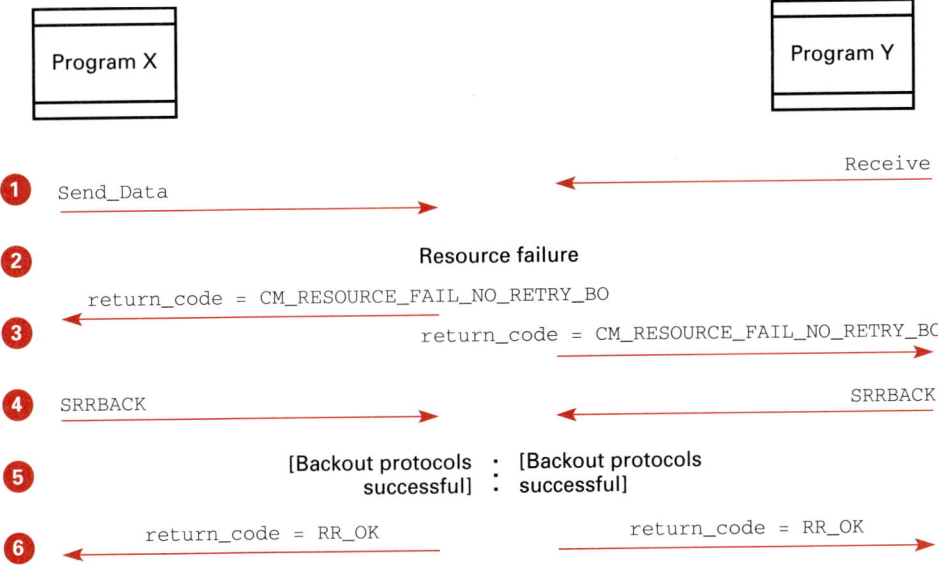

Figure 9.10 Resource failure before a Commit or Backout.

1. Program Y is in receive state.
2. Program X sends data.
3. Program Y receives a Resource-Failed notification through the return code for its Receive call. Program X receives a Resource-Failed notification through the return code for its SEND_DATA call.
4. Program X and Program Y each issue an SRRBACK call to request a Backout operation.
5. The syncpoint manager on each system works with local resource managers to back out all changes. The syncpoint managers coordinate with each other to see that all Backout operations were successful.
6. Both programs receive a return code indicating that the Backout operation was successful.

CONCLUSION This chapter described the CPI Resource Recovery Interface that provides a method of change management that allows changes that have been made to multiple resources to be coordinated. Chapter 10 describes the CPI Repository Interface that defines services that application programs can use to access the information stored in a repository.

10 THE CPI REPOSITORY INTERFACE

The SAA documentation for the CPI Repository Interface begins by characterizing a *repository* as "a place to store information." From this very general perspective, most information systems organizations already use a great number of different types of repositories, including catalogs, libraries, files, databases, and data dictionaries. However, the intent of the CPI Repository Interface is actually a bit more narrow than this very broad definition that IBM initially gives for the term repository.

IBM later goes on to provide this more detailed description of a repository:

> An organized group of information that supports business and processing activities and provides a single point of control for the management and sharing of that information.

Access to a repository is controlled by a software product called a *repository manager*, which provides services for the definition, collection, manipulation, and control of the information stored in the repository. The CPI Repository Interface defines sets of services to be provided in the SAA environments and the way in which an application program can request these services. At the time of writing, there is only one software product that implements the CPI Repository Interface—*Repository Manager/MVS* that operates in the large-system MVS environment.

A repository, as defined by IBM, potentially has a great many uses in the information systems environment and can be used to store almost any type of information. The initial use to which IBM is putting the repository, and its repository management products, is to store all the information necessary to control the application development process in an Integrated Computer Aided Software Engineering (I-CASE) environment.

We will begin our investigation of the CPI Repository Interface by examining the way in which the Repository Interface views the data stored in the repository.

THREE VIEWS OF DATA

The CPI Repository Interface is built on three views of data. These three views are essentially the same as the three views that are associated with the data stored in relational databases, although slightly different names are used. The CPI Repository Interface defines the following three data views:

- **Conceptual view.** The conceptual view is a global, or repositorywide view of the information stored in the repository. It consists of an entity-relationship model that describes all the information contained in the repository. The entity-relationship model consists of a set of data definitions and data associated with the data definitions (meta-data).
- **Logical view.** A logical view is a subset of the conceptual view. A particular logical view describes the data that a particular program—called a *tool* in repository terminology—has access to. It specifies the way the tool processes the data and how the tool interacts with the user of the tool.
- **Storage view.** The storage view defines the way in which repository information exists in physical storage. The storage view is specific to a particular operating environment and is implementation-dependent.

ENTITY-RELATIONSHIP MODEL

The information stored in the repository is organized using entity-relationship modeling techniques. An *entity-relationship model* describes the data stored in the repository as representing entities and the relationships that exist between them.

An *entity* is anything that can be uniquely identified and about which information can be stored, such as a person, a place, a thing, an event, or even an abstract concept. A *relationship* is an association that exists in the real world between two things. A relationship can exist between two entities, between two relationships, or between an entity and a relationship.

Entities

An *entity type* is a class or group of entities that have the same characteristics. A particular occurrence of an entity is called an *entity instance*. The characteristics associated with an entity type are called *attributes*. Each attribute represents a particular type of information that is stored about an entity. An entity instance consists of the set of attribute values that are associated with a specific entity instance of a given entity type. Figure 10.1 shows a representation of an entity type with its attributes.

Figure 10.1 The SUPPLIER entity type and its attributes.

Each entity type must have one attribute whose values uniquely identify each entity instance. This attribute is called the *key attribute*. In an entity diagram with attributes, the first attribute listed is the key attribute. So in Fig. 10.1, SUPPLIER_NUMBER is the key attribute.

Relationships

A relationship is a connection, or association, between two entities, two relationships, or an entity and a relationship. A *relationship type* is a class or group of relationships that connect members of the same two groups. The groups being connected can be two entity types, two relationship types, or an entity type and a relationship type. An entity type can also be connected to itself, as can a relationship type. Figure 10.2 shows two relationship types. The first, SUPPLIER_ SUPPLIES_PART, is an association between the entity types SUPPLIER and PART. The second, PARENT_USES_COMPONENT, associates the PART entity type with itself. Since a relationship type always represents a connection between two things, it is said to be *binary*. Even when the relationship connects an entity type to itself, the connection is between two entity instances in the entity type and thus is binary.

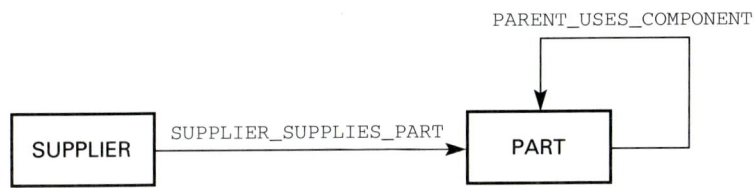

Figure 10.2 Relationship types.

A relationship type is also *bidirectional*. A relationship always has a *primary* direction and an *inverse* direction. For a given direction, a relationship type has a source, where it originates, and a target, where it terminates. The source and target for the primary direction are the target and source, respectively, for the inverse direction. Figure 10.3 illustrates this. The relationship name SUPPLIER_SUPPLIES_ PART corresponds to the primary direction and has SUPPLIER as its source and PART as its target. The relationship name PART_IS_ SUPPIED_BY_SUPPLIER, shown in parentheses, is for the inverse direction and has PART as its source and SUPPLIER as its target.

A *relationship instance* is an association between two instances of an entity or a relationship type. Each relationship instance must be uniquely identified

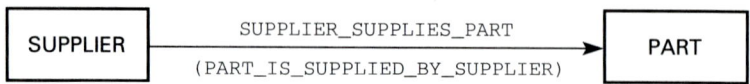

Figure 10.3 Relationship types are bidirectional.

within the relationship type. This is done with the *relationship key*, which consists of the combination of the key of the source instance and the key of the target instance.

The CPI Repository Interface allows certain properties to be defined for a relationship type. These include the following:

- **Instance Control Property.** Describes the relationship between the source and target as one-to-one, one-to-many, many-to-one, or many-to-many.
- **Mandatory Property.** Specifies whether or not the source or target instances can exist independently of the relationship instance.
- **Controlling Property.** Specifies whether deleting a relationship instance automatically triggers deletion of the source and/or target instance.
- **Ordered Property.** Specifies whether the relationship type can be used to retrieve instances of the target type in a sequence other than the key sequence.

Dependent Entities

A *dependent entity type* is a special entity type that allows more than one entity instance to have the same key value. For example, a QUOTATIONS entity type could be defined that represents prices quoted for different parts. However, several parts might have the same price, leading to multiple instances with the same key. To provide a way of uniquely identifying each instance, the QUOTATIONS entity type is made the target of a relationship type, which is called the owning relationship type. The source of the owning relationship type can be either an entity type or a relationship type. The key of the dependent entity type is then combined with the key of the source entity type to provide a unique identifier for each instance.

Figure 10.4 illustrates the dependent entity type QUOTATIONS. Its owning relationship type is SUPPLIER_QUOTES_PRICE_FOR_ PART, and the source for that relationship is the relationship type SUPPLIER_SUPPLIES_PART. The key of QUOTATIONS is then combined with the keys for SUPPLIER_SUPPLIES_PART, which are SUPPLIER_NUMBER and PART_NUMBER. The combined key then uniquely identifies each QUOTATIONS entity instance.

Aggregations

A set of entity types and relationship types can be collectively defined as an *aggregation type*. An aggregation type can group entity and relationship types in a single hierarchical structure. An example of an aggregation type is shown in

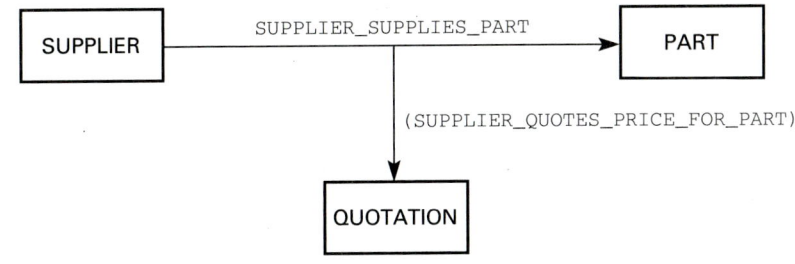

Figure 10.4 Dependent entity types.

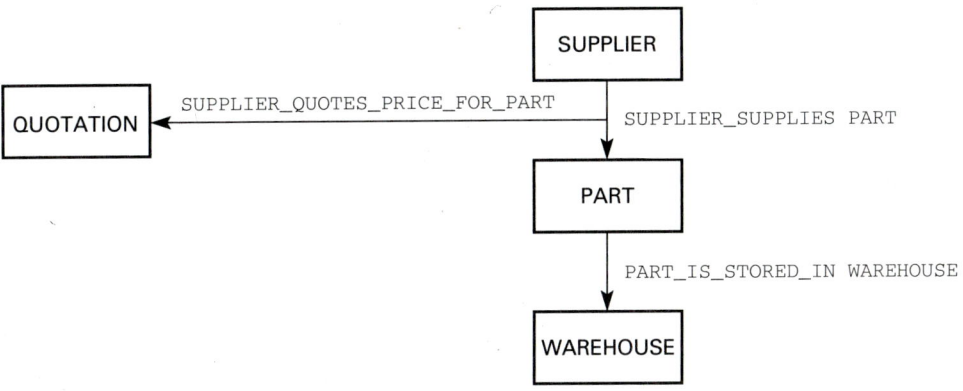

Figure 10.5 Aggregation type.

Fig. 10.5. An *aggregation instance* consists of an instance of the root entity type (SUPPLIER) and all instances of entity types subordinate to the root entity type. Locking can be performed at the aggregation instance level.

Policies

Policies can be defined as part of an entity-relationship model. These policies apply across the entire model. Types of policies that can be defined include:

- **Derivation Policies.** Certain entity attributes can be defined as consisting of values that are derived from other values in the entity-relationship model rather than values that are stored directly. When this is the case, *derivation policies* can specify the conditions for deriving the values and the expressions used in the derivation to create the values.
- **Integrity Policies.** Both entity types and relationship types can have *integrity policies* defined for them. Integrity policies for entity types specify the criteria for determining whether entity attribute values are valid. For relationship types, integrity policies define criteria for creating and deleting relationship instances.

- **Trigger Policies.** Trigger policies cause an action to be taken based on the state of data at a particular point in time. Trigger policies can be associated with either an entity type or a relationship type.

THE REPOSITORY AND AD/CYCLE

The CPI Repository Interface itself does not define any particular entity-relationship model but instead provides facilities that allow the users of the Repository Interface to define their own entity-relationship models. However, the Repository Manager/MVS product that implements the CPI Repository Interface does include a detailed entity-relationship model called the *information model*, which is intended to be used in the I-CASE environment to support application development. A number of I-CASE tool vendors are working in partnership with IBM to implement a detailed architecture called *AD/Cycle*. IBM's key SAA solution in the application development environment is *AD/Cycle*.

As we introduced in Chapter 1, AD/Cycle comprises a set of I-CASE tools, with a development platform, that is designed to enhance the productivity and manageability of the application development process. The AD/Cycle tools support all phases of the application development lifecycle, including requirements gathering, analysis, design, coding, testing and debugging, and maintenance. The development platform is based on the information model that IBM supplies with its Repository Manager/MVS product. The Repository Manager/MVS product, and the information model that it defines, provides services that enable all the various I-CASE tools provided by a variety of vendors to be highly integrated.

At the time of writing, the repository information model and the AD/Cycle strategy are both undergoing extensive development. It is not possible at this time to speculate on how successful IBM's AD/Cycle strategy is likely to be. There are several factors that are working against IBM's initial repository and AD/Cycle strategies.

IBM's initial repository manager implementation operates in the large-system MVS environment, and, thus, the initial orientation of AD/Cycle was to coordinate I-CASE application development using a large-system processor to maintain the repository. At the time of writing, most I-CASE application development tools are designed to operate on personal computers. And the emphasis in many information systems organizations is on moving toward a client-server application environment, in which smaller processors can take over many of the tasks that have traditionally required large-system processors to perform. Therefore, some organizations are beginning to question the long-term viability of an approach to I-CASE that requires a central repository managed by a large-system processor. At the time of writing, about two years after the initial shipment of the Repository Manager/MVS product, very few of its customers are actually using IBM's repository.

However, the concept of the repository has great strategic importance in the I-CASE environment. It is likely that in the future, the CPI Repository Interface may be implemented in other environments so that the AD/Cycle application development framework is not so dependent on large-system processors for its implementation and deployment.

In the remainder of this chapter, we describe the functions that the CPI Repository Interface defines for working with entity-relationship models and for accessing the information stored in a repository.

REPOSITORY FUNCTIONS

A *repository function* is a construct that provides access to repository data and allows it to be processed using repository services. A repository function consists of the following components:

- **Logical Data View.** A *logical data view* describes data used by a repository function. This data can include repository data, data passed to and from other functions invoked by this function, and data used within the repository function. The logical data view consists of a set of structures called *templates*.
- **Nonprocedural Logic.** *Nonprocedural logic* for a repository function consists of policies that have been defined specifically for that function.
- **Procedural Logic.** *Procedural logic* consists of a set of code that has been written in a programming language. Such a set of code is called a *tool program* and performs processing not performed by policies, such as data editing and calculations. A tool program also can include requests for repository services. The programming languages currently supported for writing tool programs are PL/I and C.

TEMPLATES

A *template* defines a block of structured storage used as part of a repository function. The CPI Repository Interface defines the general format used for a template, which contains both data fields and control information. There are different types of templates that are used for different purposes. The different types are described next.

Entity Type Templates

A template can correspond to an entity type. Its data fields then correspond to entity attributes of the entity type. There may be data fields for all or only some of the entity attributes. This type of template is used to access and manipulate repository information. It can be used to access, add, delete, or update entity instances and to add and delete relationship instances.

For a template that maps to a dependent entity type, the template must contain data fields that map to the key attribute of the entity type and also the key attribute or attributes for the source of the owning relationship type. This allows each entity instance being processed to be uniquely identified.

A template array can be defined to process a series of entity instances. The template array consists of a set of identical templates. Each template is an element of the array, and the number of elements comprises the extent of the array. When a template array is used, the specified repository service operates on all the elements in the array.

Parameter Templates

A repository function can call other functions as well as requesting repository services. Data is passed between the calling and called function in the form of parameters, using a parameter template. The calling function and the called function each have a template defined. Fields that have the same name in the two templates are copied from the calling function template to the called function template when the called function is invoked. The fields are copied in the opposite direction when the called function finishes processing and returns control to the calling function.

Working Storage Templates

Template fields can be defined for use as working storage areas by the repository function. These fields are used for local processing and do not map to anything outside the function.

TEMPLATE FORMAT The CPI Repository Interface defines the general format to be used for a template. Box 10.1 describes the components of a template. The initial fields contain control information that is used to specify the action the repository manager is to take and to return status information after the action has been taken. The Repository Interface also defines specific values and their meanings for call return codes and call state indicators. The control information is followed by data fields, which can be either fixed length or variable length.

TEMPLATE TREES Templates that map to entity types can be connected to one another in a hierarchical structure called a *template tree*. Figure 10.6 shows an example of a template tree. The template tree is formed by defining connections between the entity templates. For each template connection between two entity templates, there must be a corresponding relationship type defined that relates the two entity types associated with the templates. A template can be the target of only one template connection, although it can be the source of more than one connection. A template tree can be used to access a

BOX 10.1 Template components.

Control Fields

- **ACODE (Action code).** Represents the action to be taken on the data associated with this template.
- **AQUAL (Action qualifier).** Specifies an option related to the action code when the action can be performed in more than one manner.
- **CSI (Call state indicator).** Indicates the results of the action performed on the template. This field provides more specific information about an error condition generally identified by the call return code.
- **CRC (Call return code).** Indicates the results of the action performed on the template. This field provides a general indication of the results of processing.
- **LOI (Last output index).** When a template array is being used, this field indicates the number of instances retrieved following a retrieve action.

Data Fields

- **FSI (Field state indicator).** Indicates whether a data field has a value assigned to it and whether the value has caused any problem, such as truncation.
- **Length (Current length value).** For a variable-length field, the current length of the field.
- **Value (Field value).** The current value of the field.

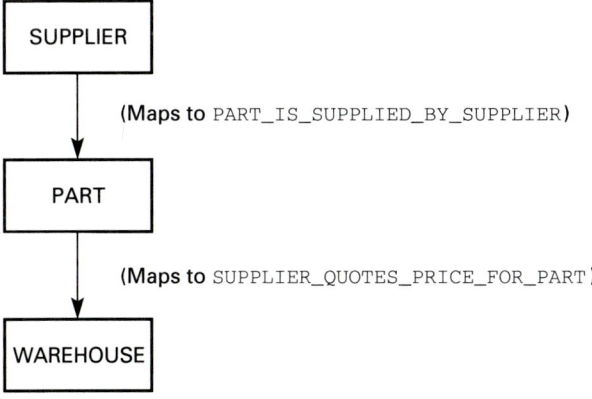

Figure 10.6 Template tree.

set of data in the repository. For example, the template tree shown in Fig. 10.6 could be used to access all parts, and for each part, suppliers that supply that part and price quotations for the part from suppliers that supply that part.

The highest level template is called the *root template*, and lower level templates are called *subordinate templates*. A template that has subordinate templates is called a *parent template*; a template with no subordinates is a *leaf template*. A path in a template tree from the root template to a leaf template is called a *branch*. Template arrays can be included in a template tree but only as leaf templates. Different template trees can be constructed that correspond to the same entity-relationship model by choosing different root templates. This is illustrated in Fig. 10.7.

USING TEMPLATES FOR RETRIEVAL

When a repository function retrieves data, the way in which the data is retrieved depends on the template and whether or not it is part of a template tree. A template has a *domain*, which is the sorted set of entity key attribute values available to the template at a particular point in time. If the template is not part of a template tree, or is the root template, its domain is the set of all entity instances. If the template is a subordinate template in a template tree, its domain is determined by its parent template. The parent template has a cursor whose position is at the most recently retrieved or added entity instance. The domain of the subordinate template is the set of entity instances that are descendants of the parent entity instance pointed to by the cursor.

With the template tree shown at the top of Fig. 10.7, for example, the domain for the SUPPLIER template is the set of all supplier numbers. Once a particular supplier instance has been accessed and is associated with the SUPPLIER cursor, the domain for the PART template is the set of all part numbers supplied by that supplier. For a particular part number supplied by the supplier (pointed to by the PART cursor), the domain of the WAREHOUSE template is all warehouse locations in which the part is stored.

REPOSITORY FUNCTION POLICIES

Policies can be defined as part of a repository function in order to perform nonprocedural logic. These policies apply only when their function operates. Types of policies that can be defined include the following:

- **Derivation Policies.** Derivation policies specify conditions for deriving template field values and the expressions used to derive those values.
- **Integrity Policies.** Integrity policies are defined for template fields. They specify the range of values that the field is allowed to contain.
- **Trigger Policies.** Trigger policies can be associated with templates and repository functions. They cause an action to be taken based on the state of data or logic at a particular point in time.

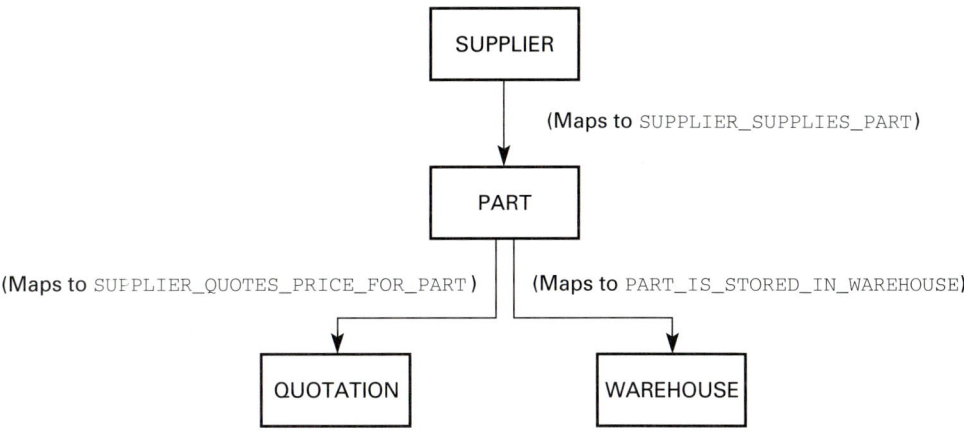

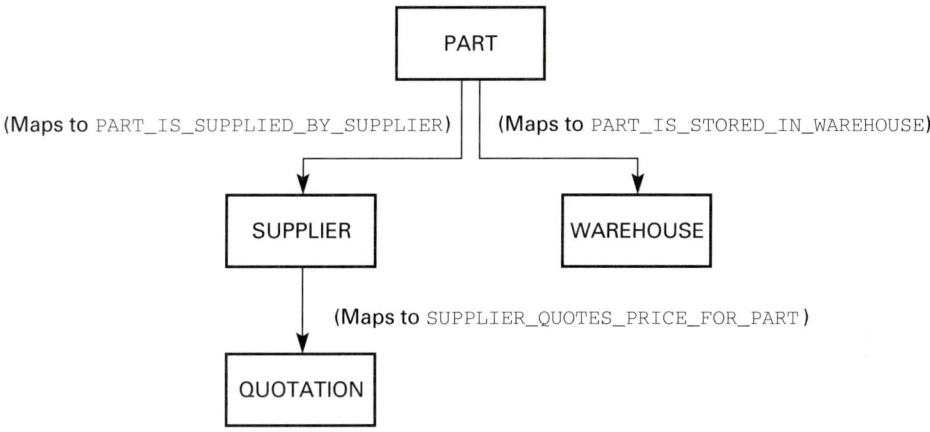

Figure 10.7 Different template trees from the same entity-relationship model.

TOOL PROGRAMS   In addition to templates and policies, a repository function can have procedural logic, in the form of a *tool program*, defined for it. A tool program contains template structures, requests for repository services, calls to other repository functions, and logic for any other processing that needs to be performed.

The template structures correspond to the templates that have been defined for the function. The way in which template structures are defined as part of a tool program is specific to a particular language and operating environment. The CPI Repository Interface does define sets of repository services that a tool program can request and the general syntax used to call these services. It also defines a set of built-in functions that can be called by other functions.

REPOSITORY SERVICES

A repository function uses repository services to perform actions on repository data accessed using one or more templates. There are two general ways in which a function can do this:

- The function may specify a repository service as the action code in an entity template and then call a general repository service routine, passing the template as part of the call.
- The function may call certain repository services directly by calling a specific repository service routine and passing it parameters.

There are two types of repository services defined as part of the CPI Repository Interface: data services and system services. These services are described next.

DATA SERVICES

Data services can be used to add, retrieve, update, or delete an entity instance, using the associated entity template. They can also be used to add or delete a relationship, using two templates that map to the source and the target of the relationship. The particular data service to be performed is specified as the action code in the template control information. In addition, a qualifier may be specified that indicates a particular way in which the action operates. Box 10.2 summarizes the data services defined as part of the Repository Interface.

CALLING DATA SERVICES

The following is an example of the PL/I coding to invoke the repository service to add an entity instance:

```
%INCLUDE SYSLIB(DWK2CONS);
   .
   .
   .
TEMPSUPP.ACODE = ACT_ADD;
TEMPSUPP.AQUAL = QUAL_KEYED;
CALL DWKT1(TEMPSUPP);
SELECT;
   WHEN (TEMPSUPP.CSI = CSI_OK) CALL ADD_OK;
   OTHERWISE CALL ADD_ERR;
END;
```

BOX 10.2   Data services.

Action	Qualifier	Description
ADD	KEYED	(1 template) Adds to the repository the entity instance defined by the template.
ADD	KEYED	(2 templates) Adds a relationship instance to the repository. The first template corresponds to the source and the second template to the target. If the relationship type is ordered, this instance is added after the last instance in the repository.
	AFTER	(2 templates) For a relationship ordered in the target direction, adds the new relationship instance immediately following the relationship instance pointed to by the target template's cursor.
	BEFORE	(2 templates) For a relationship ordered in the target direction, adds the new relationship instance immediately preceding the relationship instance pointed to by the target template's cursor.
DELETE	KEYED	(1 template) Deletes the entity instance identified by the value in the key field in the template. Any relationship instances in which this entity takes part are also deleted.
	UNQUALIFIED	(1 template) Deletes the entity instance that was retrieved by the most recent retrieval operation using this template. Any relationship instances in which this entity takes part are also deleted.
DELETE	KEYED	(2 templates) Deletes the relationship instance whose source is identified by the first template and target by the second template.
	UNQUALIFIED	(2 templates) Deletes the relationship instance corresponding to the two entities most recently retrieved using the two templates.

(Continued)

BOX 10.2 *(Continued)*

FIRST	**KEYED**	Retrieves from the template's domain the entity instance whose key value matches the value in the template key field.
	UNQUALIFIED	Retrieves the first entity instance in the template's domain.
	QUALIFIED	Retrieves the first entity instance in the domain whose key value satisfies the selection expression in the template's selection field.
LAST	**KEYED**	Retrieves from the template's domain the entity instance whose key value matches the value in the template key field.
	UNQUALIFIED	Retrieves the last entity instance in the template's domain.
	QUALIFIED	Retrieves the last entity instance in the domain whose key value satisfies the selection expression in the template's selection field.
NEXT	**UNQUALIFIED**	Retrieves from the domain the entity instance that follows the current template's cursor position.
	QUALIFIED	Retrieves the first entity instance in the domain following the current template's cursor position that satisfies the selection expression in the template's selection field.
PREVIOUS	**UNQUALIFIED**	Retrieves from the domain the entity instance that precedes the current template's cursor position.
	QUALIFIED	Retrieves the first entity instance in the domain preceding the current template's cursor position that satisfies the selection expression in the template's selection field.
UPDATE	**UNQUALIFIED**	Updates the entity instance that was most recently retrieved with this template.

The INCLUDE statement brings in declarations for Repository Interface variables, constants, and entry points. The two assignment statements set the action code and qualifier fields in the TEMPSUPP template. The constant names ACT_ADD and QUAL_KEYED are defined in the declarations brought in by the INCLUDE statement.

The CALL statement specifies DWKT1, which is the name of the repository service routine used for services that use a single template. For services that use two templates, such as adding a relationship instance, the DWKT2 service routine is used. The entity template name is specified following the service routine name.

The SELECT statement is used to check the call state indicator value returned. The Repository Interface defines the possible call state indicator and call return code values that can be returned and the meanings associated with these values. For example, the CSI_OK call state indicator value means that processing completed without error.

SYSTEM SERVICES

System services can be used to call a repository function, dynamically bind and unbind entities to templates, dynamically connect and disconnect two templates, obtain system information, and open or close a repository function. Box 10.3 summarizes the Repository Interface system services. Qualifiers are not used with system services.

BOX 10.3 System services.

- **BIND.** (1 template) Dynamically binds a template to an entity type.
- **BIND.** (2 templates) Dynamically connects two entity type templates together via a relationship type.
- **CALL.** Calls a fully integrated repository function.
- **CLOSE.** Deallocates resources from a nonfully integrated repository function.
- **INFO.** Obtains information from the repository and the operating system.
- **OPEN.** Allocates resources and establishes addressability for a nonfully integrated repository function.
- **UNBIND.** (1 template) Unbinds a dynamically bound template from its entity type.
- **UNBIND.** (2 templates) Deletes a connection between two entity templates.

CALLING SYSTEM SERVICES

The BIND, UNBIND, and CALL system services are invoked in the same way as data services.

The following code example dynamically binds a template to an entity type:

```
INVTEMP.ACODE = ACT_BIND;
CALL DWKT1(INVTEMP);
```

This code example dynamically disconnects two templates:

```
SUPPTEMP.ACODE = ACT_UNBIND;
CALL DWKT2(SUPPTEMP PARTTEMP);
```

This code example calls the DWKADD function:

```
DWKADD.ACODE = ACT_CALL;
CALL DWKT1(DWKADD);
```

When binding or unbinding a template to or from an entity type, the DWKT1 service routine is invoked. When connecting or disconnecting two templates, the DWKT2 service routine is invoked. When the CALL service is invoked, a parameter template rather than an entity template is passed. This template is discussed later in this chapter.

The OPEN, CLOSE, and INFO system services each has its own service routine that is used instead of DWKT1 or DWKT2. Also, rather than passing a template to the service routine, a series of individual parameter fields are passed. The following code example invokes the INFO system service:

```
CALL DWKIN(DWKCRC, DWKCSI, '?DATE', HOLD_DATE_LEN,
     HOLD_DATE, DATE_LEN);
```

Box 10.4 summarizes the parameters that are specified when the INFO, OPEN, and CLOSE system services are called.

BUILT-IN FUNCTIONS

In addition to repository services, the Repository Interface includes a number of built-in functions that can be invoked through the CALL system service. Most of the functions allow actions to be performed on one or more template trees. There is also a function that can be used to lock and unlock an aggregation. Box 10.5 lists the Repository Interface built-in functions.

BOX 10.4 System service parameters.

Service	Service Routine	Parameter
INFO	DWKIN	**CRC-variable.** Variable to receive the CRC value.
		CSI-variable. Variable to receive the CSI value.
		System-value-name. Name of the system-defined variable whose value is to be returned.
		Length. Length of the variable to receive the returned value.
		Receiving-variable. Name of the variable to receive the returned value.
		Length-variable. Name of the variable to receive the length of the returned value.
OPEN	DWKOP	**CRC-variable.** Variable to receive the CRC value.
		CSI-variable. Variable to receive the CSI value.
		Function-name. Name of the repository function to be opened.
		Length. Reserved field for future use.
		Reserved-parameter. Reserved field for future use.
		List-base-pointer. Name of variable to receive the address of the list of template addresses associated with the repository function being opened.
CLOSE	DWKCL	**CRC-variable.** Variable to receive the CRC value.
		CSI-variable. Variable to receive the CSI value.
		Function-name. Name of the repository function to be closed.
		List-base-pointer. Name of variable containing the address of the list of template addresses associated with the repository function being closed.

CALLING A FUNCTION

The CALL system service is used to invoke a built-in function. It can also be used to invoke user-defined functions. The CALL system service is invoked by setting the action code of a parameter template to ACT_CALL and calling the

BOX 10.5   Built-in functions.

- **DWKADD.** Adds entity instances and relationship instances for those templates in a template tree that have a key attribute value supplied.
- **DWKADDR.** Adds relationship instances for those pairs of templates in a template tree that have key attribute values supplied.
- **DWKBRWSB.** Browses all entity instances for all templates in a template tree. Browsing is done in a backward direction, from the last instance to the first for a particular cursor position of the root template.
- **DWKBRWSF.** Browses all entity instances for all templates in a template tree. Browsing is done in a forward direction, from the first instance to the last for a particular cursor position of the root template.
- **DWKDEL.** Deletes entity instances for each template in a template tree, where the key attribute field contains a value. Relationship instances in which the entity instances participate are also deleted.
- **DWKDELR.** Deletes relationship instances for those pairs of templates in a template tree, where the key attribute field in both templates contains a value.
- **DWKFIRST.** Retrieves the first entity instance for each template in a template tree.
- **DWKLAST.** Retrieves the last entity instance for each template in a template tree.
- **DWKNBOT.** Retrieves the next entity instance in each leaf template in a template tree.
- **DWKNDEP.** Retrieves the next descendant instances for the last template in each tree branch that has a template cursor position established.
- **DWKNEXT.** Retrieves the next entity instance in the root template of a template tree and its first set of descendants.
- **DWKNULL.** For template fields that map to entity attributes, sets the template field to null in all templates in a template tree.
- **DWKPDEP.** Retrieves the previous descendant instances for the last template in each tree branch that has a template cursor position established.
- **DWKPREV.** Retrieves the entity instance previous to the current entity instance in the root template and its last set of descendants.
- **DWKULCK.** Requests or releases a lock on an aggregation instance or obtains the lock status of an aggregation instance.
- **DWKUPDT.** Updates entity attribute values for each template in a template tree where the key attribute field contains a value.

service routine DWKT1. The parameter template used can be a parameter template specifically defined for the built-in function. For those built-in functions that process template trees, a universal parameter template named DWKPARM can be used in place of the function-specific template.

Using the Built-in Function Template

The template associated with a built-in function has the same name as the built-in function itself. So, the template for DWKADD—the built-in function used to add entity and relationship instances—also has the name DWKADD. The template for a built-in function contains the same control information fields as an entity template. For the built-in functions involving template trees, the template contains a data field named TMPLNAME that can be used to specify a particular template tree to be processed. The template tree is specified by placing the name of its root template in TMPLNAME. If no template name is specified, the function operates on all template trees associated with the calling function. The following code example shows how the DWKADD built-in function can be invoked using the DWKADD template:

```
DWKADD.ACODE = ACT_CALL;
DWKADD.TMPLNAME = 'SUPPTEMP';
CALL DWKT1(DWKADD);
```

The action code in the template is set to ACT_CALL, and the name of the root template (SUPPTEMP) is stored in the template name field. The call specifies DWKADD as the parameter template being used.

The DWKULCK built-in function, used to lock and unlock aggregation instances, uses the DWKULCK parameter template, which contains the data fields shown in Box 10.6.

Using the DWKPARM Template

The DWKPARM template is a general template that can be used to invoke the built-in functions that process template trees. In addition to the standard control information, the template contains two data fields:

- **DWKFNAME.** This field is used to specify the name of the function being invoked.
- **TMPLNAME.** This field is used to specify the name of the root template in the template tree to be processed. If no name is specified, all template trees associated with the calling function are processed.

The following code example shows the built-in function DWKADD being called with the DWKPARM template:

```
DWKPARM.ACODE = ACT_CALL;
DWKPARM.DWKFNAME = 'DWKADD';
DWKPARM.TMPLNAME = 'SUPPTEMP';
CALL DWKT1(DWKPARM);
```

The name of the function (DWKADD) is stored in DWKNAME, and the root template of the template tree (SUPPTEMP) is stored in TMPLNAME. The call then specifies DWKPARM as the parameter template.

BOX 10.6   DWKULCK parameter template data fields.

- **AGGNAME.** Aggregation type name
- **KEY01.** Root entity instance key 1
- **KEY02.** Root entity instance key 2
- **KEY03.** Root entity instance key 3
- **KEY04.** Root entity instance key 4
- **KEY05.** Root entity instance key 5
- **KEY06.** Root entity instance key 6
- **KEY07.** Root entity instance key 7
- **KEY08.** Root entity instance key 8
- **KEY09.** Root entity instance key 9
- **KEY010.** Root entity instance key 10
- **COMMAND.** Command
- **LOCKTYPE.** Lock type
- **USERID.** Alternate used ID
- **UPDUSR.** Update lock holder
- **DELLKCNT.** Number of delete locks
- **ADDLKCNT.** Number of add locks
- **UPDLKCNT.** Number of update locks
- **NOULKCNT.** Number of noupdate locks
- **NOUPDUSR.** Noupdate lock holders
- **NOUPDCNT.** Noupdate lock count
- **ENTITY.** Entity type name
- **RELATION.** Relationship type name
- **ERRRCODE.** Error code

FULLY INTEGRATED VERSUS NONFULLY INTEGRATED FUNCTIONS

When a function is created, it can be defined as a fully integrated function or a nonfully integrated function. If it is fully integrated, there will be only one tool program associated with the function. The function's definition includes the name of its tool program. The function can be invoked directly, and when it is, its associated tool program is called in and executed. When the tool program executes, addressability to repository data and services is established automatically, and any resources needed by the function are allocated before program initiation. Only fully integrated functions can be invoked using the CALL system service.

A nonfully integrated function can be used by more than one tool program. A tool program using a nonfully integrated function must be invoked directly, rather than being executed when the function is invoked. The program must issue an OPEN system service request for the function in order to establish addressability and allocate resources before issuing any other repository service requests. This makes the function's templates available and its policies active. When function processing is completed, a CLOSE system service request for the function should be issued to deallocate resources.

CPI REPOSITORY INTERFACE FOCUS

The CPI Repository Interface does not address all aspects of accessing a repository. For example, the interface is based on concepts associated with the entity-relationship model that is part of the repository. But the interface does not address how the various elements of the entity-relationship model—entity types, relationship types, aggregations—are defined or modified. It does define a general format for templates but not the process used to define a template, associate a template with an entity type, or define a template tree. It also does not specify the process used to define a repository function or its associated policies.

The focus of the Repository Interface is on the elements that are necessary for building tool programs. It defines the repository services and built-in functions that can be called as part of a tool program and specifies the syntax and data formats used with the various types of calls.

In actually using a repository manager product, such as Repository Manager/MVS, the information defined by the CPI Repository Interface must be supplemented by additional information contained in the documentation for an actual repository manager product.

CONCLUSION

This chapter described the CPI Repository Interface that defines how the data in a repository can be described using an entity-relationship model and how the data in the repository can be accessed. IBM's initial use of the Repository Interface is to help coordinate application development in the I-CASE environment. Chapter 11 begins Part III of this book by describing IBM's strategic architecture for computing networking: Systems Network Architecture.

PART III   **NETWORKING INTERFACES**

11 SYSTEMS NETWORK ARCHITECTURE

IBM's approach to computer networking is described in the Common Communications Support (CCS) component of SAA. As we introduced in Chapter 1, CCS defines services and protocols for computer networking that are based on two network architectures. The first of these is IBM's strategic networking architecture: *Systems Network Architecture* (SNA). The second network architecture on which CCS services and protocols are based is the international standard network architecture built on the *Reference Model for Open Systems Interconnection* (OSI Model) developed by ISO.

IBM's SNA is a proprietary IBM network architecture that is implemented by a wide range of data communication hardware and software products. As an architecture, SNA defines a set of message formats and protocols to which communication products conform. Most of the products that IBM markets for building computer networks conform to the SNA architecture. SNA is the primary network architecture included in the CCS component of SAA and is the architecture that describes IBM's strategic approach to building computer networks using IBM hardware and software products. This first chapter in Part III provides an overview of SNA concepts and facilities.

Many, but not all, of the formats and protocols defined by SNA are included in CCS. The SNA communication facilities that are included in CCS are based on a key SNA element called *Logical Unit Type 6.2* (LU 6.2). Chapter 12 provides an introduction to the terminology and concepts that are specific to the architecture of LU 6.2.

The Common Programming Interface component of SAA defines only one application programming interface for accessing networking facilities—the *CPI Communications Interface*. This API is sometimes called the *Common Programming Interface for Communications* and is abbreviated CPI-C. CPI-C is based on the communication facilities defined by SNA's LU 6.2. CPI-C is described in Chapter 13.

Although CCS defines services and protocols that are based on the OSI model, CPI does not include a standard API for accessing the OSI communication services that are defined by CCS. The details concerning APIs for accessing OSI communication facilities are defined by the actual products that provide OSI communication support. IBM's own OSI communication products implement an API that is based on CPI-C concepts, but the OSI communication product APIs are not identical to CPI-C.

Information on the CCS services and protocols that are based on the OSI model can be found in the two companion volumes to this one that describe the CCS component of SAA [1,2].

We next begin our examination of the SNA network architecture by describing what is meant by an SNA user.

SNA USERS

An SNA *user* is either a person or an application program that employs an SNA network to communicate with some other SNA user. A person interacting with the network through a nonprogrammable terminal is considered to be a user of the network. People often use an SNA network to communicate not with other people but rather to communicate with application programs. Therefore, application programs that communicate over an SNA network are also considered users of the network.

It is becoming increasingly common in the SNA environment for communication to take the form of one application program communicating with another application program, and program-to-program communication is now becoming the most important form of SNA communication. Figure 11.1 illustrates these concepts, with the dashed lines representing logical interconnections that are implemented by the network between various network users.

It is important to realize that SNA users are not themselves known to the network. The characteristics of SNA users are defined outside of the architectural definition of SNA itself.

LOGICAL UNITS

As Fig. 11.1 points out, an important purpose of an SNA network is to implement a *virtual* or *logical* path between users so that they can communicate with one another easily. In order to establish a connection with another user, each user must gain access to the SNA network. SNA defines architectural entities called *logical units* (LUs) that provide points of access through which users interact with the SNA network. A logical unit can be thought of as a *port* or *socket* into which a user plugs. An LU is not a *physical* port or plug but a *logical* one. SNA defines several logical unit types, each identified by a number, provided *transmission capabilities* and a set

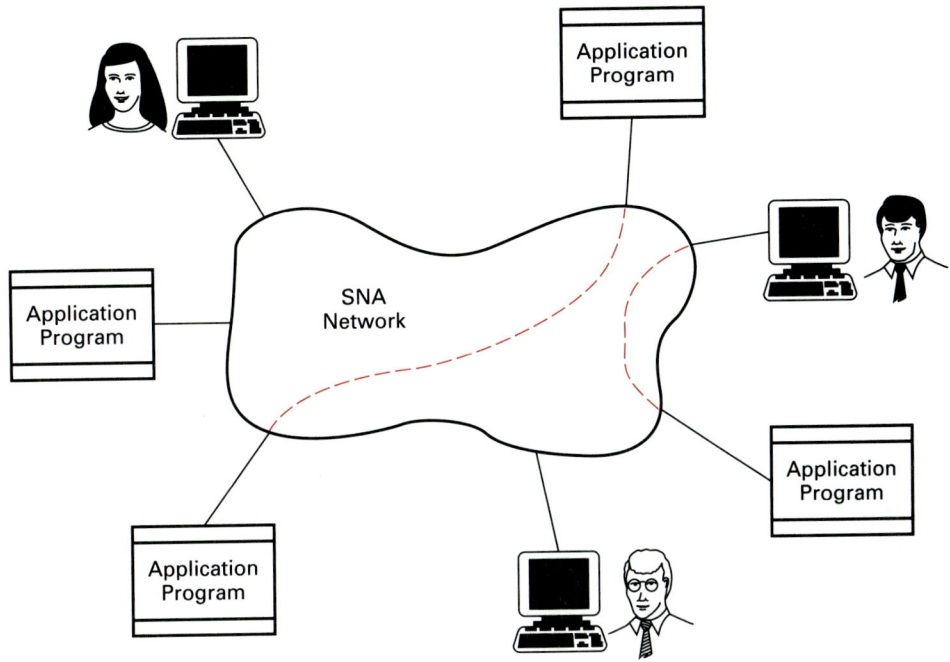

Figure 11.1 An SNA network implements logical connections between pairs of SNA users.

of *services* that are related to a particular type of user. For example, LU Type 2, or LU 2, supports communication between an application program and a user at a 3270-type display, and LU 3 supports communication between an application program and a 3270-type printer.

The Type 6 logical unit has undergone a series of architectural enhancements, and the most recent version of LU 6 is called LU 6.2. As we introduced earlier, the LU type that underlies the SNA communication facilities that are included in SAA is LU 6.2. LU 6.2 is IBM's strategic LU type and is used to support a flexible form of communication between two application programs. LU 6.2 is the only LU type for which support is included in SAA.

Figure 11.2 shows how a logical unit represents a user to the network. A logical unit provides a user with the ability to communicate with another user without one user needing to have detailed information about the other user's characteristics.

LOGICAL UNIT FUNCTIONS
Logical units perform all the functions required to maintain communication between the two SNA users, including the following:

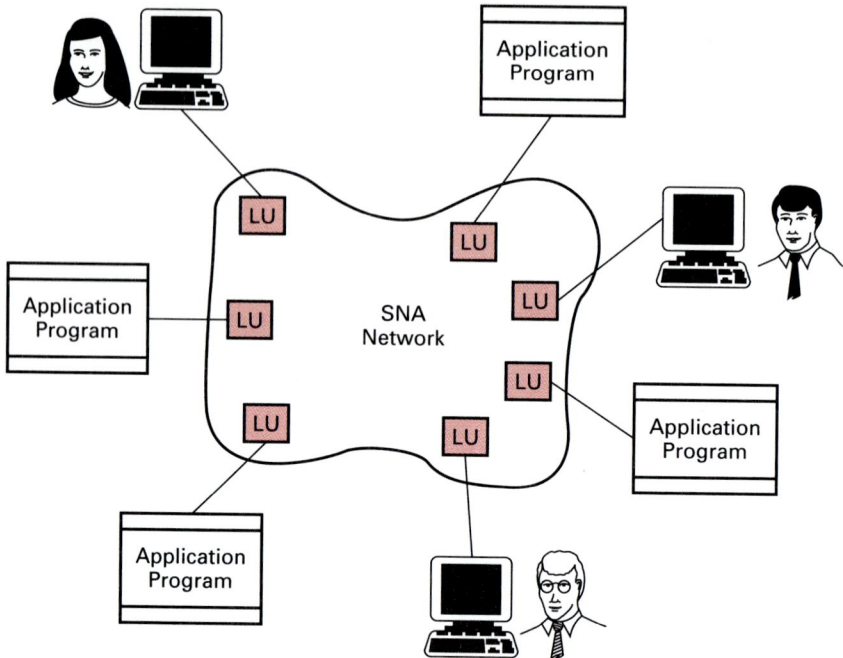

Figure 11.2 SNA logical units provide SNA users with points of access through which they access SNA communication services.

- Locating and loading the programs that are required for communication.
- Sending and receiving data units.
- Recovering from errors.
- Formatting data units appropriately for transmission through the network.
- Formatting and displaying information for their associated SNA users.

SNA users do not have to be concerned with the functions that take place in the network in transmitting data units from one logical unit to another, nor do they need to be aware of the logical or physical structure of the network. Logical units perform all the required functions that are needed to implement data transmission in such a way that the complexity of the network is hidden from the users.

PHYSICAL UNITS To SNA users, an SNA network consists *logically* of logical units that can be interconnected by logical paths that appear as simple point-to-point links between pairs of LUs. But an SNA network consists physically of various types of devices and the communication links that connect them. The devices that typically make up a network are host computing systems of various sizes, communications controllers, terminal controllers, nonprogrammable terminals, and programmable workstations.

Just as SNA users (people and programs) that use the network are not part of the architectural definition of SNA, neither are the actual devices and communication links that are used to implement the network. Instead, SNA defines architectural entities called *physical units* (PUs) to *represent* actual devices to the network. A physical unit provides the services needed to manage and use a particular type of device and to handle any physical resources, such as communication links, that may be associated with it. A physical unit is implemented by some combination of hardware, software, and microcode within the particular device that the physical unit represents.

Like logical units, SNA defines various types of physical units that correspond to network devices having varying levels of capability. Like logical units, each type of physical unit is identified by a number. Three types of physical units, corresponding to three general types of network devices, are used in today's SNA networks. Type 5 physical units are typically implemented in large-system processors, Type 4 physical units are typically implemented in communication controllers, and Type 2 physical units are typically implemented in terminal controllers, midrange systems, and personal computers.

The Type 2 physical unit (PU 2) has undergone various stages of architectural enhancement, and the most recent Type 2 physical unit is called the *Type 2.1 physical unit* (PU 2.1). The SNA protocols that concern the Type 2.1 physical unit are the SNA protocols for which support has been specifically included in SAA.

CONTROL POINTS

In addition to logical units and physical units, SNA also defines architectural entities called *control points* (CPs). A control point provides the services that a network device needs to *manage* the physical resources under its control and to establish and control the interconnections that are necessary to allow network users to communicate. Thus, a control point has a broader function than a logical unit, which represents a single user, or a physical unit, which represents a physical device and its associated resources.

SNA LOGICAL COMPONENTS

The logical components that make up an SNA network can be divided into two major categories, each of which is implemented using hardware, software, and microcode in the devices that make up the network. Figure 11.3 shows the relationships between these two major categories:

- **Network Addressable Units (NAUs).** These consist of logical units, physical units, and control points. NAUs provide the services necessary to move information through the network from one user to another and to allow the network to be controlled and managed. Each network addressable unit has a *network address* that identifies it to the other NAUs in the network.

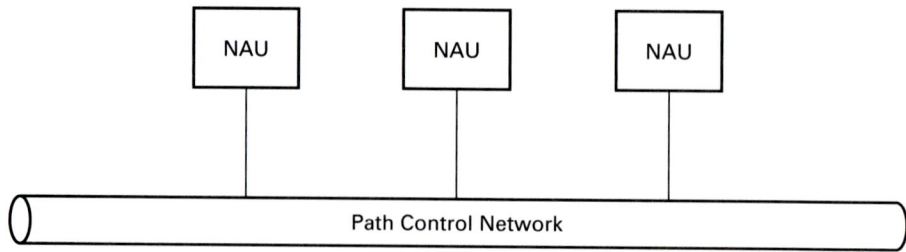

Figure 11.3 SNA logical components are divided into two major categories: network addressable units (NAUs) and the path control network (PCN).

- **Path Control Network (PCN).** These are the lower-level components that control the routing and the flow of data units through the network and handles the physical transmission of data from one device in the network to another.

Now that we have introduced all the various logical components that are implemented in network devices, we can introduce the SNA nodes that constitute the physical building blocks of an SNA network.

SNA NODES

An *SNA node* is defined as a physical point in the network that contains one or more network components. Each node contains both network addressable units and path control network components. Each SNA node corresponds to a physical device and thus contains a single SNA physical unit to represent that device to the network. A node's type corresponds to the type of physical unit it implements. Thus a node containing a Type 5 physical unit is known as a Type 5 node. The node type for which support has been specifically included in SAA is the Type 2.1 node.

If a node implements application programs or terminal devices that offer users access to the network, then the node also contains one or more logical units that correspond to the capabilities of those programs or terminals. Each node in the network also has a control point and a path control network component that together provide the services needed to enable the node to link to and communicate with other nodes.

Figure 11.4 shows how the two categories of SNA logical components are implemented by network nodes. Each terminal, controller, or computing system that conforms to SNA specifications and contains SNA components can be a node in an SNA network. These nodes, along with the transmission links that connect them and any peripheral devices attached to them, are the *physical building blocks* of SNA. They implement the network service and control capabilities required both to operate the network and to handle information exchange between network users.

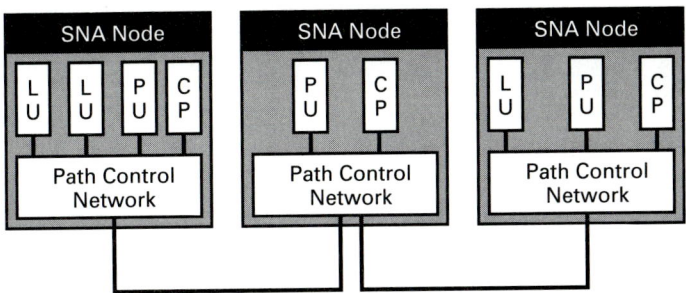

Figure 11.4 SNA network nodes implement both categories of SNA logical components.

SESSIONS

A fundamental SNA concept is that no communication takes place between network addressable units until a *session* is established between them. A session is a logical state that exists between two network addressable units to support a succession of transmissions between them to achieve a given purpose.

Many types of sessions are typically active in an SNA network at any given time. There may be sessions between physical units (PU-PU sessions), sessions between control points and physical units (CP-PU sessions), sessions between control points and logical units (CP-LU sessions), and sessions between logical units (LU-LU sessions). Some types of sessions are permanent and are automatically established when the network is brought into operation; they remain established as long as the network is operational. Other types of sessions are dynamic; they are established as required and are broken when they are no longer needed.

At any given moment in an SNA network, many concurrent sessions are in operation. Many of these separate sessions may share the same physical devices and communication links. For example, a logical unit in a host processor or in a terminal controller might be involved in multiple LU-LU sessions at one time. A logical unit located in a terminal device, on the other hand, normally participates in only one session at a time with another logical unit.

LU-LU SESSIONS

From the point of view of an SNA user, the most important type of session is an LU-LU session that is established between a pair of logical units. This type of session allows the network users that the two LUs represent to communicate with one another. SNA users perceive only LU-LU sessions; all other types of sessions are hidden from users and are used to support LU-LU sessions. In Fig. 11.5, the shaded line represents an LU-LU session that has been established between two application programs.

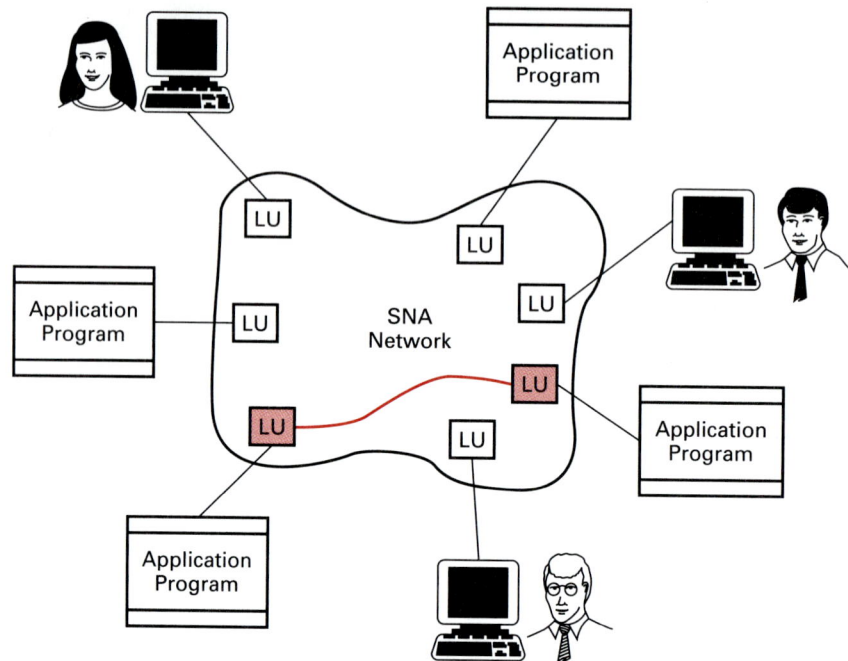

Figure 11.5 An important type of session is an LU-LU session that connects a pair of SNA users.

An LU-LU session is established using a *bind procedure*, in which the two LUs are bound together for the duration of the session. In the bind procedure an SNA command called the BIND command is sent from one LU to the other. During the bind procedure, agreement is reached between the two LUs concerning the characteristics of the session.

LU-LU Session Duration

An LU-LU session sometimes represents a temporary relationship between logical units that exists only as long as two users need to exchange data. LU-LU sessions need remain in operation only for the time needed to handle the communication requirements of their associated SNA users. With such a session, one of the LUs initiates the bind procedure to initiate a session, the two LUs exchange data units for a time, and then one of the LUs terminates the session. A logical unit is free to terminate a session at any time and can then establish a new session with some other logical unit.

An LU-LU session may also be initiated automatically when the network is started and may remain active as long as the network is in operation. This is generally the case with the Type 6.2 logical unit that supports peer-to-peer communication between programs. With a Type 6.2 LU-LU session, one of the LUs initiates the bind procedure as part of network initialization, and the LU-LU session remains active as long as the two LUs are capable of exchanging data. Various pairs of application programs can then use such a session as a resource to support *conversations* between them. Multiple conversations can use an LU-LU session, but they must use it serially, one conversation at a time.

LOGICAL UNIT AND NETWORK USER RELATIONSHIP

The relationship between SNA users and logical units is not necessarily one-to-one. Figure 11.6 shows three possibilities. The diagram at the top shows a single logical unit that represents multiple network users and can be involved in multiple sessions on behalf of those users. The second diagram shows a single application program that uses a single LU to communicate with two other programs at the same time. The diagram at the bottom shows how two logical units can have multiple concurrent LU-LU sessions, called *parallel sessions*, established between them.

SNA NETWORKING FACILITIES

The initial orientation of SNA was to support a hierarchical form of communication in which relatively simple terminals at the bottom of the hierarchy communicated with application programs running in powerful processors at the top of the hierarchy. However, SNA has evolved to also support peer-to-peer communication between pairs of application programs. SNA now includes support for two fundamentally different types of network facilities: hierarchical *subarea networking* facilities and *advanced peer-to-peer networking* (APPN) facilities. The following sections introduce the two major forms of SNA networking.

Subarea Networking Facilities

The networking facilities used to construct a hierarchical SNA network are called *subarea networking* facilities and a hierarchical SNA network is called a *subarea network*. Hierarchical networks are constructed using all three types of nodes that we described earlier: Type 5 host computer nodes, Type 4 communication controller nodes, and Type 2 peripheral nodes. A simple subarea network is shown in Fig. 11.7.

In a subarea network, LUs are normally implemented only in Type 2 and Type 5 nodes. Type 4 nodes provide an intermediate node routing capability that allows an LU in any Type 2 peripheral node to communicate with an LU in any Type 5 node. Limited support is also provided for communication between an LU in one Type 5 node and an LU in another Type 5 node. But subarea networking facilities do not allow an LU-LU session to be set up between one Type 2 node and another Type 2 node.

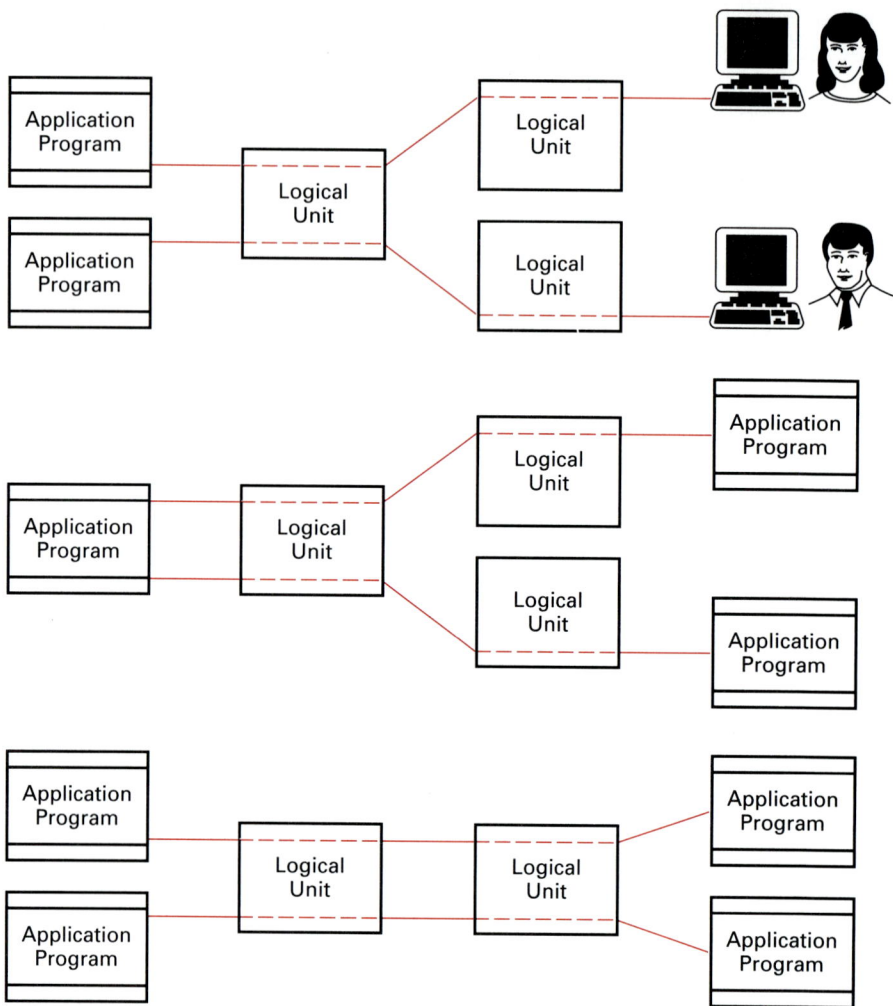

Figure 11.6 The relationship between SNA users and logical units is not necessarily one-to-one.

Advanced Peer-to-Peer Networking Facilities

As midrange systems and personal computers have become increasingly important in the IBM computing environment, the need for interconnecting smaller systems in peer networks has arisen. To meet this need, IBM has extended SNA to allow smaller processors to be interconnected using SNA formats and protocols without requiring the services of the subarea networking facilities implemented by large-system processors and communication con-

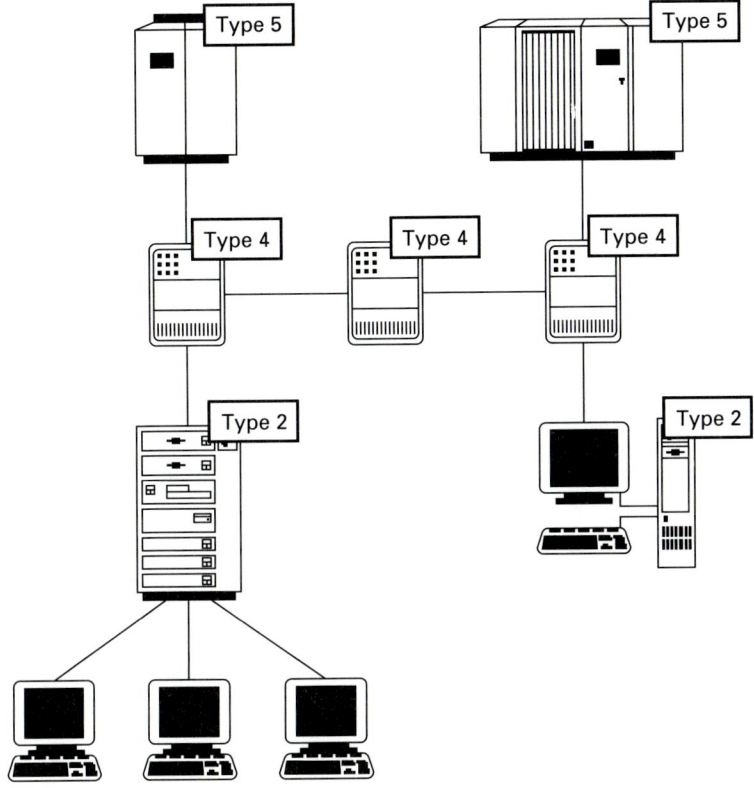

Figure 11.7 A simple hierarchical subarea network.

trollers. The networking facilities that are part of SNA for interconnecting smaller processors in peer networks is called *Advanced Peer-To-Peer Networking* (APPN). A network constructed using APPN facilities is called an *APPN network*. All the nodes in an APPN network are Type 2.1 nodes, of which there are three variations:

- APPN network nodes
- APPN end nodes
- Low entry networking (LEN) nodes

APPN end nodes can automatically configure themselves into an APPN network. To attach a LEN node to an APPN network requires more manual system configuration to be performed. APPN network nodes perform the routing function and can be used as intermediate systems to which APPN end nodes and LEN nodes can be attached. A simple APPN network having all three Type 2.1 node variations is shown in Fig. 11.8.

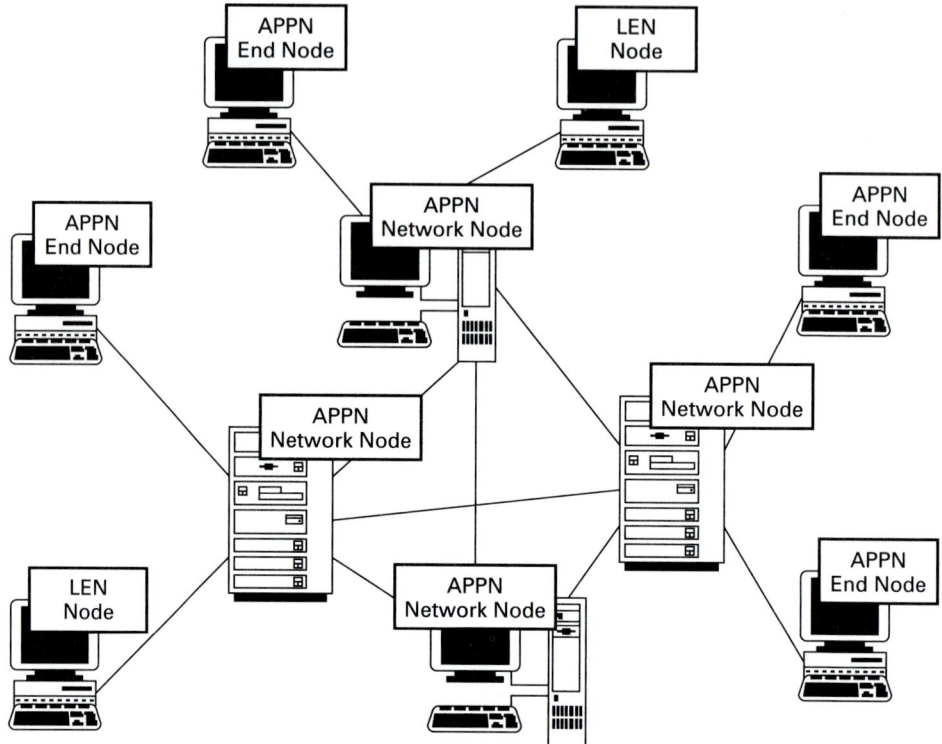

Figure 11.8 A simple peer network using advanced peer-to-peer networking (APPN) facilities.

Hybrid Networks

Each of the two types of SNA network facilities can be used alone, or they can be combined to form hybrid networks. Individual APPN networks can be interconnected using the facilities of a subarea network as a backbone, as shown in Fig. 11.9. Alternatively, individual subarea networks can be interconnected using the facilities of an APPN network as a backbone.

SNA FUNCTIONAL LAYERS

A basic concept underlying all network architectures is the division of network functions into well-defined functional layers. Each functional layer shields the layers above it from the complexities of the layers below. A network architecture defines two aspects of the layering structure:

- **Services.** A given layer is responsible for providing a specific set of *services* to the layer above it. These services define an interface between any two adjacent layers in a particular communicating node, as represented by the vertical arrows in Fig. 11.10.

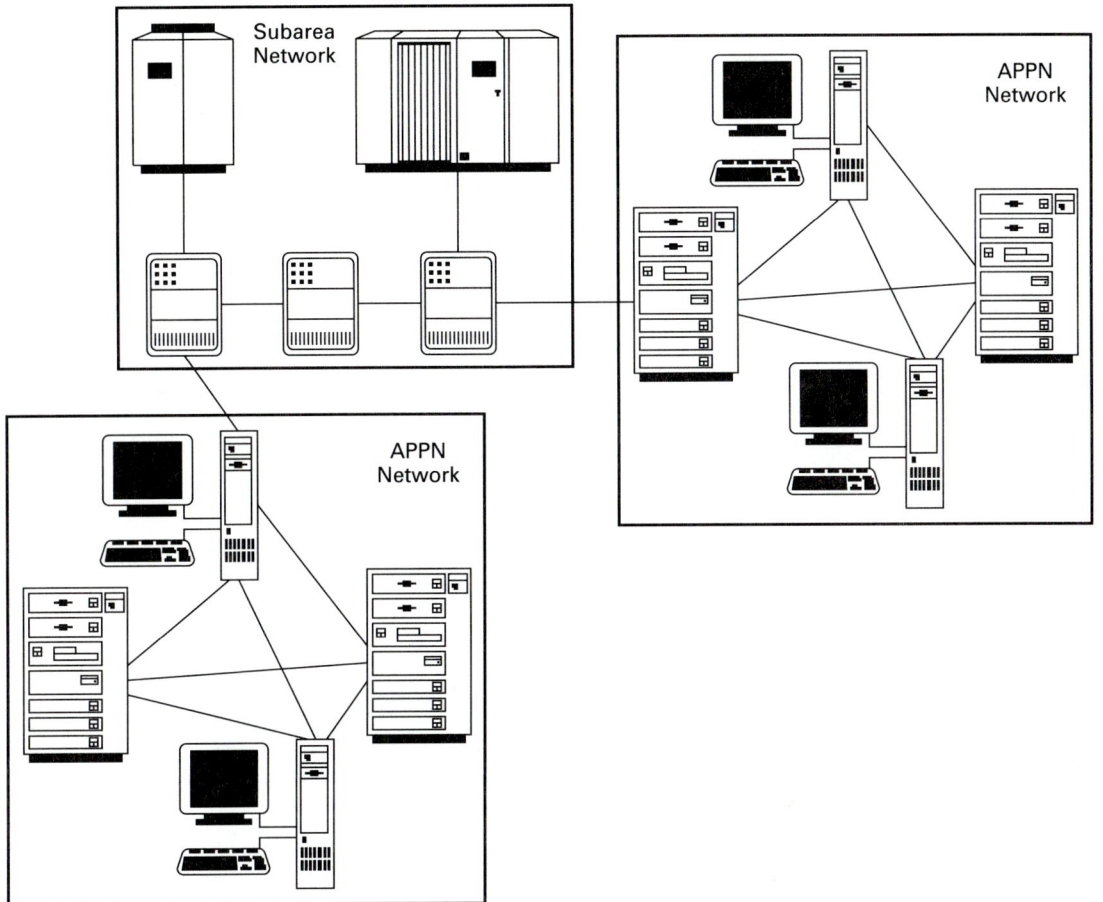

Figure 11.9 The services of a subarea network can be used as a backbone to interconnect two or more APPN networks.

- **Protocols.** *Protocols* are represented by the horizontal arrows in Fig. 11.10. When two nodes communicate, any layer in the first node appears to communicate directly with its complementary (or peer) layer in the second node. Protocols define the rules by which the communication takes place between peer layers in two communicating systems.

Following this principle, the functions of SNA are broken into layers, with each layer providing a different set of services to the layer above it. Figure 11.11 illustrates the seven major SNA functional layers and shows how the SNA functional layers relate to the two major SNA logical component categories, the network addressable units (NAUs), and the path control network. Box 11.1 describes the functions of the seven SNA layers.

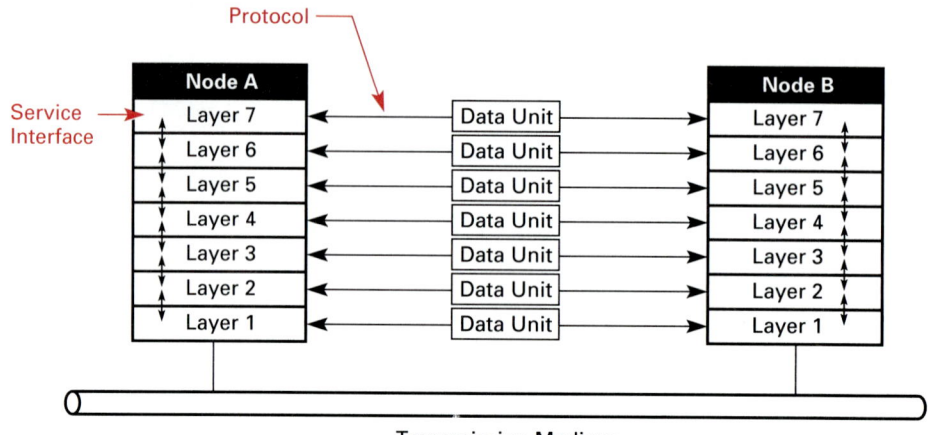

Figure 11.10 Services and protocols.

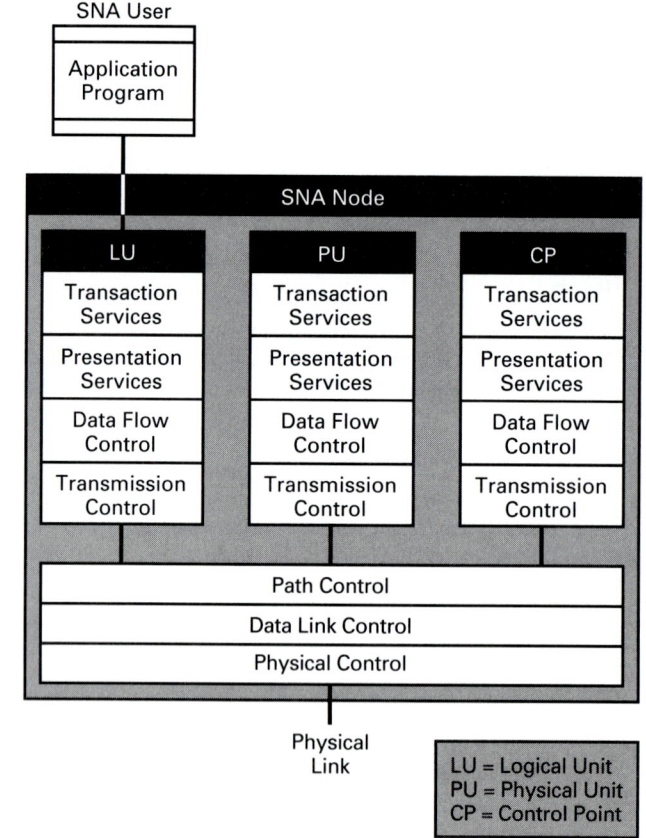

Figure 11.11 Relationship between SNA layers and SNA logical components.

BOX 11.1 SNA functional layers.

- **The Physical Control Layer.** The *Physical Control* layer is concerned with the transmission of streams of bits across a physical circuit. The Physical Control layer does not assign any significance to the bits being transmitted. For example, it has no concern with how many bits make up each unit of data, nor does it have any concern with the meaning of the data being transmitted. Various methods of physical transmission can be employed in an SNA network, including the use of computer channels, telephone lines, satellite links, microwave transmission, and local area network transmission media. The Physical Control layer must deliver bits in the same sequence in which they were submitted and must notify the Data Link Control layer of any faults that are detected.

- **The Data Link Control Layer.** The *Data Link Control* layer is responsible for the transmission of data between two SNA nodes over a particular physical circuit. Major functions of the Data Link Control layer are to manage the flow of data units over the link and to detect and possibly recover from transmission errors.

- **The Path Control Layer.** The *Path Control* layer is concerned with routing data from one node in the network to the next as a data unit moves through the network. A physical path may pass over many separate links through several nodes. Path Control layer functions include determining the next node in the path and the data link to use to reach it. Path Control can also segment a data unit if necessary before it is sent over the link and then reassemble it, and it can combine multiple data units for transmission as a block.

- **The Transmission Control Layer.** The *Transmission Control* layer keeps track of the status of sessions that are in progress, controls the pacing of data flow within a session, and sees that the data units sent within a session are all received in the proper sequence. The Transmission Control layer also defines an optional data encryption/decryption facility that can be used to implement security protection facilities.

- **The Data Flow Control Layer.** The *Data Flow Control* layer is concerned with the overall integrity of the flow of data during a session between two network addressable units. This involves assigning sequence numbers to data units, determining the way in which sending and receiving is to be coordinated, determining the types of response that are required to requests that are received by a node, and grouping data units into logical units of work using entities called *chains* and *brackets*.

(Continued)

BOX 11.1 *(Continued)*

- **The Presentation Services Layer.** The *Presentation Services* layer is responsible for formatting session data for different presentation media. This layer is also responsible for coordinating the sharing of resources through a synchronization process and for loading, invoking, and processing the programs that are required for communication over Type 6.2 LU-LU sessions. SNA users interface with the Presentation Services layer when requesting services directly of a logical unit.

- **The Transaction Services Layer.** The *Transaction Services* layer is the layer in which programs called *service transaction programs* operate. A service transaction program is a component whose functions are architecturally defined and that performs services for certain types of SNA users. Service transaction programs perform such functions as operator control of LU-LU sessions, document distribution and interchange, and distributed file and database access. An SNA user can request the services of a service transaction program that runs in the Transaction Services layer, or it can request the services of the Presentation Services layer directly, thus bypassing the Transaction Services layer. The Transaction Services layer also provides a set of configuration services for activating and deactivating SNA resources, session services for controlling the operation of sessions, and management services for managing overall network operation.

Path Control Network Layers

The Physical Control, Data Link Control, and Path Control layers are implemented in the path control network components of an SNA node. These layers are responsible for implementing protocols that handle the transmission of data units from node to node along the path the data unit takes through the network.

Network Addressable Unit Layers

The Transmission Control, Data Flow Control, Presentation Services, and Transaction Services layers are implemented within network addressable units. These layers are responsible for implementing those protocols that are concerned with *end-to-end transmission* of data units between a pair of network addressable units. The way in which the path control network implements the virtual circuit, which often consists of multiple physical connections, is transparent to the layers in the network addressable units.

Service Transaction Programs

The actual services of a logical unit are performed by the Presentation Services, Data Flow Control, and Transmission Control layers. An SNA user can interact with the logical unit directly, in which case the user makes requests of the Presentation Services layer. Alternatively, a user can request the services of an intermediary called a *service transaction program* that runs in the Transaction Services layer. The service transaction program then requests LU services on behalf of the user. Figure 11.12 illustrates how a user can request the services of a logical unit on either of these two levels.

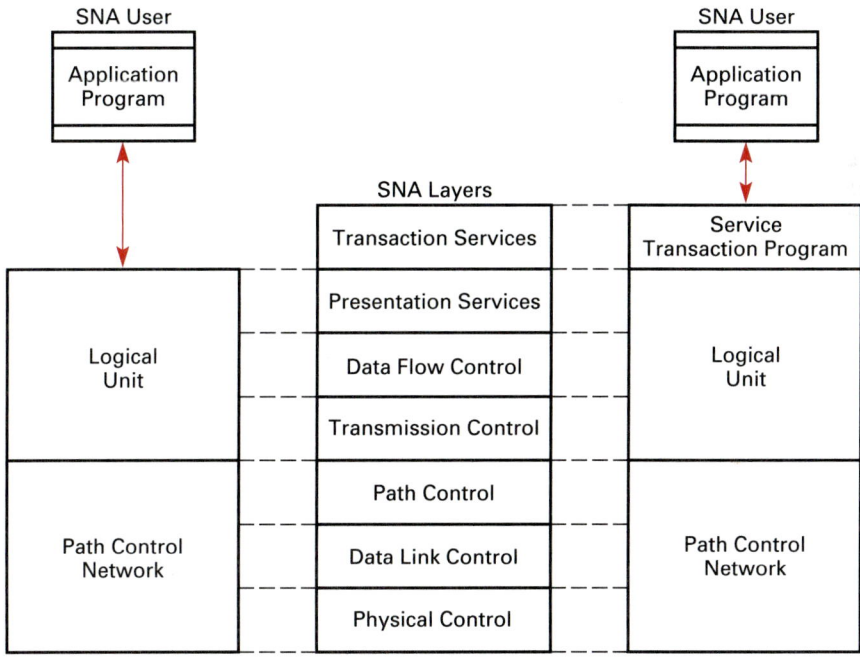

Figure 11.12 SNA logical unit communication services can be requested on two levels.

The set of services that a particular service transaction program provides to a user is architecturally defined. An example of an SNA service transaction program is an implementation of the Distributed Data Management (DDM) architecture that provides SNA users with access to the data in distributed files and databases.

CONCLUSION

SNA is IBM's strategic approach to computer networking and is the primary network architecture for which support is included in SNA. SNA includes subarea networking facilities for constructing hierarchical networks using large-system processors and advanced peer-to-peer networking facilities for constructing peer networks of smaller processors. The SNA formats and protocols that are specifically addressed by SAA are those formats and protocols that concern the LU 6.2 and the Type 2.1 node.

Chapter 12 describes in more detail the terminology and facilities that are associated with Logical Unit Type 6.2.

REFERENCES

1. James Martin, Kathleen Kavanagh Chapman, and Joe Leben, *Systems Application Architecture: Common Communications Support: Distributed Applications.* Prentice-Hall, Englewood Cliffs, NJ, 1992.

2. James Martin, Kathleen Kavanagh Chapman, and Joe Leben, *Systems Application Architecture: Common Communications Support: Network Infrastructure.* Prentice-Hall, Englewood Cliffs, NJ, 1992.

12 LOGICAL UNIT 6.2 ARCHITECTURE

As we introduced in Chapter 11, LU 6.2 is IBM's strategic SNA logical unit type and is the only LU type for which support is specifically included in SAA. All of IBM's new equipment and software designed for creating distributed computing applications provides an implementation of LU 6.2.

The logical unit types defined by earlier versions of SNA were oriented toward communication between application programs and terminals. They defined communication protocols oriented to simple, hierarchical forms of communication between a large-system processor and simpler terminal devices. With these LU types, communication typically operates in a master/slave fashion, where one of the communicating partners has greater responsibility for error recovery. LU Type 6.2 supports a more general-purpose, program-to-program protocol that avoids many of the limitations associated with the terminal-oriented LU types. With LU 6.2, there is symmetry of operation, in which both of the communicating applications are given equal control and may both share responsibility for error recovery processing.

The LU 6.2 architecture defines the semantics of a set of architected communication services that can be invoked in a standard manner by cooperating application programs and can be used for communication over an SNA network.

LU 6.2 FUNCTIONS To support distributed computing applications, LU 6.2 provides capabilities in three major functional areas:

- **Communications.** The primary goal of LU 6.2 is to provide the ability for programs to communicate in a standardized manner across an SNA network.
- **Distributed Error Recovery.** LU 6.2 communications is particularly well suited to distributed transaction processing that typically involves the control and coordination of resources that are distributed across a network. When failures

occur, it is important to be able to restore affected distributed resources to their original states and to resume communications from the point of failure. LU 6.2 provides protocols that address this type of error recovery processing.

- **Resource management.** LU 6.2 provides services necessary for managing the distributed resources that are used in implementing distributed transaction processing systems.

LU 6.2 VERSUS APPC

Logical Unit 6.2 (LU 6.2) is the formal name of the architecture that describes the logical unit type that is used to provide peer-to-peer, any-to-any connectivity in the SNA environment. *Advanced Program-to-Program Communication* (APPC) is a related term that is often used to describe the function of an implementation of the LU 6.2 architecture. The term Advanced Program-to-Program Communication and the acronym APPC are also sometimes used in the names of IBM software products that implement the LU 6.2 architecture. For example, *APPC/PC* is the name of an IBM software product for personal computers running the DOS operating system that provides LU 6.2 communication services in the personal computer environment.

ARCHITECTURAL LAYERS

As we saw in Chapter 11, SNA users are often application programs that use the services of the SNA network to communicate with other application programs. The LU 6.2 architecture has a transaction processing orientation, and the LU 6.2 architecture typically uses the term transaction program to refer to the programs that are communicating across the network using LU 6.2 facilities. Transaction programs are the programs that users employ to solve specific business problems or to achieve some business objective.

An SNA network can be used for something as simple as a file transfer from a mainframe to an intelligent workstation, or it can be used for something as complex as a distributed system having many transaction programs on many interconnected processors all communicating with one another to handle a complex user application.

As we introduced in Chapter 11, an SNA logical unit implements three layers of SNA (see Fig. 12.1):

- Presentation Services
- Data Flow Control
- Transmission Services

The path control network below the LU implements another three layers of SNA:

- Path Control
- Data Link Control
- Physical Control

The functions that the layers of the path control network perform are transparent to an LU 6.2 implementation. The LU requests services of the path control network in routing data from a source computing system to a destination computing system.

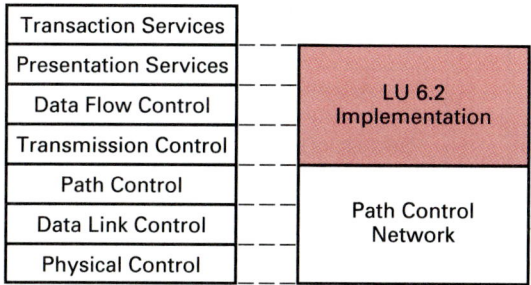

Figure 12.1 SNA architectural layers.

INTERFACING WITH LU 6.2

Figure 12.2 reviews the two methods by which an application program can request the services of an LU 6.2 implementation. One way that an application program can access an LU 6.2 implementation is shown on the left in Fig. 12.2. Here, the program directly requests the architected services that the LU 6.2 implementation provides. This interface takes place at the Presentation Services layer of SNA.

Alternatively, as shown on the right in Fig. 12.2, a program can interface with an architected service transaction program which, in turn, requests the services of an LU 6.2 implementation on behalf of the user program. An architected service transaction program runs in the Transaction Services layer of SNA. Examples of architected service transaction programs that are available are implementations of the following SNA-related architectures:

- SNA Distribution Services (SNADS)
- Document Interchange Architecture (DIA)
- Distributed Data Management (DDM)

IBM intends for LU 6.2 to be the communications base for what will eventually become a distributed operating system. Service transaction programs running on top of LU 6.2 will provide common services across dissimilar operating systems.

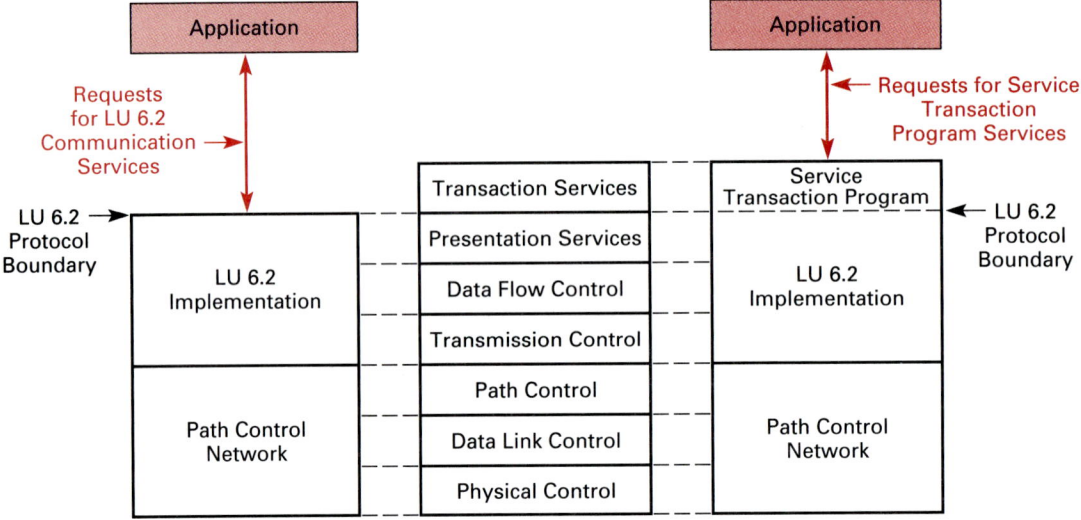

Figure 12.2 Two methods of invoking LU 6.2 services.

For example, a user will be able to request a file transfer in the same manner regardless of what type of processors are involved at the source and the destination of the file transfer.

ARCHITECTED PROTOCOL BOUNDARY

The requirement for any-to-any connectivity necessitates a standardized *protocol boundary* so that all application programs request LU 6.2 communication services in the same manner. The LU 6.2 protocol boundary sets standards for

- How the application program requests a particular service of an LU 6.2 implementation.
- How the LU 6.2 implementation delivers that service to the application program.

The protocol boundary is defined in terms of two things:

- **Protocol Boundary Verbs.** LU 6.2 protocol boundary verbs represent all the LU 6.2 communication functions that an application program can request. For example, a protocol boundary verb named MC_SEND_DATA defines a function that an application program can invoke to send data to another application program.
- **Protocol Boundary States.** These represent all the allowable conditions that can exist at the protocol boundary. These states determine which of the protocol boundary verbs a program is allowed to issue while the protocol boundary remains in a particular state.

PROTOCOL BOUNDARY VERB SEMANTICS VERSUS PROGRAMMING SYNTAX

The LU 6.2 architecture defines the *semantics*, or *meaning*, of each protocol boundary verb. But it does not define any particular programming syntax that must be used to implement the verbs.

Some implementations of LU 6.2 define commands or routines that have names that are the same or similar to the names of the LU 6.2 protocol boundary verbs. On the other hand, other implementations of LU 6.2 implement commands or routines that have different names than the LU 6.2 protocol boundary verbs. Later in this chapter, we will see how the LU 6.2 protocol boundary verbs are implemented by some commonly used LU 6.2 implementations.

CONVERSATIONS

An LU-LU session is used to connect Type 6.2 LUs with one another. Application programs use *conversations* to communicate with one another. A conversation employs an LU-LU session between the two logical units that represent the communicating programs. However, a conversation is much simpler conceptually than an LU-LU session. Transaction programs view only the conversation itself, and the complexities involved in coordinating communication over the underlying LU-LU session used to support the conversation is hidden from the transaction programs.

Once an LU-LU session is started to connect two Type 6.2 LUs, the session ordinarily remains active until it is terminated by a network operator or by some system process. However, a conversation uses an LU-LU session as a resource only for the duration of a conversation. Once a conversation completes, the session that it used is freed-up for use by some other conversation.

Only one conversation at a time can use a particular session between two LUs. If there must be multiple conversations active between two LUs at the same time, then there must be multiple parallel sessions active between the two LUs, one session for each active conversation.

APPLICATION PROGRAM VIEW OF LU 6.2

As we have described, application programs that communicate over an LU 6.2 conversation view only the conversation itself; they are isolated from the underlying session that is used to support the conversation. The application programs view only the LU 6.2 protocol boundary and are not aware of the SNA data flows that take place in implementing the conversation. One application program talks directly to another application program over an LU 6.2 conversation by issuing implementations of the LU 6.2 protocol boundary verbs.

A conversation that connects two application programs is similar to a phone call. All you need to know is the number of the person you're calling in order to conduct a conversation. There is no need to understand anything about how the telephone network operates. In a similar manner, an application program needs to know only the name of the partner application program and the name of the LU at which the partner application program is located. There is no need to know anything about the session that is established between the LUs. Nor is there any need to know anything about the structure of the underlying communication network that is used to implement the session between the LUs.

SYNCHRONIZATION

With information systems that employ distributed transaction processing techniques, the resources that are required to process a particular transaction can be distributed throughout the network. A number of separate application programs, all of which may be running on different machines, may work cooperatively in performing the required processing. In such systems, synchronization capabilities are particularly important. LU 6.2 offers three levels of capability for synchronization processing:

- **No Synchronization.** The logical unit provides no synchronization services.
- **Confirm Synchronization.** A definite response is required by each cooperating program after that program has completed the processing of a transaction. This allows all application programs to agree that processing has been completed without error. At this level, any error recovery is the responsibility of the programs that are involved in processing a transaction.
- **Syncpoint Synchronization.** Certain resources are defined to the logical unit as *protected*. The LU is then responsible for the commitment of changes to these protected resources. If an error occurs at any time during the processing of a transaction, it is the responsibility of the LU to automatically back out any changes that were made to protected resources during the processing of the transaction. A resynchronization capability is also provided to handle failures that occur during synchronization processing. The two LUs exchange information on the status of protected resources at the time of the failure and then perform the processing necessary to restore the resources to a synchronized state. LU 6.2 syncpoint synchronization provides a similar type of commit and backout capability as that defined by the CPI Resource Recovery Interface described in Chapter 9.

PARALLEL SESSIONS

LU 6.2 defines, as an option, the use of multiple sessions between the same two logical units. Multiple sessions between the same logical units are called *parallel sessions*. Some implementations of LU 6.2 support only a single-session environment; others support parallel sessions.

In a single-session environment, only one conversation can be active at a time between two logical units, and all conversations between the logical units share the same session. If a transaction program attempts to start a conversation, the conversation is allocated if the session is available. If the session is busy, either the transaction program is informed that it should try again later or it waits until the session is available, at which time the conversation is allocated.

In a parallel-session environment, a new conversation can always be allocated if there is a session available. If no session is available, it may still be possible to allocate a conversation by starting a new session. A new session will be created if the number of sessions between the two logical units has not reached an implementation-defined maximum session limit.

SESSION MODE SETS

Parallel sessions are placed into groups called *session mode sets*. Each session mode set generally corresponds to some set of performance characteristics that are chosen by the user. For example, suppose the following three session mode sets have been defined:

- **Mode Set 1.** Sessions that use terrestrial links for fast response applications.
- **Mode Set 2.** Sessions that use satellite links for high throughput applications.
- **Mode Set 3.** Sessions that use secure links for sensitive applications.

Each application program must specify the name of the mode set from which the session should be chosen when it attempts to allocate a conversation. LU 6.2 will then choose a session only from the group in the requested mode set. If all the sessions in a mode set are busy, LU 6.2 will not attempt to choose an available session from another mode set. All sessions within a particular session mode set must have similar characteristics, including the same highest synchronization level, security support, class of service, and maximum data unit size.

GENERALIZED DATA STREAM

Implementations of LU 6.2 carry data over the network in the form of an SNA data stream called a *Generalized Data Stream* (GDS). The units of data that are carried in a Generalized Data Stream take the form of blocks of data, called *GDS variables*, that are formatted as shown in Fig. 12.3.

Each GDS variable begins with a 2-byte length field followed by a 2-byte ID field. The first bit of the length field serves as a continuation flag that allows a large logical record to be carried in multiple GDS variables. Each architecture defined by IBM that uses the GDS format is assigned one or more ID field values

Figure 12.3 General Data Stream (GDS) variable format.

to allow the data associated with one architecture to be distinguished from the data associated with the others. Box 12.1 lists some of the GDS ID values that are used by the LU 6.2 architecture.

BOX 12.1   Common LU 6.2 GDS variable uses.

GDS ID	Type of Data
X'1210'	Change Number of Sessions
X'1211'	Exchange Log Names
X'1213'	Compare States
X'12A0'	Workstation Display Passthrough
X'12E1'	Error Log
X'12E2'	PIP Subfield Data
X'12F1'	Null Structured Field
X'12F2'	User Control Data
X'12F3'	Map Name
X'12F4'	Error Data
X'12F5'	PIP
X'12FF'	Application Data

MAPPED AND BASIC CONVERSATIONS

LU 6.2 supports two types of conversations: *mapped* conversations and *basic* conversations. Application programs that use LU 6.2 communication facilities generally work with mapped conversations. Basic conversations are typically used only by special-purpose system programs. The characteristics of both mapped and basic conversations are described next.

Mapped Conversations

With mapped conversations, application programs work only with application data and are not concerned with formatting the data stream that is required for communication. In a mapped conversation, LU 6.2 facilities automatically format the application data using the GDS syntax and provide the necessary header information. The application data is then extracted by LU 6.2 facilities from the GDS variables and is passed to the receiving program in its original form.

Basic Conversations

With a basic conversation, a sending program must itself format the data to be transmitted in the form of GDS variables containing the proper header information. A receiving program must then be able to interpret the GDS header information in order to extract the application data from the GDS variables in the data stream. Programs that use basic conversations are typically specialized system programs, written in assembler language, that have a requirement for manipulating the information contained in the GDS variable headers.

LU 6.2 PROTOCOL BOUNDARY

As we have already introduced, LU 6.2 specifies a *protocol boundary* that defines, in a standardized manner, the semantics of the LU 6.2 communication services that programs can request. The protocol boundary defines a set of architected communication services that are described in terms of a set of *protocol boundary verbs* with their associated parameters. Although we have now seen that the protocol boundary verbs do not constitute a set of programming language commands that an actual program issues, we often describe them as if they were programming language commands in describing the way programs invoke the LU 6.2 architected services in performing communication functions.

The standardization of the LU 6.2 protocol boundary allows application developers that are designing and coding distributed transaction processing systems to design these systems based on the common functions that LU 6.2 makes available. During the design phases of a distributed application, designers need not be concerned about differences between particular products or with their ability to communicate with each other across a network. The LU 6.2 protocol boundary provides a common conceptual basis upon which to design a distributed system.

For those who are responsible for implementing products that provide an application programming interface (API), the LU 6.2 protocol boundary verbs specify the facilities that the product must offer if it is to be considered an implementation of LU 6.2.

LU 6.2 FUNCTIONAL INTERFACES

The LU 6.2 protocol boundary comprises several functional interfaces. Each functional interface is defined by a different set of protocol boundary verbs.

Conversation Verbs

One functional interface consists of a set of conversation verbs. These are divided into three groups:

- Basic conversation verbs
- Mapped conversation verbs
- Type-independent verbs

Basic conversation verbs and mapped conversation verbs are similar and are used to perform essentially the same functions. As we have seen, mapped conversation verbs perform data stream formatting, while basic conversation verbs assume that the application program performs the data stream formatting. Type-independent verbs are verbs that can be issued by an application program that is participating in either a mapped or a basic conversation. User transaction programs typically issue only type-independent verbs and mapped conversation verbs.

Box 12.2 lists the functions of the conversation verbs and the type-independent verbs and shows how the verbs can be grouped into categories according to their functions.

Conversations are created by stringing together an appropriate sequence of the protocol boundary verbs to perform a given application function. Simple conversations can be created using only verbs from the first three categories. More complex conversations can be created by adding conversation synchronization verbs. Still more complex conversations can be created by adding verbs from the remaining three categories.

Control Operator Verbs

The control operator verbs are used in controlling certain aspects of the sessions established between two logical units. The control operator verbs are listed in Box 12.3. These verbs include functions for controlling the number of sessions supported for a particular logical unit, for activating and deactivating LU-LU sessions, and functions for allowing access to system definition parameters for the local logical unit. Control operator verbs are not typically used in application programs, and many implementations of LU 6.2, including the CPI Communications Interface, do not provide the capabilities for performing control operator verb functions.

SAMPLE CONVERSATIONS The architected services defined as part of the LU 6.2 protocol boundary support a number of different types of conversation flows. The following sections provide examples of the data exchanges that take place during the operation of three simple LU 6.2 conversations. The conversation flows are described using the LU 6.2 protocol boundary verbs and do not reference any particular application programming interface that is being used to request the LU 6.2 services.

ONE-WAY CONVERSATION WITH NO CONFIRMATION Figure 12.4 shows an example of a conversation flow that implements a simple one-way conversation with no confirmation in which a single data record is sent from Program X to Program Y. The following are the steps involved in carrying out the conversation:

BOX 12.2   LU 6.2 conversation verbs.

Allocating and Deallocating Conversation

- **ALLOCATE and MC_ALLOCATE.** Used to allocate a conversation with a remote program.
- **DEALLOCATE and MC_DEALLOCATE.** Used to terminate a conversation.

Sending Data

- **SEND_DATA and MC_SEND_DATA.** Used to cause data to be sent over a conversation to the remote program.
- **FLUSH and MC_FLUSH.** Used to cause data being held in the LU's send buffer to be transmitted.

Receiving Data

- **RECEIVE_AND_WAIT and MC_RECEIVE_AND_WAIT.** Used to wait until data arrives and then to receive the data.
- **PREPARE_TO_RECEIVE and MC_PREPARE_TO_RECEIVE.** Used to cause a program to change from the send state to the receive state.
- **POST_ON_RECEIPT and MC_POST_ON_RECEIPT.** Used to request posting of a conversation when data or other information is available to be received.
- **RECEIVE_IMMEDIATE and MC_RECEIVE_IMMEDIATE.** Used to receive data that is immediately available but does not wait for data to arrive.
- **TEST and MC_TEST.** Used to determine whether a conversation has been posted or whether a request-to-send notification has been received.
- **WAIT.** Used to wait for posting to occur on any conversation from among a list of conversations.
- **CONFIRM and MC_CONFIRM.** Used to send confirmation requests to a remote program to determine if the program has successfully received data.
- **CONFIRMED and MC_CONFIRMED.** Used to send confirmation replies in response to CONFIRM or MC_CONFIRM.

(Continued)

BOX 12.2 *(Continued)*

- **PREPARE_FOR_SYNCPT and MC_PREPARE_FOR_SYNCPT.** Used to cause the protected resources associated with the conversation to be prepared to advance to the next synchronization point.
- **SET_SYNCPT_OPTIONS.** Changes the options that govern the operation of the SYNCPT, BACKOUT, PREPARE_FOR_SYNCPT, and MC_PREPARE_FOR_SYNCPT verbs.
- **SYNCPT.** Used in conjunction with various parameters on other verbs to advance all protected resources to the next synchronization point.
- **BACKOUT.** Used in conjunction with various parameters on other verbs to restore all protected resources to their status as of the last synchronization point.

Notifying The Partner Program that an Error Has Occurred

- **SEND_ERROR and MC_SEND_ERROR.** Used to inform the remote program that an error has occurred. The program issuing the SEND_ERROR or MC_SEND_ERROR is placed in the send state and the remote program is placed in the receive state.

Requesting Permission to Send

- **REQUEST_TO_SEND and MC_REQUEST_TO_SEND.** Used by the local program that is in the receive state to inform the remote program that the local program would like to be placed into the send state in order to begin sending data.

Requesting Information About a Conversation

- **GET_TP_PROPERTIES.** Used to return information about the program that issues the verb.
- **GET_TYPE.** Used to return type of conversation, which can be basic or mapped.
- **GET_ATTRIBUTES.** Used to return information about a conversation, including mode name, partner LU name, and synchronization level.

1. Program X begins this one-way conversation by invoking the LU 6.2 MC_ALLOCATE service with SYNC_LEVEL of NONE, indicating no synchronization processing. The MC_ALLOCATE service assigns the conversation to a session and queues up an allocation message for later transmission. As long as the LU's buffer is not filled, the data is not yet sent.

BOX 12.3 LU 6.2 control operator verbs.

Control Operator Verbs — Session Number

- **INITIALIZE_SESSION_LIMIT.** Used to establish the maximum number of sessions that can be active for a particular logical unit.
- **RESET_SESSION_LIMIT.** Used to reset to zero the session limit for a particular logical unit.
- **CHANGE_SESSION_LIMIT.** Used to request a change in the session limit.
- **PROCESS_SESSION_LIMIT.** Used in conjunction with the INITIALIZE_SESSION_LIMIT, RESET_SESSION_LIMIT, and CHANGE_SESSION_LIMIT verbs to change session limits.

Control Operator Verbs — Session Activation and Deactivation

- **ACTIVATE_SESSION.** Used to activate a session given a specified mode name.
- **DEACTIVATE_CONVERSATION_GROUP.** Used to deactivate a session that is associated with a specified conversation group ID.
- **DEACTIVATE_SESSION.** Used to deactivate a session.

Control Operator Verbs — System Definition Parameters

- **DISPLAY.** Used to return the values of the system definition parameters, including the total LU-LU session limit, the remote LU name, the set of properties associated with a particular mode name, and session limits for local LU and mode combinations.
- **DEFINE.** Used to set or modify system definition parameters.
- **DELETE.** Used to delete all LU system definition parameter values that have been defined by DEFINE.

2. Program X then invokes the MC_SEND_DATA service, which causes data to be queued up for later transmission. Again, if the buffer is not filled, the data is not sent.
3. Program X requests the termination of its side of the conversation by invoking the MC_DEALLOCATE service. This terminates the execution of Program X and causes a deallocation message to be queued up. Now, whether or not the LU's buffer is filled, all the queued up messages and data are sent over the LU-LU session to the partner LU.
4. When the allocation message is received by the logical unit on the other end of the LU-LU session, the LU locates Program Y, loads it into memory, and starts its execution.

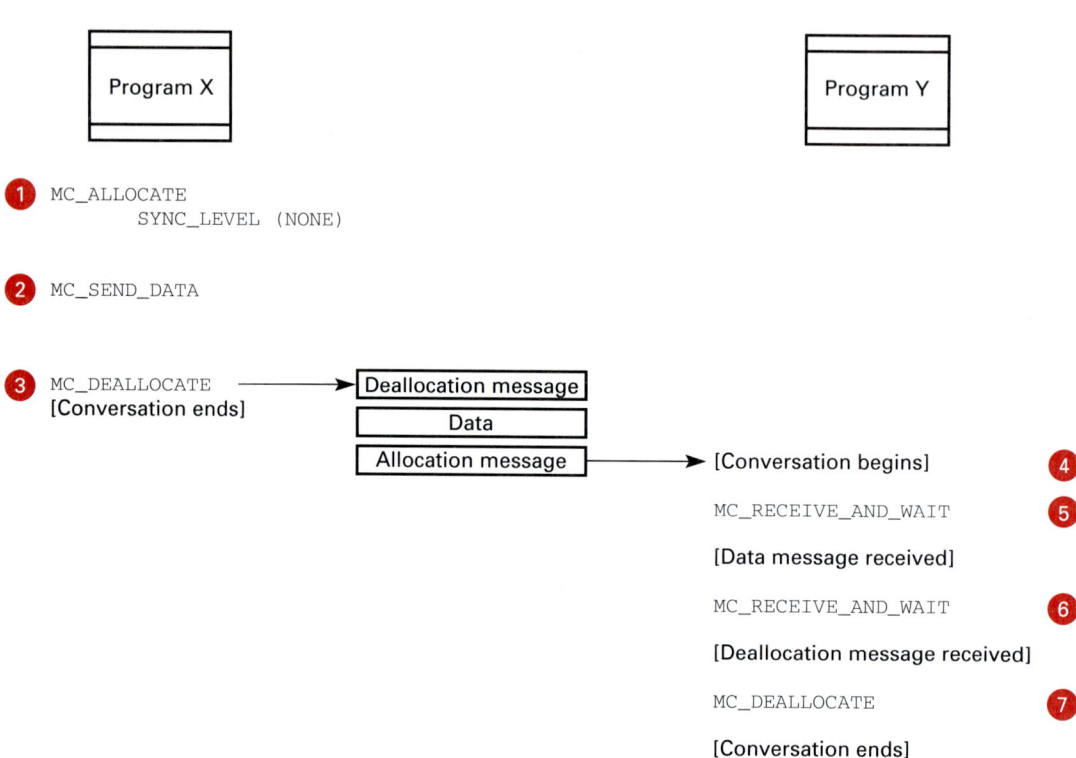

Figure 12.4 One-way conversation with no confirmation.

5. Program Y begins by invoking the MC_RECEIVE_AND_WAIT service, which receives the data Program X sent. (The LU has already processed the allocation message and removed it from the queue.)

6. The second MC_RECEIVE_AND_WAIT receives the deallocation message, indicating that there is no more data to receive over the conversation.

7. Program Y terminates its side of the conversation by invoking the MC_DEALLOCATE service.

A conversation using the data flow in Fig. 12.4 is an example of a conversation in which the programs on each side of the conversation execute at different times. Program X finishes its processing and terminates its side of the conversation before Program Y even begins executing.

ONE-WAY CONVERSATION WITH CONFIRMATION

Figure 12.5 shows an example of a one-way conversation with confirmation. Processing is similar to that for a one-way conversation with no confirmation except that Program X does not terminate

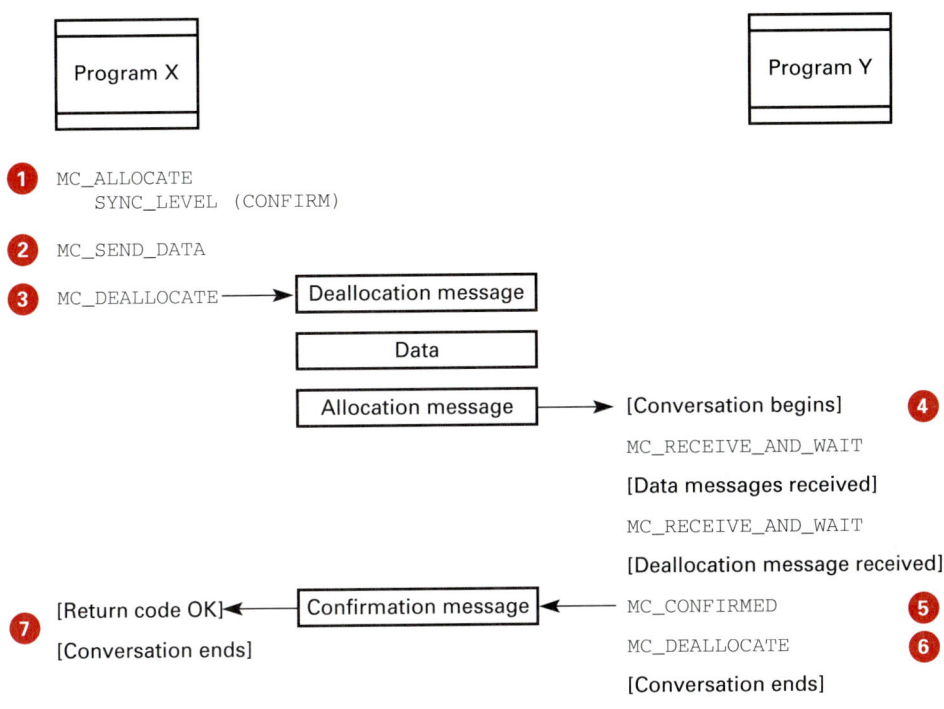

Figure 12.5 One-way conversation with confirmation.

its end of the conversation until it receives a confirmation reply from Program Y.

1. Program X begins this synchronous conversation by invoking the MC_ALLOCATE service with a SYNC_LEVEL of CONFIRM, requesting confirmation synchronization. This allocates a session and queues up an allocation message for transmission.
2. Program X next invokes the MC_SEND_DATA service, causing the data to be queued up for transmission.
3. Program X signals that it is finished sending data by invoking the MC_DEALLOCATE service. This causes a deallocation message to be queued up and begins transmission of the queued up messages and data. This time, as the data flows, the MC_DEALLOCATE service causes Program X to wait until Program X's LU receives a confirmation message from the partner LU.
4. Program Y processes the received data as in the previous conversation.
5. After Program Y receives the deallocation message, it completes its processing and, if all is well, invokes the MC_CONFIRMED service. This causes a confirmation message to be queued up.
6. Program Y then invokes the MC_DEALLOCATE service to end its side of the conversation. This causes the confirmation message to be transmitted over the LU-LU session.

7. When the other LU receives the confirmation message, the MC_DEALLOCATE service invoked by Program X completes, Program X finishes its processing, and the conversation ends.

A conversation using the data flow in Fig. 12.5 is an example of a conversation in which both programs execute concurrently. Program X does not finish its processing and terminate its side of the conversation until it gets a confirmation from Program Y.

TWO-WAY CONVERSATION

Figure 12.6 shows an example of a two-way conversation. Here the programs alternately send and receive data until one of the programs invokes the MC_DEALLOCATE service. When a final confirmation is received from the other program, the conversation ends.

A program can explicitly invoke the MC_PREPARE_TO_ RECEIVE service to indicate to the partner that it can begin sending data. Invoking MC_PREPARE_TO_RECEIVE causes a Send message to be queued up. The use of the MC_PREPARE_TO_RECEIVE service is optional. A program can simply invoke the MC_RECEIVE_ AND_WAIT service, and the Send message will be generated automatically.

DISTRIBUTED TRANSACTION EXAMPLE

Most of the examples in this chapter have referred to a single conversation between two application programs. However, actual business solutions may involve groups of related conversations that work together to produce a given result. Figure 12.7 illustrates the structure of a possible simple distributed transaction.

TPA is running in a large-system processor and is started as a result of something keyed by a terminal operator. Assume that this is a manufacturing application and that the terminal operator is ordering a product. In order to respond to the operator's request, TPA determines that it needs information from three different plants. It then allocates a conversation with application programs running on distributed processors running at each of the plants and makes requests for data from each of them.

Each conversation that TPA starts is a separate conversation that uses an SNA session for communication, but all the conversations are part of the same distributed transaction. TPB may determine that information is needed from other remote locations (other plants or even outside vendors) in order to determine whether the product order request can be successfully satisfied. It then starts conversations with processors at the required locations and makes requests for required data. TPD does the same.

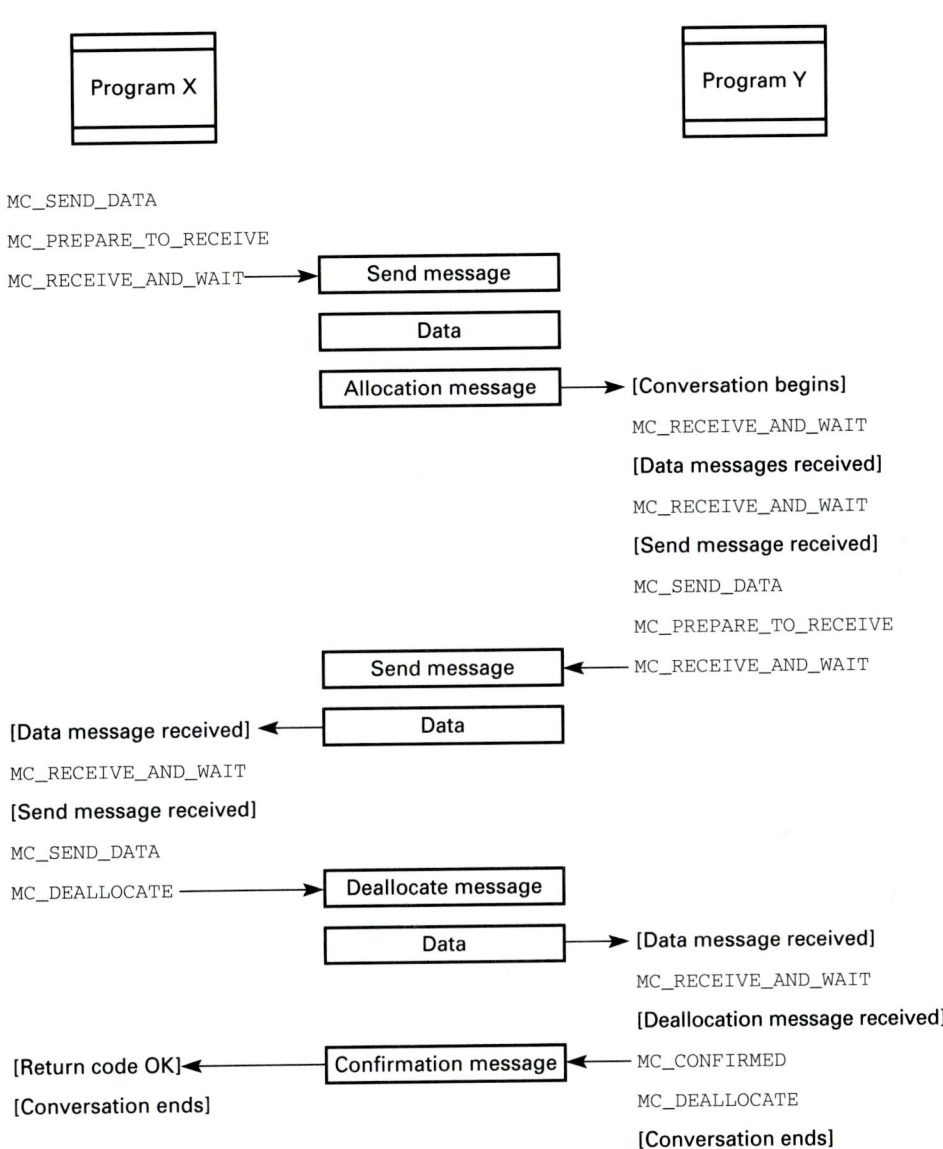

Figure 12.6 Two-way conversation.

Assume that all the conversations are taking place in real time while the original terminal operator is waiting for a response to the original product-ordering request. Suppose TPE and TPF respond positively to the requests made by TPB. TPB can then respond positively to TPA. TPC also responds positively to TPA. Assume TPG responds negatively to TPD, perhaps saying that a part that is

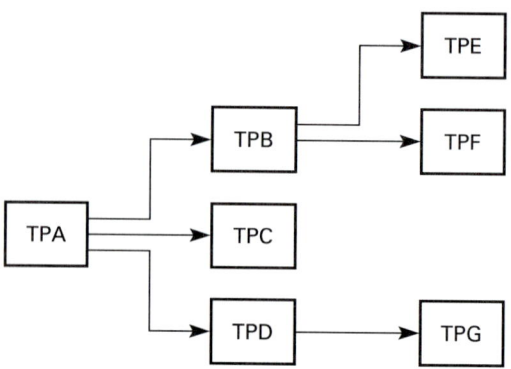

Figure 12.7 Distributed application.

required to construct the product is not available. TPD then responds negatively to TPA. TPA may now want to inform the terminal operator that the transaction failed and could not satisfy the product-ordering request. It may also want to roll back any changes that were made as a result of the processing performed by any of the application programs involved in this distributed transaction.

Such a distributed conversation is complex. However, LU 6.2 provides the tools needed for building such distributed applications. For example, synchronization facilities are supported by LU 6.2 implementations that allow all the application programs to synchronize their processing, even though the application programs are all running on separate distributed processors.

In implementing this distributed application, TPA must allocate separate conversations with TPB, TPC, and TPD to request and receive the required data. One way to handle this is to conduct each conversation separately, one at a time, using synchronous processing. Another method is to use asynchronous processing to conduct multiple conversations concurrently. We will examine both methods next.

Synchronous Processing Example

TPA would first conduct a conversation with TPB, using two-way conversation techniques similar to that shown in a previous example. When the conversation with TPB is terminated, TPA would conduct a conversation with TPC, and then with TPD. The problem with this technique is that the conversations take place in a serial fashion. The exchange with TPC does not begin until the exchange with Program B has been completed.

Asynchronous Processing Example

As an alternative to the previous procedure, TPA can issue three MC_ALLOCATE verbs to allocate all three conversations at once. TPA can then issue MC_SEND_DATA verbs to all three partner application programs so they can complete their processing concurrently. The following sequence of events takes place:

1. TPA issues an MC_PREPARE_TO_RECEIVE verb to change the protocol boundary at Program A's LU to receive state for each transaction without explicitly causing a wait to occur.
2. TPA issues three MC_PREPARE_TO_RECEIVE verbs, one over the conversation with TPB, one over the conversation with TPC, and one over the conversation with TPD.
3. TPA issues the MC_POST_ON_RECEIPT verb to cause TPA to be informed when data is available to be read on a conversation.
4. TPA issues an MC_POST_ON_RECEIPT verb for each of the three conversations.
5. TPA then issues a WAIT verb to cause it to wait for a message to be received from any of the three application programs it is in conversation with. The first time TPA issues the WAIT verb, it lists all three conversations as resources. TPA then regains control when a record is available to be read from any of the conversations for which it is waiting. The WAIT returns a parameter that indicates which conversation has a record available to be received. We will assume the record came from the conversation with TPC.
6. TPC now issues an MC_SEND_DATA followed by an MC_FLUSH, thus making data available for TPA to receive over its conversation with TPC.
7. TPA then issues an MC_RECEIVE_IMMEDIATE verb to read the data that is now available from TPC.
8. TPA then performs whatever processing is required as a result of receiving the data from TPD, including sending a confirmation to TPC, thus allowing that conversation to end. In the meantime, it is possible that one of the other two application programs may also have sent data to TPA on their conversations.
9. TPA can issue an MC_TEST verb to determine if there is data available from either of the other two conversations. TPA issues MC_TEST for each of the two remaining conversations to determine if data is waiting. If not, TPA issues another MC_POST_ON_RECEIPT for each of the two remaining conversations and issues a WAIT listing the remaining two conversations.
10. Similar processing continues until TPA has received data from the remaining two application programs and has terminated those conversations. TPA can then reply to the original request and terminate its processing.

MAPPING BETWEEN SYNTAX AND SEMANTICS

In the data flows just described, we showed the LU 6.2 services that cause each of the flows to take place by referencing the LU 6.2 architected services that are associated with each of the flows. However, as we introduced earlier, the actual services provided by a specific implementation of LU 6.2 may not necessarily correspond one-to-one with the LU 6.2 protocol boundary verbs. For example, to perform the functions of the MC_ALLOCATE service to allocate a mapped conversation, a particular LU 6.2 implementation may require an application program to invoke a series of functions to provide all of the information necessary to completely invoke the MC_ALLOCATE service.

By the same token, a single service provided by an LU 6.2 implementation may perform the functions defined by two or more LU 6.2 architected services. Each implementation of LU 6.2, however, is required to specify precisely how each of the LU 6.2 architected services is mapped to the actual services the LU 6.2 implementation provides.

OPEN VERSUS CLOSED LU 6.2 IMPLEMENTATIONS

LU 6.2 implementations are classified as either *open* or *closed*. An open implementation supports an application programming interface that user programs can employ to request LU 6.2 communication services. All the functions available in the implementation's API can be mapped to the protocol boundary verbs that define LU 6.2 architected services. All programmable implementations are open implementations.

A closed implementation does not support an API and has all required transaction programs written as part of the LU 6.2 implementation. Closed implementations typically take the form of nonprogrammable devices, such as terminal controllers or printers that perform a limited set of functions.

APPLICATION SUBSYSTEM LU 6.2 IMPLEMENTATIONS

Prior to the development of SAA, each application subsystem, such as CICS and other programs that provide open implementations of the LU 6.2 architecture, defined its own application programming interface. The API defined by CICS is one example. A CICS application program sends data using the command EXEC CICS SEND. In response to this, CICS performs the functions associated with the LU 6.2 MC_SEND_DATA architected service. This is shown conceptually in Fig. 12.8.

APPC LU 6.2 IMPLEMENTATIONS

As discussed earlier in this chapter, many LU 6.2 implementations have the term APPC in their titles. A typical APPC product provides an application programming interface that has a close mapping between API functions and the LU 6.2 protocol boundary verbs. For example, each protocol boundary

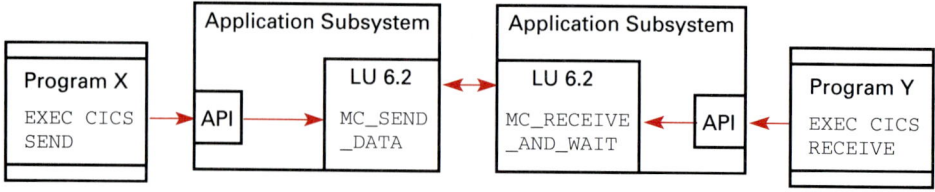

Figure 12.8 CICS LU 6.2 application program interface.

verb function typically has a corresponding API function with a similar name, as shown in Fig. 12.9.

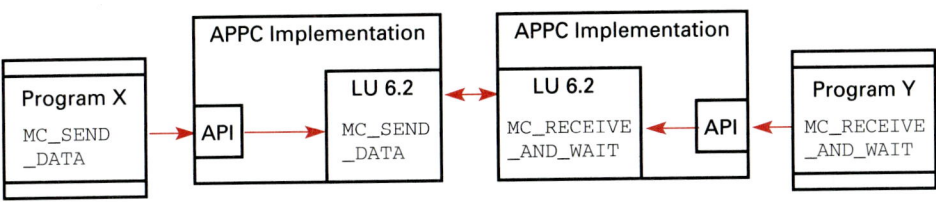

Figure 12.9 Typical APPC product application program interface.

CPI COMMUNICATIONS INTERFACE

The CPI Communications Interface, described in Chapter 13, also defines an application programming interface for requesting LU 6.2 communication services. This API—often called Common Programming Interface for Communications (CPI-C)—defines a simplified, standardized API that a program can use to request the services described by the LU 6.2 protocol boundary verbs. CPI-C is the only LU 6.2 API for which support is specifically included in SAA. The CPI-C API defines a set of callable services that a program, written in any of the SAA programming languages, can issue via a standard subroutine call mechanism to access LU 6.2 communication services. This is shown in Fig. 12.10.

CPI-C assigns default values for much of the information that must be supplied to fully specify all the information required in the parameters of LU 6.2 protocol boundary verbs. Thus, with CPI-C, the application programmer often needs to supply less information in requesting CPI-C callable services than would be necessary when using other LU 6.2 APIs, such as that of a typical APPC product.

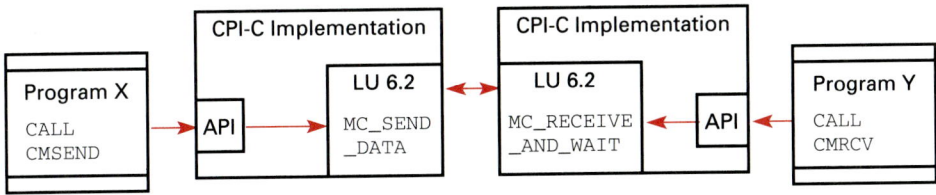

Figure 12.10 CPI-C LU 6.2 application program interface.

DESIGNING LU 6.2 CONVERSATION FLOWS

Even though two different LU 6.2 implementations define different API syntaxes, they all use the same protocol for communication. Therefore, it is possible for any LU implementation to interoperate with any other implementation. IBM recommends a simple method for designing an LU 6.2 conversation that operates in a mixed environment in which two different LU 6.2 APIs are used.

The conversation's overall flow should be designed in a generic fashion using the LU 6.2 architected protocol boundary verbs as if those verbs were actual programming language statements. Doing so allows the semantics of the interactions that occur between the two communicating programs to be defined in an implementation-independent manner. Once the conversation flow has been designed, the developer of the program at each end of the conversation can translate the LU 6.2 protocol boundary verbs into the appropriate programming statements required by the LU 6.2 implementation being used on that side of the conversation.

CONCLUSION The Logical Unit 6.2 architecture defines the communication services for which support is included in SAA for the SNA environment. LU 6.2 defines a set of architected communication services that an implementation of the LU 6.2 architecture provides to application programs. These communication services allow application programs to communicate with one another in a uniform way over an SNA network. Chapter 13 describes the CPI Communications Interface that defines a standardized API for requesting LU 6.2 communication services.

13 THE CPI COMMUNICATIONS INTERFACE

The *CPI Communications Interface* defines an application programming interface—often called *Common Programming Interface for Communications* (CPI-C)—that can be used for requesting LU 6.2 communication services. CPI-C defines a simplified, standardized API that can be used to request most of the architected communication services defined by the LU 6.2 protocol boundary verbs. As described in Chapter 12, the LU 6.2 protocol boundary defines the *semantics* of the LU 6.2 communication services, while CPI-C defines a specific API *syntax* by which these services can be requested by an application program. The CPI-C syntax defines a set of callable services that a program, written in any of the SAA programming languages, can issue via a standard subroutine call mechanism to access LU 6.2 communication services.

CPI-C CONCEPTS

CPI-C is built on the same basic concepts as LU 6.2, as illustrated in Fig. 13.1. Communication between two programs takes place using a conversation. The conversation uses an underlying LU-LU session for the exchange of data across an SNA network. The LU-LU session must be an LU Type 6.2 session. The intention with CPI-C is to provide a single API that will be available in all the SAA computing environments for accessing LU 6.2 communication services. However, as shown by the conversation between Program X and Program Z in Fig. 13.1, a program that uses the CPI-C API can communicate with a program that uses an implementation of LU 6.2 with a different API, such as an APPC implementation.

CPI-C supports both kinds of LU 6.2 conversations: mapped conversations and basic conversations. As discussed in Chapter 12, with mapped conversations the application programs exchange data records in formats meaningful to the programs. LU 6.2 facilities are responsible for formatting the data in the form of GDS variables for transmission across the network. With basic conversations, the application programs are responsible for GDS variable formatting and must include the GDS header information as part of each logical record.

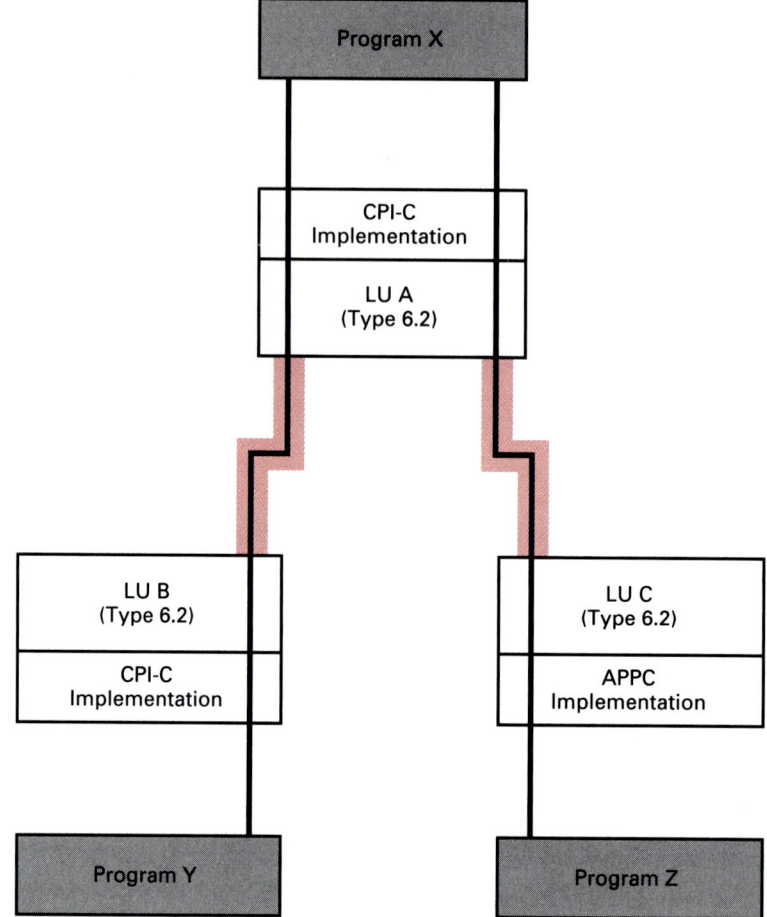

Figure 13.1 CPI-C programs communicate using a Type 6.2 LU-LU session as a resource.

As shown in Fig. 13.1, a single application program can be involved in multiple conversations. CPI-C assigns a different **conversation_id** to each conversation. This **conversation_id** is included as a parameter on CPI-C calls, thus allowing CPI-C to determine to which conversation each call applies.

CPI-C CALLS

CPI-C programs communicate with each other by making program calls that access LU 6.2 services. CPI-C divides the calls into two categories:

- **Starter Set Calls.** The *starter set* calls permit simple transfers of data between two programs and assume the two programs use a default set of conversation characteristics defined in the CPI-C documentation. Box 13.1 describes the callable services included in the starter set. The name in parentheses is the actual name used in a subroutine call to access the service. The longer, more descrip-

BOX 13.1 Starter set CPI-C callable services.

Services for Allocating a Conversation

- **Initialize_Conversation (CMINIT).** A program that intends to allocate an outgoing conversation begins by issuing a call to the Initialize_Conversation service. The Initialize_Conversation service initializes values for various conversation characteristics in preparation for allocating the conversation through a call to the Allocate service.

- **Accept_Conversation (CMACCP).** A program that intends to accept an incoming request for the allocation of a conversation begins by issuing a call to the Accept_Conversation service. The Accept_Conversation service initializes values for various characteristics that will apply to the incoming conversation.

- **Allocate (CMALLC).** A program that has issued a call to the Initialize_Conversation service issues a call to the Allocate service to actually establish a conversation. The value of the **conversation_type** characteristic determines whether the conversation is a mapped or a basic conversation. The value of the **TP_name** characteristic specifies the name of the partner program.

Services for Sending and Receiving Data

- **Send_Data (CMSEND).** A program issues a call to the Send_Data service to send data over a conversation to the remote program. When issued during a mapped conversation, this call sends a single data record to the remote program.

- **Receive (CMRCV).** A program issues a call to the Receive service to receive information over a conversation from the remote program. The information received can be data, information about the status of the conversation, or a request for confirmation.

Services for Deallocating a Conversation

- **Deallocate (CMDEAL).** A program issues a call to the Deallocate service to terminate its side of a conversation.

tive name that precedes it is a *pseudonym* used in the CPI-C documentation to describe the call's function.

- **Advanced-Function Calls.** The *advanced-function* calls are used to perform more specialized processing than is possible using the starter set. These calls provide for synchronization services and for the monitoring of data transfer operations. Box 13.2 describes the callable services that make up the advanced-function calls.

BOX 13.2   Advanced-function CPI-C callable services.

Services Used During Data Transfer

- **Flush (CMFLUS).** Used to empty the local LU's send buffer for a given conversation. When the LU receives a Flush request, it sends any information it has buffered to the remote LU. The buffered information can come from Allocate, Send_Data, or Send_Error calls.

- **Prepare_To_Receive (CMPTR).** Used to change a conversation from Send state to Receive state in preparation for receiving data. This call's exact function is determined by the value of the **prepare_to_receive_type** conversation characteristic and may include the same function as the Confirm call.

- **Request_To_Send (CMRTS).** Used to notify the remote program that the local program would like to enter the Send state for a given conversation.

- **Send_Error (CMSERR).** Used to inform the remote program that the local program detected an error during the processing of a conversation. If the conversation is in the Send state, the Send_Error service forces the LU to flush its send buffer.

- **Test_Request_To_Send_Received (CMTRTS).** Used by a program to determine whether a Request_to_Send notification has been received from the remote program for the specified conversation.

Services for Determining Conversation Characteristics

- **Extract_Conversation_State (CMECS).** Used to determine the current conversation state for a conversation.

- **Extract_Conversation_Type (CMECT).** Used to determine the value of the **conversation_type** characteristic for a conversation.

BOX 13.2 *(Continued)*

- **Extract_Mode_Name (CMEMN).** Used to determine the value of the **mode_name** characteristic for a conversation.

- **Extract_Partner_LU_Name (CMEPLN).** Used to determine the value of the **partner_LU_name** characteristic for a conversation.

- **Extract_Sync_Level (CMESL).** Used to determine the value of the **sync_level** characteristic for a conversation.

Services for Setting Conversation Characteristics

- **Set_Conversation_Type (CMSCT).** Used to set the value of the **conversation_type** characteristic for a conversation. It overrides the value assigned with the Initialize_Conversation call.

- **Set_Deallocate_Type (CMSDT).** Used to set the value of the **deallocate_type** characteristic for a conversation. It overrides the value that was assigned when either the Initialize_ Conversation or the Accept_Conversation call was issued.

- **Set_Error_Direction (CMSED).** Used to set the value of the **error_direction** characteristic for a conversation. It overrides the value that was assigned when the Initialize_Conversation or Accept_Conversation call was issued.

- **Set_Fill (CMSF).** Used to set the value of the **fill** characteristic for a conversation. It overrides the value that was assigned by the Initialize_Conversation or Accept_Conversation call.

- **Set_Log_Data (CMSLD).** Used to set the values of the **log_data** and **log_data_length** characteristics for a conversation. It overrides the values that were assigned with the Initialize_Conversation or Accept_Conversation call.

- **Set_Mode_Name (CMSMN).** Used to set the values of the **mode_name** and **mode_name_length** characteristics for a conversation. It overrides the system-defined value.

- **Set_Partner_LU_Name (CMSPLN).** Used to set the value of the **partner_LU_name** characteristic for a conversation. It overrides the current value for the **partner_LU_name.**

(Continued)

BOX 13.2 *(Continued)*

- **Set_Prepare_To_Receive_Type (CMSPTR).** Used to set the value of the **prepare_to_receive_type** characteristic for a conversation. It overrides the value that was assigned by the Initialize_Conversation or Accept_Conversation call.
- **Set_Receive_Type (CMSRT).** Used by a program to set the value of the **receive_type** characteristic for a conversation. It overrides the value that was assigned by the Initialize_Conversation or Accept_Conversation call.
- **Set_Return_Control (CMSRC).** Used to set the value of the **return_control** characteristic for a given conversation. It overrides the value that was assigned with the Initialize_ Conversation call.
- **Set_Send_Type (CMSST).** Used by a program to set the value of the **send_type** characteristic for a conversation. It overrides the value that was assigned with the Initialize_Conversation or Accept_Conversation call.
- **Set_Sync_Level (CMSSL).** Used by a program to set the value of the **sync_level** characteristic for a given conversation. The **sync_level** characteristic is used to specify the level of synchronization processing between the two programs and determines whether or not the programs support the use of the Confirm and Confirmed calls. Set_Sync_Level overrides the value that was assigned with the Initialize_Conversation call.
- **Set_TP_Name (CMSTPN).** Used by a program to set the value of the **TP_name** characteristic for a given conversation. It overrides the current value.

Services for Handling Confirmation

- **Confirm (CMCFM).** Issued by a program to send a request for a confirmation to the remote program. After issuing a call to the Confirm service, the program waits for a confirmation reply from the remote program.
- **Confirmed (CMCFMD).** Issued in response to receiving a request for a confirmation to send a confirmation reply to the remote program. The local and remote programs use the Confirm and Confirmed calls to synchronize their processing.

CPI-C CONVERSATION CHARACTERISTICS

CPI-C maintains a set of values that identify characteristics associated with a given conversation. Box 13.3 lists the CPI-C conversation characteristics. A

BOX 13.3   Conversation characteristics.

- **Conversation_state.** Identifies the current conversation state for this program. The conversation state determines which actions can be taken next.
- **Deallocate_type.** Specifies the type of deallocation to be performed. Deallocation can be normal or abnormal and can require confirmation or a commit operation before deallocation.
- **Conversation_type.** Identifies the conversation as basic or mapped.
- **Error_direction.** Specifies whether an error was detected in data received or when the program was preparing to send data.
- **Fill.** Specifies whether the program is to receive data based on logical records or the **requested_length** parameter.
- **Log_data.** Specifies program-unique error information to be logged.
- **Log_data_length.** Specifies the length of **log_data.**
- **Mode_name.** Specifies the network properties that the session used for this conversation must have.
- **Mode_name_length.** Specifies the length of **mode_name.**
- **Partner_LU_name.** Identifies the name of the LU associated with the remote program.
- **Partner_LU_name_length.** Specifies the length of **partner_LU_name.**
- **Prepare_to_receive_type.** Specifies the type of Prepare_To_Receive processing to be performed for this conversation.
- **Receive_type.** Identifies a subsequent Receive call as Receive_and_Wait or Receive_Immediate.
- **Return_control.** Specifies when control is returned to a program after it issues an Allocate call.
- **Send_type.** Specifies information to be sent along with the data and whether the data is to be sent immediately or buffered.
- **Sync_level.** Specifies the synchronization level (**none, confirm,** or **sync_point**) that can be used for this conversation.
- **TP_name.** Specifies the name of the remote program.
- **TP_name_length.** Specifies the length of **TP_name.**

set of characteristics is established for each application program for each conversation in which it is a partner. The application program has access to these characteristics and, in some cases, can set them to different values. There are several different ways in which characteristic values are established.

Default Values

To establish a conversation, an application program issues an Initialize_Conversation call, requesting that CPI-C initialize a conversation with a specified partner. As a result of this call, CPI-C assigns a set of default values as the characteristics for this conversation for this program. The program then issues an Allocate call to actually start the conversation. When the partner program for this conversation is loaded and executed by the partner LU, it issues an Accept_Conversation call. CPI-C then assigns a set of default values as the characteristics for the partner program.

Extracting and Setting Values

Certain CPI-C calls allow an application program to view or modify the value of a characteristic. For example, when an application program issues an Initialize_Conversation call, the **conversation_type** characteristic is normally assigned a default value corresponding to a mapped conversation. If the program wished to use a basic conversation, it would issue a Set_Conversation_ Type call to change the value of **conversation_type** before issuing the Allocate call. The **conversation_type** value in effect when the Allocate is issued determines the default value for **conversation_type** characteristic assigned to the partner program. Either program can check the type of conversation by issuing an Extract_Conversation_ Type call.

Side Information

In order to establish a conversation, an application program must specify certain initialization information, called *side information*. Side information includes

- **Partner_LU_name.** This identifies the name of the LU the partner program is using.
- **Mode_name.** This identifies properties of the session used for this conversation, such as class of service.
- **TP_name.** This identifies the name of the partner program.

With CPI-C, side information is supplied and maintained by system administrators independently of the application programs that use it. Side information is stored in a table, with each table entry consisting of a **partner_LU_name,** a **mode_name,** and a **TP_name.** A symbolic destination name, or **sym_dest_** name, is associated with each table entry. An Initialize_Conversation call can include a symbolic destination name as an input parameter, allowing the side information to be used to establish the conversation. An application program can also use the appropriate Set calls to specify this information directly.

CPI-C CALL TO LU 6.2 VERB MAPPING

The CPI-C calls correspond quite closely to the architected services defined by the LU 6.2 protocol boundary verbs, as shown in Box 13.4. The correspondence between LU 6.2 verbs and CPI-C calls is not always one-to-one. However, CPI-C provides the same range of functions through the use of characteristic values in combination with calls. For example, LU 6.2 defines two types of receive services, RECEIVE_AND_WAIT and RECEIVE_IMMEDIATE. In CPI-C, there is a single Receive call that can be used to request either type of service by setting the **receive_type** characteristic to the proper value before issuing the call.

Similarly, the **send_type** characteristic can be used with the Send_Data call to request a combination of services. By having **send_type** set to an appropriate value, the Send_Data call can perform the combined functions of a SEND_DATA verb followed by a FLUSH verb, a SEND_DATA followed by a CONFIRM, a SEND_DATA followed by a DEALLOCATE, or a SEND_DATA followed by a PREPARE_TO_RECEIVE.

LU 6.2 FUNCTIONS NOT SUPPORTED

There are certain LU 6.2 functions that have not been included in the CPI Communications Interface. The services defined by the LU 6.2 verbs POST_ON_RECEIPT, WAIT, and TEST(POSTED) are not available through CPI-C calls. These LU 6.2 services allow a program that issues multiple RECEIVE_IMMEDIATE calls for different conversations to wait until data arrives over one of the conversations and to then be informed which conversation has data waiting to be received. Such an application was described in Chapter 12. CPI-C allows a program to issue the RECEIVE_IMMEDIATE type of Receive call for multiple conversations, but it does not support the LU 6.2 waiting and posting functions. A program that wishes to receive data concurrently over multiple conversations must make arrangements to periodically issue each RECEIVE_IMMEDIATE type of Receive call to see if data has been received from that conversation.

CPI-C also does not support features related to certain LU 6.2 parameters, including PIP data, LOCKS=LONG, MAP_NAME, and FMH_DATA. Security parameters can be established for a conversation as default values, but the program is not able to examine or modify them.

BOX 13.4 LU 6.2/CPI-C correspondence.

LU 6.2 Protocol Boundary Verbs	**CPI-C Calls**
MC_ALLOCATE, ALLOCATE	Allocate (CMALLC) Initialize_Conversation (CMINT) Set_Conversation_Type (CMSCT) Set_Mode_Name (CMSMN) Set_Partner_LU_Name (CMSPLN) Set_Return_Control (CMSRC) Set_Sync_Level (CMSSL) Set_TP_Name (CMSTPN)
MC_CONFIRM, CONFIRM	Confirm (CMCFM)
MC_CONFIRMED, CONFIRMED	Confirmed (CMCFMD)
MC_DEALLOCATE, DEALLOCATE	Deallocate (CMDEAL) Set_Deallocate_Type (CMSDT) Set_Log_Data (CMSLD)
MC_FLUSH, FLUSH	Flush (CMFLUS)
MC_GET_ATTRIBUTES, GET_ATTRIBUTES	Extract_Mode_Name (CMEMN), Extract_Partner_LU_Name (CMEPLN), Extract_Sync_Level (CMESL)
MC_POST_ON_RECEIPT, POST_ON_RECEIPT	[none]
MC_PREPARE_FOR_SYNCPT, PREPARE_FOR_SYNCPT	[none]
MC_PREPARE_TO_RECEIVE, PREPARE_TO_RECEIVE	Prepare_To_Receive (CMPTR)
MC_RECEIVE_AND_WAIT, RECEIVE_AND_WAIT, MC_RECEIVE_IMMEDIATE, RECEIVE_IMMEDIATE	Receive (CMRCV)
MC_REQUEST_TO_SEND, REQUEST_TO_SEND	Request_To_Send (CMRTS)
MC_SEND_DATA, SEND_DATA	Send_Data (CMSEND)
MC_SEND_ERROR, SEND_ERROR	Send_Error (CMSERR)
MC_TEST, TEST	Test_Request_To_Send_Received (CMTRTS)
BACKOUT	[none]

BOX 13.4 *(Continued)*

```
GET_TP_PROPERTIES              [none]
GET_TYPE                       Extract_Conversation_Type (CMECT)
SET_SYNCPT_OPTIONS             [none]
SYNCPT
WAIT
[none]                         Accept_Conversation (CMACCP)
                               Extract_Conversation_State (CMECS)
                               Set_Error_Direction (CMSED)
                               Set_Fill (CMSF)
                               Set_Prepare_To_Receive_Type (CMSPTR)
                               Set_Receive_Type (CMSRT)
                               Set_Send_Type (CMSST)
```

SUPPORT FOR SYNCHRONIZATION POINT PROCESSING

The LU 6.2 architecture defines a two-phase commit protocol to protect changes to distributed resources. The LU 6.2 two-phase commit protocol involves synchronization points and the use of commit and backout services. These services are described by the LU 6.2 SYNCPT and BACKOUT protocol boundary verbs. CPI-C does not include calls to directly provide these services. However, CPI-C can be used in conjunction with the CPI Resource Recovery Interface, described in Chapter 9, to request commit and backout services.

When a program issues a resource recovery call, CPI-C passes information to the program's conversation partner. If the program issues a Commit call, the partner program receives a Take_Commit notification in the **status_received** parameter of its Receive call. The partner program can then issue its own Commit or Backout call to complete the synchronization process.

If a program issues a Backout call, or if a failure or problem causes the syncpoint manager to initiate a backout operation, a Take_Backout notification is passed to the partner program as a **return_code** value. The return code can be associated with any of the following calls:

- Confirm
- Extract_Conversation_State
- Prepare_to_Receive
- Receive
- Send_Data
- Send_Error

The partner program can then issue a Backout call to complete the backout process.

SAMPLE CPI-C CONVERSATIONS

Chapter 12 showed examples of sample conversations using LU 6.2 protocol boundary verbs. Some of those conversation flows are repeated here, showing how CPI-C calls could be used to implement those same conversations.

ONE-WAY CONVERSATION WITH NO CONFIRMATION

Figure 13.2 shows a one-way conversation with no confirmation. The calls are shown using their pseudonyms for readability. The Initialize_Conversation call interacts with the local CPI-C implementation and causes conversation characteristics to be initialized for Program X. The Allocate and Send_Data calls place data in a buffer, and the Deallocate call forces the messages and data in the buffer to be sent. When the allocation message is received by the partner LU, Program Y is loaded and executed. It issues an Accept_Conversation call to initialize its conversation characteristics and then uses Receive calls to receive the data and the Deallocation

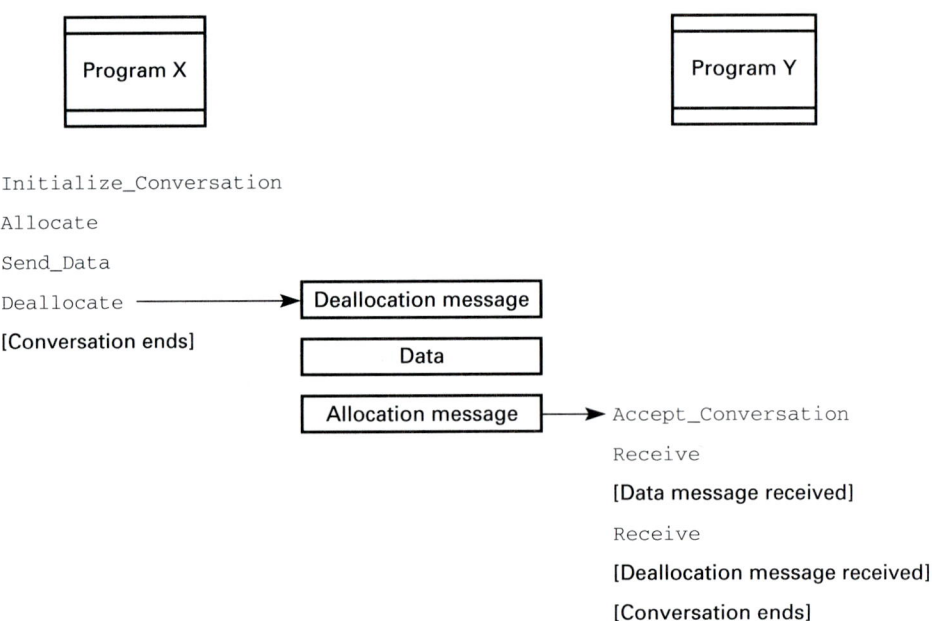

Figure 13.2 One-way conversation with no confirmation.

message. When the deallocation message is received, the conversation ends. It is not necessary for Program Y to issue a Deallocate call.

ONE-WAY CONVERSATION WITH CONFIRMATION

Figure 13.3 shows a one-way conversation with confirmation. The **deallocate_type** characteristic is set to a value of CONFIRM prior to issuing the Deallocate call. When application Program Y receives the deallocation message with the confirm request, it issues a Confirmed call, and the conversation ends on both sides.

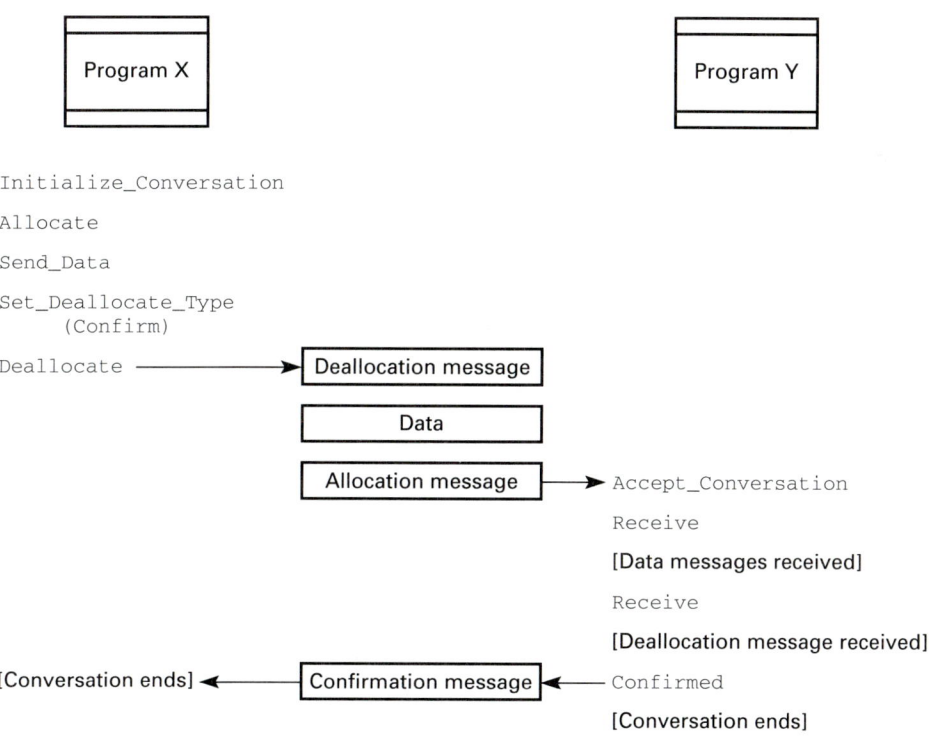

Figure 13.3   One-way conversation with confirmation.

TWO-WAY CONVERSATION

Figure 13.4 illustrates a two-way conversation, where the sending program causes the change in direction of the data flow by issuing a Prepare_To_Receive call. This change of direction could also be accomplished by issuing the Send_Data call with the **send_type** characteristic set to the proper value.

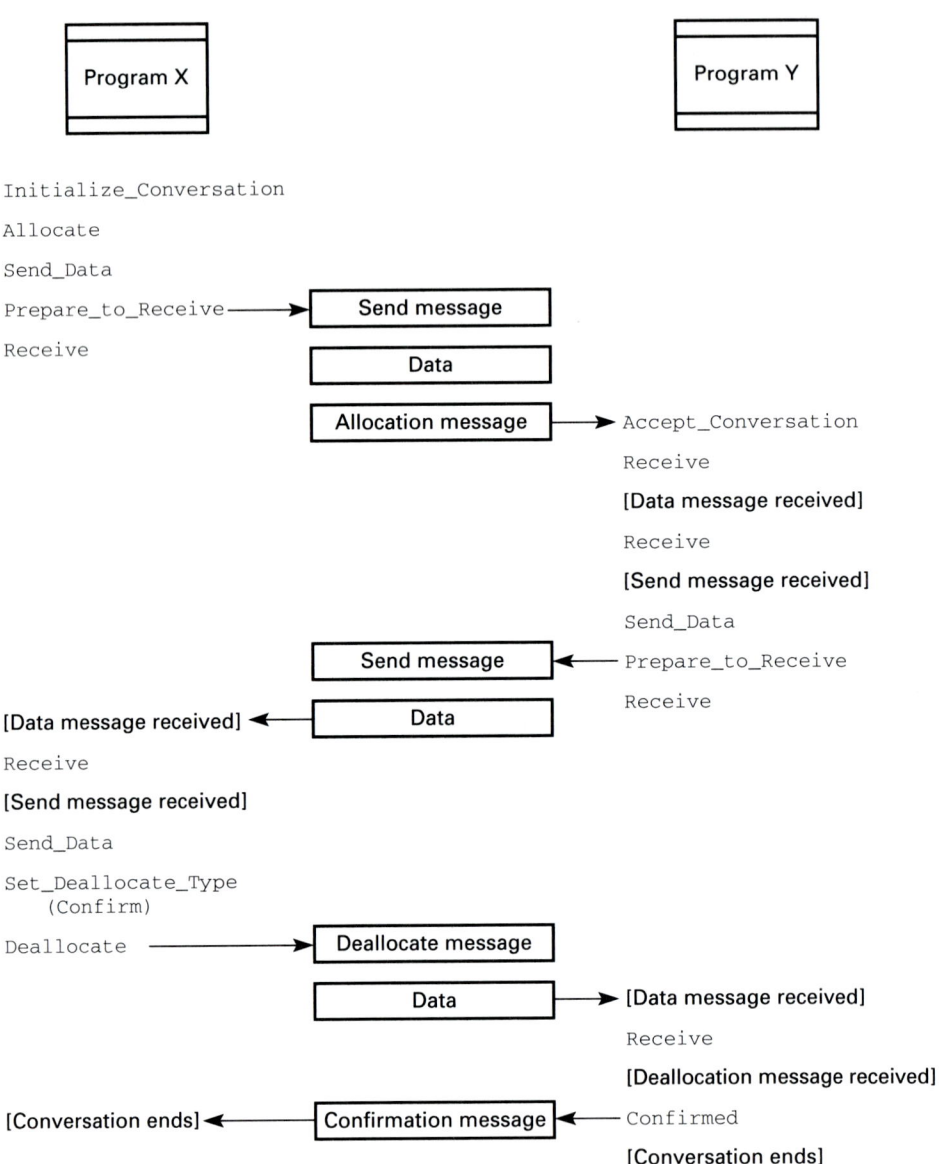

Figure 13.4 Two-way conversation.

PROTECTED CONVERSATION WITH COMMIT PROCESSING

In order to use resource recovery services, a conversation must be designated as a protected conversation. A conversation is established as protected by setting its **sync-level** characteristic to the value CM_SYNC_

POINT before allocating the conversation. Figure 13.5 illustrates a protected conversation with a successful commit operation.

Program Y issues a Commit call. This causes a Take_Commit notification to be sent to Program Y as the **status_received** parameter on its Receive call. Program Y then issues a Commit call. The syncpoint managers on both systems perform the procedures necessary to implement the two-phase commit protocol to commit changes made to protected resources. Return codes are then passed back to Program X and Program Y indicating that the Commit calls completed successfully. The programs are then able to continue processing, sending, and receiving additional data.

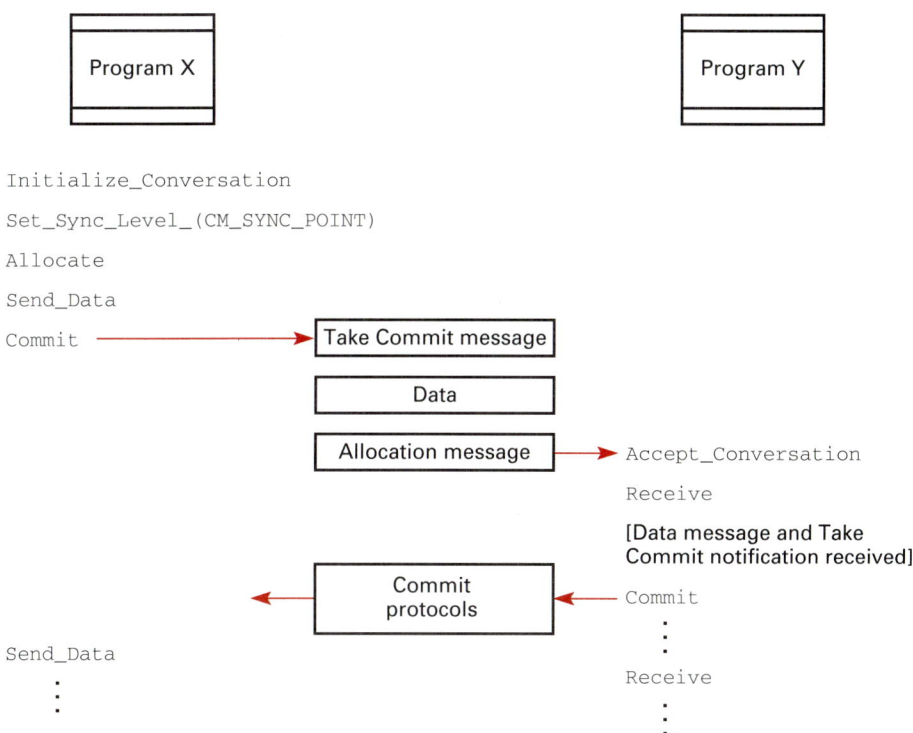

Figure 13.5 Protected conversation with a successful Commit operation.

DISTRIBUTED TRANSACTION EXAMPLE

Figure 13.6 shows how asynchronous distributed transaction processing can be performed using CPI-C calls. Each conversation is initialized, allocated, and sent data. Receive (Immediate) calls are issued in turn for each conversation until data is received from one of the conversations. Processing is then performed for that conversation.

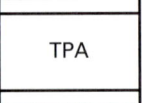

```
Initialize_Conversation(TPB)
Allocate
Send_Data

Initialize_Conversation(TPC)
Allocate
Send_Data

Initialize_Conversation(TPD)
Allocate
Send_Data
    ⋮
```

(Repeat the following until data received)

```
Set_Receive_Type (Immediate)
Receive (TPB)
```
(Check return code for data received)

```
Set_Receive_Type (Immediate)
Receive (TPC)
```
(Check return code for data received)

```
Set_Receive_Type (Immediate)
Receive (TPD)
```
(Check return code for data received)

Figure 13.6 Asynchronous distributed transaction processing.

CONCLUSION This chapter described the application programming interface defined by the CPI Communications Interface for accessing LU 6.2 communication services in the SNA environment. Chapter 14 begins Part IV on User Interfaces by examining the Common User Access component of SAA.

PART IV USER INTERFACES

14 COMMON USER ACCESS INTERFACES

Several of the CPI interfaces deal with the way in which an application displays information to or accepts information from the end user. The CPI Dialog Interface (Chapter 16) includes facilities for panel display and user interaction with the panel. The CPI Presentation Interface (Chapter 17) addresses the display of different types of information, including text using a variety of fonts, vector graphics, and raster images. The information may be displayed on either a workstation screen or a printer. The interface also supports different methods of end user interaction with the application. The CPI PrintManager Interface (Chapter 18) provides an application with a way to control the printing of information.

Other elements of SAA are also concerned with the user interface and with ways of presenting information. As described in Chapter 1, the Common User Access (CUA) component of SAA is a set of rules and guidelines for developing the interface between an application and the end user. These rules and guidelines underlie both the CPI Dialog Interface and the CPI Presentation Interface, so that these interfaces can be used to develop user interfaces that are consistent with CUA. The Common Communications Support (CCS) component of SAA includes specifications for the data stream and object architectures that are used to support complex applications that work with different types of data objects, such as text, graphics, images, and formatted data. These data stream and object architectures allow data objects to be easily interchanged between applications or presented on a display screen or printer. The CPI Presentation Interface and CPI PrintManager Interface both offer support for displaying complex forms of information involving text, graphics, and images. In this area the CPI and CCS interfaces work together to handle document presentation functions for an SAA application.

This chapter introduces the rules and guidelines defined by the CUA component of SAA. Chapter 15 introduces CCS data stream and object architectures. Chapters 16, 17, and 18 explore the specific CPI interfaces that are related to the user interface.

CUA USER INTERFACE MODELS

The CUA component of SAA specifies the characteristics of the dialog that takes place between a person and an application in terms of two things:

- The *appearance* of information that computing applications display on the screen.
- The methods users employ for *interacting* with that displayed information using a keyboard or a pointing device, such as a mouse.

As part of SAA, CUA must define standards and guidelines for the user interface that are usable in a consistent manner in any of the SAA computing environments. One of the key differences between SAA environments concerns the type of device that is used to implement the user interface. The two devices most commonly used are

- **Nonprogrammable Terminal.** A *nonprogrammable terminal* (NPT) is typically a text-based display station, such as a 3270 display.
- **Programmable Workstation.** A *programmable workstation* (PWS) is typically a personal computer with a graphics display.

In order to handle the great differences in capability between text-based terminals and graphics-based personal computers, CUA defines two major *interface*s that are associated with three *models* of user interaction:

- **CUA Advanced Interface.** The most important of the two CUA interfaces is the *CUA Advanced Interface,* designed to be used in developing applications that use graphics-based personal computers for communication with the user. The Advanced Interface defines the *graphical model* of user interaction.
- **CUA Basic Interface.** CUA also defines the *CUA Basic Interface,* designed to be used by applications that employ less sophisticated text-based terminals to implement the user interface. The Basic Interface defines two models for user interaction: the *text subset of the graphical model* and the *entry model*.

ADVANCED INTERFACE GRAPHICAL MODEL

With the graphical model defined by the CUA Advanced Interface, the entire terminal screen is called the *workplace*. The CUA workplace, illustrated in Fig. 14.1, is used to display graphical representations of the *objects* residing in the workplace that we can manipulate. These often take the form of small graphic images called *icons*. The CUA workplace environment defines three different types of objects, examples of which are illustrated in Fig. 14.1:

- **Data Objects.** Data objects are used to contain or convey information. A data object might represent a data file containing a memo, a chart, an application program, or any other collection of data.

- **Container Objects.** Container objects are used to hold other objects. A common example of a container object is a *folder*. A folder is an electronic simulation of a file folder that is used simply to group together collections of other objects, including other folders.
- **Device Objects.** A device object typically represents a device that is part of the computer system. For example, a device object might represent the mouse that is attached to the computing system.

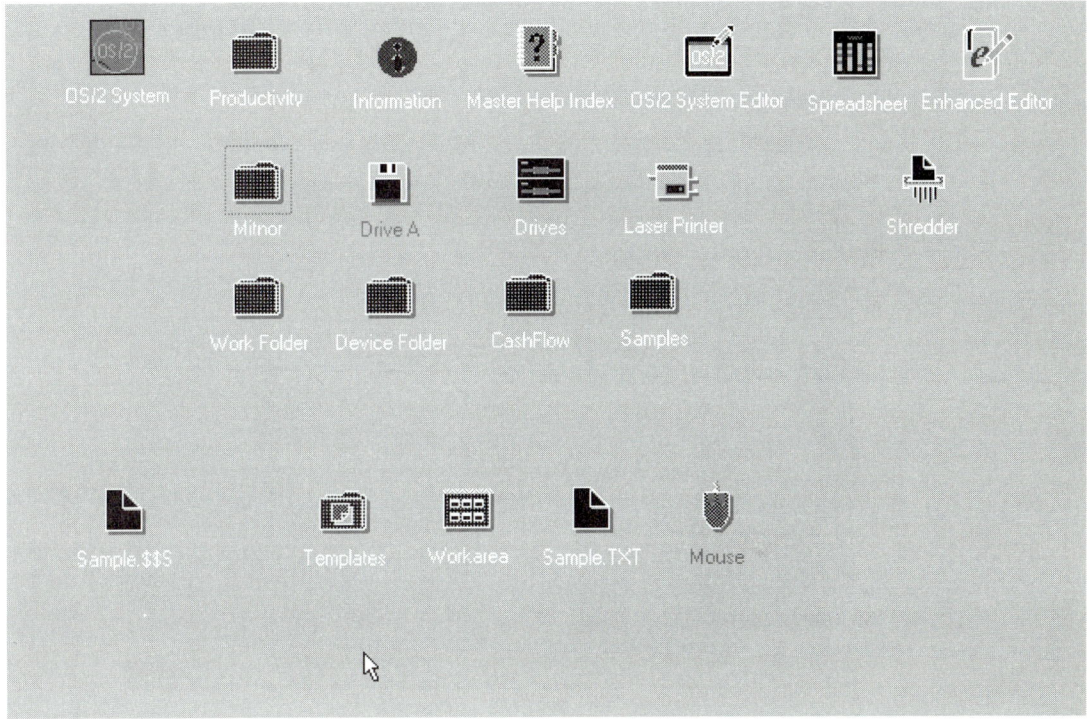

Figure 14.1 The CUA Advanced Interface workplace.

WINDOWS

Windows are primary components of the graphical model. CUA defines a window as a bounded portion of a screen that displays related information. There are two major types of windows that an application can display:

- **Primary Windows.** A *primary* window is used to present a particular view of an object or group of objects.
- **Secondary Windows.** A *secondary* window is always associated with a particular primary window and is used to present information that is associated with the information displayed in the primary window.

WINDOW COMPONENTS
The CUA Advanced Interface defines a set of standard window components so that all windows have a consistent appearance and the user can interact with applications using the same general techniques. The main window components defined by the CUA Advanced Interface are shown in Fig. 14.2. They include a *window title bar*, *window borders*, *scroll bars*, *window sizing buttons*, and a *menu bar*. The area of the window below the menu bar is used to present object information. Some windows may also have a *status area* immediately below the menu bar. Some windows also have an *information area* below the scroll bar.

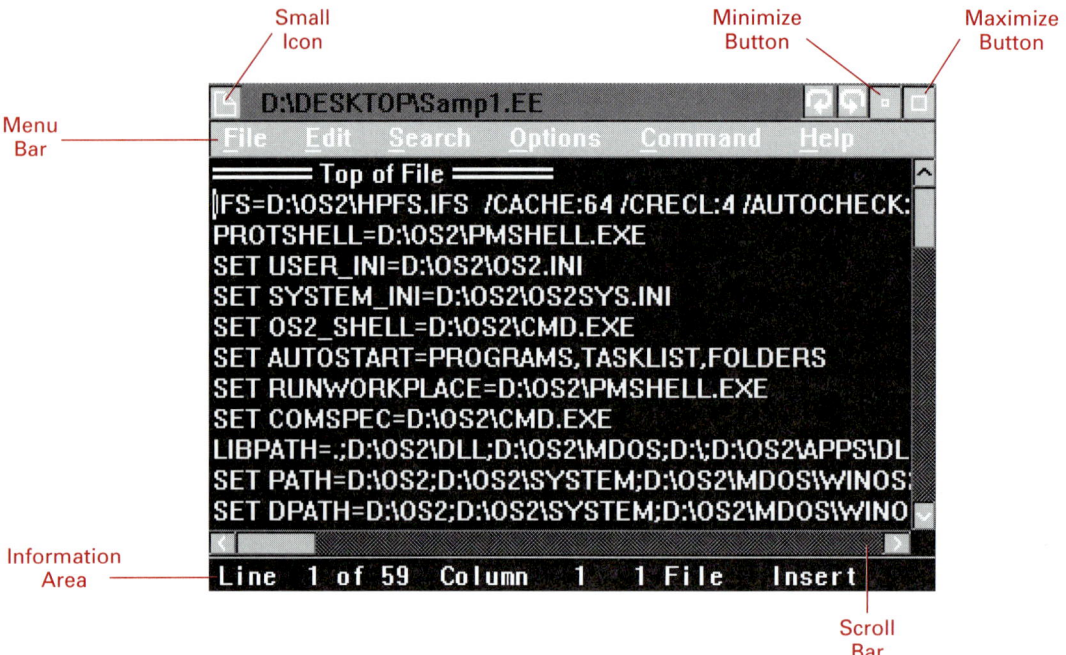

Figure 14.2 Window components.

Window Title Bar

The *window title bar* gives the name of the object the window is associated with. In addition to the object's name, the title bar also contains a *small icon*. The small icon is a smaller version of the icon that represented the object before its window was opened. We can use the small icon to perform the same actions that we can perform using the object's large icon when its window is not displayed. We can also use the small icon to display a System pulldown menu that lists actions that can be performed on a window as a whole.

Also included in the title bar are *window sizing buttons*. The window sizing buttons are shortcuts for changing the size of the window. The *maximize button* increases the size of the window so it fills the whole screen. The *minimize button* minimizes the window so it again takes the form of the object's icon.

Window Borders

An open window has visually distinctive borders. We can put the pointer on any of the borders and use the mouse to make the window any size we like. We can also place the pointer on the title bar and move the window around the screen.

Window Body Area

The central area of the window is used to present object information. *Scroll bars* are used when the application needs to display more information than the window can hold. We can use the scroll bars to control the portion of the information that the window displays.

The *menu bar* lists the major categories of *actions* that we can perform on this object. Some of the menu bar entries represent standard actions that apply to many types of applications.

Some windows also contain an information area at the bottom of the window. The *information area* can provide information about an object or choice that is currently selected or about the normal completion of a process. Some windows can also contain a *status area*. It's similar to the information area but appears just below the menu bar.

SECONDARY WINDOWS

A secondary window is similar in appearance to a primary window but typically has fewer components. For example, the secondary window shown in Fig. 14.3 has no window sizing buttons. Often a secondary window supports only a few possible actions. In this case, the actions are displayed in a set of *pushbuttons* at the bottom of the window.

An application can use three different types of secondary windows:

- **Action Windows.** Sometimes, in choosing an application action, additional information must be supplied before the request can be processed. An *action window* is used to gather the additional information needed.
- **Message Windows.** Applications also use secondary windows to display messages. Messages are displayed when something has happened in response to a request or when an unexpected condition has occurred. CUA defines three types of messages:
    - **Information Messages.** An *information message* indicates that a condition has occurred where no action can be or needs to be taken.

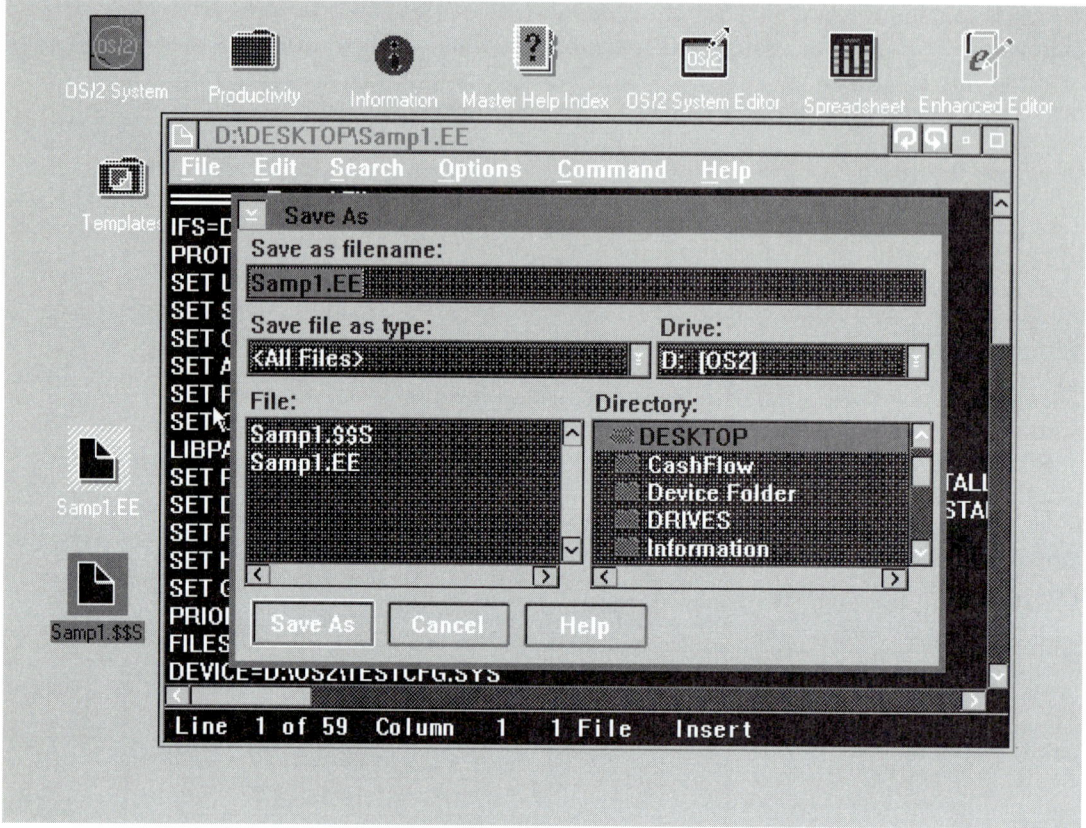

Figure 14.3 Secondary window.

- **Warning Messages.** A *warning message* tells the user that a condition has occurred that may require some corrective action.
- **Action Messages.** An *action message* indicates that processing can't continue until some explicit action is taken. Each type of message is indicated by a particular symbol.

• **Help Windows.** Another common use that applications make of secondary windows is to display *help information.* CUA defines several different types of help information:

- **General Help.** *General help* gives a brief overview of the function of the window from which help was requested.
- **Contextual Help.** *Contextual help* describes the particular object or choice currently being worked with.
- **Using Help.** *Using help* provides information on how to use the help facility itself and describes the different help options that are available.
- **Help Index.** A *help index* provides an alphabetical listing of all the topics for which help is currently available.

- **Keys Help.** *Keys help* provides a listing of key assignments and mouse button assignments that the application defines.
- **Tutorials.** *Tutorials* provide comprehensive, online instructional information for the application.

CONTROLS

The CUA Advanced Interface defines the appearance of certain types of fields, called *controls*, that allow the user to select choices or enter information. CUA also defines standard ways of interacting with these fields.

Menu Controls

An important form of control defined by the Advanced Interface is the *menu* that presents a list of choices. The Advanced Interface defines four forms of menus that applications can use:

- **Menu Bar.** The primary window for most applications displays a *menu bar* that lists the broad categories of actions that are available.

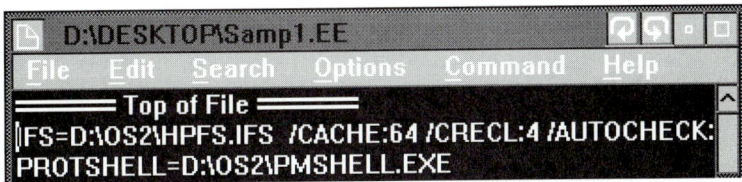

- **Pulldown Menus.** We use the menu bar to display a *pulldown menu* for each of the choices in the menu bar.

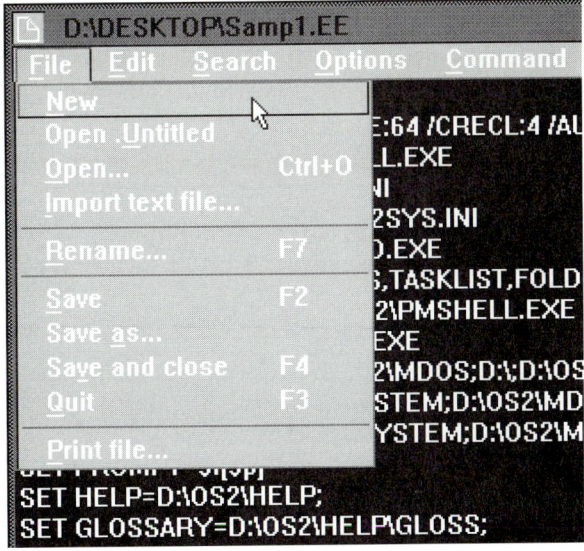

- **Pop-up Menus.** A *pop-up menu* for a particular object provides choices related to that object. We can display any object's pop-up menu using the mouse.

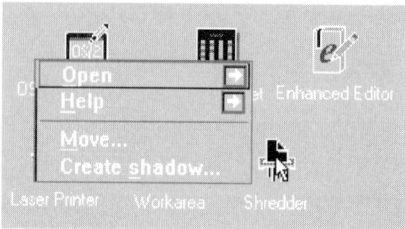

- **Cascaded Menus.** A particular choice in a menu may include an *arrow*. Selecting such a choice displays a *cascaded menu* that provides a set of additional choices associated with the main choice.

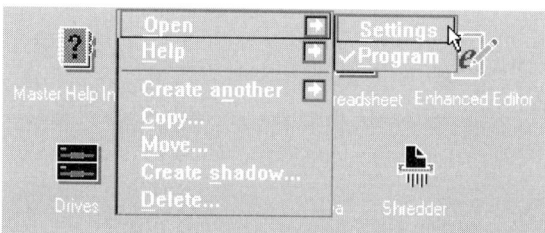

In addition to the various types of menus, CUA defines a number of additional types of controls that are described in the following sections.

Push-button Control

A *push-button control* represents a single choice that can be selected. When a number of pushbuttons are displayed, the pushbutton for the default action can be highlighted. Pressing the Enter key on the keyboard selects the default action.

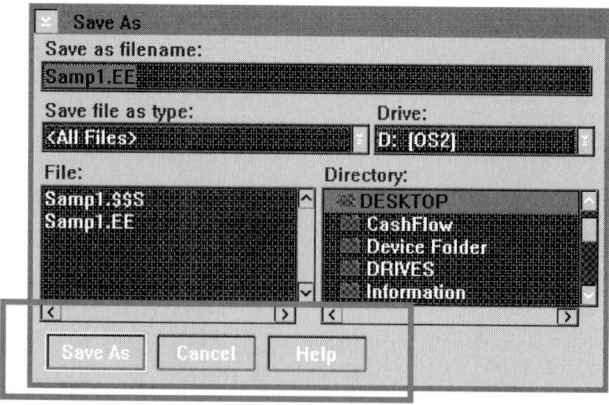

Radio Button Control

A *radio button control* consists of a group of circles followed by text describing each choice. Radio buttons are used when we can select only one of the displayed choices. The selected choice is indicated by a dot in the center of the circle.

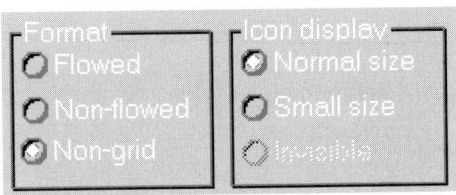

Value Set Control

A *value set* consists of a single-choice selection field in which the choices are typically represented using graphical elements, rather than radio buttons and text. Highlighting is used to indicate the selected choice.

Slider Control

A *slider* is used to select from a continuous range of available values. Moving the slider bar selects the appropriate value.

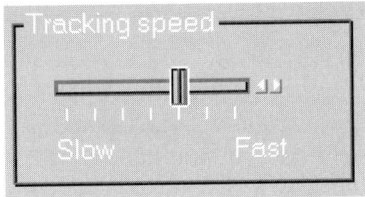

Check Box Control

A *check box* is used to indicate a choice that can be either selected or not selected. With a set of check boxes, we can select any number of the displayed choices.

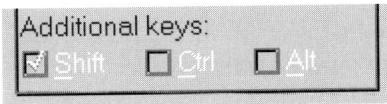

List Box Control

A *list box* consists of a box that contains a scrollable list of choices. A list box can allow either a single choice or multiple choices. A scroll bar is used to scroll through the list. The set of choices in a list box can be either fixed or variable.

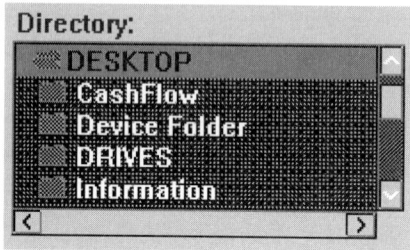

Drop-down List Control

A *drop-down list* is a list box that initially shows a single choice and a downward pointing arrow. When the down arrow is selected, the rest of the list box appears.

Entry Field Control

An *entry field* consists of a rectangular box containing one or more lines for entering data. An entry field can be scrollable when more data can be entered than can be displayed on the screen.

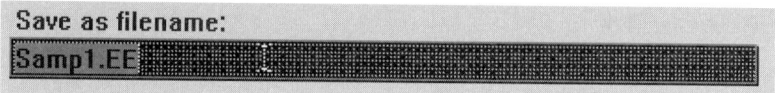

Combination Box Control

A *combination box control* consists of an entry field and a list box. We can enter information into the entry field directly or select one of the choices from the list box. The selected choice then appears in the entry field.

Drop-down Combination Box Control

A *drop-down combination box* consists of a combination box that initially displays only the entry field portion and a downward pointing arrow. If the arrow is selected, the list of choices is displayed.

Spin Button Control

A *spin button control* consists of an entry field in which we can select a value by scrolling through a ring of choices. Spin buttons are commonly used when there is a fixed set of possible values.

Notebook Control

A *notebook control* is used to display data or choices that can be organized into distinct groups. The groups are contained in sections indicated by tabs. The tabs let us move from one section of the notebook to another. Each section in the notebook can have one or more pages, and we can move from page to page within each section.

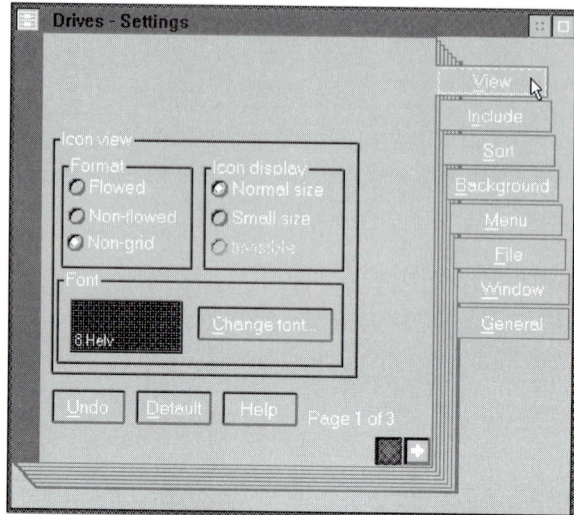

INTERACTION TECHNIQUES

The CUA Advanced Interface defines two different types of devices that can be used to interact with a computing application—a *mouse* or other similar pointing device and a *keyboard*. Although it is possible to interact with some Advanced Interface applications using a keyboard alone, the mouse is generally an important element in the user interface.

The Advanced Interface defines specific interaction techniques for the following types of interaction:

- **Data entry.** Data can be entered in either insert or replace mode. Certain control keys, such as Delete, Backspace, and Tab, have defined functions during data entry.
- **Selection.** Selections can be made using a mouse, with the *point-and-click* technique. This involves moving the pointer and pressing one of the mouse buttons. Selection is made using the keyboard by moving the cursor and performing a selection action or by entering a mnemonic.
- **Scrolling.** Scrolling can be performed by interacting with the scroll bar or by using keyboard keys that have been defined to have scrolling functions.
- **Window manipulation.** Windows can be moved, resized, opened, and closed using window elements, such as window borders, window sizing buttons, and the System pulldown menu.
- **Object manipulation.** Objects can be moved, copied, and created by interacting directly with the icons that represent them in the workplace.

STANDARD ACTIONS

The Advanced Interface also defines a number of standard actions to be included in pulldown and pop-up menus and in pushbuttons. It recommends including these actions in an application where their use is appropriate. For example, CUA recommends always including a Help choice in the menu bar, with the following standard actions included in the Help pulldown menu:

- **Help Index.** Displays an alphabetical index of all help topics available within the application.
- **General Help.** Displays a brief overview of the function of the window from which Help was requested.
- **Using Help.** Displays information about how to use the help facility.
- **Tutorial Help.** Displays an online tutorial about the application.
- **Product Information.** Displays information about the product being used, such as a logo, version information, or a copyright notice.
- **Keys Help.** Displays a list of all key and mouse button assignments available as part of this application. CUA recommends including Keys Help as a help index topic, but a specific application may also include it in the Help pulldown.

These choices cause the display of different types of help information. Menu bar choices for which CUA recommends standard actions are listed in Box 14.1.

BOX 14.1 Standard menu choices.

- **File.** The *File* pulldown menu provides choices that affect the object being viewed in the window as a whole, such as opening it, printing it, and saving it.
- **Selected.** The *Selected* menu contains choices that can be applied to an object, or set of objects, that have been selected from within the window. The choices may be similar to the File menu choices but are applied to selected objects rather than to the object associated with the window. For example, the window may be a view of a container object, and the Selected choices could apply to individual data objects stored in the container.
- **Edit.** The *Edit* menu contains choices related to editing operations that can be performed on an object and to operations that affect which objects are selected.
- **View.** The *View* menu has choices related to how an object is displayed. This can include the type of view, the objects to include, the sequence to use, and when the view is updated.
- **Options.** The *Options* menu offers choices that allow the user to customize an application. Most choices in the Options window will be application-specific.
- **Windows.** The *Windows* menu presents choices that allow the user to manage other windows associated with this window.
- **Help.** The *Help* menu provides access to various forms of help information and facilities.

CUA also defines a set of standard actions for inclusion in pushbuttons and provides recommendations for their use in different types of windows. These actions are listed in Box 14.2.

BOX 14.2 Standard pushbutton actions.

- **OK.** Causes the application to accept any changes the user has made in the window and removes the window.
- **Close.** Removes the window without affecting an active process or application associated with the window.
- **Stop.** Causes an associated process or application to end and removes the window.
- **Continue.** Resumes a process or application that had been interrupted by the operating environment.
- **Retry.** Causes an operation to be retried after an error has occurred.
- **Apply.** Causes any settings changes that have been made to be applied without removing the window used to make the changes.
- **Reset.** Returns any changed settings choices in the window to their last saved value.
- **Cancel.** Removes the window without making any changes that were specified in that window.
- **Pause.** Temporarily suspends a process or application.
- **Resume.** Causes a process or application that was suspended to continue.
- **Help.** Causes contextual help information to be displayed.

CUA BASIC INTERFACE MODELS

Applications conforming to the CUA Basic Interface display information in the form of *panels* where one panel occupies the entire terminal screen. As indicated earlier, the CUA Basic Interface defines two models of user interaction—a text subset of the graphical model and an entry model.

Panel Appearance

Figure 14.4 shows an example of a panel conforming to the text subset of the graphical model. It can contain a *menu bar*, a *work area*, a *panel title*, a *panel ID*, a *message area*, a *command area*, and a *function key area*. The menu bar, or *action bar*, as it is sometimes called, is used to call up pulldown menus that allow

```
      Find    Add    Help
                           Hotel Selector
   Select one from each group by typing the number.
   Then select an action.

            Name of city  _ 1. New York
                            2. Paris
                            3. Tokyo

            Price category _ 1. Budget
                             2. Moderate
                             3. Expensive
                             4. Luxury



   Reformatting is complete. Enter to continue.
   Command ===> sent stat.rpt to tony ▮_____
   F1=Help    F3=Exit    F10=Actions    F12=Cancel
```

Figure 14.4 CUA Basic Interface panel format.

the user to make choices. Below the menu bar is the *work area* of the panel. It is used to display application-specific information. Below the work area of the panel is a *message area*. The application uses this area to display messages to the user. The Basic Interface defines three types of messages: information messages, warning messages, and action messages. A panel can optionally contain a *command area* below the message area. If the application supports one, it can be used to enter commands. At the bottom of the panel is the *function key area*. The application uses it to display actions that can be invoked by pressing function keys.

As with the Advanced Interface, we can use a text subset menu bar to display a *pulldown menu*, as shown in Fig. 14.5. A pulldown menu details the specific actions that are associated with that menu bar entry.

The other user interface model defined by the CUA Basic Interface is called the *entry model*. Figure 14.6 shows an example of the entry model panel format defined by the CUA Basic Interface. It is similar to the text subset panel format except that there is no menu bar.

Controls

The Basic Interface does not include all the types of controls defined by the Advanced Interface. The controls that are part of the Basic Interface include the following:

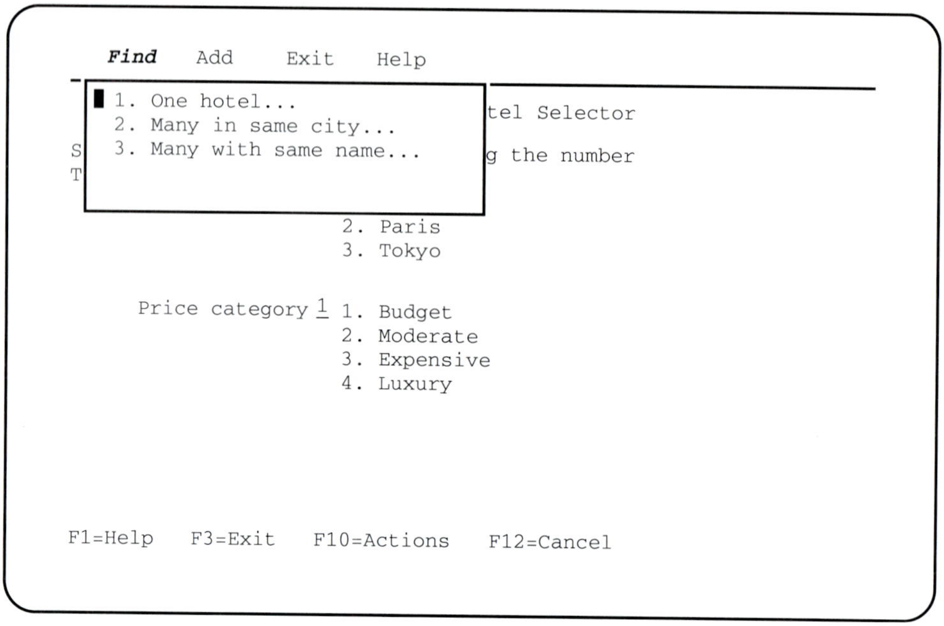

```
    Find   Add    Exit   Help
    ┌─────────────────────┐
    ■ 1. One hotel...     │ tel Selector
    │ 2. Many in same city...
  S │ 3. Many with same name... │ g the number
  T │                     │
    └─────────────────────┘
                     2. Paris
                     3. Tokyo

         Price category 1  1. Budget
                           2. Moderate
                           3. Expensive
                           4. Luxury




  F1=Help    F3=Exit    F10=Actions    F12=Cancel
```

Figure 14.5   CUA Basic Interface pull-down menu.

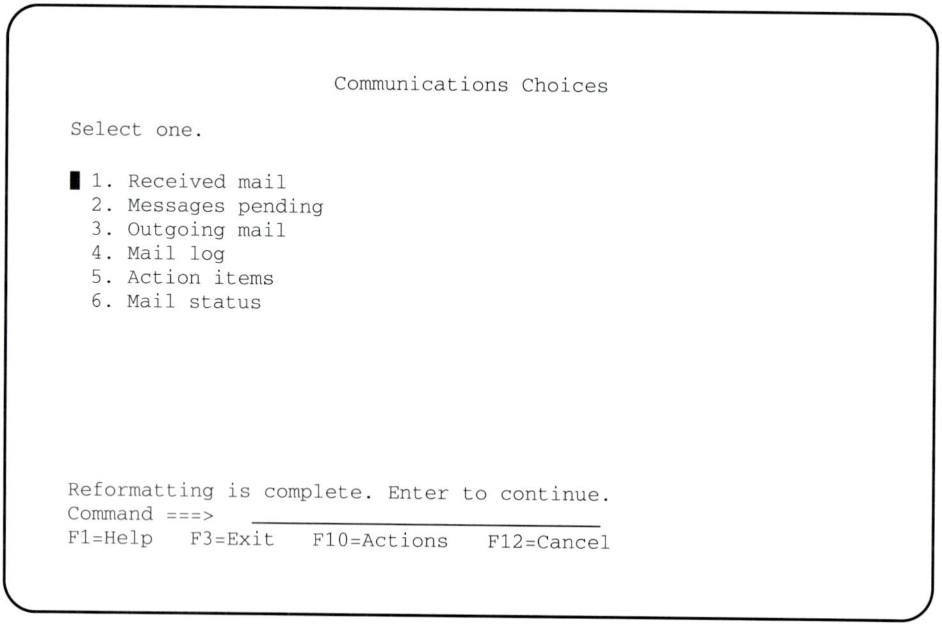

```
                      Communications Choices

   Select one.

   ■ 1. Received mail
     2. Messages pending
     3. Outgoing mail
     4. Mail log
     5. Action items
     6. Mail status




  Reformatting is complete. Enter to continue.
  Command ===> _____
  F1=Help    F3=Exit    F10=Actions    F12=Cancel
```

Figure 14.6   CUA Basic Interface entry model panel.

- **Menu bar and pulldown menus.** The menu bar lists broad categories of actions that are available. Pulldown menus display specific choices available for a given menu bar entry.
- **Single-choice field.** With a *single-choice field,* the user must select one and only one choice. To select a choice, the user enters a number or mnemonic associated with the choice in an entry field that is part of the selection field.
- **Multiple-choice field.** With a *multiple-choice field,* the user can select any number of choices or choose none of the entries. The user selects a choice by entering a slash in the entry field next to each of the desired choices.
- **Selection list.** A *selection list* is a selection field in which the list of choices in the selection list may vary from one execution of the application to another. There may be more items in the list than can fit on the screen, and scrolling is used to display them all. A selection list can be single- or multiple-choice.
- **Action list.** An action list has instructions and a list of action codes at the top. It has a list of choices, each with an associated entry field. To select choices, the user enters one of the action codes in the action entry field. The user can select different actions for different choices.

Pop-Up Windows

An application conforming to the text subset of the graphical model can also display *pop-up windows,* as shown in Fig. 14.7. They can be used to extend the dialog or to display additional information, such as help or messages. The pop-up

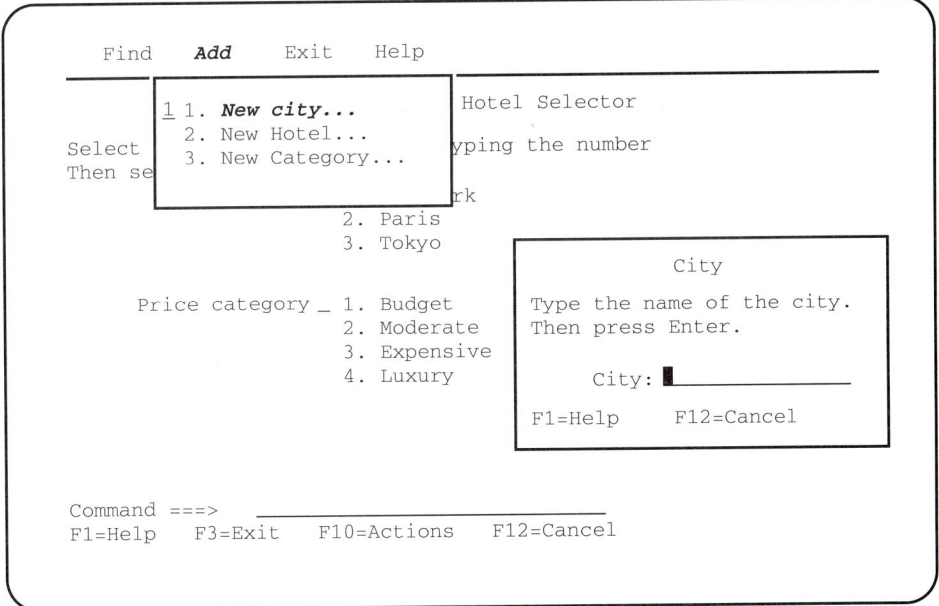

Figure 14.7 CUA Basic Interface pop-up window.

window shown in Fig. 14.7 is an example of a *dialog box*. It displays additional information that is needed to completely specify this action. An application can also display pop-up windows to allow us to enter commands or to display prompts and help information.

Interaction

When using a nonprogrammable terminal, the user interacts with an application using the keyboard. CUA does not support the use of a mouse or other pointing device with nonprogrammable terminals. Selections are typically made by entering a number or mnemonics associated with a particular choice or by entering a particular selection character alongside a choice. Various control keys are used for scrolling and with data entry operations.

As with the Advanced Interface, the Basic Interface defines standard actions that an application should include in the menu bar and its pulldown menus when the actions are appropriate. The Basic Interface also defines standard actions to be associated with function keys that are basically equivalent to the Advanced Interface push-button actions.

Model Differences

There are two primary differences between the text subset and the full graphical model. The text subset does not use icons or other graphical elements, and windows are not movable or sizable and do not have window title bars or window borders. The entry model does not support the use of pulldown menus, and the use of pop-up windows is optional. If the application does not use pop-up windows, it typically uses full-screen panels to conduct the dialog and to display prompt and help information.

Except for Help windows, pop-up windows, the equivalent of secondary windows, are modal. The user must complete the interaction with the pop-up window and either submit or cancel it before being allowed to interact with any of the field in the underlying panel.

CONCLUSION

This chapter has introduced the characteristics of the Common User Access interface component of SAA. Chapter 15 introduces the elements of the Common Communications Support component that are directly associated with the presentation of information.

15 COMMON COMMUNICATIONS SUPPORT USER INTERFACES

The Common Communications Support component of SAA is the SAA element that is concerned with how computing applications or computing application components communicate over a network. This chapter describes the user interfaces that are associated with CCS.

CCS DATA STREAM AND OBJECT ARCHITECTURES

The elements of the CCS component of SAA that are directly connected with the presentation of information are *transmission objects* and *data streams*:

- **Transmission Objects.** *Transmission objects* are entities containing the types of data that can be combined to create a finished product, such as a document, a data file, or a database. In many cases, the data exchanged in distributed computing applications takes the form of documents that are exchanged among application programs. A document containing many different types of data, such as text, graphics, and bit-mapped images is called a *compound document.* Data in a compound document is carried in entities called *objects.* CCS includes a series of architectures that are used to define the formats of the various types of transmission objects that can be carried over a network.

- **Data Streams.** A data stream is a continuous, ordered stream of data elements conforming to a particular format. Transmission objects, as well as other types of data, are carried in a data stream. CCS data stream architectures define the structure and content of the types of data streams supported in CCS. Like the transmission objects, CCS data streams are also associated with the applications that use the network for communication.

TRANSMISSION OBJECTS

Transmission objects contain the types of data that can be combined to produce a finished product, such as a document, a data file, or a database. These transmission objects can carry data in the form of text, graphics, images, formatted data, and font resources. The transmission objects included in CCS are defined in *object content architectures* (OCAs) that describe the format and content of the transmission objects. Those object content architectures for which support is included in CCS are as follows:

- **Presentation Text Object Content Architecture.** The *Presentation Text Object Content Architecture* (PTOCA) defines the structure and content of objects that contain text that has been formatted for display.
- **Graphics Object Content Architecture.** The *Graphics Object Content Architecture* (GOCA) defines the structure and content of graphic objects that contain such elements as lines, arcs, and character strings.
- **Image Object Content Architecture.** The *Image Object Content Architecture* (IOCA) defines the structure and content of objects that contain bit-mapped images.
- **Formatted Data Object Content Architecture.** The *Formatted Data Object Content Architecture* (FD:OCA) is used to express the format and meaning of data elements that are stored in files and databases.
- **Font Object Content Architecture.** The *Font Object Content Architecture* (FOCA) defines the structure and content of objects that contain information about type fonts that can be used to control the appearance of printed or displayed text.

DATA STREAMS

A CCS *data stream* is a continuous, ordered string of data elements that conforms to a defined format and is destined for a printer, a workstation, or another program. CCS includes architectures for five different types of data streams that application programs can generate and transmit over a network.

- **Mixed Object Document Content Architecture.** The *Mixed Object Document Content Architecture* (MO:DCA), which is often pronounced such that it rhymes with vodka, defines a data stream used to carry the transmission objects making up a compound document. A MO:DCA data stream consists of objects and control information. The individual object content architectures introduced previously define the structure of transmission objects of various types that can be included as part of a MO:DCA data stream.
- **Intelligent Printer Data Stream.** An *Intelligent Printer Data Stream* (IPDS) carries compound document objects that are destined for an all-points-addressable output device, such as a laser printer or typesetter. IPDS supports presentation of high-quality text, image, vector graphics, and bar code data and control of device functions such as duplexing and media-bin selection.
- **3270 Data Stream.** A *3270 Data Stream* is used for transmitting data between an application program and a 3270-type terminal. A 3270 data stream contains user data, commands, and control codes that govern the processing and formatting of data. For data sent from a program to a terminal, the data stream controls how information is formatted and displayed on the device's display screen or

printer. For data sent from a terminal to a program, the data stream controls how the program interprets the data.

- **Revisable Form Text Document Content Architecture.** The *Revisable Form Text Document Content Architecture* (RFT:DCA) defines a data stream that carries text that is easily updatable and is used to store and exchange text documents in an office system. An RFT:DCA data stream contains both text representing the content of the document and control information that specifies how the document is to be formatted. RFT:DCA specifies the structure used within the data stream to represent both text and control codes and how systems are to interpret the text and control codes. Revisable form text documents are in a form that permits them to be easily modified by anyone who receives the document or has access to it.

- **Character Data Representation Architecture.** The *Character Data Representation Architecture* (CDRA) can be used in conjunction with text data contained in a transmission object. It is used to identify the encoding method used to generate the graphic character set, called a *code page,* used to display or print each character of the text data. The current IBM CCS documentation classifies CDRA as defining a fifth type of data stream. However, CDRA is not an actual data stream architecture in the same sense as MO:DCA, IPDS, RFT:DCA, and the 3270 data stream. Rather, CDRA is used to define the structure and semantics of information ordinarily contained within a transmission object. But we are classifying CDRA with the data stream architectures for consistency with the CCS documentation.

DOCUMENT DATA STREAM ENVIRONMENTS

In the SAA environment, information to be shared between communicating application programs is transmitted among them in the form of data streams.

Each data stream has a structure that is defined by an architecture and is understood by each of the applications that must interpret the information carried in the data stream. The structure and content of a data stream are influenced by the environment in which the data stream is used. For example, a data stream that is transmitted from one application program to another in a distributed application may not require any device-specific control information. But a data stream that is being carried from an application program to a presentation device, such as a display or a printer, may require device-specific control information that controls device functions.

SAA recognizes three separate processing environments in which a data stream can be processed:

- The interchange environment
- The interactive environment
- The presentation environment

The following sections discuss each of these processing environments.

THE INTERCHANGE ENVIRONMENT

The *interchange environment* involves the exchange of documents between applications. In this environment, data is shared between applications. In order to store, retrieve, and process the shared data, it must be in a commonly understood format. The applications must be able to accurately interpret the data stream, both in terms of content and appearance. One example of a possible use for the interchange environment is to send a document from a host computing system to a programmable workstation for processing. The RFT:DCA and MO:DCA data streams that are included in CCS are designed to provide commonly understood formats for interchanging documents between applications.

THE INTERACTIVE ENVIRONMENT

A document may also need to be processed using a nonprogrammable workstation, such as a 3270 display station. This type of processing characterizes the *interactive environment*. In this environment the data that makes up the document must be able to be displayed at the terminal, edited, stored, and retrieved. The data stream used in this environment must support control information and formatting appropriate to the display and data entry characteristics of the device being used for presentation. The recommended data stream structure for this environment is the 3270 data stream, which is specifically designed for use with the 3270 family of terminal equipment.

THE PRESENTATION ENVIRONMENT

A document may also be presented on an output device such as a printer. The *presentation environment* is intended for such an application. In this environment the data stream used must facilitate the use of device-specific functions and provide for the management of device resources and the handling of error conditions. Typically, the data is displayed only, and the data stream does not need to support editing and composition functions. The *Advanced Function Printer Data Stream* (AFPDS) is an older data stream that was developed to define printer data streams for all-points-addressable printers where the objects being printed may contain different data types, such as text and images. Many products generate AFPDS data streams. When an AFPDS data stream is to be sent to a specific type of printer, the AFPDS data stream is typically converted to the *Intelligent Printer Data Stream* (IPDS) format, in which control information has been inserted that is specific for the particular printer device being used.

ENVIRONMENTS AND DATA STREAMS

An example of the relationship between the different environments and the data streams they employ is illustrated in Fig. 15.1. Notice that the MO:DCA data

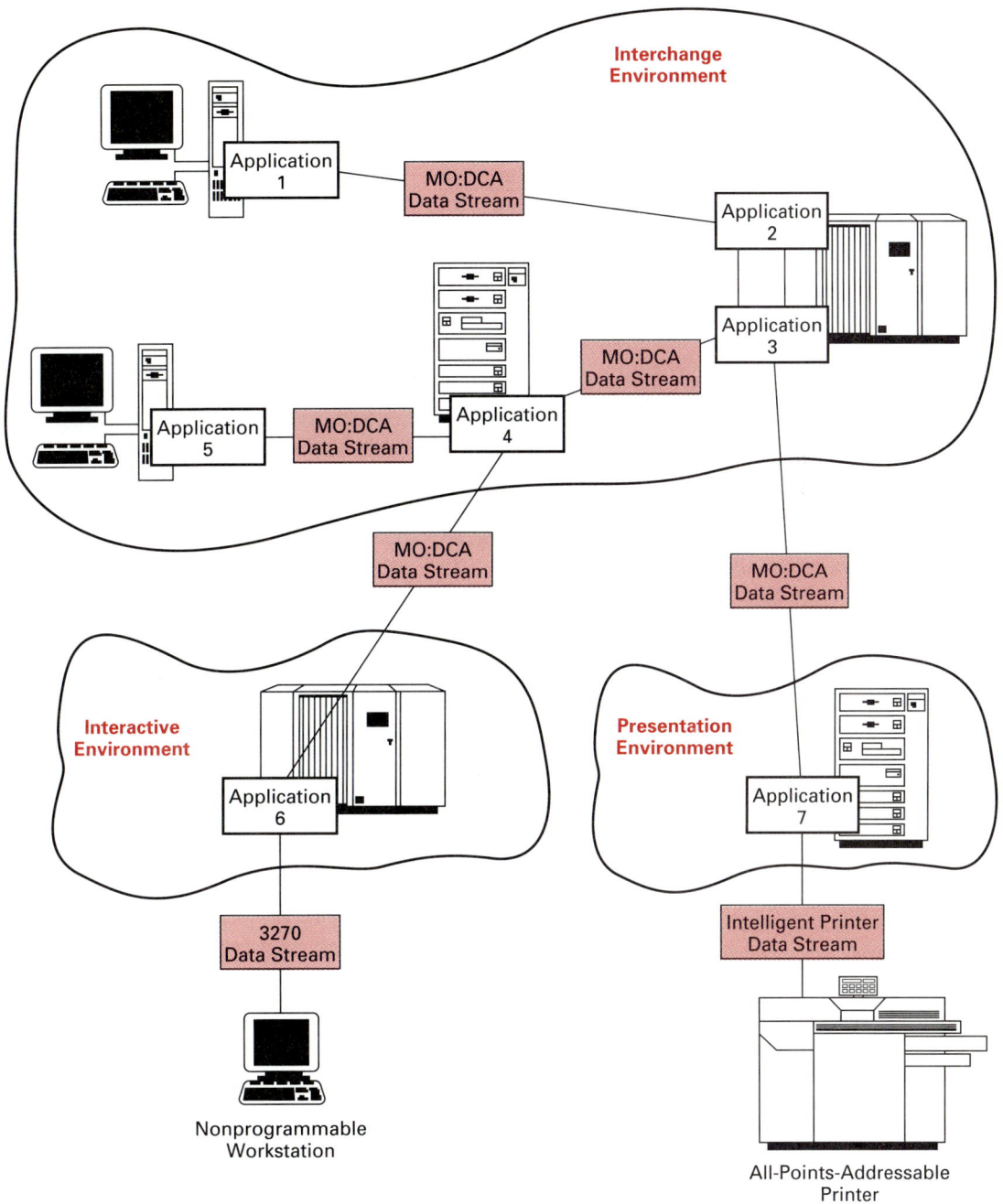

Figure 15.1 Data streams used in the three document processing environments.

stream is used when documents are exchanged between applications running on various types of processors in the interchange environment and also when they are conveyed from one environment to another.

OBJECT CONTENT ARCHITECTURES

Of the object content architectures included in CCS, the ones that are most directly reflected in the CPI interfaces are the Graphics Object Content Architecture (GOCA) and the Font Object Content Architecture (FOCA). The following sections discuss each of these object content architectures.

GRAPHICS OBJECT CONTENT ARCHITECTURE

The *Graphics Object Content Architecture* (GOCA) addresses the creation, modification, and presentation of transmission objects that represent pictures consisting of vector, or line-drawn, graphics. The architecture includes functions not only for the presentation of the graphic object on a display screen or printer device but also for direct manipulation of the object in an interactive environment.

The initial version of the architecture (Version 0), which is the version included in CCS, supports the use of graphics objects in presentation and resource documents. A second version of the architecture (Version 1), also known as the *Extended Graphics Object Content Architecture* (GOCA Extended), provides additional facilities and supports the use of graphics objects in revisable documents as well as in presentation and resource documents. At the time of writing, GOCA Extended has not been included in CCS.

PRIMITIVES

GOCA provides facilities for drawing complex pictures. A picture is made up of one or more elements called *primitives*. The types of primitives that can be drawn include the following:

- **Lines.** Line primitives include straight lines, curved lines, and boxes.
- **Areas and Paths.** Areas and paths are two-dimensional primitives that are filled with a pattern.
- **Character Strings.** A character string consists of text characters and information about the character set or font used to draw the characters.
- **Markers.** A marker is a symbol used to indicate a position.
- **Images.** Images are digitized pictures that are stored and manipulated as a two-dimensional array of data, called *image points,* where each point has a particular visual quality. Image data is sometimes referred to as *raster data.*

Each primitive has its own set of *primitive attributes*, such as line width, line style, or shading associated with it. In addition, there may be a set of *drawing attributes*, such as color, that apply to all the primitives.

DRAWING ORDERS AND SEGMENTS Each primitive that makes up a picture is produced by a *drawing order* that defines the primitive's characteristics. The drawing orders associated with the different types of primitives are shown in Box 15.1. Drawing orders are grouped

BOX 15.1 Drawing orders.

Line Drawing Orders

- **LINE.** Draws one or more contiguous straight lines using absolute values for points.
- **RELATIVE LINE.** Draws one or more contiguous straight lines using relative values for points.
- **ARC.** Draws a curve based on a start point, a middle point, and an end point. The arc is drawn by scaling the shape defined by the SET ARC PARAMETERS order.
- **FULL ARC.** Draws a complete circle or ellipse based on a center point and a multiplier value that specifies how much the circle or ellipse defined by the SET ARC PARAMETERS order is to be scaled.
- **PARTIAL ARC.** Draws a curve based on a center point, a multiplier, and start and sweep angles. The center point and multiplier determine a full arc. The start angle and sweep determine how much of the arc is included.
- **FILLET.** Draws a curve based on a set of points that are described in the FILLET order's parameters. Imaginary lines connect the points and then a curve is drawn tangential to the lines. The curve is tangential to the first line at its start point, to intermediate lines at their midpoints, and to the last line at its end point.
- **SHARP FILLET.** Draws a curve based on a set of points and a set of sharpness-specification parameters. The sharpness-specification parameters determine points through which the curve must pass between the points where it is tangential to a line.

(Continued)

BOX 15.1 *(Continued)*

- **BEZIER CURVE.** Draws a curve based on a set of points. The points are processed in sets of four, and the curve is defined by a set of parametric equations based on the four points.
- **BOX.** Draws a box based on the corner positions of a rectangle and the lengths of the horizontal and vertical axes of an ellipse. The lengths of the axes determine the shape of the corners.
- **BEGIN AREA.** Marks the beginning of an area definition and is followed by drawing orders that generate each of the primitives that define the area's boundary.
- **END AREA.** Marks the end of an area definition.
- **BEGIN PATH.** Marks the beginning of a path definition and is followed by drawing orders that generate the figures, character strings, or markers that define the path.
- **END PATH.** Marks the end of a path definition.
- **CHARACTER STRING.** Draws a character string using the specified attributes.
- **MARKER.** Draws a marker using the specified symbol and attributes.
- **BEGIN IMAGE.** Marks the beginning of an image definition.
- **IMAGE DATA.** Draws one row of image points using the specified attributes to determine the appearance of each point.
- **END IMAGE.** Marks the end of an image definition.

together in collections called *segments*. A segment is a named set of drawing orders with their associated attributes. Attributes included in a segment determine the appearance of the primitives being drawn. If a required attribute for a primitive is not included in the segment, a default value is used for that attribute. Standard defaults for attribute values are defined as a general part of the environment. Box 15.2 lists drawing attributes, which can be specified for any type of primitive. Box 15.3 contains line attributes. Box 15.4 lists pattern attributes, which are used with area and path primitives. Box 15.5 contains character attributes, used with character string primitives. Box 15.6 shows marker attributes.

The location and size of each primitive is specified in a drawing order in terms of points that exist in a *coordinate space*. The various coordinate spaces that are defined by GOCA are described later in this chapter.

BOX 15.2   Drawing attributes.

- **Foreground Color.** Determines the color in which the foreground bits of the primitive are drawn. The value of the attribute acts as an index into a color table. Either a standard architecture-defined table or an environment-defined table can be used.
- **Background Color.** Determines the color in which the background bits of the primitive are drawn.
- **Mix.** When a primitive is drawn in the graphics presentation space, it may overlap picture elements that have already been drawn and have their own color attributes. The mix attribute determines how the color of the foreground bits of the primitive being drawn is combined with an existing color in the graphics presentation space. Mixing is done by combining color attribute values and determining a new value that is then used as the index into the color table. The way in which the values are combined is determined by the mix attribute. Different methods that can be specified are as follows:
  — **Or.** The two color attribute values are ORed together.
  — **Overpaint.** The color attribute of the primitive being drawn is used.
  — **Leave Alone.** The color attribute from the graphics presentation space is used.
- **Background Mix.** Determines how the color of the background bits of the primitive being drawn is combined with an existing color in the graphics presentation space.

BOX 15.3   Line attributes.

- **Line Type.** Determines the style of the line used in drawing, such as solid, dotted, dashed, and so on.
- **Line Width.** Specifies the width of the line used in drawing. It is specified in multiples of a standard line width.
- **Line End.** Specifies the type of ending of stroked lines, such as flat, square, or round.
- **Line Join.** Specifies the type of joining of stroked lines, such as round, bevel, or miter.
- **Stroke Width.** Specifies the length of the perpendicular to the path used in stroking a path.

BOX 15.4 Pattern attributes.

- **Pattern Set.** Specifies the symbol set or font from which the pattern symbol is taken.
- **Pattern Symbol.** Specifies the particular symbol used as a fill pattern.
- **Pattern Reference Point.** Specifies the position at which the first symbol is placed. The symbol is then repeated in both directions from there.

BOX 15.5 Character attributes.

- **Character Precision.** Specifies the level of accuracy required in presenting a character. Possible values are
  — **Precision 1.** Each character is positioned at the nearest character cell or more precisely if possible; the size and angle of the character may be ignored.
  — **Precision 2.** Each character is positioned as accurately as possible; size and angle may be ignored.
  — **Precision 3.** Each character is positioned as accurately as possible; size and angle are implemented as accurately as possible.
- **Character Shear.** Specifies the horizontal shear of the character string.
- **Character Angle.** Specifies the angle of the baseline of the character string.
- **Character Cell.** Specifies the size of the cell in which characters are drawn.
- **Character Direction.** Specifies the direction in which characters in the string are drawn relative to the baseline. This can be left-to-right, right-to-left, top-to-bottom, or bottom-to-top.
- **Character Set.** Specifies the character set or font that determines the graphic symbol drawn for each character.
- **Character Extra.** Specifies the additional increment to be added to character positions within a character string.
- **Character Break Extra.** Specifies the additional increment to be added to character positions following a break character in a character string.

BOX 15.6   Marker attributes.

- **Marker Precision.** Determines the level of accuracy required in presenting the marker. Possible values are the same as for character precision.
- **Marker Cell.** Specifies the size of the cell in which the marker is drawn.
- **Marker Set.** Specifies the symbol set or font from which the marker symbol is taken.
- **Marker Symbol.** Specifies the particular symbol that is used as the marker.

PICTURE GENERATION

A picture is generated, or drawn, on a particular presentation medium by executing the segments that make up the picture. When a segment is executed, the drawing orders that make up the segment are interpreted, and an appropriately shaped and shaded portion of the picture is mapped into a coordinate space. Execution of a segment begins with the first drawing order in the segment and continues, order by order, until the last drawing order has been executed. As part of the drawing process, *resources* may be used that are part of the data stream environment. These resources include a *color table* that associates an index with a color definition and a *font/symbol set* that associates a local identifier with a particular set of graphic symbols. In addition to the segment and resource data used to construct the picture, there are a number of internal *controls* that can influence the final appearance of the picture.

Chained Segments

A collection of segments can be chained together to form a picture. When segments are chained, after each segment has completed execution, control is passed to the next segment in the chain, and that segment is then executed. In this way the entire picture can be generated by invoking the execution of the first segment in the chain.

Called Segments

A segment can also call another segment, causing the called segment to be executed. After the called segment is executed, control returns to the calling segment. Called segments are often used to define subpictures that may be used in multiple places.

Transmission Mode

In order to start picture generation, data stream transmission must take place with the proper transmission mode in effect. The mode in effect can be *immediate*, *store*, or *store and draw*. In immediate mode, transmitted chain segments are executed and then discarded. In store mode, transmitted chain segments are stored for later execution. In store and draw mode, chain segments are both executed and stored. Transmitting a chained segment in either immediate or store and draw mode starts the picture generation process.

COORDINATE SPACES AND TRANSFORMATIONS

As we have already described, primitives are drawn based on coordinates that exist in a coordinate space. One of the major functions defined in GOCA is the way in which coordinates specified in drawing orders are mapped to a standard coordinate system. The standard coordinate system is then mapped to coordinates associated with the presentation medium. The process of mapping from one coordinate system to another is called a *transformation*, or *transform*.

Drawing Order Coordinate Space

The different coordinate spaces and transformations used for presentation of graphic objects are illustrated in Fig. 15.2. When a segment is executed, the subpicture generated by the segment is created in the *drawing order coordinate space* using coordinates specified in the drawing orders in the segment. Each segment has its own drawing order coordinate space.

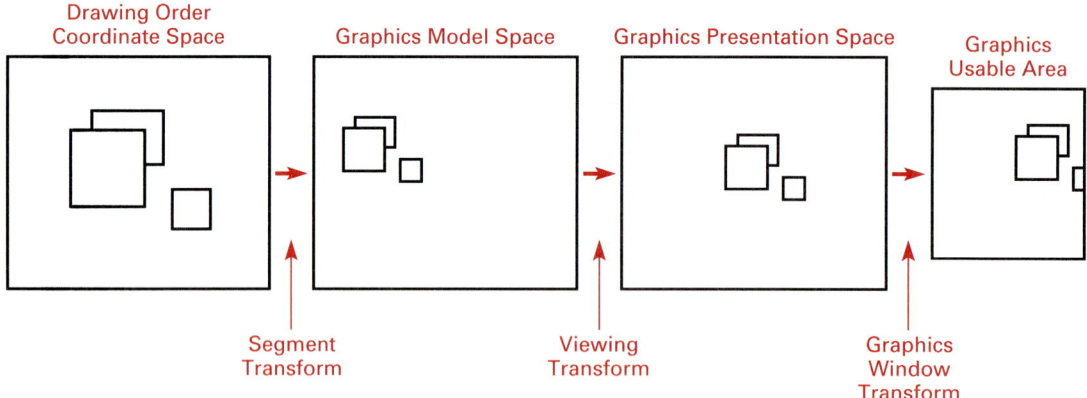

Figure 15.2 Coordinate spaces and transformations.

Graphics Model Space

The *model transform* maps the subpicture in the drawing order coordinate space to a standard coordinate system used for the entire picture and places the subpicture in a new space called the *graphics model space*. This transform may involve translating coordinates and rotating or scaling the subpicture. The segment transform can be changed during the execution of a segment. This allows different portions of a segment to be generated using different drawing order coordinate systems and allows all of them to be mapped to a consistent coordinate system in the graphics model space.

Graphics Presentation Space

After a picture or model has been constructed in the graphics model space, the *viewing transform* then maps it to the *graphics presentation space*. The graphics presentation space is the application user's view of the picture that is generated. The viewing transform is based on how the model is to be viewed and can involve operations such as panning or zooming. The *viewing window* function defines a rectangular area within the graphics model space with sides parallel to the graphics model space boundaries. When a picture is generated in the graphics model space, any primitives that cross the viewing window or lie outside it are clipped. Only the portion of the primitive that is inside the viewing window is mapped to the graphics presentation space by the viewing transform.

Usable Area

The model in the graphics presentation space is device independent. To be presented on a particular device, it must be mapped to the coordinate space used by the actual presentation medium. This coordinate space is called the *usable area*. The *graphics window transform* maps the model from the graphics presentation area to the usable area. This transformation may again involve clipping or scaling of the picture. Both the usable area and the graphics window transform are defined outside of GOCA. They are the responsibility of the data stream environment and not of the object environment.

Called Segments

When one segment is called by another segment, the called segment has its own drawing order coordinate space and graphics model space. The resulting model must then be mapped to the coordinate space used by the calling segment. This mapping is accomplished with an *instance transform*, which maps the graphics model from the called segment's graphics model space to the calling segment's drawing order coordinate space. The instance transform is specified by the calling segment. This process is illustrated in Fig. 15.3. Once the model has been mapped to the calling segment's drawing order coordinate space, it goes through

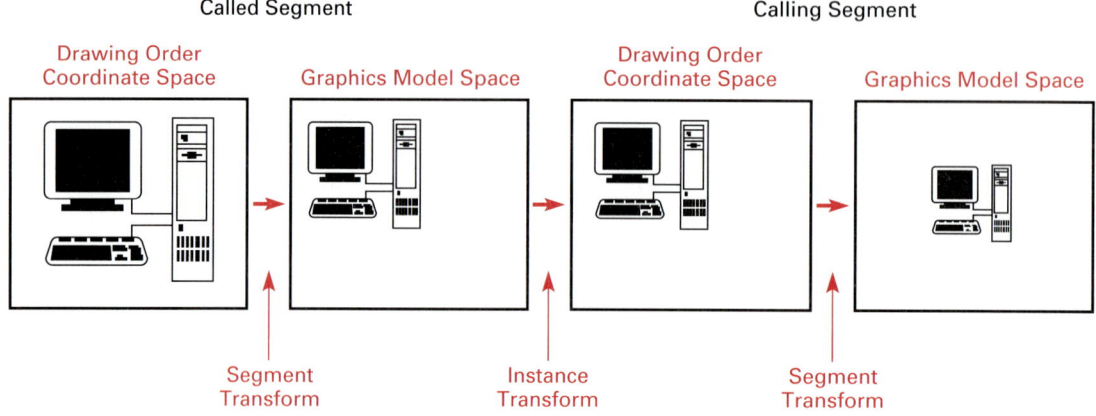

Figure 15.3   Transformation with a called segment.

the normal sequence of transformations to the graphics model space, graphics presentation space, and usable area.

GOCA EXTENDED   The facilities described here as part of GOCA are taken from a second version of GOCA, known as GOCA Extended. The facilities included as part of GOCA Extended that are not included in GOCA Version 0 include the following:

- The SHARP FILLET, BEZIER CURVE, and BOX drawing orders
- Paths and path clipping
- The use of bitmaps as pattern symbols and image primitives
- The ability to set color and mix attributes for each type of primitive
- The line attributes stroke width, line end, and line join
- The character attributes, character extra, and character break extra

At the time of writing, CCS includes only GOCA Version 0 and not GOCA Extended.

FONT OBJECT CONTENT ARCHITECTURE   The *Font Object Content Architecture* (FOCA) defines a model for defining *font resources*. A *font* is a set of graphic character symbols that share a characteristic design. Figure 15.4 shows examples of charac-

This is an example of Adobe Times.
This is an example of Adobe Helvetica.
`This is an example of Adobe Courier.`

Figure 15.4   Three sample fonts.

ters from the Times, Helvetica, and Courier fonts that are marketed by Adobe Corporation. Adobe fonts are commonly used in printers that implement the PostScript page description language used in many popular laser printers. A particular font can come in different *sizes*, where a size value specifies the height of a typical character. Type size is measured in *points*, with 72 points approximately equal to one inch. A font can also have different *typefaces*. A typeface corresponds to a particular weight, posture, and proportion. Commonly available typefaces in a typical font include roman, italic, and bold. Examples of three typefaces for the Times font are shown in Fig. 15.5.

This is an example of Adobe Times Roman.
This is an example of Adobe Times Italic.
This is an example of Adobe Times Bold.

Figure 15.5   Three typefaces in the Adobe Times font.

FONT RESOURCES   A *font resource*, as defined by the Font Object Content Architecture, consists of a collection of graphic character patterns and associated parametric information that represents a particular type family in one or more typefaces and type sizes. The parametric information identifies the font resource and its general characteristics and provides the information needed to position characters and generate character shapes for text data.

FONT REFERENCING   Documents must carry with them font referencing information that allows an appropriate font resource to be identified and used when the document is formatted and presented. A font resource can be identified by specifying its name or by specifying descriptive font information. If descriptive information is specified, the font resource that best matches those parameters is selected.

Font referencing also includes character mapping, which involves associating text data in the document with appropriate graphic characters in the font. Text is usually encoded by using a code point to represent each graphic character in the document. A code page takes the form of a table that associates a character identifier with each code point. The graphic characters in a font are then mapped to the code points of one or more code pages.

THE FOCA APPROACH

FOCA is designed to provide a consistent way of referencing and accessing font resources so that documents that use fonts can more easily be interchanged between applications and systems and still be presented in a consistent manner. FOCA does this by precisely defining the set of parameters needed to specify and reference font resource objects. FOCA does not define the syntax or format used to store the graphic character patterns that make up a font. This is left to specific implementations. FOCA also does not define the syntax used for font references. This is defined as part of the overall data stream architectures, such as MO:DCA or IPDS.

The parameter set defined by FOCA can be divided into five categories:

- **Font-Descriptive Parameters.** Font-descriptive parameters identify and describe a font resource. This information is used to assure that the correct font is used during processing. The various font-descriptive parameters are listed in Box 15.7.

- **Font-Metric Parameters.** Certain standard measurements are used for graphic characters in FOCA. Font-metric parameters provide measurement information, such as character height, width, and spacing for the font as a whole. The font-metric parameters are listed in Box 15.8.

- **Character-Metric Parameters.** Character-metric parameters provide specific measurement information for each character in a font, and the parameters are repeated for each character and each rotation of that character. The parameters are summarized in Box 15.9.

- **Character-Shape Parameters.** Character-shape parameters provide information needed to determine the exact appearance of each graphic character pattern when it is used for presentation. The information applies to the font as a whole. However, a font resource may support multiple representation techniques, such as bitmap, vector, and conic sections. The character-shape parameters, listed in Box 15.10, are repeated for each technology supported.

- **Code Page Parameters.** Code page parameters supply the information needed to map code points to graphic character patterns in a font resource. A given font resource may support one or more code pages, with the code page parameters repeated for each code page supported. The parameters are listed in Box 15.11.

BOX 15.7 Font-descriptive parameters.

- **Average Weighted Escapement.** The arithmetic average of the escapement of all, or some subset of, the characters in a font.
- **Cap-M Height.** The height above the baseline for uppercase character shapes is usually equal to the height of the uppercase letter M.
- **Character Rotation.** The rotation of the character box relative to the character baseline.
- **Em-Space Increment.** The character increment for an em-space in this font.
- **Family Name.** The common name for the font design.
- **Font Local Identifier.** A numeric identifier assigned temporarily to a font resource within the context of another object.
- **Font Type.** Whether the font is a bit-mapped or outline (vector) font.
- **Font Typeface Global Identifier.** The unique number assigned to the font typeface.
- **Horizontal Font Size.** The width of the font space character.
- **Inline Direction.** The direction in which successive characters appear in a line of text.
- **Italics.** Whether the graphic characters are upright or italics.
- **Kerning Pair Data.** Whether or not kerning pair data is available for one or more character rotations.
- **Maximum Vertical Font Size.** The maximum vertical size for scaling purposes.
- **Minimum Vertical Font Size.** The minimum vertical size for scaling purposes.
- **Negative Image.** Whether graphic characters are positive or negative images.
- **Nominal Character Slope.** The slope, or stem incline, of the graphic characters of this font.
- **Nominal Vertical Font Size.** The vertical size of the font as specified by the font designer.
- **Outline Font.** Whether or not the graphic characters in the font are overstruck.

(Continued)

BOX 15.7 *(Continued)*

- **Primary Graphic Character Set Global Identifier.** The GCSGID number assigned to the graphic character set.
- **Proportional Spacing.** Whether the font is monospaced or proportionally spaced.
- **Resource Name.** The character string that identifies this resource object.
- **Typeface Name.** The common name of the typeface.
- **Transformable Font.** Whether or not this font can be transformed (scaled, rotated, or sheared).
- **Underscored Font.** Whether or not the graphic characters in this font are underscored.
- **Uniform Character Box Font.** Whether or not all the character boxes in the font are of uniform height and width.
- **Weight Class.** The visual weight, or thickness of stroke, of the graphic characters in the font.
- **Width Class.** The relative change from the normal aspect ratio (width to height ratio) for the character shapes in the font.
- **X-Height.** The height of the body, not including ascenders, of lowercase graphic characters above the baseline.

BOX 15.8 Font-metric parameters.

- **Default Baseline Increment.** The nominal distance between character reference points in the vertical direction.
- **External Leading.** The amount of white space, in addition to the font vertical size increment, that can be added to the interline spacing without degrading the aesthetic appearance of the font.
- **Figure Space Increment.** The character increment used for numerals.
- **Internal Leading.** The nominal amount of white space above and below the character shapes of the font that provides interline spacing.
- **Kerning Bit.** Whether or not there can be negative A-space and C-space values.
- **Kerning Pair Character 1.** The first character in a pair of characters for kerning.
- **Kerning Pair Character 2.** The second character in a pair of characters for kerning.
- **Kerning Pair X-Adjust.** The required escapement adjustment in the X direction for the pair of kerning characters just specified.
- **Maximum Baseline Extent.** The space parallel to the baseline that can be used to place characters.
- **Maximum Baseline Offset.** The maximum distance of any character in a font from the character baseline to the upper edge of the character box after it has been rotated.
- **Maximum Character Box Height.** The height of uniform character boxes or the maximum height of variable character boxes.
- **Maximum Character Box Width.** The width of uniform character boxes or the maximum width of variable character boxes.
- **Maximum Character Increment.** The maximum character increment for all characters of the font.
- **Maximum Descender Depth.** The maximum descender depth for all characters of the font.
- **Maximum Lowercase Ascender Height.** The maximum ascender height of the lowercase characters a-z.
- **Maximum Lowercase Descender Depth.** The maximum descender depth of the lowercase characters a-z.
- **Measurement Units.** The unit base and units per unit base in both the X and Y directions.

(Continued)

BOX 15.8 *(Continued)*

- **Minimum A-Space.** The most negative or least positive A-space value for this font.
- **Space Character Increment.** The initial or default value of the character increment for the space character.
- **Subscript Horizontal Font Size.** The recommended horizontal font size for subscript characters.
- **Subscript Vertical Font Size.** The recommended vertical font size for subscript characters.
- **Subscript X-Axis Offset.** The recommended vertical offset from the character baseline to the character baseline for subscript characters.
- **Subscript Y-Axis Offset.** The recommended horizontal offset from the character escapement point to the reference point of a subscript character.
- **Superscript Horizontal Font Size.** The recommended horizontal font size for superscript characters.
- **Superscript Vertical Font Size.** The recommended vertical font size for superscript characters.
- **Superscript X-Axis Offset.** The recommended vertical offset from the character baseline to the character baseline for superscript characters.
- **Superscript Y-Axis Offset.** The recommended horizontal offset from the character escapement point to the reference point of a superscript character.
- **Throughscore Position.** The recommended displacement from the character baseline for drawing throughscores.
- **Throughscore Width.** The recommended width of throughscores for a font.
- **Underscore Position.** The recommended displacement from the baseline for drawing underscores.
- **Underscore Width.** The recommended width of underscores for a font.
- **Uniform A-Space.** The smallest A-space for all characters in a font.
- **Uniform Baseline Offset.** Whether or not the baseline offset is uniform for all characters in a font.
- **Uniform Character Increment.** Whether or not the character increment is uniform for all characters.

BOX 15.9 Character-metric parameters.

- **A-Space.** The distance from the character reference point to the leftmost side of the (bounded) character box.
- **Baseline Offset.** The distance from the character baseline to the topmost edge of the character box.
- **B-Space.** The width of the (bounded) character box.
- **Character Box Height.** The height of the character box.
- **Character Box Width.** The width of the character box.
- **Character Box Increment.** The sum of the A-space, B-space and C-space values.
- **C-Space.** The distance from the rightmost side of the (bounded) character box to the escapement point.
- **Descender Depth.** The descender depth of the character.
- **Graphic Character Global Identifier.** The registered identifier for this character.

BOX 15.10 Character-shape parameters.

- **Design Resolution X.** The intended presentation resolution in the X direction for this character shape representation technology.
- **Design Resolution Y.** The intended presentation resolution in the Y direction for this character shape representation technology.
- **Pattern Data.** The actual pattern shape data for this character-representation technology.
- **Pattern Data Alignment.** The byte alignment of the beginning of each character's pattern data.
- **Pattern Data Count.** The total quantity of shape data, in number of bytes.
- **Pattern Data Offset.** The size of the pattern data for each character.
- **Pattern Technology Identifier.** The technology used for character shape representation.

> **BOX 15.11   Code page parameters.**
>
> - **Code Point.** The integer sequence assigned to a graphic character.
> - **Encoding Technique.** The encoding technique used for code points in the code page.
> - **Invalid Coded-Character.** Whether this coded character is valid or not.
> - **No-Presentation.** Whether this coded character is presented.
> - **No-Increment.** Whether this character causes incrementing.
> - **Primary Code Page Global Identifier.** The CPGID value assigned to this code page.
> - **Section Number.** A number assigned to a group of not more than 256 code points.
> - **Unspecified Coded-Character Identifier.** The registered identifier for the graphic character used whenever a font object does not have character information for a particular code point.

MO:DCA DATA STREAM

The *Mixed Object Document Content Architecture* (MO:DCA) defines the syntax and semantics of a composite document data stream carrying one or more transmission objects. A MO:DCA data stream can contain various types of transmission objects, including *data objects* containing text, graphics, images, and formatted data; *resource objects* that describe such things as type fonts; and *methods* that describe the presentation intent of objects in a revisable document. In addition to the objects themselves, a MO:DCA data stream also contains control information. MO:DCA control information defines three things:

- **Document Logical Structure.** The *logical structure* of the document describes the document's content.
- **Document Layout Structure.** The *layout structure* of the document defines how the document is to be ultimately presented on an output device.
- **Presentation Space.** The *presentation space* defines the coordinate space within which document content is presented.

DOCUMENT LOGICAL STRUCTURE

In MO:DCA, a revisable document has a *logical structure* consisting of a series of logical elements. The logical structure defines the relationships that exist between the document's logical elements. For example, a document might consist of *sentences*, *list items*, and *figures*, all arranged into a series of *paragraphs*. Paragraphs, in turn, may be grouped into *subsections*, *sections*, and *chapters*. A document might also include other element types, such as *front matter*, *table of contents*, *appendices*, and an *index*. When we define a particular piece of a document's content, we define that piece as a particular type of logical element. The logical structure we define for the document specifies how each logical element relates to all the other logical elements. The logical structure we define may also have an impact on how each element is presented. For example, identifying a piece of content as a *footnote* may determine where on a page or where in the document the footnote will be placed once the document is formatted for presentation.

DOCUMENT LAYOUT STRUCTURE

In addition to its logical structure, a document also has a *layout structure* that governs how the data that makes up the document will be arranged when it is presented. A document's layout structure is typically specified in terms of *page sets*, individual *pages*, and *areas* within each page. Individual data objects within the data stream are then mapped to the areas that are defined. The layout structure may also define the relationship that exists between the individual pages and the presentation medium. For example, a particular type of presentation device may allow two pages to be displayed at the same time. And for a printed presentation medium, it might be possible for pages to be printed on both the front and the back of the paper.

PRESENTATION SPACE

The MO:DCA presentation space uses a hierarchy of coordinate systems. Each coordinate system consists of an X axis and a Y axis, with only positive X and Y directions included. An example of a MO:DCA coordinate system is shown in Fig. 15.6. The orientation of the axes and the location of the origin point (0,0) depend on the orientation of the medium. Coordinate systems are defined for the medium (X_m, Y_m), the page (X_p, Y_p), and object areas (X_{oa}, Y_{oa}). Coordinate systems are also specified by the object content architectures and are used in formatting a data object for presentation before it is mapped to a data area.

RELATIONSHIP OF MO:DCA TO THE OBJECT CONTENT ARCHITECTURES

The MO:DCA architecture and the object content architectures are distinct from one another but are intended to be used together. Each of the object content architectures allows a different type of data object to be individually created, edited, stored, and

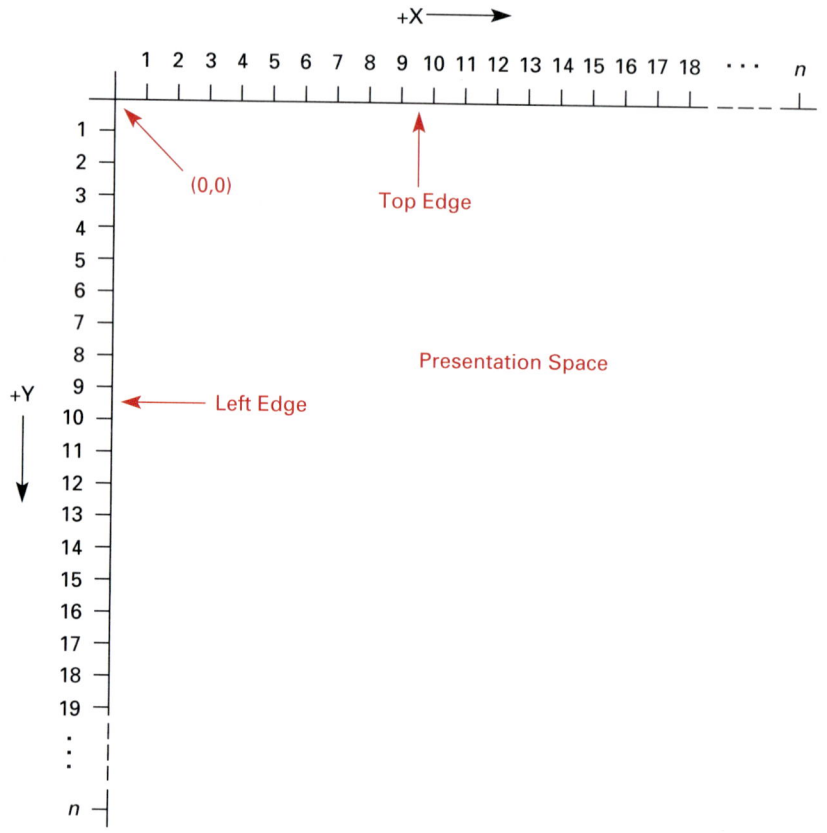

Figure 15.6 MO:DCA presentation space coordinate system.

retrieved. With MO:DCA, objects of different types can be combined to form a *compound document*. MO:DCA specifies the means by which a document's logical structure and the layout structure are defined.

As discussed earlier, MO:DCA defines a presentation space—made up of pages and areas within pages—into which data objects are mapped for presentation. MO:DCA is responsible for the location and size of each area and for the positioning of each area within a page. Individual objects, consisting of data and control information, are mapped to page areas for presentation. The object content architecture definitions determine the content and appearance of each data object within the area. For example, MO:DCA may specify that a given text object be positioned at a certain offset from the page origin. The object content architecture for text data, however, is responsible for defining how that text data is to be placed within the area. For example, the Presentation Text Object Content Architecture (PTOCA) specifies such characteristics as the spacing to be used between words and between lines.

MO:DCA COMPONENTS

In addition to data objects that make up pages, a MO:DCA data stream can contain other components that are used to define the logical structure and layout structure of the document and to specify processing control information for the document. The major components that can be carried in a MO:DCA data stream are as follows:

- **Logical Structures.** Used to define the logical structure of the document. In MO:DCA, a document's logical structure is typically organized hierarchically and can be represented as a tree structure. A logical structure consists of logical elements. A logical element can be a *basic logical element,* which is one that is not composed of other logical elements. These are the leaves in the tree structure. A *composite logical element* is one that consists of other logical elements. The very highest level logical element, in this case the document, is called the *logical document root.*

- **Logical Elements.** Used to identify the logical meaning of a particular data object and to assign values to attributes associated with the data. For example, a logical element component might be used to identify an illustration and to specify attributes for it, such as where to place it in the document relative to other objects and whether or not to draw a frame around it.

- **Layout Structures.** Used to define the layout structure of the document. As with a document's logical structure, a document's MO:DCA layout structure is also typically hierarchical.

- **Pages.** Used to contain a series of data objects. The layout structure and processing control information associated with the page define object areas within the page and determine functions such as positioning, replication, modification, orientation, and size of the object areas.

- **Overlays.** Used to provide templatelike patterns of data that can be merged with data from data objects for presentation.

- **Data Objects.** Used to contain data and formatting control information. Data objects are mapped to object areas for presentation. The data and control information that are part of a data object determine the actual appearance of that object within the object area.

- **Page Segments.** Used to define a collection of data objects that can be repeated on multiple pages.

- **Resource Groups.** Used to define different types of objects that can be referenced and retrieved from elsewhere in the data stream. A resource group can contain pages, overlays, data objects, fonts, and page segments.

- **Environment Groups.** Used to define processing control information for the document. This control information includes space definitions, formatting descriptions, measurement system definition, suppression activation, assignment of external identifiers to internal data stream references, and number of copies.

- **Suppressions.** Used to prevent the presentation of specific elements of a document when it is being displayed or printed.

- **Macros.** Used to define a group of structured fields that can be used repeatedly and can be customized at process time through the specification of parameter values.

INTELLIGENT PRINTER DATA STREAM

The *Intelligent Printer Data Stream* architecture defines the data stream used to send the objects making up a compound document to an all-points-addressable printer. The data stream is device-specific and contains control information and recovery sequences appropriate to a specific type of device. IPDS supports the use of text, image, vector graphic, and bar code data. It allows output from different applications to be combined as part of a composed page.

IPDS uses a hierarchy of presentation spaces, consisting of the following:

- **Physical Page.** A physical page is the medium on which information is placed. It has boundaries for width and depth and usually consists of paper.
- **Logical Page.** A logical page is a rectangular area in which data is formatted for presentation.
- **Data Block.** A data block is a rectangular area within a logical page in which a particular type of data is formatted.

An example of this hierarchy of presentation spaces is shown in Fig. 15.7. Different areas within the logical page are used for different types of data. Text

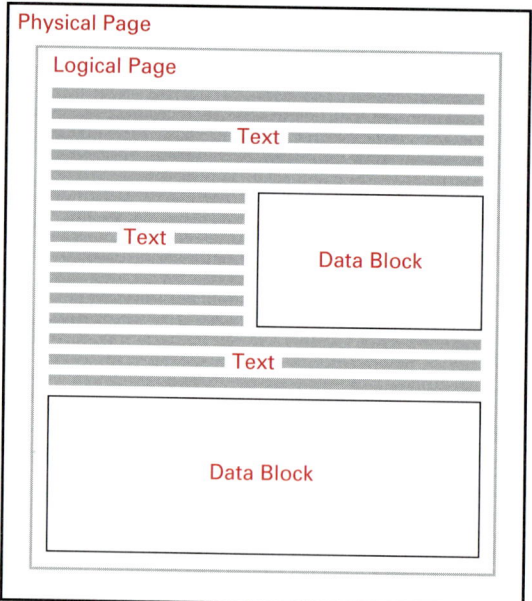

Figure 15.7 IPDS presentation hierarchy.

data contains lines of character information that can be positioned anywhere on the page. Text control information specifies positioning and orientation for the text data. Data blocks can contain image, graphic, or bar code data. Each data block is mapped to a specified location within a logical page.

DATA OBJECTS

The IPDS data stream is fully paginated and object-oriented. A document consists of one or more pages, and each page is a self-contained entity. A page may be composed of elements of text, image, or graphics. Each element exists in the data stream as a discrete object, and, as with the MO:DCA data stream, the architectural definition of the object is independent of the definition of the data stream environment itself. The data stream provides a description of the environment and defines a coordinate space on the logical page into which each data object is mapped. Each data object has its own coordinate space used for the formatting of the data in the object.

RESOURCES

With IPDS devices, it is possible to store resources in the printer for later use. These resources include the following:

- **Overlays.** Sets of data that can be combined with the data in a logical page. Overlays are often used as electronic forms to give a standard format to the logical pages being printed.
- **Page Segments.** Sets of one or more data blocks that can be included as part of a logical page.
- **Fonts.** Sets of characters in a particular type style and size. A font defines the character shapes used for the presentation of data.

IPDS COMMANDS

The IPDS data stream carries control information in the form of commands. IPDS commands are grouped into different function sets. The different types of commands include:

- **Device Control Commands.** Used to change the printer's operating state, to specify control information used in processing logical pages, to request information about the printer and its capabilities and resources, and to specify certain physical processing options.
- **Text Commands.** Used to present text data as part of a logical page, overlay, or page segment.
- **IM and IO Image Commands.** Used to present image raster data as part of a logical page, overlay, or page segment.
- **Graphics Commands.** Used to present vector graphic data as part of a logical page, overlay, or page segment.

- **Bar Code Commands.** Used to present bar code data as part of a logical page, overlay, or page segment.
- **Page Segment Commands.** Used to store, delete, and present page segment information.
- **Overlay Commands.** Used to store, delete, and present overlay information.
- **Loaded-Font Commands.** Used to store and delete font information.

CONCLUSION

This chapter described the user interfaces that are associated with the Common Communications Support component of SAA. CCS is the SAA element that is concerned with how computing applications or computing application components communicate over a network. Chapter 16 describes the CPI Dialog Interface that defines a set of *dialog services* that computing applications can use to manage the dialog that takes place between the user and the application.

16 THE CPI DIALOG INTERFACE

When an application executes in an SAA computing environment, the *CPI Dialog Interface*, which is typically implemented by a component called a *Dialog Manager*, provides a set of *dialog services* that the application uses to manage the dialog that takes place between the application and the user. These services provide for displaying information to the user and for accepting requests and data from the user. To use the CPI Dialog Interface, the application defines certain objects, such as *panels*, *messages*, and *commands*, using a *dialog tag language* (DTL). Definitions for these objects, formatted according to the rules of the dialog tag language, are compiled by the Dialog Manager and stored in libraries. When the application is executed, the application requests dialog services using subroutine calls. The Dialog Manager uses the dialog objects that have been stored in libraries as resources in providing the requested dialog services.

The CPI Dialog Interface specification that is part of the Common Programming Interface defines the general syntax of the dialog tag language that the application developer uses to define dialog objects and of the call statements that are used to invoke dialog services.

THE CPI DIALOG INTERFACE AND CUA

The CPI Dialog Interface can be used, with minimal effort on the part of the application developer, to develop a user interface for an application that is compliant with the CUA graphical model. When the CPI Dialog Interface is used to provide the user interface for an application, the interface generated is consistent with CUA guidelines in appearance and interaction. The application uses the dialog tag language to define various dialog objects used by the application. It also includes appropriate calls at points in its logic where it wishes to use particular dialog services. The Dialog Manager is then responsible for formatting and displaying panels and for managing user interactions with the panels. With this approach, the primary responsibility for seeing that the application's user interface conforms with the CUA rules and guidelines rests with the Dialog Manager rather than with the application.

Presentation

Standard window elements, such as the window title bar, window borders, window sizing icons, and scroll bars, are provided by the Dialog Manager for application-defined panels. The Dialog Manager makes available many, but not all, of the controls defined by the CUA graphical model. The controls available include menu bars (action bars), pulldown menus, radio buttons, check boxes, pushbuttons, list boxes, and entry fields. When these controls are used, the Dialog Manager is responsible for formatting them according to CUA guidelines. Other controls are not directly available through the CPI Dialog Interface. An application can also define messages and various types of help text. The Dialog Manager again is responsible for seeing that this information is presented as defined by CUA.

The CPI Dialog Interface supports the use of primary and secondary windows, although with some restrictions. An application can display only one primary window at a time. When secondary windows (pop-up windows) are used to display messages or to extend the dialog, the windows cannot be resized by the user, and the user must complete interaction with the pop-up window before returning to the underlying primary window.

Interaction

When a user interacts with window elements or controls in a panel, the Dialog Manager is responsible for supporting the different interaction techniques defined by CUA. The results of user interactions—selection of a choice or entry of data—are passed to the application via variables. The application is not concerned at all with the way in which the interaction takes place; the interaction is handled by the Dialog Manager, not by the application.

The application retains the responsibility for determining which of the CUA standard actions are to be included in the action bar and its pulldown menus and in pushbuttons. For most of the standard actions, the application is also responsible for providing the processing that is required. The CPI Dialog Interface does define processing support for standard actions associated with the help function through built-in commands that it defines.

Basic Interface Support

The CPI Dialog Interface assumes that the application runs on a programmable workstation. The formatting and interaction techniques that it supports, then, are designed to be consistent with the CUA graphical model. However, the interface does include elements that allow panels to be developed that are consistent with the Basic Interface. These elements allow a panel to include and use a command area, to display panel IDs, and to display currently active function keys in a function key area.

DIALOG ELEMENTS

The CPI Dialog Interface defines a set of *dialog elements* that can be defined using the dialog tag language. These elements are combined, as needed, to define an application's dialog structure. These elements include the following:

- **Application Panels.** A panel is an arrangement of information that is grouped together for display to the user as part of the dialog between the application and the user. An application panel can contain information for display only as well as selection fields and data entry fields with which the user interacts.
- **Help Panels.** A help panel contains information that assists the user with some part of the application. It is displayed in response to a user's request for help.
- **Help Index.** A help index is a listing of help topics that are available in the different help panels defined for an application.
- **Messages.** A message consists of information that is displayed in response to a particular user action or in response to the occurrence of some event.
- **Application Command Table.** The CPI Dialog Interface provides a command facility that allows the user to signal that certain actions should be taken. There are built-in commands that provide standard actions, such as requesting help or exiting a dialog. An application command table can be used to add application-specific commands or to change the action associated with a built-in command.
- **Key Mapping List.** The user may be able to execute a command through the use of a particular key. A key mapping list is a listing of the keys that have been assigned to different commands for this application.

DIALOG SERVICES

The dialog services that are part of the CPI Dialog Interface provide three major functions:

- **Display Services.** These are used to control the display of panels and messages to the user. These services also control the user's interactions with the application, which may involve making selections, entering data, specifying actions to take, or scrolling information that appears on the screen.
- **Control Services.** These are used to begin and end a dialog, by activating and deactivating the Dialog Manager.
- **Variable Services.** These allow an application to use variables to communicate with the Dialog Manager. Variables can be used to provide information to be displayed in a panel or message, to store information entered by the user, to indicate action and selection choices, or to provide access to system information.

In the following sections, we will look at each of these types of services in more detail.

DISPLAY SERVICES

With the CPI Dialog Interface, panels and messages are displayed in windows. The CPI Dialog Interface supports the use of three types of windows:

- **Primary Windows.** A primary window is the display area in which the dialog between the user and the application takes place. A dialog application can use only one primary window, and the window is used to display a succession of panels. The user is allowed to move and change the size of the primary window.
- **Pop-up Windows.** Pop-up windows are used for transient interactions related to the primary window, such as displaying messages. When a pop-up window is displayed, the user cannot interact with the underlying primary window. The user must complete the interaction with the pop-up window before being allowed to interact again with the primary window. A pop-up window can be moved but not resized by the user.
- **Help Windows.** Help windows are used to display help information. A secondary window is used to display help information. The user can switch back and forth between the help window and the underlying window from which Help was requested. The user can move and resize the help window.

Display services can be used to display application panels, either in the primary window or in a pop-up window and to display messages. Box 16.1 describes the dialog services that fall into the display services category.

BOX 16.1 Display services.

- **DISPLAY.** Displays a panel and then allows the user to interact with it. If a panel name is specified, that panel is displayed; otherwise, the current panel is refreshed. A message to be displayed on the panel and the initial cursor position can also be specified. Once the panel is displayed, the user can make selections or enter data into entry fields. The Dialog Manager validates data as it is entered. When the user's interaction is complete, the Dialog Manager returns entered data to the application.
- **ADDPOP.** Initiates and positions a pop-up window. Subsequent display service requests display panels in the pop-up window.
- **REMPOP.** Removes a pop-up window. If a series of pop-up windows have been used, either the last window or all windows can be removed.

CONTROL SERVICES

Control services are used to begin and end a dialog. The service calls used for control services are listed in Box 16.2.

BOX 16.2   Control services.

- **DMOPEN.** Initializes communication between the Dialog Manager and the application so that the application is able to issue dialog service requests.
- **DMCLOSE.** Completes the scope of a DMOPEN call and terminates communication between the application and the Dialog Manager.

VARIABLE SERVICES

There are two types of variables that can be used with the CPI Dialog Interface—dialog variables and system variables.

- **Dialog Variables.** *Dialog variables* are defined by the application, either explicitly or implicitly. They can be used as part of a panel or message to provide information to be displayed, to store data entered by the user, or to record the results of an action specified or selection choice made by the user. A variable is explicitly defined with the VDEFINE service call. A variable is implicitly defined by including its name where a variable can be used in a service call, panel, message, or command table. The dialog variables for a particular dialog are stored in a dialog variable pool.
- **System Variables.** *System variables* provide for the exchange of special information between the application and the Dialog Manager. For example, system variables can be used by the application to access date and time information, to determine the location of the cursor when the user exits a panel, or to pass a window title to the Dialog Manager for use in the window title bar.

The service calls that are available as part of variable services are shown in Box 16.3.

SERVICE CALL FORMATS

The CPI Dialog Interface defines the general syntax to be used with each of the service calls and also shows specific syntax examples for use with C, COBOL, FORTRAN, or the Procedures Language. Figure 16.1 shows the general format of the DISPLAY service call, which is used to display a panel or message

BOX 16.3 Variable services.

- **VCOPY.** Provides the application program with a copy of specified dialog variables.
- **VDEFINE.** Used to define dialog variables for the function pool. It allows the Dialog Manager to directly access variables within a function program. As part of the call, the format of the variable is specified.
- **VDELETE.** Removes variables from the function pool that were previously defined through the VDEFINE service.
- **VREPLACE.** Updates the value of a variable in the function pool.
- **VRESET.** Resets the function pool to empty.

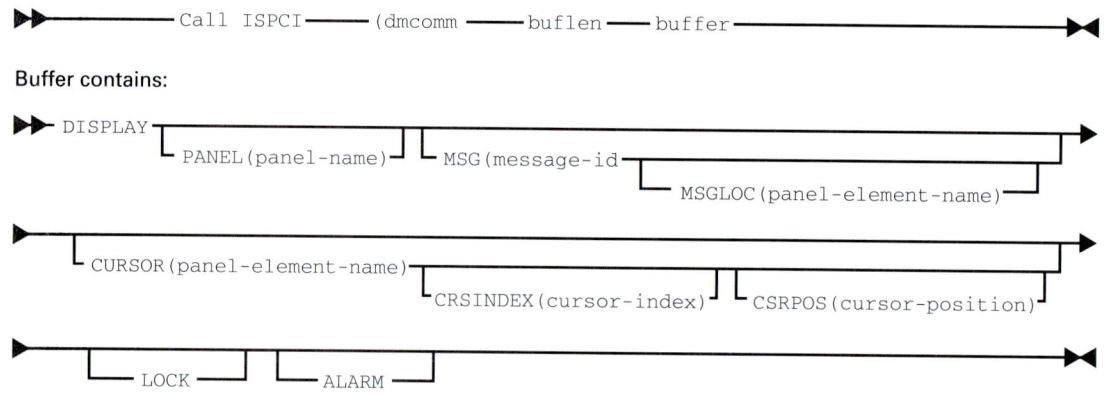

Figure 16.1 Format of the DISPLAY call.

to the user. Box 16.4 shows how this call could be coded in each of the supported languages.

For C, COBOL, and FORTRAN, the call includes the following:

- **Dmcomm.** The Dialog Manager communication area, or **dmcomm,** is an area of storage that has been defined within the application and is used by the Dialog Manager to convey information associated with a service request, such as a return code and error information.
- **Buflen. buflen** is the length of the buffer used as part of the call.
- **Buffer.** The **buffer** is used to pass the name of the service being requested and any parameters associated with the service. In this example, the name of the service is DISPLAY, and two parameters are specified: the name of the panel to display (DMM001) and the name of the field where the cursor is to be initially located (NAME).

BOX 16.4 Call syntax examples.

C Syntax Example

```
ISPC12 (&dmcomm,buflen,buffer,&lng,errmsg);
```

COBOL Syntax Example

```
CALL 'ISPC12' USING DMCOMM BUFLEN BUFFER
              LNG ERRMSG.
```

FORTRAN Syntax Example

```
CALL ISPC12 (DMCOMM, BUFLEN, BUFFER, LNG, MSGNAME)
```

Procedures Language Syntax Example

```
DISPLAY PANEL(panel-name) MSG(message-id)
        CURSOR(field-name)
        DMCOMM(dmcomm-variable)
```

For the Procedures Language, the service name and parameters are specified directly in the CALL statement, rather than being passed in a buffer.

USING THE DIALOG TAG LANGUAGE

As we mentioned earlier, the CPI Dialog Interface includes a dialog tag language that is used to define dialog elements. The language consists of a set of *tags*, or control words, that are used to specify the characteristics of elements. The dialog tag language is based on the *Standard Generalized Markup Language* (SGML), which is an established international standard. Figure 16.2 describes the general syntax used with tags and shows a sample dialog element definition. The LINES tag specifies that the text that follows should be displayed as entered and not wrapped around from one line to the next.

In addition to a tagname that identifies the tag, a tag may include attributes that provide information used in processing the tag. The following PANEL tag is used to begin the definition of an application panel:

```
<panel NAME=panel003 HELP=help010 KEYLIST=keyl001>
```

The attributes included in this example are used to provide the following information:

- **NAME=panel003.** Gives the name **panel003** to this panel.
- **HELP=help010.** Identifies the name of the help panel (**help010**) to be used as extended help for this panel.
- **KEYLIST=keyl001.** Identifies the name (**keyl001**) of a list of keys and their corresponding commands. This determines which key assignments are active when this panel is displayed.

```
<tagname attributes>
   .
   .
   text and other content
   .
   .
</tagnames>
```

Tag Syntax

```
<lines>
text for line 1
   indented text for line 2
more text for line 3
        text
        text
        text
</lines>
```

Tag Example

Figure 16.2   Tag syntax and example.

DEFINING AN APPLICATION PANEL

DTL *panel definitions* describe the format of the panels the application displays and define the various fields in the panel through which the user interacts with the application. DTL panel definitions also specify the details of any field processing that the Dialog Manager should provide when the panel is displayed. Tags can be used to define a panel title, top and bottom instructions, an action bar and associated pulldown menus, panel body areas, information, selection and entry fields, scrollable areas and fields, a message area, a command area, and a pushbutton or function key area. Tags can also associate a help panel with the panel being defined.

The tags that are described in this chapter have been taken from the CPI Dialog Interface specification that is current as of the time of writing. IBM has indicated that as the dialog tag language evolves, new tags will be added to the CPI Dialog Interface specification. The dialog tag language, as described in the CPI Dialog Interface specification, will most likely be expanded over time to include additional tags that are used in products that implement the CPI Dialog Interface.

The various tags that can be used in creating a panel definition are shown in Box 16.5. Figure 16.3 shows a sample panel definition. The tags and panel text are shown in a generalized format; the exact coding that would be used depends

BOX 16.5   Panel definition tags.

General Tags

- **Pandef (Panel Default).** Provides default information for any panel referencing it.
- **Panel (Panel).** Identifies the beginning of a panel. It can be used to specify an associated help panel, panel depth and width, panel title, initial cursor placement, and a key list for the function key area.
- **Topinst (Top Instruction).** Specifies instructions to be displayed at the top of the panel.
- **Botinst (Bottom Instruction).** Specifies instructions to be displayed at the bottom of the panel.
- **Cmdarea (Command Area).** Defines the command area and the text and placement of the command field prompt.

Panel Body Area Tags

- **Area (Area).** Identifies a scrollable portion of a panel.
- **Region (Region).** Specifies how fields on a panel are arranged.
- **Divider (Divider).** Provides a separator between panel areas.

Action Bar Tags

- **Ab (Action Bar).** Defines an action bar.
- **Abc (Action Bar Choice).** Identifies an action bar choice and its associated pulldown menu.
- **Pdc (Pulldown Menu Choice).** Defines a choice within a pulldown menu.
- **Pdsep (Pulldown Menu Separator).** Draws a line between choices in a pulldown menu.
- **M (Mnemonic).** Designates a mnemonic for an action bar or pulldown menu choice.

Selection and Entry Field Tags

- **Dtacol (Data Column).** Identifies column widths for subsequent entry and selection fields. The Dialog Manager then vertically aligns the fields and provides dot leaders.
- **Dtafld (Data Field).** Defines an entry field. Parameters include a dialog variable name, a help panel name, and prompt text to be displayed.

(Continued)

BOX 16.5 *(Continued)*

- **Dtafldd (Data Field Description).** Provides additional descriptive text for a data field.
- **Selfld (Selection Field).** Defines a selection field. The particular type of selection field is specified as a parameter.
- **Choice (Choice Item).** Identifies a choice within a selection field. A help panel name can be specified.
- **M (Mnemonic).** Designates a mnemonic for a selection field choice.
- **Lstfld (List Field).** Defines a vertically scrollable list made up of columns of data.
- **Lstcol (List Column).** Identifies a column within a list field.

Information Tags

- **Info (Information).** Identifies protected information to be displayed as part of a panel. Other information tags can be used to format the information text.
- **Dl (Definition List).** Used along with the **dt** (Define Term), **dd** (Define Description), **dthd** (Define Term Column Heading), and **ddhd** (Define Description Column Heading) tags to define a list of terms and their corresponding definitions.
- **Fig (Figure).** Specifies that following text is not to be word-wrapped and should be set off by a border or spacing. A **figcap** tag can be used to supply a caption.
- **Hn (Heading Level *n*).** Identifies main topics and subtopics of information.
- **Lines (Lines).** Specifies that the following text is not to be word-wrapped.
- **Li (List Item).** Identifies an item in a list. The following text is indented from the current level of the list. Used with the **ol, sl,** and **ul** tags, which identify the type of list.
- **Lp (List Part).** Identifies text that is part of the current list item.
- **Note (Single-Paragraph Note).** Identifies following text as a single-paragraph note.
- **Nt (Multiple-Paragraph Note).** Identifies following text as a single- or multiple-paragraph note.
- **Ol (Ordered List).** Identifies an ordered list of items. The items are formatted as an indented list with order identifiers (1, 2, . . . a, b . . .).

BOX 16.5 *(Continued)*

- **P (Paragraph).** Identifies the following text as a paragraph.
- **Parml (Parameter List).** Identifies parameter terms and their descriptions, using the **pt** (Parameter Tag) and **pd** (Parameter Description) tags.
- **Sl (Simple List).** Identifies a simple list of terms, formatted as an indented list with no item identifiers.
- **Ul (Unordered List).** Identifies an unordered list of terms. The items are formatted as an indented list with bullets, hyphens, and dashes used as item identifiers.

```
<panel name=panel1 help=mainh depth=10 width=50
       keylist=actkeys>Car Selector
 <ab>
   <abc><m>File
      <pdc><m>New
         <action run=New>
      <pdc><m>Open...
          .
          .
          .
   <abc><m>Help
 </ab>
 <dtafld datavar=salesnum>Salesperson Number
 <selfld type=single pmtwidth=28 pmtloc=above>Choose
    Vehicle type
      <choice checkvar=car>Car
         <action setvar=truck value=0>
      <choice checkvar=truck>Truck
         <action setvar=truck>
   <selfld>
</panel>
```

Figure 16.3 Sample panel definition.

on the particular language being used to create the application and the specific implementation of the CPI Dialog Interface that is being used.

DEFINING MESSAGES

DTL *message definitions* describe messages that the application displays to the user. The **msg** tag defines a message. It can specify the message text, the severity level of the message, and a help panel to be associated with the message. The CPI Dialog Interface provides for the definition and display of messages of three different severities:

- **Information.** Indicates to the user that a normal action is in progress or has completed.
- **Warning.** Indicates that a potentially undesirable condition could occur.
- **Action.** Indicates that an exception condition has occurred and that the user must take an action related to the condition before processing can continue.

Figure 16.4 contains an example of a message definition. An application requests the display of a message through the **msg** parameter on a **display** service call. The message is displayed in a message pop-up window. An alarm is sounded when a warning or action message is displayed.

```
<msg suffix=0 msgtype=action>A valid file
     name must be entered.
```

Figure 16.4 Sample message definition.

DEFINING A COMMAND TABLE

Commands are issued by the user to request a particular action. Commands can be issued in three ways:

- By selecting the command as a pulldown menu choice.
- By pressing a key that has been assigned to that command.
- By typing the command name in a command entry field.

The CPI Dialog Interface provides built-in commands that perform certain standard actions. These are listed in Box 16.6. An application can use a command table to define new commands and specify different actions to take for built-in commands. Figure 16.5 contains an example of a command table definition. The **cmdtbl** tag identifies the beginning of a command table. A **cmd** tag is then used to define each command in the table. The **cmd** tag specifies both an external and an internal name for the command. The internal name is used for defining pulldown menu choices and mapping to keys. The external name is used when a command name is entered in a command entry field. A **cmdact** tag defines the action to be taken when the command is invoked. One of the standard actions can be specified, or the command can be passed to the application for processing.

```
<cmdtbl applid=cars>
  <cmd name=open>Open
    <cmdact action=passthru>
  <cmd name=close>Close
    <cmdact action=passthru>
</cmdtbl>
```

Figure 16.5 Sample command table definition.

BOX 16.6 Built-in commands.

- **ACTIONS.** Switches the cursor to the action bar.
- **BACKWARD.** Scrolls a scrollable field up.
- **CANCEL.** Removes the current pop-up window.
- **ENTER.** Initiates processing of the current panel.
- **EXIT.** Requests that the current function be ended.
- **EXHELP.** Displays help text for an entire panel.
- **FKA.** Turns the display of the function key area on or off.
- **FORWARD.** Scrolls a scrollable field down.
- **HELP.** Displays help text for a panel field, message, command, or entire panel, depending on the cursor position.
- **HELPHELP.** Displays help for help text.
- **INDEX.** Displays the help index.
- **KEYS.** Displays keys help text.
- **PANELID.** Turns display of panel identifiers on or off.
- **RETRIEVE.** Displays previously entered commands in an active command entry field.

DEFINING KEY MAPPING LISTS

A *key mapping list* associates commands with keys that can be used to execute them. The following tags are used for a key mapping list:

- **Keyl.** Identifies a key mapping list and gives it a name by which it can be referenced within a panel definition.
- **Keyi.** Associates a command with a particular key.

HELP FACILITIES

The dialog tag language contains facilities for defining help panels and for giving them identifying names. A help panel can be associated with a particular dialog element—such as an application panel, selection field, entry field, message, and so on—as they are defined using the dialog tag language. When a user requests help for an element, the Dialog Manager retrieves the appropriate help panel and displays it. The CPI Dialog Interface provides the following types of help information:

- **Extended Help.** Help on an application panel as a whole and the task it performs.
- **Contextual Help.** Help for a particular item, based on the position of the cursor when help is requested. The item can be
    - an action bar or pulldown menu choice
    - a selection field, selection list, or selection field choice
    - an input field, list field, or list field column
    - a message
- **Reference Phrase Help.** Help for a particular word or phrase in the text of a help panel.
- **Command Help.** Help that provides a list of the commands the user can enter in the command entry field plus help for each of the commands in the list.
- **Keys Help.** Help that describes the mapping of keys to commands supported by this application.
- **Tutorial help.** Help that presents a detailed tutorial on how to use the application or a specific function within it. The structure and content of the tutorial is determined by the application.
- **Help for Help.** Help on how to use the help facility.
- **Help Index.** Help that provides a list of all help topics in the application.

The Dialog Manager controls user interactions with help panels, including switching between an application panel and a help panel.

DEFINING HELP PANELS

Help panels are defined in much the same way as application panels. The tags used to define help panels are shown in Box 16.7. The **help** tag defines the beginning of a help panel and gives it a name. The **area** tag can be used to define a scrollable area. The various information tags shown in Box 16.5 can also be used to format information text in a help panel. An **rp** tag can be used to identify a reference phrase within the panel text and to associate a help panel with that phrase.

BOX 16.7 Help panel tags.

- **Help (Help).** Begins the definition of a help panel.
- **Area (Area).** Identifies a scrollable portion of a panel.
- **Info (Information).** Identifies protected information to be displayed as part of a panel. Other information tags can be used to format the information text.

An **icmd** tag can be used to associate the help panel with a particular command. When help is requested for that command, this help panel is displayed.

When certain dialog elements are defined, a help panel can be associated with the element by specifying the help panel name as part of the element's dialog tag language definition. The Dialog Manager then displays the appropriate help panel when the user requests help for that element. Elements for which a help panel name can be specified include

- Application panel **(panel, pandef)**
- Action bar and pulldown menu choices **(abc, pdc)**
- Selection fields and choices **(selfld, sellst, choice)**
- Input fields and columns **(dtafld, lstfld, lstcol)**
- Messages **(msg)**

DEFINING A HELP INDEX

A help index is a list of help topics that are available to the user. The CPI Dialog Interface allows the user to specify search words and will then display help topics associated with the search words. The **itop** and **isyn** tags are used to build the help index and to provide the information needed to match a search word with certain topics.

The **itop** tag associates a help panel with a topic. When that topic is selected from the help index, the associated help panel is displayed. The **itop** tag also specifies the text that is to be displayed as the index entry for the topic. One or more root words are associated with the topic through the **itop** tag. When the user enters search words, the search words are translated into root words, and the root words are used to identify a topic in the topic index.

The **isyn** tag is used to define the mapping from search words entered by the user to root words. The **isyn** tag defines one root word and one or more synonyms that are to be mapped to that root word. Figure 16.6 contains an example of the use of the **itop** and **isyn** tags. The **itop** tag defines "Copying a File" as an entry in the help index and associates a help panel with the entry. The root

```
<help...>
<itop roots = 'copy file'>Copying a File
    :
</help>

<help>
<isyn root=copy>copy copying duplicate
               duplicating
<isyn root=File>data information file
               document documents
    :
</help>
```

Figure 16.6 Help index example.

words for this entry are "copy file." The **isyn** tags define synonyms for copy and file. If the user enters "duplicate data" as search words, they are mapped to "copy file," and the "Copying a File" topic would be included in the resulting help index listing.

REQUESTING HELP   There are several built-in commands that can be used by the user to request different forms of help:

- **HELP.** Displays contextual help for a panel field, choice, or message, based on the position of the cursor. If the cursor is in the command entry field, a list of commands is displayed. If the cursor is on a command in the command list, help for that command is displayed. The F1 key must always be assigned to the HELP command.
- **EXHELP.** Displays the help panel associated with the application panel being displayed.
- **HELPHELP.** Displays help for help information.
- **INDEX.** Provides access to the search facility of the help index.
- **KEYS.** Displays keys help. The help panel to be displayed for keys help is named in the **zkeyhelp** system variable, which can be set by the application.

DEFINING VARIABLES   Variables are often used to pass values between the Dialog Manager and the application. For example, when the user enters data into an entry field, the Dialog Manager uses a variable to pass the data to the application. When the user makes a choice, a variable can be used to indicate to the application which choice was selected. Variables can also be used to pass values from the application to the Dialog Manager for display to the user.

The CPI Dialog Interface defines several processing functions for variables. Sometimes the internal value used for a variable is different from the value that is displayed. The CPI Dialog Interface provides a mapping function that can be used to translate from internal values to display values. Mapping can also be performed on data entered by the user, in order to convert the data into a format more suitable for processing by the application. Validation checks can be defined that the Dialog Manager applies to data entered by the user. Assignment lists can also be defined that assign values to one variable based on the values of some other variable. Mapping and validation checks can be specified for individual variables or for a variable class. Variable classes and their associated mappings and validation checks are defined in variable class tables. A variable class table applies across an entire application.

Box 16.8 lists the tags that can be used in defining variables. They allow the application developer to supply the characteristics of a specific variable and assign it to a variable class, define an assignment list for a variable, define validation checks for a variable or variable class, and define translation lists for a variable or variable class.

BOX 16.8 Variable tags.

- **Varlist (Variable List).** Establishes the access technique for specific variables.
- **Vardcl (Variable Declaration).** Establishes characteristics for specific variables.
- **Assignl (Assignment List).** Identifies the beginning of an assignment list.
- **Assigni (Assignment Item).** Defines an entry in an assignment list and provides the association between a value in one variable and the value to be assigned to another.
- **Checkl (Check List).** Defines a list of validity checks to be applied to a variable or class of variables. Multiple checklists referencing the same variable or variable class are ANDed together.
- **Checki (Check Item).** Defines a single validity check within a checklist. Multiple check items within a checklist are ORed together.
- **Xlatl (Translate List).** Identifies the beginning of a translate list used to map between internal dialog variable values and values displayed for the user or entered by the user. A translate list can be defined for a specific variable or a variable class.
- **Xlati (Translate Item).** Defines a single set of mapping values within a translate list.
- **Clstbl (Variable Class Table).** Defines a variable class table.
- **Varclass (Variable Class).** Defines information related to a variable class. The **checkl, checki, xlatl,** and **xlati** tags can be used within the scope of a **varclass** tag.

CONCLUSION

This chapter described the CPI Dialog Interface that is implemented by Dialog Manager components that can assist the application developer in creating CUA-compliant user interfaces. Chapter 17 describes the CPI Presentation Interface that defines application services relating to displaying and printing text, graphics, and image information.

17 THE CPI PRESENTATION INTERFACE

The *CPI Presentation Interface* is another application programming interface defined by the Common Programming Interface component of SAA. The CPI Presentation Interface provides services to a computing application that concerns the display and printing of text, graphics, and image information. Many of the functions defined by the CPI Presentation Interface are designed to support the creation, manipulation, display, and storage of graphic pictures. The CPI Presentation Interface also supports the definition and use of different type fonts, including double-byte character set fonts, and the display of images that are defined pixel by pixel, rather than as geometric constructs.

The CPI Presentation Interface defines a general windowing system that supports the display of multiple windows on the display screen and allows users to move and resize windows. In addition, it provides functions that are related to the user interface. The user interface functions are designed to display data using window formats that are consistent with CUA guidelines and to allow the user to interact with the displays using CUA interaction techniques. With its support of graphics and window capabilities, the CPI Presentation Interface allows the development of a user interface that is fully consistent with the CUA advanced interface graphical model.

CPI PRESENTATION MANAGER IMPLEMENTATIONS

IBM's initial implementation of the CPI Presentation Interface is the *Presentation Manager* component of the OS/2 operating system that runs on IBM personal systems and compatible personal computers. In this chapter we will use the term *presentation manager* as a generic term to refer to any implementation of the CPI Presentation Interface.

WINDOWS

CPI Presentation Interface user interface processing is based on the use of CUA advanced interface *windows*. As we described in Chapter 14, a window is an area of a display screen used to present information related to a particular application. Multiple windows can be displayed on the screen at the same time, as shown in Fig. 17.1. Here the windows all belong to a single application. There can also be windows displayed by multiple applications on the screen, as shown in Fig. 17.2. Windows may overlap one another, restricting what is visible of a particular window.

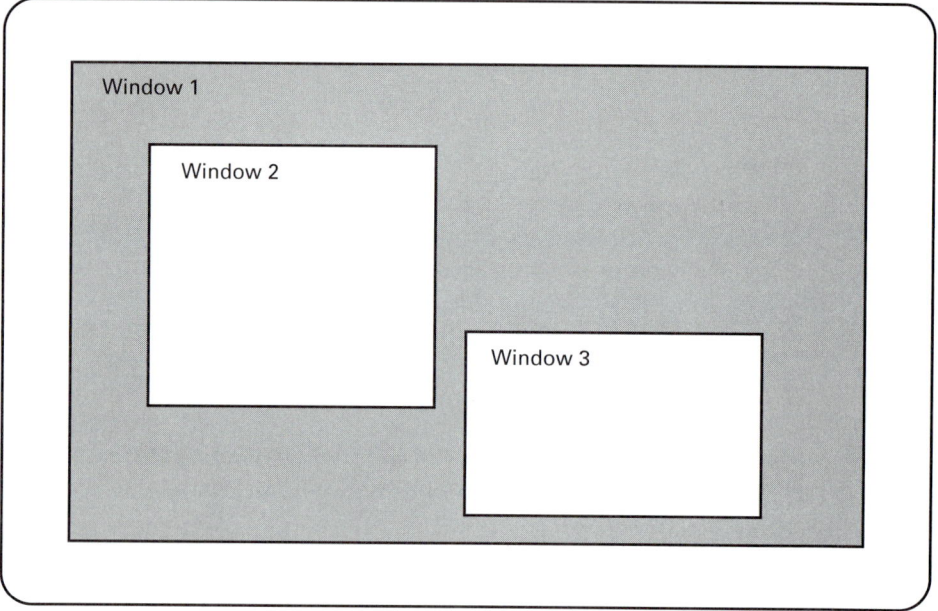

Figure 17.1 Multiple windows.

WINDOW HIERARCHIES

Windows are related to one another in a hierarchical manner. The display screen as a whole is called the *desktop*. Each application has at least one *main window*, which is positioned relative to the desktop. A main window can have one or more *child windows*, and a child window can also have its own child windows. A *child window* is positioned relative to its *parent window*. Child windows that have the same parent window are called *siblings*. Siblings are displayed in a particular visual order, called the *z-order*. When the windows overlap, this determines which sibling is displayed as the topmost window, which is directly underneath it, and so on down the group of windows.

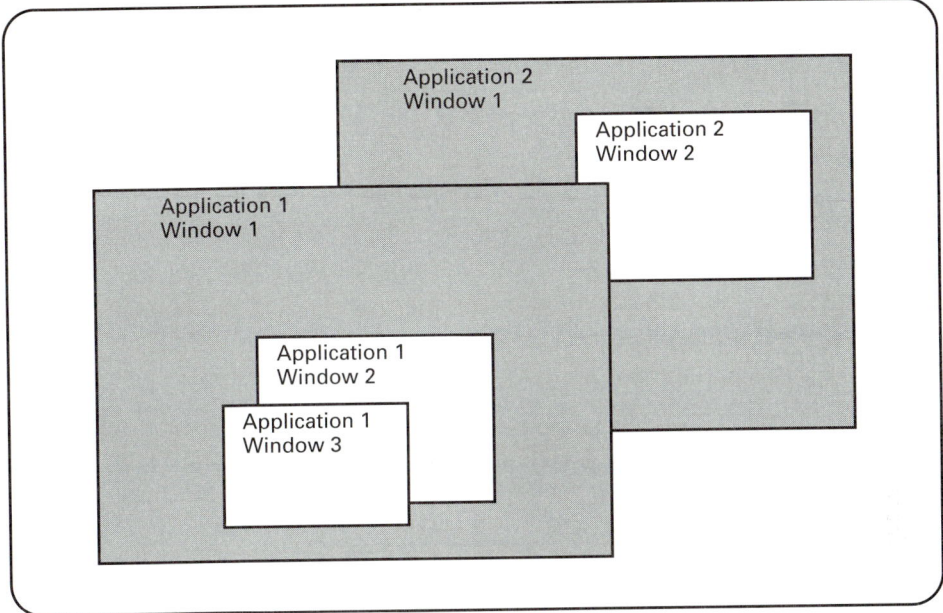

Figure 17.2   Overlapping windows.

Figure 17.3 shows the hierarchy, or logical relationship, that might exist for a collection of windows. If the z-order is from left to right in the hierarchy, then the windows appear as shown in the bottom of the figure. Main window A appears on top of main window B. Child windows A1, A2, and A3 appear on top of each other as specified by the z-order. Child windows B1 and B2 show that windows do not have to overlap one another if there is space to display them separately.

WINDOW POSITIONING

When a window is displayed, it will be in a specified position and be a specified size, as determined by the application and the presentation manager. The CPI Presentation Interface defines facilities that allow the user to alter the position or size of a window on the screen. When one main window is moved or changed, other main windows are unaffected. When a parent window is moved or changed, its children are moved and resized along with it.

The facilities to alter the position or size of a window operate independently of the application. However, the application may choose to be aware of changes and handle any data reformatting or reorganization that may be necessary because of changes to the window. Window resizing operations include maximizing the window (changing it to the application-defined maximum size) or minimizing it (changing it to the application-defined minimum size.)

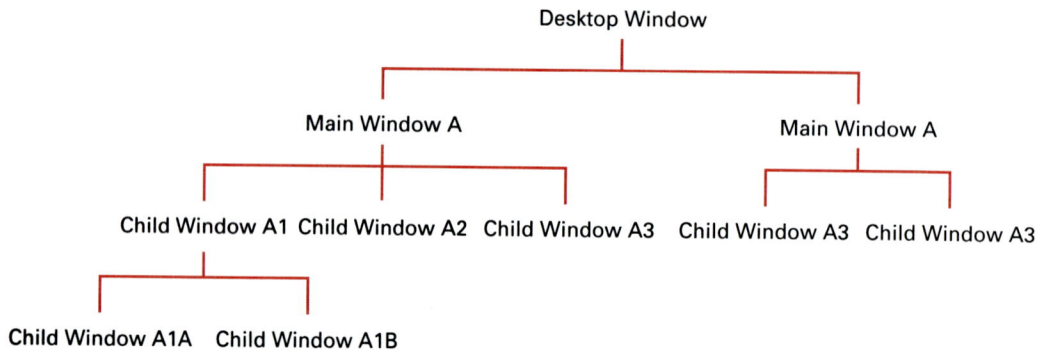

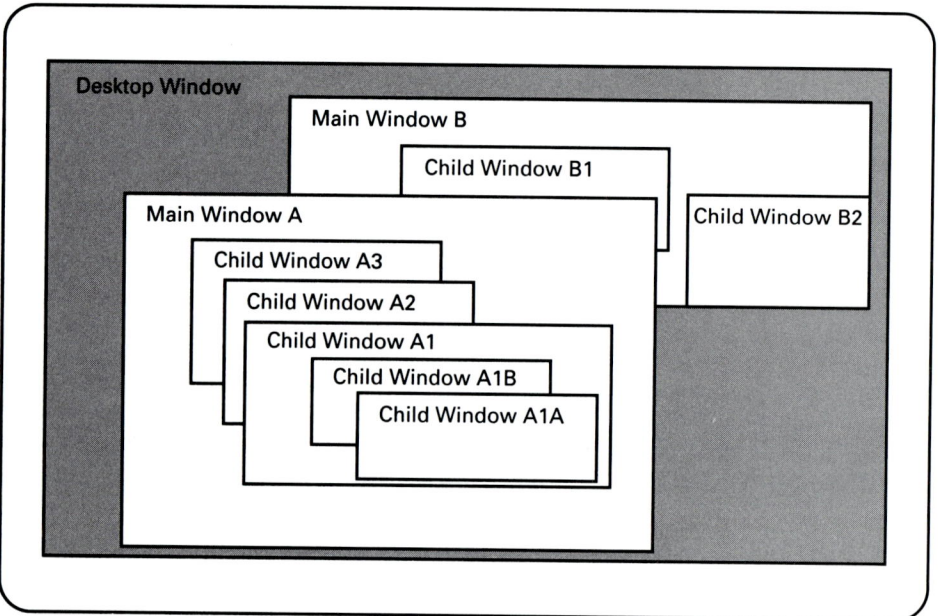

Figure 17.3   Window hierarchy.

WINDOW INTERACTIONS

Windows are the mechanism used to display information to the user and to accept inputs from the user. The user can interact with a window using either a keyboard or a pointing device, such as a mouse. The *cursor* is a symbol on the screen that indicates the position at which the next keyboard interaction will take place. The window that contains the cursor is the *focus window*. The focus window and its children are shown on top of other windows. The main window related hierarchically to the focus window is the *active window*. The active window and its children are shown on top of other main windows.

The *pointer* is a symbol on the screen that indicates where the next pointing device interaction will take place. The movement of the pointer is under user control and is not confined to a specific window. It can be used to select an object within a window or to select some other window with which to interact. When a window is selected, the related main window becomes the active window, and the application establishes the focus window.

WINDOW CHARACTERISTICS

Each window has associated with it a *window procedure* that is used to process input and output events that are associated with that window. An application can provide its own window procedure, or it can use a standard window procedure that is provided by a presentation manager implementation of the CPI Presentation Interface. More than one window can use the same window procedure. The set of windows that share a window procedure is called a *window class*. A window also has a set of *window style* properties. These properties affect the appearance and behavior of a window. For example, one window style attribute can be used to specify that the window be given its maximum size when it is created. A window class can also possess a set of properties, called the *class style*. A particular window class, for example, may have a class style that specifies that a window should be redrawn when its size is changed. Each window in a window class possesses the properties that make up the class style. A window can also have individual window style properties defined for it.

When an application defines a window, it defines the window's window class, which determines the window procedure and class style that apply to this window. The application can also define the properties that make up the window style for a particular window. In addition to providing standard window procedures, the CPI Presentation Interface also defines standard window classes that can be used by the application when defining windows. Many of the standard window procedures and window classes that are part of the CPI Presentation Interface define facilities that are conformant with the CUA component of SAA. They are designed to make it easy to develop a user interface for an application that is consistent with CUA standards and guidelines.

MESSAGES

The application and a presentation manager implementation of the CPI Presentation Interface work cooperatively to maintain a dialog with the user of the application. To do this, the application requests services of the presentation manager. For example, the application may request that the presentation manager display a window on the screen. At times, the presentation manager may also request services from the application. When the presentation manager is moving a window, for instance, it may need the application to redraw the window in its new position or to redraw other windows that have been uncovered by the move. In any interaction between the application and the presentation manager, the partner that is requesting a service is called the *service requester* and the partner that performs the service is called the *service provider*.

Service requests take the form of *messages*. Each message is associated with a particular window and is processed by the window procedure associated with that window. Messages are generated in several different ways. An application may generate a service request message by issuing a CPI Presentation Interface call. Depending on the type of call, the message is either placed on the presentation manager's message queue or is passed to the window procedure for the window associated with the message. The window procedure may be one defined by the application or one defined by the CPI Presentation Interface and provided by the presentation manager. The window procedure processes the message and provides the requested function.

User interactions also generate messages. When a user makes a selection or enters data, the presentation manager generates a message that provides information about the interaction. Based on the window that received the user interaction, the message is posted to the application's queue or sent directly to the appropriate window procedure. System events can cause messages to be generated. Also, when a service request message is being processed, additional messages may be generated by the service provider. Message flow and message processing constitute a critical part of the CPI Presentation Interface.

A window procedure provides a defined response to each message that it receives, which might be a change to displayed data or a change to internally or externally stored data. A window class is defined by the responses it provides to the different types of messages that can be sent to a window of that class.

SYNCHRONOUS AND ASYNCHRONOUS MESSAGE PROCESSING

Messages, and the services they request, can be processed either synchronously or asynchronously. With *synchronous service provision*, the service requester must wait for the message to be processed and the service to be completed before continuing with processing. When the request is for a synchronous service, the message is sent directly to the service provider. With *asynchronous service provision*, the service requester can continue with other processing in parallel with the service provision. When the request is for an asynchronous service, the message is posted to a queue associated with the service provider.

APPLICATION STRUCTURE

Each window has a window procedure associated with it. When an application creates a window, it either provides a window procedure for it or specifies that a standard window procedure in the presentation manager should be used. The presentation manager can request services from the application, either by posting messages to the application's queue or by sending messages directly to window procedures that are part of the application.

An application typically requests services by issuing calls to the presentation manager. The presentation manager then processes the messages generated by the call. A function call may result in a message that is processed by a window procedure in the application. For example, when an application issues a call to create a window, a message is generated and passed to the window procedure in the application, thus allowing the application to initialize the data in the window.

Figure 17.4 illustrates the general structure used for an application that uses the services defined by the CPI Presentation Interface. The initialization phase is used to establish a connection between the application and the presentation manager, to create the application's message queue and the windows that it uses, and to identify the message types the application will process. The main processing loop successively accesses the messages in the application's message queue. Each message is sent to a window procedure, based on the class of the window

```
Initialization
   WinInitialize          Establish association with presentation interface
   WinCreate MsgQueue     Create message queue
   WinCreateWindow        Create application windows
      .
      .
   WinSetMsgInterest      Identify messages to be
                             processed by application
      .
      .
Loop
   WinGetMsg              Get message from queue
   WinDispatchMsg         Invoke window procedure for this message
Termination
   WinDestroyWindow       Destroy application windows
   WinDestroyMsqQueue     Destroy message queue
   WinTerminate           End association with presentation interface

WindowProcedure
   IF message_ID=value1   Process based on message ID
      DO
         .
         .
      END
   ELSE IF message_ID=value2
      DO
         .
         .
      END
      .
   ELSE WinDefWindowProc  or send to default window procedure
```

Figure 17.4 CPI Presentation Interface application structure.

associated with the message. The window procedure may be defined as part of the application or may be a standard window procedure defined by the CPI Presentation Interface and provided by a presentation manager implementation. The termination phase destroys the windows and queue created for the application and disassociates the application from the presentation manager.

An application window procedure performs processing based on message IDs. Messages not specifically processed by the window procedure are passed to the default window procedure in the presentation manager.

APPLICATION RELATIONSHIP TO THE CPI PRESENTATION INTERFACE

The general relationship between the application and the CPI Presentation Interface is shown in Fig. 17.5. A presentation manager implementation of the CPI Presentation Interface acts as an intermediary between the user and the application for both user input and user output.

USER INPUT

When an input event occurs, such as the user making a selection, entering data, or moving the pointer, the presentation manager generates the messages needed for processing the event and either sends them to a window procedure or posts them to the application's message queue. The application retrieves messages from the queue and passes them to a window procedure for processing. A keyboard-related event is associated with the focus window, and a window identifier, called the *window handle*, for that window is included as part of the message. The window handle determines the queue into which the message is placed and the window procedure that is used to process it. A given window is associated with only one queue, but more than one window can be associated with the same queue. For an event relating to the pointing device, the presentation manager must determine to which window the event applies, since there may be overlapping windows under the position at which the event took place. A hit test message is sent to the window procedure for each window under the pointer, starting with the topmost window. The window procedure can claim the event by returning a specified value. If the window does not claim the event, the next window down is tested.

User input operations can occur asynchronously to the application that will process them, in that a user input operation may complete before processing has been completed for a previous input. The presentation manager buffers user inputs in the system queue before posting a message to the application's input queue. Messages in the input queue are then processed synchronously. This restriction is observed because the processing of one message may affect the way in which the next message is handled. When the application gets messages from the queue, it can use *message filtering* to retrieve only certain types of messages,

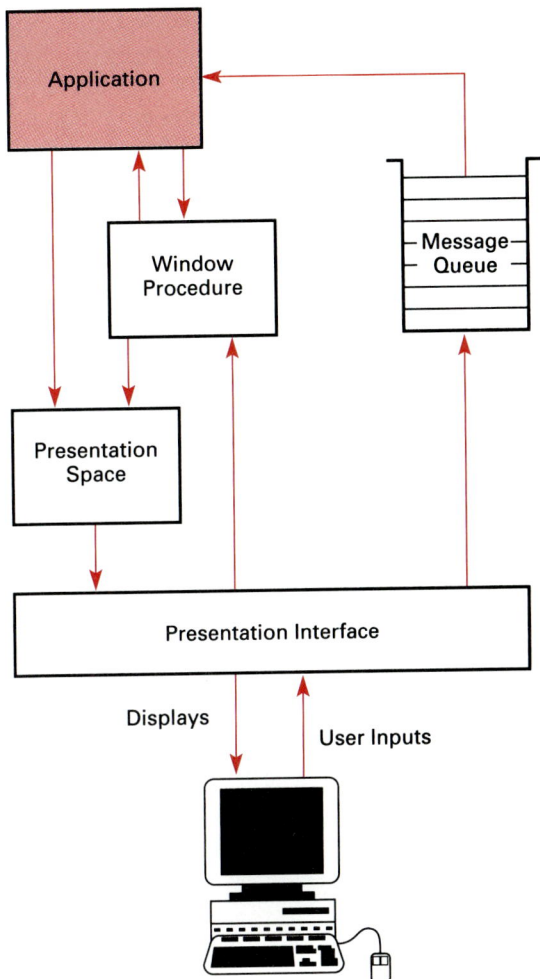

Figure 17.5 Application relationship to the CPI Presentation Interface.

such as messages associated with a particular window or its children or only messages with a message ID that falls within a particular range of IDs.

USER OUTPUT When an application has output data to display to the user, the application provides a logical specification of the data in an area called a *presentation space*. The presentation manager then associates the presentation space with a *device context* that contains the device-dependent definitions needed to present, or *draw*, the data in the presentation space on a particular device. This allows an application to define its output data in a device-independent manner and then be executed using different devices by employing different device contexts.

The presentation manager is responsible for actually displaying the data on the screen. The application is responsible for adjusting data to fit the size of the window. The application does not need to respond to the fact that a window may be partially overlaid by some other window and is not expected to reformat the data in this case.

MESSAGE PATHS   The CPI Presentation Interface defines a dialog that takes place between an application and an application user. Generally, this dialog takes the form of information flowing between the application and the user, with a presentation manager implementation of the CPI Presentation Interface acting as an intermediary. The normal flow of messages in the dialog is shown in Fig. 17.6.

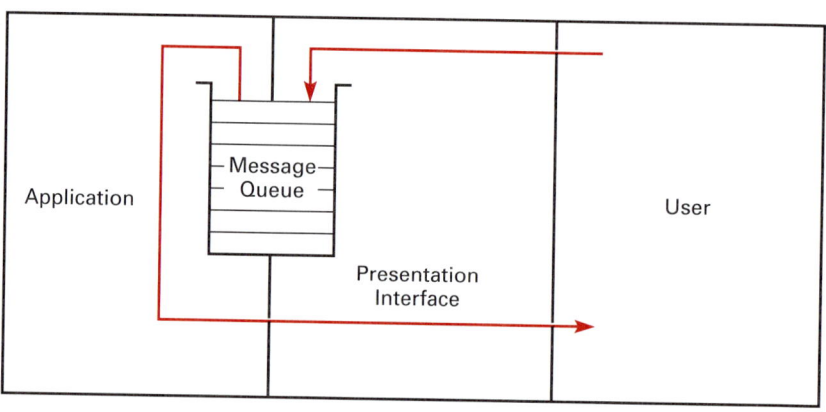

Figure 17.6   Normal message flow.

As we have seen, processing services related to this flow of information are invoked through the passing and processing of messages. The CPI Presentation Interface defines a standard window procedure that can be used for processing certain types of messages. The application can make use of these services by passing certain messages from the queue back to the presentation manager for processing after completing any application-specific processing. The use of the default window procedure is shown in Fig. 17.7.

If there are messages that require only standard processing, the application can allow the presentation manager to process them directly, without first placing them in the application's queue. The delegation of message processing to the presentation manager is shown in Fig. 17.8. This provides for more efficient processing of the messages, since the processing path length is shorter, and the overhead associated with the application processing is removed.

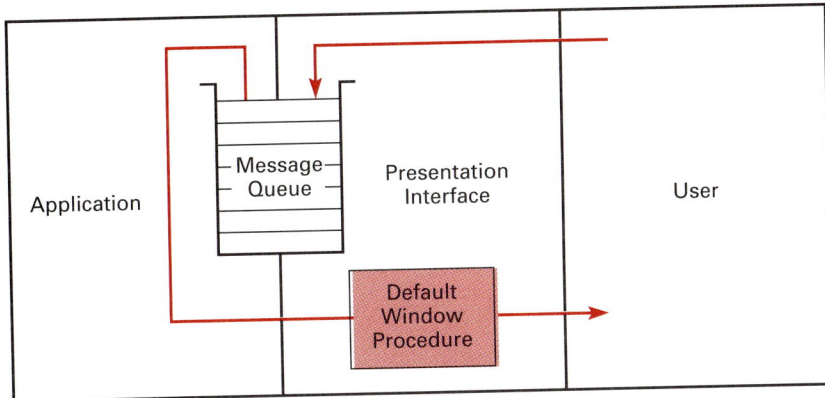

Figure 17.7 Default window procedure.

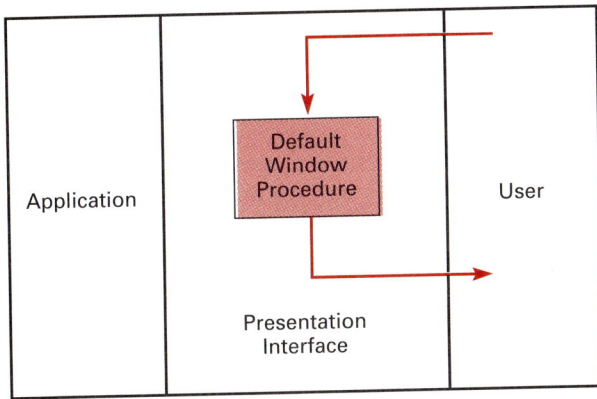

Figure 17.8 Delegating message processing to the CPI Presentation Interface.

When a computing application is distributed across two or more processors within a network, there is a potential for realizing even more efficient processing. The elements of the CPI Presentation Interface can be present on the processors that execute application functions and on the processor that executes user interface functions. Message paths for messages that require only the default window procedure can be "short-circuited" by processing them on the local user-interface processor, as shown in Fig. 17.9. They do not incur the processing overhead and time delays associated with routing messages back and forth across the network. This is an example of a form of distributed computing that SAA is designed to support.

USER INTERFACE FUNCTIONS
As we indicated earlier, the CPI Presentation Interface defines a number of facilities designed to assist application developers in implementing a user interface

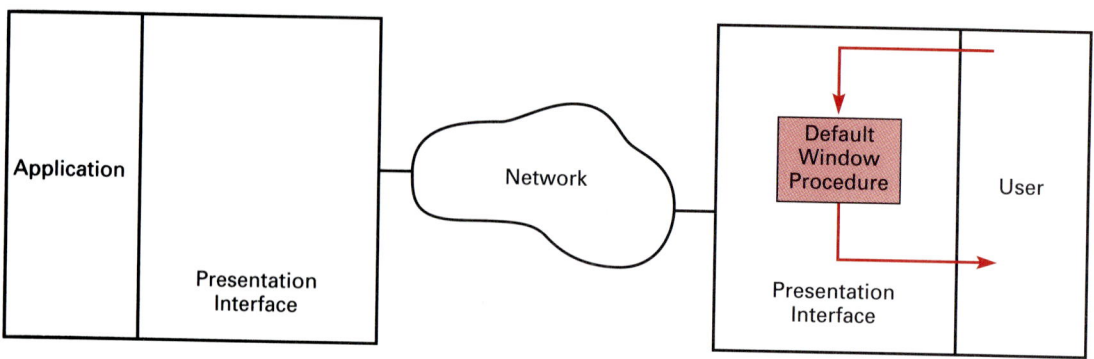

Figure 17.9 Short-circuiting of message paths.

that is consistent with CUA. These facilities include controls, a standard window definition, and a special type of window called a *dialog box* window. Each of these is described next.

CONTROLS

A control is a special-purpose window, or element in a window, with an associated window procedure that reacts to application- or user-generated events in a defined manner. Various controls are available to implement CUA-defined methods of data display and user interaction. These controls correspond closely to the controls defined in the CUA advanced interface graphical model, although not all CUA controls are explicitly addressed by the CPI Presentation Interface.

CPI Presentation Interface controls are defined to support both selection and data entry actions. Examples of what each of the following types of controls looks like can be found in Chapter 14:

- **Menu.** A series of options from which the user chooses one. Selecting a choice causes the visual appearance of the choice to change and may cause another menu to appear. The second menu offers another series of choices. A menu control can be used to define an action bar and its pulldown menus.

- **Pushbutton.** A description within a border that is used to represent an action that is performed as soon as the pushbutton is selected. Selection also causes the appearance of the item to change.

- **Radio Button.** Identifies one item in a group of selectable items. When one member of the group is selected, any previously selected item becomes unselected. The selected item is highlighted.

- **Scroll Bar.** Provides a way for the user to control the data displayed when there is more data available than will fit in the window area defined for display. The scroll bar includes scrolling arrows and a slider box.

- **Check Box.** Identifies an item within a group of selectable items where more than one item can be selected. When an item is selected, this is indicated by a checkmark within the check box.
- **List Box.** A vertical list of selectable items. If the list cannot all be displayed at one time, it can be manipulated with a scroll bar. A list box can be defined as either single choice or multiple choice.
- **Combination Box.** A combination box, or *prompted entry field,* consists of an entry field plus a list box. Data can be entered directly in the entry field or one of the items in the list box can be selected as the entry.
- **Entry Field.** One or more lines into which the user can type or edit data.
- **Static Control.** Defines an area that the application can use to display protected data. The end user is not allowed to change data that is part of a static control.

The CPI Presentation Interface defines a standard window procedure for each type of control that generates and processes messages. The window procedure and its associated window class provide the characteristic processing facilities for that control. An application can use these standard window procedures in addition to or in place of its own window procedures for the controls it uses.

Different types of controls can be combined to implement a wide variety of user interface functions, including all the interaction techniques defined by CUA. The CPI Presentation Interface includes two combinations of controls called the standard window and the dialog box window, each of which is described next.

THE STANDARD WINDOW

The *standard window* formats and displays data in a way that is consistent with the general formatting guidelines and window formats defined by CUA. The CPI Presentation Interface standard window format is shown in Fig. 17.10. The components that can be included in a standard window are described in Box 17.1. Several basic controls are used as part of a standard window. The action bar and system menu both are menu controls. The scroll bars use the scroll bar control.

A window that uses the standard window format is called a *frame window*, and the various components that make up a frame window, other than the client area, are called *frame controls*. The client area is a window implemented by the application, and its window class and style are defined by the application. The frame window is responsible for arranging the various frame controls and the client area and for controlling the arrangement if the window is resized or moved. The application is responsible for defining and controlling the content of the client area. The CPI Presentation Interface defines a standard window procedure for processing messages related to a frame window.

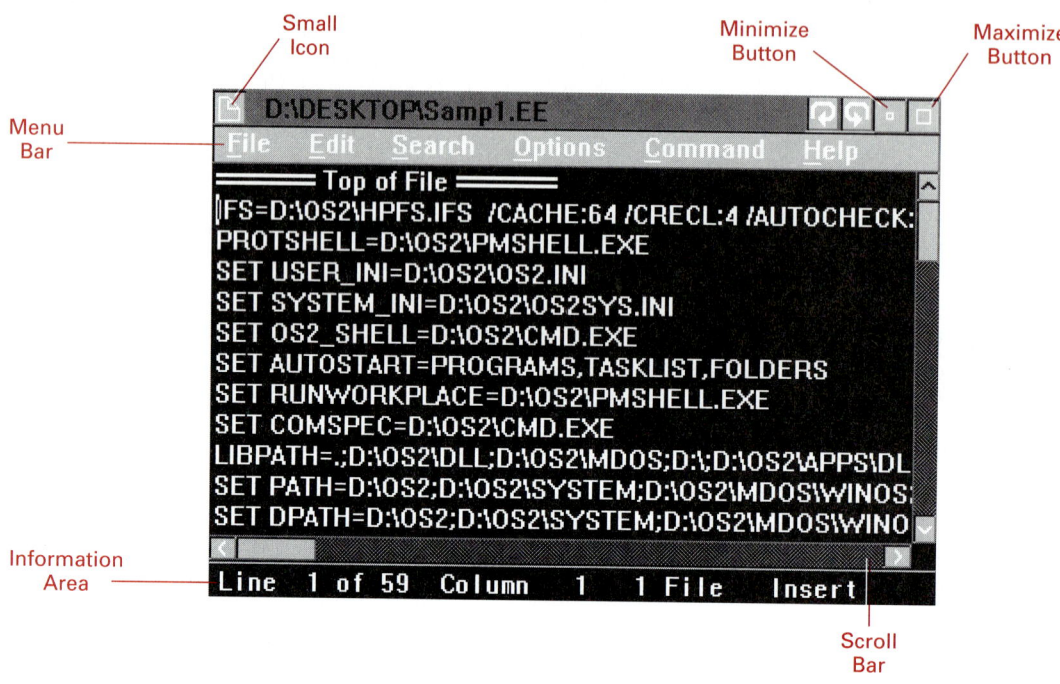

Figure 17.10 Standard window format.

DIALOG BOX

The CPI Presentation Interface also defines a special type of window, called a *dialog box*, that can be used to combine various individual controls and to deliver a collection of inputs to the application. The individual controls that make up a dialog box are called *dialog control items*. A dialog box can be used, for example, for bulk data entry. It can also be used to display formatted output.

There are two types of dialog boxes:

- **Modal.** A modal dialog box requires the user to finish input operations associated with that window or its children before being allowed to interact with another window for that application.
- **Modeless.** A modeless dialog box allows the user to interact with any of the windows of the application.

A standard window procedure is defined for processing a dialog box window.

CONTROL WINDOW MESSAGES

Control windows are defined with both a parent and an owner window. The owner window can be, but does not have to be, the parent window. When a significant

BOX 17.1 **Standard window components.**

- **Border.** The border of the standard window can have one of four formats:
  — Normal border
  — Wide border (border is selectable by the user for sizing operations)
  — Thin border
  — No border
- **System Menu.** Selection of the system menu icon generates a pulldown menu that allows the user to move or resize the window.
- **Title Bar.** Contains text that identifies the window.
- **Minimize Control.** Selecting the minimize control causes the window to assume its minimum size.
- **Maximize Control.** Selecting the maximize control causes the window to assume its maximum size.
- **Action Bar.** A menu presented horizontally across the window. Selecting a choice either causes an immediate action to take place or a pulldown menu to appear.
- **Scroll Bar Controls.** Horizontal and vertical scroll bars can be used to identify and control scrollable areas.
- **Client Area.** Contains application data presented in a window defined by the application.

event occurs, the control sends a message to the window procedure of its owner. For a frame window, the individual frame controls send messages to the frame window when an event related to the frame control occurs. For events of interest to the client area, the frame window sends messages to the window procedure of the client area window. A dialog box window receives messages from the individual dialog control items that are part of it and sends messages to its owner.

RESOURCES

The CPI Presentation Interface allows certain kinds of information to be defined and stored and then used by an application. There are different types of information, or resources, that can be used:

- **Templates.** Templates are data structures that are used to define certain types of control windows. A *dialog template* is used for a dialog box and a *menu template* for defining a menu control. The template defines each of the control items that make up the dialog box or menu control and data values associated with each control item. The application then uses the template to display the control and to receive inputs from it.

- **Mnemonics.** Mnemonics can be defined for the choices in a menu control.
- **Accelerators.** An accelerator is a key or key combination that is associated with a particular menu choice. An accelerator table can be defined for an application, showing the correspondence between keys and menu actions. An accelerator can be used to invoke an action even when the menu is not displayed, unlike mnemonics, which can be used only when the menu is visible. Thus accelerators provide the user with a shortcut for selecting an action.
- **Fonts.** Fonts, which are particular styles used to present characters, can be defined and then used by applications to present text.

THE CLIPBOARD FACILITY

The CPI Presentation Interface defines a *clipboard* facility that allows end users to transfer data from one place to another while in an application or from one application to another. Data transfer is accomplished using the following operations:

- **Cut.** Removes an identified segment of data from a window and saves it on the clipboard for later use.
- **Copy.** Makes a copy of an identified segment of data from a window and saves it on the clipboard for later use.
- **Paste.** Makes a copy of the data on the clipboard at a specified location in an application window.

CPI PRESENTATION INTERFACE SPECIFICATIONS FOR WINDOW PROCESSING

The CPI Presentation Interface specification defines a number of different elements that can be used by an application as part of window-based user interface processing. These include window function calls, window messages, standard window classes and styles, standard window procedures, and resource files. We will examine each of these in the sections that follow.

Window Function Calls

The CPI Presentation Interface defines a set of window function calls that provide a wide range of services. With these calls, an application can create, destroy, lock, show, and update windows, and set and query various window-related values. An application can control window size, position, display characteristics, and visibility, and specify a window as the active window or focus window. It can create, inspect, and destroy message queues, and dis-

Show Window

> Show Window (hwnd, NewVisibility, Success)

Call names: WinShowWindow, WISHOW

Function

This call sets the visibility state of a window.

Input Parameters

hwnd (*HWND*)
  Window handle.

NewVisibility (*BOOL*)
  New visibility state:

  TRUE Set window state visible.
  FALSE Set window state invisible.

Returns

Success (*BOOL*)
  Visibility changed indicator:

  TRUE Window visibility successfully changed.
  FALSE Window visibility not successfully changed.

Remarks

A window possesses a visibility state indicated by the WS_VISIBLE style bit. When the WS_VISIBLE style bit is set, the window is shown and subsequent drawing into the window is presented, unless that window is obscured by some other window, or at least one of the windows upward in the parent chain from **hwnd** does not have the WS_VISIBLE style.

When the WS_VISIBLE style bit is not set, the window is not shown ("hidden") and subsequent drawing into the window is not presented, even if that window is not obscured by another window.

If the value of the WS_VISIBLE style bit has been changed, the WM_SHOW message is sent to the window of **hwnd** before the function returns.

Figure 17.11 Window function call description.

patch, free, get, post, send, and wait for messages. It can process the clipboard, accelerators, the cursor, the pointer, and various types of data structures. An application may use window function calls in its mainline processing and as part of its window procedures.

Figure 17.11 shows an example of a window function call. The CPI Presentation Interface specification defines the following for each call:

- **Call Syntax.** The function call name in English and a list of its parameters.
- **Call Names.** The function call name used in the C language, and the name used in FORTRAN or COBOL.
- **Function.** A brief description of the purpose of the call.
- **Parameters.** Descriptions of the input and output parameters used with the call.
- **Returns.** A description of the possible values returned by the function call.
- **Remarks.** Additional information about the use of the function call.

As shown in the example in Fig. 17.11, a function call may cause another message to be generated and processed.

Standard Window Classes and Styles

The CPI Presentation Interface specification provides standard window classes and styles that can be used in defining a window. A window class is a set of windows that use the same window procedure. The window class is defined in terms of the processing performed and replies returned by the window procedure in response to specific messages. Box 17.2 lists the window classes predefined as part of the CPI Presentation Interface. These classes correspond to the control window types described earlier. For each class, there is a system-provided window procedure that performs the required window processing.

In addition to having a window class, a window has a set of characteristics, known as its *style*, that determine the window's appearance and behavior. The CPI Presentation Interface defines standard styles that can be used in defining windows. These styles are listed in Box 17.3. The first set of styles are class styles that apply to all windows of a particular class. These styles can be specified if a user-defined window class is created. The second set of styles are styles that can be assigned to individual windows.

System-Provided Window Procedures

There are several system-provided window procedures that are available for processing window messages, including a procedure for each of the standard control window classes listed in Box 17.2. In addition to these control window procedures, the CPI Presentation Interface also defines default window processing. A default window procedure is used for any messages that some other window procedure does not process. The system-provided window procedures are used by an application for any message that it is not prepared to process. The default procedures are also used by the control window procedures for messages that require no control-specific processing.

There is a default dialog procedure for messages related to a dialog box window and a default window procedure that can be used for any type of window message. There are also a language support window procedure and a language support dialog procedure. The language support procedures are used with appli-

BOX 17.2 Standard window classes.

- **WC_BUTTON.** Provides the facilities of a pushbutton, radio button, and check box control. It allows the user to select a choice represented by a button or box using either a pointing device or the keyboard.
- **WC_COMBOBOX.** Provides the facilities of prompted entry field control, or combination box, which combines an entry field with a list box. It allows the user to either enter a value or select a value from a list.
- **WC_ENTRYFIELD.** Provides the facilities of an entry field control. It allows the user to enter and edit a single line of text.
- **WC_FRAME.** Provides the facilities of a frame window. It displays and accepts user-entered data using standard window components.
- **WC_LISTBOX.** Provides the facilities of a list box control. It presents a list of items from which the user can make one or more selections.
- **WC_MENU.** Provides the facilities of a menu control. It presents a list of items, displayed either horizontally or vertically, from which the user is allowed to select one. Selection of an item causes the display of an associated pulldown menu, from which further choices can be made.
- **WC_MLE.** Provides the facilities of a multiline entry field control. It allows the user to enter and edit multiple lines of text.
- **WC_SCROLLBAR.** Provides the facilities of a scroll bar control. It allows the user to scroll the contents of an associated window.
- **WC_STATIC.** Provides the facilities of a static control and is used to present protected information.
- **WC_TITLEBAR.** Provides the facilities of a title bar and is used to display the window title. Highlighting of the title bar indicates the main window with which the user is interacting. The user can move a window by selecting the title bar with the pointer and then moving it.

cations written in a language like FORTRAN or COBOL that does not support reentrant procedures.

The system-provided window procedures are defined in terms of their responses to different window messages. Figure 17.12 shows an example of a message processing description from the default window procedure. The message description contains the following:

- **Name.** The message name and a description of the principle cause of the message's occurrence.
- **Parameters.** Input and output parameters used with the message. Messages always have two input parameters and one return value, which is called the reply.

BOX 17.3 Standard window styles.

Window Class Styles

- **CS_SIZEREDRAW.** Determines whether a window should be redrawn when sized.
- **CS_SYNCPAINT.** Specifies that a window should be synchronously repainted.
- **CS_MOVENOTIFY.** For a child window, specifies that it should be notified when its parent is moved.
- **CS_CLIPCHILDREN.** Specifies that the area occupied by a window's children should not be included when drawing in the parent window.
- **CS_CLIPSIBLINGS.** Specifies that the area occupied by a window's siblings should not be included when drawing in that window.
- **CS_PARENTCLIP.** Controls how a window is clipped when drawing is done in that window.
- **CS_SAVEBITS.** Specifies that the screen image of the area under a window is saved when the window is made visible.
- **CS_PUBLIC.** Indicates, when returned from a query, that the window being queried has a system-provided window class.
- **CS_HITTEST.** Causes a WM_HITTEST message to be sent to the window before it is sent any pointing device message.
- **CS_FRAME.** Specifies that the window will behave as a frame window.

Window Styles

- **WS_SYNCPAINT.** Specifies that a window should be synchronously repainted.
- **WS_CLIPCHILDREN.** Specifies that the area occupied by a window's children should not be included when drawing in the parent window.
- **WS_CLIPSIBLINGS.** Specifies that the area occupied by a window's siblings should not be included when drawing in that window.
- **WS_DISABLED.** Specifies that the window is disabled.
- **WS_MAXIMIZED.** Specifies that the window is to be created maximized.
- **WS_MINIMIZED.** Specifies that the window is to be created minimized.
- **WS_PARENTCLIP.** Controls how a window is clipped when drawing is done in that window.
- **WS_SAVEBITS.** Specifies that the screen image of the area under a window is saved when the window is made visible.
- **WS_VISIBLE.** Specifies that the window is visible.
- **WS_GROUP.** For dialog box windows, identifies the dialog items that make up a group.
- **WS_TABSTOP.** For dialog box windows, identifies a dialog item as one that can be reached using the TAB key.

- **Remarks.** A description of the processing performed for this message by the window procedure.
- **Default processing.** A description of how the default window procedure processes this message.

For control window procedures, the CPI Presentation Interface specification includes definitions of window styles that are specific to that control and a

WM_CREATE

This message occurs when an application requests the creation of a window.

Parameters

param 1

  ctldata (*PCTLDATA*)
    Control data.

    This points to a *CTLDATA* data structure initialized with the data provided in the **CtlData** parameter of the Create Window call.

    This pointer is also contained in the **create** parameter.

param 2

  create (*PCREATESTRUCT*)
    Create structure.

    This points to a *CREATESTRUCT* data structure.

Returns

reply

  result (*BOOL*)
    Error indicator:

      TRUE   Discontinue window creation.
      FALSE Continue window creation.

Remarks

This message is sent to the window procedure of the window being created, thus offering it an opportunity to initialize that window.

The window procedure receives this after the window is created but before the window becomes visible.

Default Processing

The Default Window Procedure takes no action on this message, other than to set **result** to FALSE, which is equivalent to continuing the creation of the window.

Figure 17.12   Default window procedure message processing description.

description of messages that are sent by the control to its owner window. For example, the following two styles can be used with a list box control window:

- **LS_MULTIPLESEL.** The list box control allows the end user to select more than one item at any one time.
- **LS_NOADJUSPOS.** The list box control is drawn at the size specified, which may cause parts of an item to be shown.

The WM_MEASUREITEM description, shown in Fig. 17.13, is an example of a message initiated by the list box control window procedure to notify its owner of a significant event.

The specification also includes message descriptions for messages processed by the control window procedure. There are certain messages that are specific to a particular control. The control window procedure description contains message processing descriptions for both control-specific messages and

WM_MEASUREITEM

This notification is sent to the owner of a list box control to establish the height for an item in that control.

Parameters

param 1

  listbox (*SHORT*)
    List-box identifier.

param 2

Returns

reply

  height (*SHORT*)
    Height of item.

Remarks

All items in a list box must have the same height, which must be greater than or equal to the height of the current font.

In particular, this notification is sent to the owner of a list box that has style of LS_OWNERDRAW, to offer the owner an opportunity to establish the height of an item that accommodates any special requirements for the drawing of items in that list box.

Default Processing

The Default Window Procedure does not expect to receive this message and therefore takes no action on it, other than to set **height** to the default value of NULL, which is equivalent to zero.

Figure 17.13   WM_MEASUREITEM message description.

LM_QUERYITEMCOUNT

This message returns a count of the number of items in the list box control.

Parameters

param 1 (*BIT32*)
Reserved.

   NULL   Reserved value.

param 2 (*BIT32*)
Reserved.

   NULL   Reserved value.

Returns

reply

   itemcount (*SHORT*)
     Item count.

Remarks

The List Box Control Window Procedure responds to this message by setting **itemcount** to the number of items in the list.

Default Processing

The Default Window Procedure does not expect to receive this message and therefore takes no action on it, other than to set **itemcount** to the default value of NULL, which is equivalent to zero.

Figure 17.14   LM_QUERYITEMCOUNT message description.

general messages. Figure 17.14 shows the description of the LM_QUERYITEMCOUNT message, a message that is specific to a list box control.

The Clipboard Facility

The clipboard facility is defined by the CPI Presentation Interface specification as part of general window processing. There are certain window function calls, listed in Box 17.4, that provide services related to the use of the clipboard. There are also clipboard messages, and the specification includes message processing descriptions for these messages.

Resource Files

Resources that can be used by an application as part of user interface processing include fonts, accelerator keys, and dialog and menu templates. In order for an application to make use of these types of resources, the resource must be defined in a resource file that is then compiled and made available to the application. The

BOX 17.4 Clipboard calls.

- Close Clipboard
- Empty Clipboard
- Enumerate Clipboard Formats
- Open Clipboard
- Query Clipboard Format Information
- Query Clipboard Data
- Query Clipboard Owner
- Query Clipboard Viewer
- Set Clipboard Data
- Set Clipboard Owner
- Set Clipboard Viewer

CPI Presentation Interface specification includes descriptions of the statements used to define resources.

GRAPHICS PROCESSING

The CPI Presentation Interface includes extensive facilities for processing various kinds of output. CPI Presentation Interface output can include character data displayed using various fonts; pictures created from primitive elements that include lines, arcs, and areas; and images that are specified pixel-by-pixel. Output can be presented on different types of devices, including display screens, printers, and plotters. Output can also be directed to picture interchange files that are used to send graphics objects from one CPI Presentation Interface environment to another.

PRIMITIVES

The CPI Presentation Interface defines facilities for drawing complex pictures. A picture is made up of one or more elements called primitives. The types of primitives that can be used to draw a picture include the following:

- **Straight and curved lines.** Straight lines can be drawn using a set of points or as a rectangular box. Curved lines are produced using arcs, fillets, and Bezier curves.

- **Areas.** An area is defined by its boundary, which consists of one or more closed figures. A closed figure consists of a set of straight and curved lines that are connected together with the start and end point as the same point.
- **Character strings.** A character string is a series of text characters drawn using a specified character set or font.
- **Markers.** A marker is a symbol used to indicate a position.
- **Images.** An image is a rectangular array of data where each bit represents a pixel, or display point, in the image picture.

Each primitive has its own set of *attributes*, such as color, line width, and shading associated with it.

SEGMENTS

Primitives are grouped together into collections called segments. A *segment* is a named set of primitives that defines a picture or a portion of a picture. A segment is generally used to define a discrete part of a picture that the end user may wish to manipulate as an object. Primitives are specified using either graphics calls or graphics orders. The CPI Presentation Interface specification documents both forms for specifying primitives. Figure 17.15 shows the description of the graphics call used to draw a line. Figure 17.16 shows the description of the graphics order that provides the same function. When segments are stored locally or in an interchange file, primitives are stored in the form of graphic orders.

ATTRIBUTES

Each type of primitive has attributes associated with it that determine characteristics that affect the appearance of the picture being drawn. For example, attributes specify the width and type of lines used; whether shading is applied and, if so, in what pattern; what colors are used for foreground and background; and so on. Box 17.5 lists the attributes applied to each primitive type.

PICTURE GENERATION

A picture is generated, or drawn, in a particular presentation space by executing the segments that make up the picture. When a segment is executed, the graphics calls or graphics orders that make up the segment are interpreted, and an appropriately shaped and shaded portion of the picture is mapped into a coordinate space. Execution of a segment begins with the first call or order in the segment and continues, one by one, until the last call or order has been executed.

As part of the drawing process, *resources* may be used that are part of the CPI Presentation Interface environment. These resources include a *color table* that associates an index with a color definition and a *font/symbol set*

Line

Line (hps, EndPoint, ErrInd)

Call names: Gpi/GpsLine, GI/GSLINE

Function

This call draws a straight line from the current position to the specified end point.

Input Parameters

hps (*HPS*)
  Presentation-space handle.

EndPoint (*POINT*)
  End point of the line.

Returns

ErrInd (*LONG*)
  Error indicator:

  GPI_OK   Successful.
  GPI_ERROR   Error.

Remarks

The current position is set to the end point of the line.

The line is drawn using the current values of the line color, line mix, line width, and line type attributes.

Graphic Element

  Element Type: OCODE_GCLINE

  Note that Polyline also generates this element type.

  Order: Line at Current Position.

Figure 17.15 Graphics call description example.

that associates a local identifier with a particular set of graphic symbols. The CPI Presentation Interface includes calls to create and use a color table, to create logical fonts, and to load, unload, and query fonts.

Chained Segments

A collection of segments can be chained together to form a picture. When segments are chained, after each segment has completed execution, control is passed

Line at Given Position / Line at Current Position

These orders define one or more connected straight lines, drawn from the given position or from the current position.

Line at Given Position (GLINE)
X'C1' (len, p0, p1, pn)

Line at Current Position (GCLINE)
X'81' (len, p1, pn)

Parameters

len (*GLENGTH1*)
  Length of following data

P0 (*GPOINT*)
  Coordinate data of line start.

  This parameter is only present in a Line at a Given Position order.

P1 (*GPOINT*)
  Coordinate data of first line end.

Pn (*GPOINT*)
  Coordinate data of final line end.

Figure 17.16 Graphics order description example.

to the next segment in the chain, and that segment is then executed. In this way the entire picture can be generated by invoking the execution of the first segment in the chain.

Called Segments

A segment can also call another segment, causing the called segment to be executed. After the called segment is executed, control returns to the calling segment. Called segments are often used to define subpictures that may be used in multiple places.

RETAINED DATA

When a picture is drawn, the information needed to redraw the picture may be saved by the presentation manager. This is known as *retained data*. With retained data, if a window needs to be redisplayed, for example when an overlapping window is removed, the presentation manager is able to do the redrawing without involving the application. With nonretained data, if a picture must be redrawn, the application must do the redrawing.

BOX 17.5 Graphics primitive attributes.

Line Attributes

Line color
Line mix
Line width
Geometric line width
Line type
Line end
Line join

Character Attributes

Character color
Character background color
Character mix
Character background mix
Character set
Character mode
Character box
Character angle
Character shear
Character direction

Marker Attributes

Marker color
Marker background color
Marker mix
Marker background mix
Marker set
Marker symbol
Marker box

BOX 17.5 *(Continued)*

Pattern Attributes (Areas)
Area color
Area background color
Area mix
Area background mix
Pattern set
Pattern symbol
Pattern reference point

Image Attributes
Image color
Image background color
Image mix
Image background mix

DRAWING MODE The drawing mode determines whether the primitives and attribute information needed to redraw a segment are retained by the presentation manager. Possible drawing modes are as follows:

- **Draw.** Segments are drawn immediately and not retained.
- **Retain.** Segment data is retained by the presentation manager for later drawing of the picture.
- **Draw and Retain.** Segments are drawn immediately, and segment data is retained by the presentation manager.

COORDINATE SPACES AND TRANSFORMATIONS Primitives are drawn based on coordinates that exist in a coordinate space. One of the major functions defined by the CPI Presentation Interface is the way in which coordinates specified in primitives are mapped to a standard coordinate system. The standard coordinate system is then mapped to coordinates associated with the presentation medium. The process of mapping from one coordinate system to another is called a *transformation*, or a *transform*.

World Coordinate Space

The different coordinate spaces and transformations used for the presentation of graphic objects are illustrated in Fig. 17.17. When a segment is executed, the subpicture generated by the segment is created in the *world coordinate space* using coordinates that reflect the units specified in the calls or orders in the segment. World coordinates are application-defined.

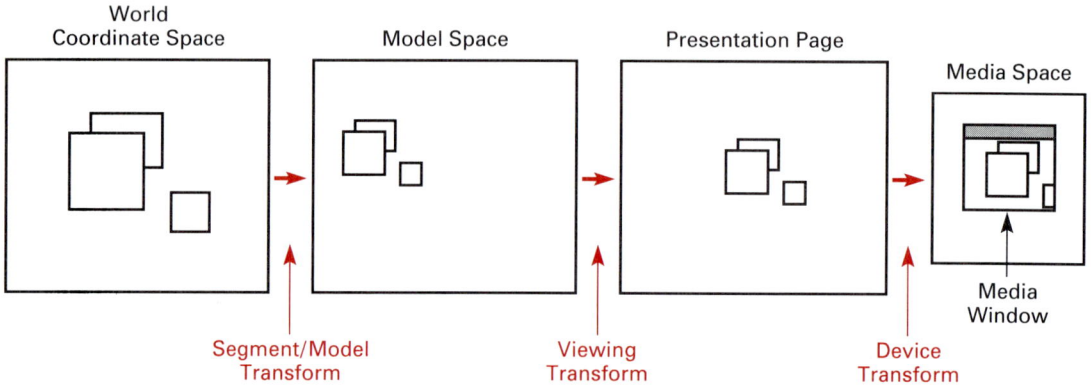

Figure 17.17   Coordinate spaces and transformations.

Model Space

The *segment/model transform* converts world coordinates to a coordinate system used for the *model space*. This transform may involve translating coordinates and rotating or scaling a segment or portion of a segment. For example, a segment that draws a particular construct, such as a wheel, might be used in more than one location within a picture and in different sizes in the different locations. A segment transform would map from the coordinates associated with the segment itself to those required in a particular location. The segment transform can be changed during the execution of a segment. A segment transform applies to an entire segment. A model transform applies to a group of primitives within a segment.

Presentation Page

After a picture or model has been constructed in the model space, the *viewing transform* then maps it to the *presentation page*. The presentation page is the application user's view of the generated picture. For a picture that consists of more than one subpicture, the presentation page is where the entire picture is assembled. The viewing transform is based on how the picture is to be viewed and can involve operations such as scrolling and scaling.

Media Window

The picture in the presentation page is device independent. To be presented on a particular device, it must be mapped to the coordinate space used by the actual presentation medium. This coordinate space is called the *media space*. For a display screen, the picture is moved into the client area of the appropriate window on the screen, called the *media window*. The *device transform* maps the picture from the presentation page to the media window. This transformation may involve clipping or scaling of the picture.

CLIPPING

Generally, the entire presentation page is mapped to the media window. However, depending on the current placement of the window on the display screen, the entire window may not be visible. The part of the media window that is visible is known as the *visible area*, and only the portion of the presentation page that maps to the visible area is displayed on the screen. When this happens, clipping occurs, and the drawing of the graphic picture is restricted to the region that is within the visible area. Any portion of the picture that falls outside the visible area is "clipped away" and not drawn.

A window may also have an area that needs to be redrawn. For example, an area that had been covered by an overlapping window now needs to be displayed again. Such an area is known as an *invalid region*. When the window display is updated, the redrawing is restricted to the invalid region, and any graphics picture being displayed is clipped to the boundaries of the invalid region.

Other types of clipping can be specified, if desired by an application. A *graphics field* can be defined within the presentation page, and then only the portion of the picture that lies within the graphic field is drawn. Similarly, a *viewing limit* can be established within the model space and then used for clipping. A *clip path* or *clip region* can be defined for clipping in the world space. A clip region is defined using rectangles, while a clip path can have an irregular shape, defined using primitives, such as lines, arcs, and even character strings. The graphic picture produced on the output device reflects the combination of all the different forms of clipping that are in effect when the picture is drawn.

GRAPHICS SPECIFICATIONS IN THE PRESENTATION INTERFACE

The CPI Presentation Interface specification defines the following elements related to the processing of graphics pictures:

- **Device Function Calls.** These calls are used to process device contexts, to determine device characteristics, and to set device modes.
- **Graphics Function Calls.** These calls are used to draw primitives, query and set attributes, process segments, control the drawing mode, define clipping and

transforms, and process metafiles used to interchange graphics between applications.
- **Graphics Orders.** Graphics orders, or drawing orders, are used to specify primitives, attributes, and other picture information, in a form that is used as part of a stored segment or a metafile. The graphics orders have similar meanings to graphics calls, and many times there is a one-to-one correspondence between them. Where graphics orders can provide the same function, the graphic call description identifies the graphics order or orders that correspond.
- **File Formats.** Standard formats are defined for use with bitmaps and interchange files.

CONFORMANCE WITH CUA

The various controls that are part of the CPI Presentation Interface can be used to develop a user interface for an application that is consistent with CUA guidelines in appearance and interaction. The windows required to implement the application's user interface can be defined with a *frame* window class. They will then be formatted in the CPI Presentation Interface standard window format, which is consistent with CUA graphical model formatting guidelines. The CPI Presentation Interface also provides support for multiple windows on the screen and for the user to move and resize the windows.

Client areas can be defined using individual controls for selection, entry, and display fields to implement the required interface to application objects and actions. The CPI Presentation Interface supports a number of, but not all, the controls defined as part of the CUA advanced interface graphical model. Controls supported include the menu bar, pulldown menus, radio buttons, check boxes, list boxes, combination boxes, pushbuttons, and entry fields.

The dialog box can be used to implement secondary windows. A dialog box can be used to provide a secondary window that extends the dialog with the user, such as a secondary window used when a particular pulldown menu choice is selected. A dialog box can also be used to implement help panels or to display messages to the user.

The CPI Presentation Interface does not directly support the three types of messages defined by the graphical model and the icons used to designate them. The CPI Presentation Interface also does not directly support the different types of help defined by CUA. The application must see that the different types of messages are formatted and processed properly, and that the different types of help information are available to the user and can be invoked in the ways defined in CUA. The application also must provide the processing required for any CUA-defined standard actions that are included in the menu bar and its pulldowns or in pushbuttons.

The CPI Presentation Interface does define methods for handling general user interactions with windows and the controls they contain. The standard frame and dialog box window procedures can be used by the application to handle the user interactions with the various controls. The presentation manager handles the interactions with individual controls as well as movement from one control to another or from one window area to another. The presentation manager, in the messages it sends to the application's window procedures, provides the logical results of the user's interactions, identifying choices selected and passing data entered to the application. The application is then responsible for providing the application-specific logic required to process the data or respond to the selection. With this approach, the primary responsibility for seeing that the application's user interface conforms with the CUA rules and guidelines rests with the presentation manager implementation rather than with the application.

CONFORMANCE WITH CCS OBJECT CONTENT ARCHITECTURES

The graphics processing facilities that are defined by the CPI Presentation Interface specification conform very closely to the capabilities defined by the Graphics Object Content Architecture (GOCA). The drawing order functions defined in GOCA, including those in GOCA Extended, have been implemented in both the graphics functions calls and the graphics orders that are defined by the CPI Presentation Interface. All the attributes in GOCA Version 0 and most of the attributes from GOCA Extended have been included in the CPI Presentation Interface. Color tables and fonts can be used as resources. The picture generation process, including the use of chaining, calling, drawing modes, transforms, and clipping, operates as described in GOCA Extended. The coordinate spaces and transforms used with the CPI Presentation Interface, although named differently, are the functional equivalents of those defined in GOCA.

The font processing facilities included in the CPI Presentation Interface are consistent with the capabilities defined by the Font Object Content Architecture (FOCA). When a logical font is created, it is based on a physical font. The physical font to use can be specified by supplying font attributes. The font attributes used in the CPI Presentation Interface are a subset of the font parameters defined by FOCA. Also, the CPI Presentation Interface allows the application to query fonts to determine their font metrics. These font metrics are, for the most part, values included in the FOCA font parameters.

CONCLUSION

This chapter has described the CPI Presentation Interface that defines services used by applications to display and print text, graphics, and image information. An implementation of the CPI Presentation Interface can be used by applications to help them create user interfaces that are in conformance with the CUA component of SAA. Chapter 18, the final chapter of this book, describes the CPU PrintManager Interface. It describes services applications can use for performing functions related to printing that are normally controlled through operating system facilities.

18 THE CPI PRINTMANAGER INTERFACE

The CPI PrintManager Interface is designed to allow applications to perform printing-related functions that are normally specified through facilities that are dependent on the operating system environment in which the programs run. With the CPI PrintManager Interface, an application is able to define print options and submit print jobs to an implementation of the PrintManager Interface, which we will call a *print manager*.

The CPI PrintManager Interface is consistent across all the SAA environments, so it helps in creating applications that can be migrated from one environment to another with little or no modification required to their printing functions. With the CPI PrintManager Interface, the way in which print jobs are submitted is independent of the type of data stream or protocols being used. Print options can be defined and print destinations specified in a way that is consistent across environments and is independent of the particular computing system at which printing takes place.

CPI PRINTMANAGER INTERFACE CAPABILITIES

The CPI PrintManager Interface defined as part of CPI provides an application with the following capabilities:

- The ability to provide an interactive interface to the end user for controlling printing functions.
- The ability to have standard sets of print options that are applied at the application level across the organization.
- The ability to have different print options and print destinations for different print jobs created within the same application.
- The ability to write multiple buffers of data and complete files within a single print job.
- The ability to specify the use of Advanced Function Printing (AFP) resources and to include those resources inline with a print job.

These capabilities are defined by the CPI PrintManager Interface through a set of functions, known as verbs, and a set of print options that can be controlled via PrintManager verbs.

PRINTMANAGER VERBS

The PrintManager verbs, as defined by the CPI Print-Manager Interface, allow an application to start and end print sessions, to query and set print options, to create and control print jobs, and to process error information. Figure 18.1 shows an example of a PrintManager verb specification. For each verb, the interface specification includes a description of the function of the verb, the parameters used with the verb, the possible values that can be returned, and programming-related information about using the verb. The various PrintManager verbs are examined in the following sections.

Print Session Verbs

The verbs that can be used to control a print session are

- **OPEN (SPROPEN).** Opens and identifies a print session.
- **CLOSE (SPRCLOS).** Ends the current print session.
- **ABORT (SPRABRT).** Aborts the current print session.

Print Option Verbs

The verbs that can be used to process print options are

- **LIST OPTIONS (SPRLOPT).** Lists the currently-defined print options.
- **QUERY OPTION (SPRQOPT).** Lists the current value for a specified print option.
- **SET OPTION (SPRSOPT).** Sets a print option to a specified value.

Print Job Verbs

The following verbs can be used to create and abort print jobs:

- **START DOCUMENT (SPRSDOC).** Starts a print job and assigns a document name to it.
- **WRITE (SPRWRIT).** Writes a buffer of data to a print job.
- **ADD FILE (SPRADDF).** Writes a file of print data to a print job. Both buffers of data and files can be written to the same print job.
- **END DOCUMENT (SPREDOC).** Ends a print job.
- **ABORT DOCUMENT (SPRADOC).** Aborts a print job and deletes any data that has been written to it.

SPRWRIT (Write)

MVS	VM	OS/400	OS/2
X	X	X	

Function

Sends a buffer of data to the print job.

Syntax

SPRWRIT (hprm, Count, Data, *success*)

Figure 4–14. Format of the SPRWRIT (Write) Verb

Parameters

hprm (HPRM)
(Input). Identifies a valid print session.

Count (LONG)
(Input). The length of the buffer of print data sent to the print job.

Data (BUFFER)
(Input). The buffer of print data sent to the print job.

Usage

Use the SPRWRIT (Write) verb to send a buffer of data to a print job.

If an error occurs, PrintManager returns to Session Active state.

For the hprm parameter, ensure that you enter a valid print-session dentifier. Otherwise, in the MVS and VM environments PrintManager will abend with X'0245', and in OS/400 a value of 0 will be returned.

Return Values

success (BOOL)
A nonzero value means the buffer of data was sent to the print job successfully, whereas a value of 0 means an error occurred.

Environment Restrictions

For PrintManager Interface applications, the maximum length of the buffer is 32K bytes in VM.

Figure 18.1 Sample CPI PrintManager Interface verb specification.

Error Verbs

The following verbs can be used to process information related to error conditions:

- **GET ERROR INFORMATION (SPRGERI).** Returns the error-information data structure associated with the most recent error.

- **GET ERROR MESSAGE (SPRGEEM).** Returns additional error information associated with the error-information data structure. The additional information consists of one or more error messages.
- **FREE ERROR INFORMATION (SPRFERI).** Frees the storage used for an error-information data structure returned by a previous Get Error Information verb.

PRINTMANAGER PRINT OPTIONS

The CPI PrintManager Interface defines a wide range of print options that define printer capabilities and data stream characteristics, select printer options to use, specify resources to be used, define various size and spacing options, and so on. Figure 18.2 shows an example of a print option specification. For each print option, the interface specification includes a description of its functions, rules, and values that are recognized by a print manager implementation of the CPI PrintManager Interface and notes about the print option's usage. One of the key uses of print options is to specify AFP resources that are used with a particular print job. These resources include form definitions, page definitions, fonts, overlays, and page segments. The print options used to specify these resources are as follows:

- **FORMDEF.** Used to specify the forms definition to be used with a print job. A forms definition provides information about the printing medium and how it is handled. This can include items, such as number of copies, overlays used, duplexing or simplexing, and placement of data on the page. An existing forms definition can be specified or one can be created using other print options that define the various printing medium characteristics that are part of a forms definition.
- **PAGEDEF.** Specifies information about the placement and formatting of line data on the print medium. This includes line length, page length, fonts, and the use of rotated printing.
- **OVERLAY.** Used to specify the use of overlays, which are collections of coded information that specify where to place boxes, lines, shading, text, logos, or graphic images on the page. Overlays can be used as a replacement for preprinted forms.

Copies

Specifies how many copies of a print job will be printed.

Validation Rule:	**RANGE**
Valid Values:	0 (decimal places), 1 (minimum), 255 (maximum)
Environment Notes:	This option is functionally supported by a printer driver in the OS/400, MVS, and VM operating systems.

Figure 18.2 Sample print option specification.

- **FONT.** Used to specify the use of fonts, which are sets of characters in a given size and style. Fonts control the appearance of text data.
- **PAGESEG.** Specifies the use of page segments. Page segments can contain text, raster graphics, or both. As with overlays, they can be placed anywhere on the page. They are typically used for items like logos, signatures, bar charts, and drawing.

Box 18.1 lists the print options that are defined as part of the CPI PrintManager Interface.

BOX 18.1   Print options.

- **BACKGRNDMIX.** Specifies the background-mix toning supported by the printer.
- **BARCODESET.** Specifies the MO:DCA-P bar code capability supported by the printer driver.
- **CAPSGRAPHIC.** Specifies the graphics capability supported by the printer.
- **CAPRASTER.** Specifies the raster capability supported by the printer.
- **CC.** Specifies the type of carriage control characters contained in a data stream.
- **CKPTLINE.** Specifies the maximum number of lines in a logical page.
- **CKPTPAGE.** Specifies the number of logical pages to be printed before taking a checkpoint.
- **CKPTSEC.** Specifies the number of seconds to elapse before taking a checkpoint.
- **CLASS.** Specifies the print output class for job scheduling.
- **COLORNUM.** Specifies the number of distinct colors supported by the printer, including reset.
- **COPIES.** Specifies how many copies of a print job to print.
- **DATACK.** Specifies which printer errors are reported.
- **DATATYPE.** Specifies the data stream type of the print job.
- **DEVDRIVERTYPE.** Identifies the printer driver.
- **DEVMODEL.** Identifies the type and model number of the printer.
- **DNLDFONT.** Specifies the number of fonts that can be downloaded to the printer at any one time.

(Continued)

BOX 18.1 *(Continued)*

- **DOCOWNER.** Specifies the print-job owner.
- **DUPLEX.** Specifies how the job will be printed on the output medium.
- **FCB.** Specifies the name of the forms control buffer (FCB) for formatting line data for a 3800-1 printer.
- **FIDELITY.** Specifies if the printer driver will try to print a file that contains errors.
- **FLASHCNT.** Specifies the number of pages to print with the forms flash specified in the FLASHNAME option.
- **FLASHNAME.** Specifies the name of a forms flash for printing images on a 3800 printer.
- **FOCASET.** Specifies the SAA font capability supported by the printer driver.
- **FONT.** Specifies the names or location of fonts to be used with a print job.
- **FOREGRNDMIX.** Specifies the foreground-mix toning supported by the printer.
- **FORM.** Specifies an installation-defined forms code that specifies the output medium for a print job.
- **FORMDEF.** Specifies the form definition for an AFP print job.
- **GDDMDEVTOKEN.** Specifies a GDDM device token.
- **GRAPHICSET.** Specifies the MO:DCA-P graphics capability supported by the printer driver.
- **HORIZRES.** Identifies the horizontal resolution of the specified device in pels (pixels) per meter.
- **IMAGESET.** Specifies the MO:DCA-P image capability supported by the printer driver.
- **INBIN.** Specifies the source for paper or other media for a print job.
- **INDEX.** Specifies the number of print positions for the left margin indentation for 3211 printers with the indexing feature.
- **JOGOUT.** Specifies offsetting of copy groups within a print job in the printer output bin.
- **LEFTMAR.** Specifies the width of the left margin in pels.
- **LINDEX.** Specifies the number of print positions for the right margin indentation for 3211 printers with the indexing feature.

BOX 18.1 *(Continued)*

- **LINECT.** Specifies the maximum number of lines to print on each output page for a JES2 line printer.
- **LPI.** Specifies the number of printed lines per inch.
- **MEDIATTRIBUTES.** Specifies output medium availability.
- **MEDIATYPE.** Specifies the type of output medium being used by the printer.
- **MEDIAXLEFTCLIP.** Specifies the left clip limit of the output medium in millimeters.
- **MEDIAXPELS.** Specifies the number of pels between the left and right clip limits of the output medium.
- **MEDIAXRIGHTCLIP.** Specifies the right clip limit of the output medium in millimeters.
- **MEDIAXWIDTH.** Specifies the width of the output medium in millimeters.
- **MEDIAYBOTTOMCLIP.** Specifies the bottom clip limit of the output medium in millimeters.
- **MEDIAYHEIGHT.** Specifies the height of the output medium in millimeters.
- **MEDIAYPELS.** Specifies the number of pels between the top and bottom clip limits of the output medium.
- **MEDIAYTOPCLIP.** Specifies the top clip limit of the output medium in millimeters.
- **MESSAGES.** Specifies the number of errors to be received before terminating the job for a job sent to an AFP printer.
- **MODCASET.** Identifies the level of MO:DCA-P supported by the printer driver.
- **MODIFYNAME.** Specifies the copy-modification module to be used to print a job on a 3800 printer.
- **MODIFYTRC.** Specifies the character-arrangement table to be used with a copy-modification module on a 3800 printer.
- **OUTDISP.** Specifies the disposition of the print job.
- **OUTMETHOD.** Specifies postprocessing operations done by the printer.
- **OUTPUTID.** Specifies the printer name.
- **OUTQ.** Specifies the output queue for the spooled output file.

(Continued)

BOX 18.1 *(Continued)*

- **OVERLAY.** Specifies the electronic overlays for a print job.
- **PAGEDEF.** Specifies the name and location of the page definition used for AFP printing of a line data print job.
- **PAGERANGE.** Specifies the beginning page and ending page of a print job.
- **PAGESEG.** Specifies the location of the page segments for a print job.
- **PRMODE.** Specifies job processing.
- **PRTDIRECTION.** Ensures page-presentation compatibility between 3800 and 3835 printers.
- **PRTENVIRONMENT.** Defines the operating system environment of the printer.
- **PRTQUAL.** Specifies the print-quality level for the print job.
- **PRTY.** Specifies the print job priority.
- **RSCSID.** Specifies the user ID of the local RSCS service machine in VM.
- **SCHEDULE.** Specifies when the spooled output file is available to a printer driver.
- **TECHNOLOGY.** Identifies the type of technology (vector, raster, impact, etc.) of the specified printing device.
- **TEXTSET.** Specifies the MO:DCA-P text capability supported by the printer driver.
- **TOPMAR.** Specifies the width of the top margin in pels.
- **TRC.** Specifies if the print data contains font table reference characters.
- **UCS.** Specifies the universal character set image, print train, or character arrangement table to be used in printing the job.
- **VERTRES.** Specifies the vertical resolution of the printer in pels per meter.
- **WRITER.** Specifies a spool program other than JES to process the job.

PRINT DESCRIPTORS

Print descriptors can be used to set default values that are used for print options that have not been set to a specific value within an application. A print descriptor can also define the values that are valid for a particular print option. These values are then used to validate the value specified for a print option as part of a SET OPTION (SPRSOPT) verb.

As defined in the CPI PrintManager Interface, either the OPEN (SPROPEN) or the SET OPTION (SPRSOPT) verb can specify the name of a print descriptor. The default values included in that print descriptor then become part of the current environment. A default value can be overridden by specifying a different value for the print option in a SET OPTION (SPRSOPT) verb.

When a print option is set with a SET OPTION (SPRSOPT) verb, the value specified is validated. If a print descriptor has been specified, the valid values and rules specified in the print descriptor are used to validate the value. The rules and values for a print option in a print descriptor can be specified as follows:

- A list of valid values.
- A range of valid values, specified with a minimum and maximum value.
- A string value, where the value can contain any alphanumeric characters and can be any length up to a defined maximum length.
- Not validated, where any value is valid.

If a particular print option is not included in the print descriptor, that print option is not valid and cannot be set to a value while the print descriptor is in effect.

If a new print descriptor is specified, the set of default values changes to that specified in the new print descriptor. Any print option values that have been explicitly set are revalidated according to the validation rules and values in the new print descriptor. Values are retained as part of the current environment only if they meet the validation criteria of the new print descriptor.

The CPI PrintManager Interface specifies how print descriptors are specified in an Open or Set Option verb and how print descriptors are used for default values and validation. However, the interface does not specify how print descriptors are defined. This is left to the individual print manager implementations.

RELATIONSHIP TO CCS

The CPI PrintManager Interface supports the use of both MO:DCA and Advanced Function Printing (AFP) data stream formats. The CPI PrintManager Interface is not responsible for formatting the data stream. This is the responsibility of the application and any resources it uses to create the data to be printed. However, the CPI PrintManager Interface defines facilities that can be used when processing a data stream in MO:DCA or AFP format. Print options can be used to query and set MO:DCA-related capabilities for fonts and for text, graphics, image, and bar code data. Other print options support the use of AFP resources, including fonts, overlays, page segments, forms definitions, and page definitions.

The AFP data stream is a device-independent data stream that allows applications to produce data to be represented on an all-points-addressable printer. The MO:DCA and AFP data stream formats are similar but not identical. Both use objects, structured fields, and component delimiters, although the specific objects supported in each vary. IBM's intent is to allow AFP applications to coexist with MO:DCA applications and to provide a common means of access to all-points-addressable devices for the two types of data streams. The CPI PrintManager Interface reflects this coexistence by supporting both the SAA-defined MO:DCA data stream as well as the non-SAA AFP data stream.

To be used with a specific device, a MO:DCA or AFP data stream is first converted to the Intelligent Printer Data Stream (IPDS) format. An IPDS data stream contains control information for the particular printer device used for presentation. This conversion for actual presentation is normally performed by a print services component, rather than by the application itself. The CPI PrintManager Interface, which is designed to be used at the application level, does not address the use of the IPDS format. However, a particular implementation of the CPI PrintManager Interface may provide this function.

CONCLUSION

This chapter has described the CPI PrintManager Interface that defines services allowing applications to perform environment-independent printing-related functions that are normally specified through facilities that are dependent on a particular operating system. This concludes this book on the Common Programming Interface component of SAA.

INDEX

A

Accelerators, 354
Access plan, 159
Action bar tags, Dialog tag language, 329
Action messages, 280
Action windows, 279
Active window, 343
AD/Cycle, 10, 198–99
ADDPOP, 324
Adobe Corporation, 307
Advanced function calls, CPI-C, 260
Advanced Function Printer Data Stream (AFDS), 296
Advanced Function Printing (AFP), 381, 382
Advanced Interface, CUA, 276–77
Advanced peer-to-peer networking (APPN) facilities, 225, 226–27
Advanced Program-to-Program Communication (APPC), LU 6.2 and, 236, 254
Aggregation(s), 196–97
Aggregation instance, 197
Aggregation type, 196
ALL, 148
ALTER TABLE statement, 157
AND, 148
ANY, 148
Application design, 29–30
  of application logic, 46–47
  of communications, 47
  components of, 31
  of data, 46
  of user interface, 45–46
Application enablers, 6
Application Generator Interface, CPI:
  application logic definition, 100–101
  application logic specification, 101–3
    application processing, 104–5
    application structure, 103–4
    special function words, 106–7
  application logic structure, 101
  data definition, 107–8
  data specification:
    data structure, 108, 109
    record specification, 108, 110
    table specification, 108, 111
  environments, 99–100
  map definition, 108–11
    map specification, 111–12
    map structure, 112, 113–115
Application logic, designing, 46–47
Application panel, Dialog interface, 328–31
Application programming interface (API), 243
Application services, CCS, 19–20
Application structure, Presentation Interface, 344–46
APPN end nodes, 227
APPN network, 227, 229

APPN network nodes, 227
Areas, 363
ASCII character set, 42–43, 44
AS/400, 6
Association control service element (ACSE), 20
Asynchronous message processing, 252–53, 344
Atomic data, 134
Attributes, 134
   entity types and, 194
   Presentation Interface, 363
Authorization, 139
   Database Interface, 158–59

B

Backout service, 186, 187, 189–91
BACKOUT statements, 180, 181
Base tables, 138
Basic conversations, 242–43, 257
Basic conversation verbs, 243, 244
BEGIN DECLARE statement, 160
BETWEEN, 148
Bidirectional relationship, 195
Binary relationship, 195
Bind procedure, 224, 225
Branch, 202
BREAK fields, Query Interface, 167
Built-in functions, 123
   Repository Interface, 208, 210
Byte-ordering, 42

C

Callable interface, Query Interface, 165
   commands, 175–77
   function calls, 172–74
   interface communications area, 175
   return variables, 175
Called segments, 303, 305, 365
Calls, CPI-C, 259–62
Candidate keys, 135
Cascaded menus, 282
CCITT Recommendation X.25, 22

CCS, 8, 17–18. *See also* User interfaces, CCS
   application services, 19–20
   data link controls, 21–22
   data streams, 18–19
   goals of, 22
   network services, 21
   objects, 18
   Presentation Interface (CPI) and, 371
   PrintManager Interface (CPI) and, 381–82
   session services, 20–21
Chained segments, 303, 364–65
Change commitment, 154
Character attributes, Graphics Object Content Architecture (GOCA), 302
Character Data Representation Architecture (CDRA), 19, 295
Character strings, 363
Check box, Presentation Interface, 351
Check box control, Advanced Interface, 283
Child window, 340
CICS (Customer Information Control System), 4
C language, 51–52, 172, 199, 325, 326
   call syntax example, 327
   constant data types, 56
   data definition and use, 52
   embedded SQL statements, 160, 161
   example of, 52, 53–55
   function calls without variables, 173
   function calls with variables, 174
   library functions, 55
   operators, 59
   preprocessor directives, 60
   statements, 55, 60
   variable data types, 57–58
   variable storage classes, 58
Class style, 343
Client/server computing, 34–35
Clipboard facility, Presentation Interface, 354, 361, 362
Clip path, 369
Clipping, Presentation Interface, 369
Clip region, 369
COBOL, 172, 177, 325, 326, 357
   call syntax example, 327
   data definition and use, 61, 63–64
   data types, 65

embedded SQL statements, 160, 161
  example of, 61, 62–63
  file organizations and access modes, 65
  function calls without variables, 173
  function calls with variables, 174
  statements, 64, 66–67
Code page, 295
Color table, 363
COLUMN fields, Query Interface, 167
Columns, 133
Combination box, Presentation Interface, 351
Combination box control, Advanced Interface, 284
Command(s):
  IPDS, 319–20
  Procedures Language, 127–28
  Query Interface, 168
Command table, Dialog Interface, 332–33
COMMENT ON statement, 157, 158
Commit operation, 271
Commit point, 154
Commit service, 185, 186, 187–88
COMMIT statements, 154, 180, 181
Commit tree, 184
Common Programming Interface (CPI), 8, 10–14
Common Programming Interface for Communications (CPI-C), 11
  calls, 258–62
  call to LU 6.2 verb mapping, 265
  concepts related to, 257–58
  conversation characteristics, 263–64
    default values, 264
    extract and setting values, 264
    side information, 264–65
  distributed transaction example, 271–72
  LU 6.2 and, 255, 265
  one-way conversation with confirmation, 269
  one-way conversation with no confirmation, 268–69
  protected conversation with Commit processing, 270–71
  support for synchronization point processing, 267–68
  two-way conversation, 269–70
Communication, 6

designing, 47
Composite key, 135
Compound document, 293, 316
Concurrency, 139
  Database Interface, 153–54
Concurrent access, 139
Conditions, Procedures Language, 123–24
Condition traps, Procedures Language, 123–24
CONFIRM, 265
Connectionless-mode network service (CLNS), 21
Connection-mode network service (CONS), 21
CONNECT statement, 162
Container objects, Advanced Interface, 277
Control operator verbs, 244, 247
Control points (CPs), 221
Controls, Advanced Interface:
  check box, 283
  combination box, 284
  drop-down combination box, 285
  drop-down list, 284
  entry field, 284
  list box, 284
  menu, 281–82
  notebook, 285
  push-button, 282
  radio button, 283
  slider, 283
  spin button, 285
  value set, 283
Controls, Basic Interface, 289–91
Controls, Presentation Interface, 350–51
Control services, Dialog Interface, 325
Control window messages, Presentation Interface, 352–53
Conversation(s), 225
  CPI-C, 263-65
    one-way conversation with confirmation, 269
    one-way conversation with no confirmation, 268–69
    protected, with Commit processing, 270–71
    two-way conversation, 269–70
  LU 6.2, 242–43

one-way conversation with confirmation, 248–50
one-way conversation with no confirmation, 244–248
two-way conversation, 250, 251
LU-LU session and, 239
Conversational application, 44
Conversation verbs, LU 6.2 and, 243–44
Cooperative processing, 32-33
Coordinate spaces:
   Graphics Object Content Architecture (GOCA), 300, 304
   Presentation Interface, 367–69
Copies, PrintManager, 376
Correlated reference, 147
CP-LU session, 223
CP-PU session, 223
CREATE INDEX statement, 158
CREATE TABLE statement, 154, 156
CREATE VIEW statement, 157
Cross System Product (CSP), 99, 100
CUA (Common User Access), 8. *See also* User interface, CUA
   Dialog Interface (CPI) and, 321–23
   interaction techniques, 17
   nonprogrammable terminal panel layout, 15
   panel and window information content guidelines, 17
   presentation, 14
   Presentation Interface (CPI) and, 370–71
   programmable workstation window structure, 16
Cursor, 152, 342
Cursor-based processing, 152–53
Curved lines, 362

D

Data:
   designing, 46
   logical data model, 138
   physical data structures, 138
   user view of, 138
Database Interface, CPI, 11, 133, 180–81
   authorization, 158–59
   concurrency, 153–54
   creating tables, 154–56
   cursor-based processing, 152–53
   data definition, 154
   defining indexes, 158
   defining views, 157–58
   DELETE statement, 152
   dynamic SQL statements, 162–64
   embedded SQL statements, 160–62
   executing SQL statements, 159–60
   FROM clause, 146
   GROUP BY clause, 150
   HAVING clause, 150
   INSERT statement, 152
   modifying tables, 157
   ORDER BY clause, 150
   other search conditions, 147–49
   package processing, 160
   queries, 143–44
   SELECT clause, 144–45
   SELECT INTO statement, 151
   SQL communications area, 162–63
   UNION operation, 151
   UPDATE clause, 151
   updating data, 151
   WHERE clause, 146–47
      subqueries, 147
Data definition:
   Application Generator Interface, 107–8
   Database Interface, 154
Data Flow Control layer, SNA, 231, 236, 237
Data items, 134
Data Link Control layer, SNA, 231, 237
Data Link Controls, CCS, 21–22
Data objects:
   Advanced Interface, 276
   IPDS, 319
Data representation:
   ASCII and EBCDIC differences, 42–43
   byte-ordering differences, 42
   double-byte character set considerations, 43–44
   floating-point format differences, 43
   zoned- and packed-decimal data differences, 43
Data services, Repository Interface, 204
   calling, 204–7
Data specification, Application Generator Interface:

Index

data structure, 108, 109
record specification, 108, 110
table specification, 108, 111
Data streams, 293, 294–95
   Common Communications Support (CCS), 18–19
   environments and, 296–98
   Mixed Object Document Content Architecture (MO:DCA), 314
DB2 (Data Base 2), 4
DEALLOCATE, 265
DECLARE CURSOR statement, 152
DELETE statement, 152
Dependent entities, 196
Dependent table, 156
Derivation policies, 197
DESCRIBE statement, 163
Desktop, 340
Device context, 347
Device Function Calls, Presentation Interface, 369
Device objects, Advanced Interface, 277
Device transform, 369
Dialog box, Presentation Interface, 350, 352, 370
Dialog control items, 352
Dialog elements, Dialog Interface, 323
Dialog Interface, CPI, 13
   basic interface support, 322–23
   Common User Access (CUA) and, 321–23
   control services, 325
   defining a command table, 332–33
   defining an application panel, 328–31
   defining help panels, 334
   defining key mapping lists, 333
   defining messages, 331–32
   defining variables, 336–37
   developing help index, 335–36
   dialog elements and, 323
   dialog services, 323–24
   display services:
      help windows, 324
      pop-up windows, 324
      primary windows, 324
   help facilities, 333–34
   interaction and, 322
   presentation and, 322

requesting help, 336
service call formats, 325–27
using the dialog tag language, 327–-28
variable services, 325
Dialog Manager, 321, 322
Dialog services, Dialog Interface, 323–24
Dialog tag language (DTL), 321, 327
Dialog template, 353
DISPLAY, 324, 325, 326
Display services, Dialog Interface, 324
Distributed computing, 30–31
Distributed data access, 33–34
Distributed database access:
   nontransparent, 37, 38
   remote unit of work processing, 37–38
   transparent, 37
Distributed Data Management (DDM), 40, 237
Distributed dialog processing, 32
Distributed document access, 36
Distributed files:
   OSI, 41–42
   SNA, 40–41
Distributed function processing, 34, 35
Distributed Relational Database Architecture (DRDA), 39–40, 41, 141–42
Distributed relational databases, 139–41
Distributed request processing, 39, 141, 181
Distributed resource processing, Resource Recovery Interface, 183–85
Distributed resources, 30, 35–36
Distributed unit of work processing, 39, 141, 181
DMCLOSE, 325
DMOPEN, 325
Document data stream environments, 295
Document Interchange Architecture (DIA), 19, 237
Document layout structure, MO:DCA, 315
Document logical structure, MO:DCA, 314–15
Domain, 202
Double-byte character set, 43–44
Draw, 347
Drawing attributes, Graphics Object Content Architecture (GOCA), 301
Drawing mode, Presentation Interface, 367

Drawing order coordinate space, 304
Drawing orders, Graphics Object Content Architecture (GOCA), 299–300
Drop-down combination box control, Advanced Interface, 285
Drop-down list control, Advanced Interface, 284
DROP statement, 157, 158, 160
Dynamic SQL statements, 160, 162–64

E

EBCDIC character set, 42–43, 44
END DECLARE statement, 160
End-to-end transmission, 232
Entities, 194–95
Entity instance, 134, 194
Entity integrity, 136–37
Entity occurence, 134
Entity-relationship model, Repository Interface:
    aggregations, 196–97
    dependent entities, 196
    entities, 194–95
    policies, 197–98
    relationships, 195–96
Entity type, 133, 194
Entity type templates, 199–200
Entry field, Presentation Interface, 351
Entry field control, Advanced Interface, 284
Entry model, 289
Error verbs, 375–76
EXEC IMMEDIATE statement, 162
EXECUTE statement, 163
EXISTS, 148
EXIT command, 175, 177
External routine, 123
Extract processing, 38, 140

F

File Formats, Presentation Interface, 370
File Transfer, Access, and Management (FTAM), 20, 41–42
FINAL TEXT fields, Query Interface, 167–68

Floating-point data, 43
FLUSH, 265
Focus window, 342
FONT, 377
Font(s), 306, 354
Font Object Content Architecture (FOCA), 18, 294, 298, 306–7, 371
    character-metric parameters, 308, 313
    character-shape parameters, 308, 313
    code page parameters, 308, 314
    font-descriptive parameters, 308, 309–10
    font-metric parameters, 308, 311–12
Font referencing, 307
Font resources, 306, 307
Font/symbol set, 363
Foreign key, 137
FOREIGN KEY clause, 156
Formatted Data Object Content Architecture (FD:OCA), 18, 294
FORMDEF, 376
FORTRAN, 172, 325, 326, 357
    call syntax example, 327
    data characteristics statements, 74
    data definition, 68
    data types, 73
    embedded SQL statements, 160, 161
    example of, 69–72
    expressions, 73
    function calls without variables, 173
    function calls with variables, 174
    processing statements, 72, 75
    program structure, 68, 74–75
Frame controls, 351
Frame window, 351, 370
FROM clause, 143, 146
Functions:
    Procedures Language, 122–23
    Repository Interface:
        calling, 209, 212
        fully integrated versus non-fully integrated, 212

G

Generalized Data Stream (GDS), 241–42
General tags, Dialog tag language, 329

GET command, 177
GRANT statement, 158, 159, 160
Graphics field, 369
Graphics function calls, Presentation Interface, 369–70
Graphics model space, 305
Graphics Object Content Architecture (GOCA), 18, 294, 298, 371
   coordinate spaces and transformations, 304–6
   drawing orders and segments, 299–303
   picture generation, 303–4
   primitives, 298–99
Graphics Object Content Architecture Extended (GOCA Extended), 298, 306
Graphics Orders, Presentation Interface, 370
Graphics presentation space, 305
Graphics processing, Presentation Interface, 362
Graphics specifications, Presentation Interface, 369–70
Graphics window transform, 305
GROUP BY clause, 150

H

HAVING clause, 150
Help facilities, Dialog Interface, 333–34
Help index, Dialog Interface, 335–36
Help panels, Dialog Interface, 334–35
Help requests, Dialog Interface, 336
Help windows:
   Advanced Interface, 280–81
   Dialog Interface, 324
Host variable, 151
Hybrid networks, 228

I

Icons, 276
Image(s), 363
Image Object Content Architecture (IOCA), 18, 294
Image points, 298
IMS (Information Management System), 4

IN, 149
INCLUDE statement, 162
Indexes, defining, 138, 158
Information area, 279
Information messages, 279
Information model, 198
Information tags, Dialog tag language, 330–31
Initiator, 42
Input, Procedures Language, 124–25, 126
INSERT statement, 152
Instance transform, 305
Integrated Computer Aided Software Engineering (I-CASE), 193
Integrated Services Digital Network (ISDN), 22
Integrity constraints:
   entity integrity, 136–37
   referential integrity, 137
Integrity policies, 197
Intelligent Printer Data Stream (IPDS), 19, 294, 296, 318–19
   commands, 319–20
   data objects, 319
   resources, 319
Interactive applications, 44
Interactive environment, 296
Interactive SQL, 159
Interchange environment, 296, 297
Interface communications area (DSQCOMM), Query Interface, 175
Internal routine, 123
Interpreter, Procedures Language, 128–29
Invalid region, 369

K

Key attribute, 195
Key mapping lists, Dialog Interface, 333
Keys, 135

L

Leaf template, 202
LIKE, 149

Line attributes, Graphics Object Content Architecture (GOCA), 301
List box, Presentation Interface, 351
List box control, Advanced Interface, 284
LM_QUERYITEMCOUNT, 361
Local processing, 31–32
Locks, 139
LOCK TABLE statement, 154
Logical unit of work, 179
Logical units, 218–19
   functions of, 219–20
   network user relationship and, 225
Logic blocks, 100
Low entry networking (LEN) nodes, 227
LS_MULTIPLESEL, 360
LS_NOADJUSPOS, 360
LU_LU session, 223–24, 257
   duration of, 224–25
LU 2, 219
LU 3, 219
LU 6, 219
LU 6.2, 219, 224
   APPC implementations, 254
   APPC versus, 236
   application program view of, 239–40
   application subsystem implementations, 254
   architected protocol boundary, 238
   architectural layers, 236–37
   conversations, 239
      one-way with confirmation, 248–50
      one-way with no confirmation, 244–48
      two-way, 250, 251
   CPI-C and, 255, 265
   designing conversation flows, 255–56
   distributed transaction example, 250–52
      asynchronous processing example, 252–53
      synchronous processing example, 252
   functional interfaces:
      control operator verbs, 244
      conversation verbs, 243–44
   functions of, 235–36
   generalized data stream and, 241–42
   interfacing with, 237–38
   mapped and basic conversations, 242–43
   mapping between syntax and semantics, 253–54
   open versus closed implementations, 254
   parallel sessions and, 240–41
   protocol boundary, 243
   protocol boundary verb semantics versus programming syntax, 239
   session mode sets, 241
   synchronization, 240

M

Main window, 340
Map definition, Application Generator Interface, 108, 110–11
   map specification, 111–12
   map structure, 112, 113–15
Mapped conversations, 242, 257
Mapped conversation verbs, 243, 244
Marker(s), 363
Marker attributes, Graphics Object Content Architecture (GOCA), 303
Maximize button, 279
Media space, 369
Media window, 369
Menu, Presentation Interface, 350
Menu bar, Advanced Interface, 279, 281
Menu controls, Advanced Interface, 281–82
Menu template, Presentation Interface, 353
Message(s):
   Dialog Interface, 331–32
   Presentation Interface, 343–44, 352–53
Message filtering, 346
Message paths, Presentation Interface, 348–49
Message windows, 279
Minimize button, 279
Mixed Object Document Content Architecture (MO:DCA), 19, 294, 296, 381, 382
   components, 317–18
   data stream, 314
   document layout structure, 315
   document logical structure, 314–15
   presentation space, 315
   relationship to object content architectures, 315–16

Mnemonics, 354
Modal dialog box, 352
Modeless dialog box, 352
Model space, 368
Model transform, 305
Multiple Virtual Storage (MVS), 4, 6
Multiple Virtual Storage/Enterprise Systems Architecture (MVS/ESA), 4

N

Network addressable units (NAUs), 221, 222, 229, 232
Network Application Support (NAS) architecture, 5
Network services, CCS, 21
Nodes, 222, 223
Nonprogrammable terminal (NPT), 276
Nontransparent distributed database access, 37, 38, 140
Normalized data structure, 134
NOT, 149
Notebook control, Advanced Interface, 285
NULL, 149

O

Object(s), 276, 293
    Common Communications Support (CCS), 18
    Query Interface, 170–72
Object content architectures (OCAs), 293, 294, 298
    relationship of MO:DCA to, 315–16
OfficeVision, 9
ON DELETE clause, 156
One-way conversation:
    CPI-C:
        with no confirmation, 268–69
        with confirmation, 269
    LU 6.2:
        with confirmation, 248–50
        with no confirmation, 244–48
Online processing, 30

interactive applications, 44
transactional applications, 44–45
OPTIONS fields, Query Interface, 168
OR, 148
ORDER BY clause, 150
OS/2, 4, 6
OS/400, 4
Output, Procedures Language, 124–25, 126
OVERLAY, 376
Owning relationship type, 196

P

Package, 159
Package processing, Database Interface, 160
Packed-decimal data, 43
PAGEDEF, 376
PAGE fields, Query Interface, 167–68
PAGESEG, 377
Panel body area tags, Dialog tag language, 329
Parallel sessions, 225, 240–41
Parameter templates, 200
Parent table, 156
Parent templates, 202
Parent window, 340
Parsing, Procedures Language, 125, 127
    numeric pattern example, 125–27
    string pattern example, 125
Partial maps, 111
Path control layer, SNA, 231, 237
Path control network (PCN), 222, 229, 232
Pattern attributes, Graphics Object Content Architecture (GOCA), 302
Physical Control layer, SNA, 231, 237
Physical units, 220–21
Picture generation:
    Graphics Object Content Architecture:
        called segments, 303
        chained segments, 303
        transmission mode, 304
    Presentation Interface, 363–64
        called segments, 365
        chained segments, 364–65
PL/I, 199

compiler-directing statements, 83
data definition, 75–76
data types and attributes, 79
embedded SQL statements, 160, 161
expressions, 80
processing statements, 77, 81–82
program structure, 76–77, 78
Pointer, 343
Policies, entity-relationship model:
  derivation, 197
  integrity, 197
  trigger, 198
Pop-up menus, 282
Pop-up windows:
  Basic Interface, 291–92
  Dialog Interface, 324
POST_ON_RECEIPT, 265
PREPARE statement, 163
PREPARE_TO_RECEIVE, 265
Presentation environment, 296, 297
Presentation Interface, CPI, 13
  application relationship to, 346, 347
  application structure, 344–46
  attributes, 363, 366–67
  clipboard facility, 354
  clipping, 369
  conformance with CCS Object Content
    Architectures, 371
  conformance with CUA, 370–71
  controls, 350–51
  control window messages, 352–53
  coordinate spaces and transformations, 367
    media window, 369
    model space, 368
    presentation page, 368
    world coordinate space, 368
  dialog box, 352
  drawing mode, 367
  graphics processing, 362
  graphics specifications in, 369–70
  implementations of, 339
  message paths, 348–49
  messages, 343–44
  picture generation, 363–64
    called segments, 365
    chained segments, 364–65
  primitives, 362–63

  resources, 353–54
  retained data, 365
  segments, 363
  specifications for window processing:
    clipboard facility, 361, 362
    resource files, 361–62
    standard window classes and styles, 356, 357, 358
    system-provided window procedures, 356–61
    window function calls, 354–56
  standard window, 351, 352
  synchronous and asynchronous message
    processing, 344
  user input, 346–47
  user interface functions, 349–50
  user output, 347–48
  windows, 340
    characteristics of, 343
    hierarchies of, 340–41
    interactions of, 342–43
    positioning of, 341–42
Presentation layer protocol, CCS, 21
Presentation Manager, 339
Presentation page, 368
Presentation Services layer, SNA, 232, 236, 237
Presentation space:
  MO:DCA, 315
  Presentation Interface, 347
Presentation Text Object Content Architecture
  (PTOCA), 18, 294, 316
Primary key, 135
Primary windows:
  Advanced Interface, 277
  Dialog Interface, 324
Primitives:
  Graphic Object Content Architecture
    (GOCA), 298–99
  Presentation Interface, 362–63
Print descriptors, PrintManager Interface, 380–81
Print job verbs, 374
PrintManager Interface, (CPI):
  capabilities of, 373–74
  print descriptors, 380–81
  print options, 376–80

relationship to CCS, 381–82
verbs, 374–76
Print options, PrintManager Interface, 376–80
Print option verbs, 374
Print session verbs, 374
Privileges, 139, 158
Procedures, Query Interface, 170
Procedures Language, 172, 177, 325
    call syntax example, 327
    conditions and condition traps, 123–24
    embedded SQL statements, 160, 161
    example of, 118
    expressing values, 119–21
    function calls without variables, 173
    function calls with variables, 174
    input and output, 124–25
    interacting with the interpreter, 128
    issuing commands, 127–28
    parsing, 125
        numeric pattern example, 125–27
        string pattern example, 125
    program logic, 122
    routines and functions, 122–23
    statements, 121–22
Procedures Language Interface, CPI. *See* Procedures Language
Process, 100
Process option, 100
Programmable workstation (PWS), 276
Prompted entry field, Presentation Interface, 351
Protected conversation, 183
Protected resources, 182
Protocol(s), 229, 230
Protocol boundary, 238, 243
Protocol boundary states, 238
Protocol boundary verbs, 238, 239, 243, 244
Pseudo-conversational application, 44
PU 2, 221
PU 2.1, 221
PU 4, 221
PU 5, 221
Pulldown menus, 281, 289
PU-PU sessions, 223
Pushbutton:
    Advanced Interface, 279
    Presentation Interface, 350

Push-button control, Advanced Interface, 282

Q

Queries:
    Database Interface, 143–44
    Query Interface, 165–66
Query Interface, CPI, 11, 133
    BREAK fields, 167
    callable interface:
        function calls, 172–74
        interface communications area, 175
        return variables, 175
    callable interface commands, 175–76
        EXIT command, 177
        SET and GET commands, 177
        START command, 176–77
    COLUMN fields, 167
    commands, 168
    object formats, 171–72
    OPTION fields, 168
    PAGE and FINAL TEXT fields, 167–68
    procedures, 170
    processing objects, 170–71
    processing query results, 168–69
    queries, 165–66
    report formatting, 167
    variables, 169–70

R

Radio button, Presentation Interface, 350
Radio button control, Advanced Interface, 283
Raster data, 298
RECEIVE_AND_WAIT, 265
RECEIVE_IMMEDIATE, 265
Reference Model for Open Systems Interconnection (OSI Model), 20, 217
Referential integrity, 137
Relational database concepts:
    authorization and privileges, 139
    concurrency, 139
    distributed relational databases, 139–41
    integrity constraints:
        entity integrity, 136–37

referential integrity, 137
keys, 135
primary key, 135
representing relationships, 135–36
SAA support for distributed database, 141–42
tables, 133–34
   properties of, 134
   views of data, 138
Relationship instance, 195
Relationship key, 196
Relationship type, 195
Remote request processing, 38, 140
Remote unit of work processing, 37–38, 140, 181
REMPOP, 324
Report formatting, Query Interface, 167
Repository Interface, CPI, 133, 193–94
   AD/Cycle and, 198–99
   built-in functions, 208, 209
      calling, 209–12
   data services, 204, 205–6
      calling, 204, 207
   entity-relationship model, 194–98
   focus of, 213
   fully integrated versus non-fully integrated functions, 213
   function policies, 202
   functions of, 199
   repository services, 204
   system services and, 207
      calling, 208
   templates and, 199–200
      format of, 200, 201
      use for retrieval, 202
   template trees, 200–202
   tool programs, 203–4
   views of data:
      conceptual, 194
      logical, 194
      storage, 194
Repository manager, 193
Repository Manager/MVS, 193, 198
Requester, 38, 140
Resource files, Presentation Interface, 361–62
Resource(s):
   IPDS, 319

Presentation Interface, 353–54, 363
Resource manager, 182
Resource Recovery Interface, CPI, 133
   calls:
      Backout service, 186
      Commit service, 185
   change commitment with distributed resources, 187–88
      Commit with partner program Backout, 189–90
      successful Backout, 190–91
      successful Commit, 188
      unsuccessful Commit, 188–89
      wide area networking, 191–92
   change commitment with local resources:
      successful Backout, 187
      successful Commit, 186
      unsuccessful Commit, 186
   distributed resource processing, 183–85
   services of, 181–82
   synchronization, 179–80
   synchronization point managers, 182–83
Responder, 42
Result table, 143
Retained data, Presentation Interface, 365
Revisable Form Text Document Content Architecture (RFT:DCA), 19, 295, 296
REVOKE statement, 159, 160
REXX, 117
ROLLBACK statement, 154
Root template, 202
Routines, Procedures Language, 122–23
Rows, 133
RPG:
   calculation specifications, 89–90, 95
   compiler directive statements, 91, 97
   control specifications, 88, 91
   embedded SQL statements, 160, 161
   example of, 84–87
   extension specifications, 89, 93
   file description specifications, 88, 92
   indicators, 90
   input specifications, 89, 94, 95
   line counter specifications, 89, 93
   output specifications, 90, 96
   program cycle, 83, 87
   program structure, 88

S

SAA (Systems Application Architecture), 3–4
  applications and solutions:
    application development, 10
    information and data, 9–10
    information processing structure, 10
  architectures, 8
  architecture versus implementation, 23–24
  development of, 4–7
  future of, 26–27
  implementation of, 26
  as an open architecture, 25–26
  strengths and weaknesses of, 24–25
  structure of, 7
  vendor support, 10
Scroll bar:
  Advanced Interface, 279
  Presentation Interface, 350
Secondary windows, Advanced Interface, 277, 279–81
Segments:
  Graphics Object Content Architecture (GOCA), 299–300
  Presentation Interface, 363
SELECT clause, 157
SELECT INTO statement, 151
Selection and entry field tags, Dialog tag language, 329–30
SELECT statement, 143, 144-45, 146, 147, 163, 165, 166, 167
SEND_DATA, 265
Server, 140
Service(s), 228, 230
Service call formats, Dialog Interface, 325–27
Service provider, 344
Service requester, 344
Service transaction programs, 233
Session(s), 223
Session layer protocol, CCS, 21
Session mode sets, 241
Session services, CCS, 20–21
SET command, 177
Siblings, 340
Side information, 264–65
Slider control, Advanced Interface, 283
Small icon, 278

SNA (Systems Network Architecture), 217–18
  control points, 221
  functional layers, 228–32
    network addressable unit layers, 232
    path control layers, 232
    service transaction programs, 233
  logical components, 221–22
  logical unit and network user relationship, 225
  logical unit functions, 219–20
  logical units, 218–19
  LU-LU sessions, 223–25
  networking facilities:
    advanced peer-to-peer networking facilities, 226–28
    hybrid networks, 228
    subarea networking facilities, 225
  nodes, 222, 223
  physical units, 220–21
  sessions, 223
  users, 218
SNA Distribution Services (SNADS), 20, 237
SNA/Management Services (SNA/MS), 20
SOME, 149
Source DDM server, 41
Special function works, Application Generator Interface, 106
Spin button control, Advanced Interface, 285
SQL, 143
  Database Interface, 145, 148–49, 159–64
  Query Interface and, 165, 166
SQL Communications Area (SQLCA), 162
SSRBACK return codes, 186
SSRCMIT return codes, 185
Standard Generalized Markup Language (SGML), 327
START command, 175, 176–77
Starter set calls, CPI-C, 258–60
Statement group, 100–101
Static control, Presentation Interface, 351
Static SQL, 159
Status area, 279
Straight lines, 362
Subarea network, 225
Subarea networking facilities, 225
Subordinate templates, 202

Subqueries, 147
Synchronization, Resource Recovery Interface, 179–80
Synchronization point, 179, 180, 181
Synchronization point managers, Resource Recovery Interface, two-phase Commit protocol, 182–83
Synchronous data link control (SDLC), 22
Synchronous message processing, Presentation Interface, 252, 344
System control, 6
System services, Repository Interface, 207
 calling, 208
SystemView, 10

T

Tables, 133–34
 Database Interface:
  creating, 154–56
  modifying, 157
 properties of, 134
Target DDM server, 41
Templates, Repository Interface, 353
 entity type, 199–200
 format of, 200, 201
 parameter, 200
 using for retrieval, 202
 working storage, 200
Template trees, 200–202
TEST(POSTED), 265
3270 data stream, 19, 294, 296
Token-ring LAN, 22
Tool programs, Repository Interface, 199, 203–4
Transactional applications, 44–45
Transaction Services layer, SNA, 232
Transformations, 304, 367–69
Transmission Control layer, SNA, 231
Transmission mode, 304
Transmission objects, 293–94
Transmission Services, SNA, 236, 237
Transparent distributed database access, 37, 140–41
Transport layer protocol, CCS, 21
Trigger policies, 198

Two-way conversation:
 CPI-C, 269–70
 LU 6.2, 250, 251
Type 2 nodes, 225
Type 2.1 nodes, 21, 227
Type 4 nodes, 225
Type 5 nodes, 225
Type-independent verbs, 243, 244

U

UNION operation, 151
Unique key, 135
UPDATE clause, 151
Usable area, 305
User input, Presentation Interface, 346–47
User interface(s), CCS:
 data stream and object architectures, 293
 data streams, 294–95
 document data stream environments, 295
 environments and data streams, 296–98
 Font Object Content Architecture (FOCA), 306–7
  font referencing, 307–8
  font resources, 307
  parameters, 308–14
 GOCA Extended, 306
 Graphics Object Content Architecture (GOCA), 298
  coordinate spaces and transformations, 304–6
  drawing orders and segments, 299–303
  picture generation, 303–4
  primitives, 298–99
 Intelligent Printer Data Stream (IPDS), 318–19
  commands, 319–20
  data objects, 319
  resources, 319
 interchange environment, 296, 297
 Mixed Object Document Content Architecture (MO:DCA) data stream, 314
  components of, 317–18
  document layout structure, 315
  document logical structure, 314–15

presentation space, 315
    relationship to object content
        architectures, 315–16
  object content architectures, 298
  presentation environment, 296, 297
  transmission objects, 293–94
User interface, CUA:
  Advanced Interface graphical model,
        276–77
    controls, 281–86
    interaction techniques, 286
    standard actions, 286–88
    windows, 277–81
  basic interface models:
    controls, 289–91
    interaction, 292
    model differences, 292
    panel appearance, 288–89
    pop-up windows, 291–92
  designing, 45–46
User interface functions, Presentation
    Interface, 349–50
User output, Presentation Interface, 347–48

V

Values, 134
Value set control, Advanced Interface, 283
Variable definition, Dialog Interface, 336–37
Variables, Query Interface, 169–70
Variable services, Dialog Interface, 325
Verbs, PrintManager Interface:
  error, 375–76
  print job, 374–75
  print option, 374
  print session, 374
Viewing limit, 369
Viewing transform, 305, 368
Views, defining, 138, 157–58

Virtual Machine (VM), 4, 6
Virtual tables, 138
Visible area, 369

W

WAIT, 265
Warning messages, 280
WHERE clause, 146–47
Wide area networking, 191–92
Window(s):
  Advanced Interface, 277–78
    action windows, 279
    help windows, 280–81
    message windows, 279–80
    window body area, 279
    window borders, 279
    window title bar, 278–79
  Dialog Interface, 324
  Presentation Interface, 340–43, 351,
        352–53
Window class, 343, 356, 357, 358
Window function calls, 354–56
Window handle, 346
Window procedure, 343, 356–61
Window sizing buttons, 279
Window style, 343, 356, 357, 358
WM_CREATE, 359
WM_MEASUREITEM, 360
Working storage templates, 200
Workplace, 276
World coordinate space, 368

X, Z

X.400 message handling system, 20
Zoned-decimal data, 43
Z-order, 340